Christine Ko~~~~~   ~rpret-
ers of Kant's moral philosophy. ~~~~   ~ small
group of philosophers who are producing a version of Kant's
moral philosophy that is at once sensitive to its historical
roots while revealing its particular relevance to contemporary problems. She rejects the traditional picture of Kant's ethics as a cold vision of the moral life which emphasizes duty at
the expense of love and value. Rather, Kant's work is seen as
providing a resource for addressing not only questions about
the metaphysics of morals, but also practical questions about
personal relations, politics, and everyday human interaction.

This collection of thirteen essays is divided into two parts.
Part One offers an exposition and interpretation of the moral
philosophy, and could serve as a commentary on *The Groundwork of the Metaphysics of Morals*. Part Two compares and
contrasts Kant's philosophy with other influential moral phi-
losophies, both historical (Aristotle, Sidgwick, Moore, and
Hume) and contemporary (Williams, Nagel, and Parfit). Two
particular focal points of her interpretation are Kant's theory
of value and his widely misunderstood doctrine of the "two
standpoints." When these ideas are fully explained, according
to Korsgaard, many of the traditional problems with and puzzles about Kant's ethics disappear.

This collection contains some of the finest work being
done on Kant's ethics and will command the attention of all
those involved in teaching and studying moral theory.

CREATING THE KINGDOM OF ENDS

Creating the Kingdom of Ends

Christine M. Korsgaard

Harvard University

PUBLISHED BY THE PRESS SYNDICATE OF THE UNIVERSITY OF CAMBRIDGE
The Pitt Building, Trumpington Street, Cambridge CB2 1RP, United Kingdom

CAMBRIDGE UNIVERSITY PRESS
The Edinburgh Building, Cambridge CB2 2RU, United Kingdom
40 West 20th Street, New York, NY 10011-4211, USA
10 Stamford Road, Oakleigh, Melbourne 3166, Australia

First published 1996
Reprinted 1997, 1999, 2000

Typeset in Trump Mediaeval

A catalogue record for this book is available from the British Library

Library of Congress Cataloguing-in-Publication Data is available

ISBN 0-521-49644-6 hardback
ISBN 0-521-49962-3 paperback

Transferred to digital printing 2004

*To my parents
Marion and Albert Korsgaard
with love and gratitude*

Contents

viii CONTENTS

Introduction

This volume contains the thirteen essays I published on Kantian ethics between 1983 and 1993. Part One consists of seven essays which are devoted primarily to the exposition, interpretation, and, in some cases, reconstruction, of Kant's moral philosophy itself. Part Two consists of six essays in which I compare and contrast Kantian ideas and approaches with those of other important moral philosophers, both in the tradition and on the contemporary scene.

The first essay in Part One provides a general survey of Kant's ideas about morality, the political state, and the ethical basis of religious faith, situating those ideas within Kant's general project of providing a critique of reason and in the historical context from which that project arose. The remaining six essays together constitute a short commentary on Kant's moral philosophy, following the order in which Kant himself presents his ideas in the *Groundwork of the Metaphysics of Morals*, but bringing in material from his other ethical works.

Two themes dominate the interpretation of Kant which I offer in these essays. The first is the theory of value that I associate with Kant's Formula of Humanity. Kant differs from realists and empiricists not merely in the objects to which he assigns value, or in the way he categorizes different kinds of value, but in the story he tells about why there is such a thing as value in the world. According to Kant, we *confer* value on the objects of our rational choices. He argues that the conception of ourselves as "ends-in-ourselves" is a presupposition of rational choice. To choose something is to take it to be worth pursuing; and when we choose things because they are important *to us* we are in effect taking *ourselves* to be important.

Reflection on this fact commits us to the conception of our humanity as a *source of value*. This is the basis of Kant's Formula of Humanity, the principle of treating all human beings as ends-in-themselves.

In one way this account resembles empiricist theories of value. The *objects* of value are just the things that are important to us, the objects of natural human interests. But the resulting values are not "subjective" or given directly by those interests. Value springs from the act of rational choice. Our commitment to the value of humanity constrains our own choices, by limiting us to pursuits which are acceptable from the standpoint of others, and extending our concern to the things which others choose. This confirms the basic intuitions behind realist theories of value: that we can't value just anything, and that there are things which we must value. But these requirements are not derived from metaphysical facts. What brings "objectivity" to the realm of values is not that certain things *have* objective value, but rather that there are constraints on rational choice.

The second theme concerns Kant's famous, or infamous, doctrine of the two standpoints, and the bearing of that on moral philosophy. In the *Groundwork of the Metaphysics of Morals*, Kant argues that a rational being "has two standpoints from which he can consider himself and recognize the laws of the employment of his powers . . ." (G 452). We can consider ourselves, in the language of the *Critiques*, as *noumena* or as *phenomena*. This view is not, as so many have supposed, an ontological or metaphysical theory according to which we exist simultaneously in two different "worlds," one somehow more real than the other. As I understand it, it goes like this: In one sense the world is given to us, it *appears* to us, and we are passive in the face of it. We must therefore think of the world as generating the appearances, as giving them to us. The world insofar as it appears to us is phenomenal; the world insofar as it generates the appearances is noumenal. We can only *know* the world as phenomenal, that is, insofar as it is given to sense, but we can *think* of it as noumenal. So there are not "two worlds," but rather one world which must be conceived in two different ways. And all of these points apply above all to ourselves. When we view ourselves as phenomena, we regard everything about ourselves, including inner appearances such as thoughts and choices, as parts of the natural world, and therefore as governed by its laws. But insofar as we are rational, we also regard ourselves as *active* beings, who are the authors of our thoughts and choices. We do not regard our thoughts and choices merely as things that *happen* to us; rather, thinking and choosing are things that we *do*. To this extent, we must view ourselves as *noumena*. And from this standpoint, we recognize laws that govern our mental powers in a different way than the laws of nature do: laws for the employment, for the *use*, of these powers; laws that show us how thinking and choosing must be *done*.

There may be problems with this way of looking at the human situation, but it does not commit us to a belief in a mysterious form of supersensuous existence. It does, however, have important implications for the way that we approach moral philosophy. The basic task of moral philosophy, for Kant, is to answer the question "What should I do?" This task is set for us by our practically rational nature, which brings with it both the capacity for and the necessity of *choosing* our actions. Choice is our plight, our inescapable fate, as rational beings. The project of critical moral philosophy is to determine what resources we can find in reason for solving the problem which reason itself has set for us. Since we are looking for laws for the employment of our powers of choice and action, we do not, in this investigation, regard ourselves as natural, causally determined beings – as the objects of scientific understanding. We regard ourselves as free, as the authors of our actions. This is not because there is any reason to deny that we are natural, causally determined beings, but because for the purpose at hand, that conception of ourselves is *irrelevant*. Moral philosophy proceeds from what I call the standpoint of practical reason.

These two themes come together in the essay from which I have derived the title of this volume, and in which I describe the account of human relationships, both personal and moral, that follows from Kant's philosophy. Treating others as ends-in-themselves is not a matter of discovering a metaphysical fact about them – that they are free and rational, and so have value – and then acting accordingly. When you respect the humanity of others you do not regard them as the objects of knowledge – as *phenomena* – at all. Instead you regard them as active beings, as the authors of their thoughts and choices, as *noumena*. To respect others as ends-in-themselves is to treat them as fellow inhabitants of the standpoint of practical reason. It is therefore to make your choices with them or at least in a way that is acceptable from their point of view – that is, to choose maxims which can serve as universal laws. To respect the humanity of others is to think and act as a legislative citizen in the Kingdom of Ends.

If I am right about this, Kant approaches moral philosophy in a very different way than the British Empiricists and their heirs in the analytic tradition do. The basic problem, set by the plight of rational agency, is "what should I do?" The approach is to raise practical questions as they are faced by the reflective moral agent herself. Moral philosophy is the extension and refinement of ordinary practical deliberation, the search for practical reasons. This makes Kant's enterprise very different from that of philosophers who talk about morality and the moral agent from the outside, third-personally, as phenomena that are in need of explanation. Kant's arguments are not *about* us; they are addressed *to* us.

Failure to grasp this difference or to grasp its depth and significance has bedeviled the English-speaking world's reception of Kant. Where the goal is not to explain but to address, the very standards of success are different. First-personal questions require first-personal answers. Misguided emulation of science has been a recurring source of confusion in the philosophy of the modern world. One manifestation of this is that so many philosophers suffer from an unreflective tendency to pose all philosophical questions in epistemological terms. How do we *know* that anything has value, and which things have it? This way of looking at ethical problems suggests from the start that their solution will turn out to be, in a broad sense, *technological:* a matter of finding some piece of knowledge which we can then apply. But there is no need to assume that reason's guidance of practice must look like *that.* It may lie instead in the provision of principles of practical reason – principles that govern choice in the same way that the principles of logic govern thought in general and the principles of the understanding govern the formation of our beliefs about nature. Since such principles are in the first instance addressed *to us,* the philosophical question about them is not so much how we know them as why we have to conform to them. Or rather, those two questions become one. In answering the second we will already have answered the first.

The misunderstandings of Kant's ideas which have resulted from misconstructions of his project have been unusually extreme. But this general form of misunderstanding is common in philosophy. I believe that most philosophical views that have gained any currency in the tradition either are extremely plausible or can be made so by a little generous reconstruction. Views that have been held and developed by intelligent people over long periods of time are unlikely to be infected by logical errors and elementary mistakes, or to be refuted by local arguments. Usually the "standard objections" that one school of thought raises against another are question-begging in deep and disguised ways; in fact they presuppose the first school's way of looking at things. Philosophers are at their best when the task is the internal development of a philosophical position into a plausible and systematic view; the criticism of an opponent's position is normally the weakest part of a philosophical work. Deep disagreements among good philosophers spring from large-scale differences of approach and outlook; these are what are really at stake.

This conception of the subject makes determining the choice among opposing philosophical positions both more difficult and more interesting. The philosophical tradition – and, in my view, the contemporary philosophical scene – present us with a true embarrassment of riches. We are or should be perplexed at being confronted with so many seemingly contrary and plausible views. Our perplexity begins to dissipate when we come to see that the proponents of different views are raising and therefore answering somewhat different questions. We will only know what to think, however, when we can find once again the common human plight or worry that motivates them to ask these different questions. The correct view is not going to be the one left standing when the contradictions and absurdities of all the others have finally been exposed. It is going to be the one that answers best to the human concerns which motivate the study of philosophy in the first place.

I would like to think that this conception of the subject is illustrated, even if imperfectly, by the second set of essays. These essays are comparative, and their general aim is to show that the more obvious disparities between Kant's view and some of the more powerful philosophical alternatives can be explained in terms of deeper differences in approach and outlook. Of course I also think that once these differences are correctly understood, Kant's views emerge as the more compelling.

The first three essays are linked by a concern with issues in value theory. I compare Kant with philosophers who, at least as far as value theory is concerned, represent the rationalist tradition: Aristotle, G. E. Moore, and Thomas Nagel. There are in fact important similarities between Kant's account of value and the accounts given by these three philosophers, but there is also, in each case, an essential difference. The work of each essay is to bring out the similarity and then to show where the difference lies and why it matters. Aristotle's idea of a good that is "final without qualification," Moore's idea of an "intrinsic" good, and Nagel's idea of an "agent-neutral" value are all designed to do work which in Kant's theory is done in a rather different way by the idea that humanity is the "unconditioned condition" of all value. When the similarity in the function of these concepts is brought into focus, we can then ask which succeeds best at the job. Or, in the case of the essay on Aristotle, perhaps I should say best *for us*, for there I trace the ethical difference to a larger difference in the metaphysical views possible in the ancient and modern worlds.

The last three essays also have a common theme, but it is a little more difficult to articulate. These essays contrast Kant's views with those of philosophers who – again, so far as the issues under discussion are concerned – represent empiricist strains in moral philosophy: David Hume and Bernard Williams, Henry Sidgwick, and Derek Parfit. These philosophers argue, in various ways, that the content of the principles of practical reason is shaped and controlled by facts about the world. Hume and Williams argue that the possible content of rational principles is limited by our motivational capacities. Sidgwick argues that rational principles must employ concepts which can be applied to natural objects without vagueness or ambiguity, and that only the principle of utility meets this criterion. And Parfit's famous attacks on some familiar dictates of practical reason depend not only on his unusual views about the metaphysics of personal identity, but also on his assumption that the content of rational principles depends on such metaphysical facts. I argue that these philosophers misconceive the relation between practical reason and the world. Practical reason is not shaped by the world but rather shapes it, by showing us how we must shape it. Against Hume and Williams I argue that the principles of practical reason, if there are such principles, give us motives. Against Sidgwick I argue that the concepts of ethics cannot be applied without ambiguity to natural objects because they are and must be ideal concepts if they are to shape our aspirations. And against Parfit I argue that it is because we occupy the standpoint of practical reason, not because of our metaphysical constitution, that we are faced with the task of constructing a unified personal identity. The theme here is the familiar Kantian one: practical reason – in fact, reason – is not something we find in the world but something we bring to it.

Philosophy is a cooperative enterprise. How could it be otherwise? Philosophical arguments can succeed only if their audience can recognize themselves, their plight, the human condition, in the way that those arguments are presented. Yet every person's mind has a set of natural, almost primitive biases: towards the big picture or the intricate detail, towards similarity and system or distinction and difference, towards the careful conservation of territory already mapped out and won, or the radical challenge to received ways of conceiving things. These biases are not bad in themselves, but left uncorrected, they threaten to turn your individual voice into a merely idiosyncratic one. The way to get on in philosophy is to let your natural mental proclivities do their utmost and then call in your teachers and friends and students and critics to correct the negative effects of your biases. I have been lucky in my teachers and friends and students and critics, and it is not possible here to mention the many people who have helped me to write the essays that follow. But we owe a special kind of debt to the people with whom we regularly discuss our philosophical views, and to those working on the same problems, who give us confidence when they agree and spur us to further efforts when they don't. I have benefited in these ways from the work and conversation of Charlotte Brown, Charles Crittenden, Tim Gould, Barbara Herman, Tom Hill, Peter Hylton, Scott Kim, Arthur Kuflik, Onora O'Neill, Andy Reath, Jay Schleusener, and Tamar Schapiro, who helped me to prepare this collection. I would also like to take this occasion to express my deep gratitude for the regular and generous help I received from the late Manley Thompson. And finally I would like to thank my teacher, John Rawls.

Abbreviations for Kant's works

References to and citations of Kant's works are given parenthetically in the text, using the abbreviations below, and for most works citing the page numbers of the relevant volume of *Kants gesammelte Schriften* (published by the *Preussische Akademie der Wissenschaften*, Berlin), which appear in the margins of most translations. The volume numbers are listed at the end of the entries below. The *Critique of Pure Reason*, however, is cited in its own standard way, by the page numbers of both the first (A) and second (B) editions. The *Lectures on Ethics* are cited only by the page number of the translation. The translations from which I have quoted are listed below.

ANTH   *Anthology from a Pragmatic Point of View* (1798), trans. Mary Gregor. The Hague: Martinus Nijhoff, 1974. (VII)

C1   *Critique of Pure Reason* (1st ed. 1781, 2nd ed. 1787), trans. Norman Kemp Smith. New York: Macmillan, St. Martin's Press, 1965.

C2   *Critique of Practical Reason* (1788), trans. Lewis White Beck. The Library of Liberal Arts, 1956. Formerly published in Indianapolis by Bobbs-Merrill, now published in New York by Macmillan. Hereinafter referred to simply as Library of Liberal Arts. (V)

C3   *Critique of Judgment* (1790), trans. J. H. Bernard. New York: Hafner Library of Classics, 1951. (V)

CBHH   "Conjectural Beginnings of Human History" (1786), trans. Emil L. Fackenheim in *Kant On History*, ed. Lewis White Beck. Library of Liberal Arts, 1963. (VIII)

END   "The End of All Things" in Kant (1794), trans. Robert E. Anchor in *Kant On History*, cited above. (VIII)

G   *Groundwork of the Metaphysics of Morals* (1785), trans. Lewis White Beck as *Foundations of the Metaphysics of Morals*. Library of Liberal Arts, 1959. (VI)

ID   *On the Form and Principles of the Sensible and Intelligible World* (The "Inaugural Dissertation," 1770), trans. G. B. Kerferd and

D. E. Walford in *Kant: Selected Pre-Critical Writings and Correspondence with Beck*. Manchester: Manchester University Press and New York: Barnes & Noble, 1968. (II)

IUH "Idea for a Universal History from a Cosmopolitan Point of View" (1784), trans. Lewis White Beck in *Kant On History*, cited above. (VIII)

LE *Lectures on Ethics* (1775–1780). Drawn from the lecture notes of Theodor Friedrich Brauer, Gottlieb Kutzner, and Chr. Mrongovious by Paul Menzer in 1924, trans. Louis Infeld. Indianapolis: Hackett Publishing, 1980.

MM The General Introduction to *The Metaphysics of Morals* (1797), trans. James Ellington in *Immanuel Kant: Ethical Philosophy*, Indianapolis: Hackett Publishing, 1983. The two main parts of the work are listed separately below. (VI)

MPJ *The Metaphysical Principles of Justice* (1797), trans. John Ladd. Library of Liberal Arts, 1965. (VI)

MPV *The Metaphysical Principles of Virtue* (1797), trans. James Ellington in *Immanuel Kant: Ethical Philosophy*, cited above. (VI)

OQ "An Old Question Raised Again: Is the Human Race Constantly Progressing?" trans. Robert Anchor in *Kant On History*, cited above. (VII)

PE *Enquiry Concerning the Clarity of the Principles of Natural Theology and Ethics* (the so-called "Prize Essay," 1763), trans. G. B. Kerferd and D. E. Walford in *Kant: Selected Pre-Critical Writings and Correspondence with Beck*, cited above. (II)

PFM *Prolegomena to Any Future Metaphysics* (1783), trans. P. Carus, revised by Lewis White Beck. Library of Liberal Arts, 1950. (IV)

PP *Perpetual Peace* (1795), trans. Lewis White Beck in *Kant On History*, cited above. (VIII)

R *Religion within the Limits of Reason Alone* (1793), trans. Theodore M. Greene and Hoyt H. Hudson. La Salle, Illinois: Open Court, 1934. Rpt. New York: Harper Torchbooks, 1960. (VI)

SRL "On a Supposed Right to Lie from Altruistic Motives" (1797), trans. Lewis White Beck in *Immanuel Kant: Critique of Practical Reason and Other Writings in Moral Philosophy*. Chicago: University of Chicago Press, 1949. Rpt. in New York: Garland, 1976. (VIII)

TP "On the Common Saying: 'This May Be True in Theory but It Does not Apply in Practice'" (1793), trans. H. B. Nisbet in *Kant's Political Writings*, ed. Hans Reiss. Cambridge: Cambridge University Press, 1970. (VIII)

WE "What Is Eniightenment?" (1784), trans. Lewis White Beck in *Kant On History*, cited above. (VIII)

PART ONE

Kant's moral philosophy

1 An introduction to the ethical, political, and religious thought of Kant

... reason has no dictatorial authority; its verdict is always simply the agreement of free citizens, of whom each one must be permitted to express, without let or hindrance, his objections or even his veto. (C1 A738–39/ B766–67)

Critique of Pure Reason

For Immanuel Kant the death of speculative metaphysics and the birth of the rights of man were not independent events. Together they constitute the resolution of the Enlightenment debate about the scope and power of reason. In the *Critique of Pure Reason* Kant shows that theoretical reason is unable to answer the questions of speculative metaphysics: whether God exists, the soul is immortal, and the will is free. But this conclusion prepares the way for an extension in the power of practical reason.[1] Practical reason directs that every human being as a free and autonomous being must be regarded as unconditionally valuable. In his ethical writings Kant shows how this directive provides a rational foundation for morality, politics, and a religion of moral faith. Bringing reason to the world becomes the enterprise of morality rather than metaphysics, and the work as well as the hope of humanity.

A CHILD OF THE ENLIGHTENMENT

Immanuel Kant was born in Königsberg, Prussia, on 22 April 1724, into a devout Pietist family. His father was a harness-maker and the family was not well off. But Kant's mother recognized her son's intellectual gifts, and the patronage of the family pastor Franz Albert Schultz (1692–1763), a Pietist theology professor and preacher, enabled Kant to attend the Collegium Fridericianum and prepare for

3

the university. He studied at the University of Königsberg from 1740–47, resisting pressure to choose one of the faculties and taking courses eclectically instead.[2] He was influenced by his teacher Martin Knutsen (1713–51), a Wolffian rationalist who taught philosophy and physics, and who took an interest in the developments of British philosophy and science. Knutsen introduced Kant to the works of Newton.

From 1747–55 Kant worked as a private tutor in the homes of various families near Königsberg, and pursued his interests in natural science. In 1755 he was granted the right to lecture as a *Privatdozent* (an unsalaried lecturer who is paid by lecture fees) at Königsberg. In order to earn a living Kant lectured on many subjects including logic, metaphysics, ethics, geography, anthropology, mathematics, the foundations of natural science and physics. We have testimonials to the power of Kant's lectures throughout his life: his audiences were large, and his ethics lectures are reported to have been especially moving.[3] In 1770 Kant was finally appointed to a regular professorship, the chair of logic and metaphysics at Königsberg. He lectured there until 1797. He died on 12 February 1804.

Kant never left the Königsberg area, but there are reports of his extraordinary ability to visualize, on the basis of written accounts, places and things he had never seen.[4] In a footnote to the preface of *Anthropology from a Pragmatic Point of View*, Kant complacently remarks:

A city such as *Königsberg* on the River Pregel – a large city, the center of a state, the seat of the government's provincial councils, the site of a university (for cultivation of the sciences), a seaport connected by rivers with the interior of the country, so that its location favors traffic with the rest of the country as well as with neighboring or remote countries having different languages and customs – is a suitable place for broadening one's knowledge of man and the world. In such a city, this knowledge can be acquired even without traveling. (ANTH 120n)

Kant's parents died when he was young, and he had little contact with his family after that. He never married. The regularity of his habits, perhaps due to the poverty of his early life and to his poor health, is well known. He only once got into trouble with the authorities. The events of his life were those of his intellectual life, and the political events in which he took such interest. His reawakening to the problem set by the skepticism of Hume; his conversion to a morality based on the worth of humanity under the influence of Rousseau; and the American and French Revolutions formed the important episodes of his life.

In Enlightenment Germany the intellectual world was dominated by an extreme form of rationalism called the Leibniz-Wolffian philosophy. Christian Wolff (1679–1754) is generally considered one of the two founders of the German *Aufklärung*. Wolff constructed his philosophy from the ideas of Leibniz and Thomistic scholasticism. He took mathematics as a model, and believed that philosophy should be a universal deductive system, with every conclusion derived by syllogistic reasoning from necessary premises. Like Leibniz, Wolff based his system on the principles of contradiction and sufficient reason.[5] Wolff also believed that the principle of sufficient reason could be derived from the principle of contradiction, for there would be a contradiction in the insufficiently determined existence of a merely possible thing.[6] While human beings need to use empirical methods in our search for the reasons of things, in principle it should be possible to cast the sciences in a completely deductive form. The existence of God can be proved by ontological, cosmological and teleological arguments; and because we know that God exists we know that this is the Best of All Possible Worlds. The soul is simple and immortal, and, since actions other than those one performs are logically possible, the will is free.[7] Wolff's ethics is based on the idea that the will is necessarily motivated by the good – that is, by the perception of a perfection achievable by action. Wolff thought it contradictory to perceive a perfection and not desire it, so in Kantian terms we may say that he believed that the moral principle is analytic.[8] Seeking perfection will bring us happiness, and the perfection of each person harmonizes with the perfection of every other. Immoral conduct is the result of confusion about what is good. Moral goodness is to be achieved through the clarification and correction of our ideas.

The influence of this system of dogmatic metaphysics on the thought of *Aufklärung* Germany can hardly be overestimated. Because he taught in the university, lectured in German, and wrote in German as well as Latin, Wolff had more direct influence than Leibniz himself. Wolff was the first philosopher to produce a full-fledged

system in the German language, and he invented the technical philosophical vocabulary that was used by his successors.[10] Wolff's ideas
were also presented in popular form in books written "for the la-
dies," and spawned the Societies of the Friends of Truth, whose
members pledged not to accept or reject beliefs except for sufficient
reason.[11] Kant was educated in the Wolffian system, and long after
he had rejected it he described Wolff as "the greatest of all the dogmatic philosophers" (C1 B xxxvi). Wolff's students taught in univer-
sities all over Germany and wrote many of the textbooks that German professors were required to use in their courses. One of the
most influential of them – Alexander Gottlieb Baumgarten (1714–
62) – wrote the textbooks Kant used in his courses on metaphysics
and ethics.

Of course this extreme rationalism did not go unchallenged. The
followers of the other founder of the *Aufklärung*, Christian Thomasius (1655–1728), attacked the conception of philosophy embodied in
the Leibniz-Wolffian system. Some were anti-metaphysical, and
wanted philosophy to play a more popular, non-academic role. More
important to the student of ethics is the fact that Thomasius himself,
and others who opposed Wolffian rationalism, were associated with
Pietism. Pietism, the religion of Kant's own family, emphasized inner
religious experience, self-examination and morally good works; and
Pietist theologians believed in a strong connection between morality
and religion. When Wolff was appointed rector at the University of
Halle, a Pietist center, his inaugural lecture was "On the Practical
Philosophy of the Chinese." Wolff claimed that the moral philosophy
of Confucius shows that ethics is accessible to natural reason and
independent of revelation. As a result, Wolff's Pietist enemies per-
suaded Frederick Wilhelm I to banish Wolff.

A later challenge to the Leibniz-Wolffian philosophy came when
Germans began to study the British Empiricists, especially Hume. In
Berlin after the middle of the century a movement called "popular
philosophy" flourished under the influence of Frederick the Great,
overlapping in its membership with the Berlin Academy which Frederick had revitalized. Both groups were interested in the philosophical traditions of France and Britain, and the works of Locke, Berkeley,
Shaftesbury, Hutcheson, Hume, Reid, and Rousseau were translated.
Moral sense theory was much admired, by Kant among others. Thus,
rationalism in ethics was opposed both by the appeal to religion and

the appeal to moral feeling and happiness. After the middle of the
century rationalist metaphysics too came increasingly under attack.

And so in 1763 the Berlin Academy offered a prize for the best
essay on the topic "Whether metaphysical truths generally, and in
particular the fundamental principles of natural theology and morals, are not capable of proofs as distinct as those of geometry; and if
they are not, what is the true nature of their certainty, to what
degree can this certainty be developed, and is this degree sufficient
for conviction [of their truth]?"[11] One of the competitors was Kant,
although he did not win the prize, which went to Moses Mendelssohn (1729–86). In his essay Kant denies that metaphysics has
the same method as mathematics. The difficulty is that the concepts
of metaphysics cannot be established synthetically the way the concepts of mathematics can. In mathematics the concepts create their
objects, and we can be certain that they contain what we have put
into them. Philosophy, on the other hand, has to analyze concepts
which are given to it obscurely (PE 276–78; 283ff.). Yet metaphysics
is still seen to be possible and capable of a certainty sufficient for
conviction: we must draw our inferences only from those predicates
of a concept of which we are certain, and not jump to the conclusion
that we have arrived at a complete definition (PE 292–93). Kant's
ethical views in this essay display a curious combination of influences from Wolff and Hutcheson. The moral principles are the
Wolffian "do the most perfect possible by you" and "do not do that
which would hinder the greatest possible perfection realizable
through you" (PE 299). Yet these principles are merely formal and so
empty until we know what is perfect. For this reason ethics fails to
have the requisite certainty. For, Kant says, a principle of obligation
tells us that we ought to do something. Either we ought to do something as a means to an end, in which case we can prove the principle,
but it is not a case of moral obligation; or we ought to do something
as an end, in which case the principle is unprovable. Fortunately,
Hutcheson has shown us that the subordinate principles that give
ethics content are objects not of knowledge but of unanalyzable
feeling (PE 299). It is yet to be determined whether the primary
principles of obligation are based on the faculty of knowledge or of
feeling (PE 300).[12] Kant's conclusions are in one sense the reverse of
those he will ultimately reach: it is speculative metaphysics which
will be left unfounded, and practical philosophy which will be set on

a firm basis. Yet in the prize essay we see Kant set for himself the questions that will lead to his mature views: the question of the status of pure concepts, in metaphysics, and the question of rational determinability of ends and imperatives, in ethics.

THE CRITICAL PHILOSOPHY

Throughout the 1760s and 1770s Kant was working out the views that would constitute the critical philosophy. Kant published little in this period, but we know that he worked on ethics as well as metaphysics and decided against moral sense theory. In the Inaugural Dissertation[13] of 1770 Kant says:

So *moral philosophy*, in as much as it supplies the first *principles of critical judgement*, is only cognised by the pure intellect and itself belongs to pure philosophy. And the man who reduced its criteria to the sense of pleasure or pain, Epicurus, is very rightly blamed, together with certain moderns who have followed him to some extent from afar, such men as Shaftesbury and his supporters. (ID 396)

We also have the *Lectures on Ethics*, notes taken by Kant's students in his ethics courses sometime in the years 1775–80, and the views in these are close to Kant's critical views. And we have Kant's own testimony, in a fragment written in the 1760s, of the profound influence exercised on his moral views by Rousseau, whose works he was reading.[14]

Although Kant's moral views were developing, their articulation had to await the working out of his conclusions about the status of metaphysics. The first edition of the *Critique of Pure Reason* appeared in 1781. Its conclusions overthrew the dogmatic metaphysics of the Leibniz-Wolffian philosophy; Mendelssohn referred to its author as "the all-destroying Kant."[15] In fact, Kant's aim was not to destroy, but to circumvent the skepticism of Hume. In the *Prolegomena to Any Future Metaphysics*, Kant reports:

I openly confess my recollection of David Hume was the very thing which many years ago first interrupted my dogmatic slumber and gave my investigations in the field of speculative philosophy a quite new direction. . . .

1. . . . first tried whether Hume's objection could not be put into a general form, and soon found that the concept of the connection of cause and effect

was by no means the only concept by which the understanding thinks the connection of things a priori, but rather that metaphysics consists altogether of such concepts. I sought to ascertain their number; and when I had satisfactorily succeeded in this by starting from a single principle, I proceeded to the deduction of these concepts, which I was now certain were not derived from experience, as Hume had attempted to derive them, but sprang from the pure understanding. (PFM 260)

Hume and Kant agree that metaphysical principles such as "every event has a cause" are not analytic. In an analytic judgment the predicate is contained in the concept of the subject. A judgment that is not analytic is synthetic. If metaphysical principles are synthetic, we cannot lay them down as definitions and derive truths from them by the principle of contradiction. They must be demonstrated. But Hume showed that "every event has a cause" could not be derived from experience. Although not analytic, the judgment must be *a priori* – knowable by pure reason. In the *Critique of Pure Reason*, Kant provides the needed demonstration – or "deduction" – of the synthetic *a priori* principles of the understanding. "Hitherto it has been assumed that all our knowledge must conform to objects." Instead, we must suppose that objects must conform to our knowledge. For "we can know *a priori* of things only what we ourselves put into them" (C1 Bxvi–Bxviii). But Kant's deduction only licenses our use of the principles of pure understanding for objects *as we experience them*, that is, as "phenomena." It does not provide us with a justification for applying them to things as they are in themselves – to "noumena."

In this way Kant rescues the metaphysical basis of natural science from Humean skepticism. But he does so at great cost to speculative metaphysics, for the traditional proofs of God, immortality and freedom are undermined. Kant has not shown that there is no God, immortality or freedom, but rather that these things are beyond the limits of theoretical understanding. Yet theoretical reason, in its search for the unconditioned – for the completeness of its account of things – compels us to ask whether these things are real. Human reason, the opening lines of the *Critique of Pure Reason* tell us, is compelled by its nature to ask questions it is unable to answer.

These conclusions set the problems for Kant's practical philosophy. First, the moral law itself must be a synthetic *a priori* principle (G 420). For, as Kant had already emphasized in the prize essay, "The formula in which all obligation is expressed is: One *ought* to do this or that and leave the other" and "every ought expresses a necessity of the action" (PE 298). But an ought statement cannot be derived from experience, which merely tells us how things are, and does not provide the required necessity. It must, therefore, be known *a priori*. But the moral ought cannot be established analytically. The argument for this, in the Second Section of the *Groundwork of the Metaphysics of Morals* (1785), picks up where the prize essay left off 22 years before. Hypothetical imperatives – principles which instruct us to do certain actions if we want certain ends – are analytic. While their material content comes from a law of nature telling us that a certain action is a means to a certain end, the necessity expressed in the "ought" comes from a principle that is analytic for the will:

Whoever wills the end, so far as reason has decisive influence on his action, wills also the indispensably necessary means to it that lie in his power. This proposition, in what concerns the will, is analytical; for, in willing an object as my effect, my causality as an acting cause, i.e. the use of the means, is already thought, and the imperative derives the concept of necessary actions to this end from the concept of willing this end. (G 417)

Willing something is determining yourself to be the cause of that thing, which means determining yourself to use the available causal connections – the means – to it. "Willing the end" is already posited as the hypothesis, and we need only analyze it to arrive at willing the means. If you will to be able to play the piano, then you already will to practice, as that is the "indispensably necessary means to it" that "lie in your power." But the moral ought is not expressed by a hypothetical imperative. Our duties hold for us regardless of what we want. A moral rule does not say "do this if you want that" but simply "do this." It is expressed in a categorical imperative. For instance, the moral law says that you must respect the rights of others. Nothing is already posited, which can then be analyzed. In the prize essay Kant had thought that this meant that the moral principle could not be established. Now he concludes instead that the categorical imperative is synthetic *a priori*, and requires a "deduction," like the deduction that established the principles of the pure understanding for the realm of experience.

The second result of the *Critique of Pure Reason* that bears on ethics concerns the issues of speculative metaphysics: God, freedom and immortality. As already noted, Kant concluded that these could not be objects of theoretical knowledge. In fact, the attempt to determine whether they are realities gives rise to antinomies: apparently equally good arguments on both sides of the question. The most important of these, concerning freedom, will serve as an example. Freedom, as Kant understands it, is a special kind of causality – first or spontaneous causality, unconditioned by any prior cause. One may argue that there can be no first cause, on the grounds that it would violate the rule that every event has a cause. On the other hand, one may argue that there must be a first cause, since the sufficient cause of anything must include all the causes that have led up to it, and there can be no sufficient cause if this is an infinite regress (A444–52/B472–80). Christian August Crusius (1715–75), a Pietist critic of Wolff whom Kant admired, had written about the antinomies, appealing to them as evidence of the limitations of human reason, and the need for reliance on faith and revelation.[16] Kant now resolves the antinomies by appeal to his distinction between noumena and phenomena. The antinomies show how important this distinction is, for without it reason must be seen as giving rise to contradictions and skepticism will be justified. In some cases, the antinomy is generated by a sort of equivocation – phenomena are treated as if they were noumena, and both of the arguments are false (A505–6/B533–34). In other cases, it turns out that one of the arguments is true of phenomena, while the other could be true – although we do not know that it is – of noumena. The antinomy of freedom takes the latter form. In the phenomenal world, because it is temporal and causality is temporal succession according to a rule, every event has a cause, and there can be no freedom. But the noumenal world does not exist in time and a spontaneous causality is possible, though not knowable, in it (A536–41/B564–69).

This leaves room for belief in the freedom of the will, which is the foundation of morality (A542–58/B570–86). As we will see, freedom of the will is important to Kant not merely for the familiar reason that we cannot be held accountable if we are not free, but because it provides both the content of morality and its motive. Kant will ask "how would a free will with nothing constraining or guiding it determine its actions?" and he will argue that the answer is "by the moral law" (C2 29). This solves the problem set by the antinomy, although only from a practical point of view. For reason says that there must be an uncaused cause in the noumenal world if an unconditional explanation of the phenomena can be given. Unless there is such a cause, the world is not, by the standards of human reason, intelligible. Speculative theoretical reason, however, cannot tell us what this cause would be. Practical reason, in providing us with the moral law, answers this question. This, according to Kant, provides us with a "credential" for believing in the reality of the moral law, and so in the freedom of our own wills (C2 48). Once Kant discovers that there is a moral basis for belief in the freedom of the will, he uses the same method to show that there is a moral basis for belief in God and immortality.

UNIVERSAL LAW AND HUMANITY

The views sketched above are not worked out until Kant writes the *Critique of Practical Reason* (1788). But first Kant produced a short book destined to become the main text for the study of his ethics, the *Groundwork of the Metaphysics of Morals* (1785). The purpose of this work is "the search for and establishment of the supreme principle of morality" (G 392). His plan was then to write a *Metaphysics of Morals*. In Kant's terminology, a "critique" investigates the legitimacy of applying pure rational principles and their concepts to objects; while a "metaphysics" sets forth those principles and their implications. The Third Section of the *Groundwork* contains a deduction of the moral law and so is a critique of practical reason; at the time he wrote this work, he thought that that would be sufficient. Later he saw that the moral law could be validated in a different way, and the *Critique of Practical Reason* was the result.[17] But we must turn to the *Groundwork* and the *Metaphysics of Morals* to get the substance of Kant's ethics, for in the second *Critique* the problem of validating the moral law and showing how it fits into his system supplants Kant's interest in its formulation and application.

Kant's method in the First Section of the *Groundwork* is analytic: he uses examples in order to analyze our ordinary conception of a good will and to arrive at a formulation of the principle on which such a will acts. A good will is easily distinguished from one that acts from an indirect inclination, doing the right thing merely as a means to some ulterior end, a "selfish purpose." The difficult thing is to distinguish a good will from a will that has a "direct inclination" to do something that is (as it happens) right (G 397ff.). For instance, there are people "so sympathetically constituted that without any motive of vanity or selfishness they find an inner satisfaction in spreading joy, and rejoice in the contentment of others which they have made possible" (G 398). Having a natural inclination to do what coincides with duty is not the same thing as acting from duty, so for clarity we must contrast this case with one where the duty is done without natural inclination. Take someone whose mind is "clouded by a sorrow of his own which extinguished all sympathy with the lot of others" or one who is "by temperament cold and indifferent to the sufferings of others" (G 398). If such a person is nevertheless beneficent, it must be from a good will. What is the principle on which he or she acts? We see, first, that such a person does his or her duty just because it is his or her duty. Furthermore, we see that what makes him or her do it – and so what makes it his or her duty – is not simply its purpose. For the naturally sympathetic person and the unsympathetic but beneficent person both have the same purpose, helping others, although one has this purpose because of a direct inclination and the other has it from duty. *Both* are contrasted with the selfish man who does the right thing for an ulterior purpose, such as fear of punishment or hope of reward.

Duty, then, is not a matter of having certain purposes. If we remove all purposes – all material – from the will, what is left is the formal principle of the will. The formal principle of duty is just that it is duty – that it is law. The essential character of law is universality. Therefore, the person who acts from duty attends to the universality of his/her principle. He or she only acts on a maxim that he or she could will to be a universal law (G 402). In this way Kant moves from the idea that a good will is one that acts from duty to a principle that can be used to tell us what our duties are.[18]

In the Second Section Kant reaches the same point by another route: the investigation of rational action. "Everything in nature works according to laws. Only a rational being has the capacity of acting according to the conception of laws, that is, according to principles" (G 412). The principle that you give to yourself, that you act on, Kant calls a "maxim." Your maxim must contain your reason for action: it must say what you are going to do, and why. If your maxim is one that it is rational to act on, it meets certain tests, commands of reason expressed in imperatives. Your action must be a means to your end, and (unless it is morally required) your end must be consistent with your happiness. These tests are embodied in the two kinds of hypothetical imperatives, those of skill and prudence. But there is also an imperative that tells us what we must do, regardless of our private purposes. This is the moral or categorical imperative, and because it is independent of all material, we know that "there is nothing remaining in it except the universality of law as such to which the maxim of the action should conform" (G 421). So from the very idea of a categorical imperative we can tell that it says: "Act only according to that maxim by which you can at the same time will that it should become a universal law" (G 421; C2 27).

But how can you tell whether you are able to will your maxim as a universal law? On Kant's view, it is a matter of what you can will *without contradiction*. This is important, for it helps to secure the categorical character of the results – any agent who applies the contradiction test should get the same result, regardless of his/her private interests. To determine whether you can will your maxim at the same time as its universalization without contradiction, you envision trying to will your maxim in a world in which the maxim is universalized – in which it is a law of nature. You are to "Ask yourself whether, if the action which you propose should take place by a law of nature of which you yourself were a part, you could regard it as possible through your will" (C2 69). Contradiction may arise in two ways: if the maxim cannot even be *conceived* as a law of nature without contradiction, it is contrary to strict or perfect duty; if it can be conceived but could not be *willed* without contradiction, it is contrary to broad or imperfect duty (G 424).

The best example of the first sort of contradiction concerns a man whose maxim is to make a false promise in order to get some money, which he knows he will be unable to repay. To see whether this can be willed as a universal law, we imagine a world in which this is, so to speak, the standard procedure for getting ready money – it is a law of nature that anyone who needs money tries to get it this way. Then we imagine the agent trying to will to act on his maxim in that world. Kant tells us that this gives rise to a contradiction because such universalization would make "the promise itself and the end to be accomplished by it impossible; no one would believe what was promised to him but would only laugh at any such assertion as vain pretense" (G 422). It is important to notice the sense in which this is a contradiction. Kant's view, as we saw earlier, is that hypothetical imperatives are analytic, because they express a relation of conceptual containment. The negation of an analytic statement is a contradiction. The man in the example derives his maxim from a hypothetical imperative: "If you want some ready money, you ought to make a false promise." This imperative is derived from a causal "law" – that false promising is a means to getting ready money – combined with the analytic principle that whoever wills the end wills the means. The causal "law" in question, however, turns out to be no law at all, because false promising could not be the *universal* method of getting ready money. The efficacy of a lying promise depends on the fact that it is exceptional, for people believe promises only because they are normally made in good faith, and lend money on the basis of them only because they believe them. In willing the universalization of his maxim, the deceitful promiser wills a world in which promises of this kind are not normally in good faith and therefore will not be accepted. This means that they will not be a means to getting ready money, and that the hypothetical imperative from which the deceitful promiser derives his own maxim will be falsified. This is where we get the contradiction: the lying promiser who attempts to will the universalization of his maxim wills the denial of the analytical principle on which he himself proposes to act, and the denial of an analytical principle is a contradiction.[19] Later critics claim that undermining the efficacy of promises is only a contradiction if promises are themselves necessary. But Kant's point in the example is more modest than that; it is not intended to establish that promises are necessary. Promises are necessary for the man in the example, because *he* proposes to use a promise as the means to his own end.[20] This is why Kant says that he cannot will his maxim and its universalization *at the same time*. Whenever you propose to perform an action whose efficacy depends on its exceptional character, you get a contradiction of this kind.

The other kind of contradiction arises when you attempt to will the universalization of some policy which would undermine the will's efficacy more generally. For instance, if you try to will a universal policy of neglecting talents and powers, you contradict your will because these serve you for "all sorts of possible purposes" (G 423). If you try to will a universal policy of not helping others, you contradict your will because you yourself, as a finite rational being, are often in need of assistance.[21] Kant is not offering an egoistic reason for an actual agreement here. Imagining yourself in a world without assistance is a thought experiment to determine whether you can will your maxim as a universal law. The duty of helping others holds even if you do not in fact get any assistance from anyone else, or have any real hope that you will.

At this point Kant has only told us what the categorical imperative is if there is one (G 425). But just as the laws of the understanding had to be established by a deduction showing that they apply to the world of experience, the categorical imperative must be established by showing that it actually applies to the human will. "The possibility of reason thus determining conduct must now be investigated" (G 427). While this possibility cannot be established until the critical argument of the Third Section, the rest of the Second Section prepares the way.

Kant begins from his thesis that one always acts with some end in view. Ends may provide us with reasons positively, as purposes to be achieved, or negatively, as things we must not act against. If there is a categorical imperative, there must be an objective end, one determined by reason itself and so attributed to every rational will; when we act on the categorical imperative, this will be the end we have in view (G 427–28; MPV 385). What would this end be? This kind of absolute value cannot be found in the objects of our desires, for they get their value from the fact that we desire them. Nor can it be found in our desires themselves, or in the various objects around us available for use as means. Rather, Kant says, "man, and, in general, every rational being exists as an end in himself" (G 428).

This conclusion harks back to the claim with which the *Groundwork* opens: the only thing which has unconditional value is a good will. A thing has conditional value if its value depends on whether certain conditions hold. For instance, the value of the means depends on the value of the end it serves; and the value of an object of desire depends on whether satisfying the desire will really contribute to the person's happiness. Even happiness is not valuable in all cases, and so is conditional. A thing has unconditional value if it has its value in itself and so has it under all conditions. Ultimately all value must spring from a source which is unconditionally valuable, for as long as we can question the value of something, we have not reached the end of its conditions. Kant's view is that only a good will has unconditional value of this kind. Since it is the objects of our own choices which we take to be good, and those objects do not have value in themselves, the source of value must be something that rests in us. It is not our needs and desires, for those are not always good. It must, therefore, be our humanity, our rational nature and capacity for rational choice. This is not different from saying it is a good will, for rational nature, in its perfect state, is a good will (G 428–29; C2 57–67; 87).

Kant says that the principle "rational nature exists as an end in itself" is a subjective principle of human actions, but that since every rational being holds it, it must be taken to be objective as well (G 429). Because each of us holds his/her own ends to be good, each of us regards his/her own humanity as a *source of value*. In consistency, we must attribute the same kind of value to the humanity of others. These considerations establish humanity as the objective end needed for the determination of the will by a categorical imperative. It is a negative end, one that is not to be acted against, rather than a purpose to be achieved. This leads Kant to a new formulation of the imperative, the Formula of Humanity: "Act so that you treat humanity, whether in your own person or in that of another, always as an end and never as a means only" (G 429).[22]

Kant then treats the same set of examples he used earlier, showing how the immoral maxims involve a violation of the unconditional value of humanity. Violations of perfect duty occur when the power of rational choice definitive of humanity is made subordinate to other, merely conditional goods. A suicide, for instance, treats his/her own humanity as something he/she can throw away for the sake of his/her comfort (G 429; MPV 422–23). Anyone who uses deceptive or coercive methods to undermine the freedom of choice and action exercised by others also violates perfect duty. The lying promiser uses the lender as a mere means because he tricks him into giving away his money rather than allowing him to *choose* whether or not to do so. He thus treats his having the money, a conditional good, as if it were more important than the other's humanity. Coercion (except to protect rights) and deception are unjustifiable no matter what end they serve, for a good end is an object of every rational will, and reason is "just the verdict of free citizens" (C2 62; C1 A739–40/B767).[23]

Although humanity is not a purpose to be achieved, we can act in a way that expresses a positive value for it, and imperfect duty is violated when we do not. We ought to realize our humanity by developing our talents and powers, our rational capacities. We ought to acknowledge that others are sources of value by treating their chosen ends as good, and pursuing their happiness as they see it (MPV 388). All human activities and pursuits are to be regarded as good as long as everyone can in principle agree to them. "This principle of humanity and of every rational creature as an end in itself is the supreme limiting condition on the freedom of the actions of each man" (G 430–31). The same idea is implicit in the Formula of Universal Law: for your reason to be sufficient, it need only be universalizable. Adoption of humanity as the unconditional end leads to the conduct which the Formula of Universal Law prescribes.

CATEGORIES OF DUTY: THE METAPHYSICS OF MORALS

In the *Groundwork*, a footnote to the first discussion of the four examples warns the reader that Kant will make his own division of duties when he writes the *Metaphysics of Morals*. He says that he has adopted the division normally in use by the schools, with one difference: he thinks that there are inner as well as outer perfect duties (G 421n). When Kant did publish the *Metaphysics of Morals* (1797) he introduced a more rich and complicated classification of duties. Before moving to the question of how Kant establishes the validity of the moral law, I will describe the system of duties that Kant sets out in his later work.[24]

The *Metaphysics of Morals* is divided into two parts: the *Metaphysical Principles of Justice* and the *Metaphysical Principles of Virtue*. The *Metaphysical Principles of Justice* deals with *Recht*, right, and is concerned with the question how natural and acquired rights are possible, and how they give rise to political society. The duties it deals with are "outer": the sense in which you "have a duty" not to interfere with the freedom and property of another is that the other is authorized to use coercion against you if you do (MPJ 231). Rights arise from the Universal Principle of Justice: "act externally in such a way that the free use of your will is compatible with the freedom of everyone according to a universal law" (MPJ 231). This principle is analytic, since one may arrive at it by analyzing the notion of external freedom (MPJ 231; MPV 396). Freedom can only be limited by itself – your freedom is as extensive as possible consistent with the same freedom for others. Anything that prevents a hindrance to freedom is consistent with freedom. So, if someone tries to undermine your freedom and you use coercion against him/her, that is consistent with freedom – with universal freedom and so with *his* or *her* freedom. It follows by the law of contradiction that a right is united with the authorization to use coercion against anyone who violates it (MPJ 231–233). We have an innate right to freedom, and we may acquire property rights. This is because of the Juridical Postulate of Practical Reason, according to which external objects may be property. Kant sees ownership as necessary for the use of objects as means. An object that cannot be owned cannot be effectively used, and so is, from a practical point of view, nothing at all. It would be inconsistent with freedom to limit it by nullifying the means it might use, so it follows that it must be possible for objects to be property (MPJ 246). A property right is correlated with an outer duty – a duty of justice. To say "this is my book" means that the imperative "you ought not to take this book" has acquired categorical or moral status. In this way outer duties – things that others may legitimately make us do or refrain from – are established. They are extensions of our innate right to freedom.

The *Metaphysical Principles of Virtue* deals with inner duties, duties of virtue. A duty of virtue differs from one of justice in several ways. First, a duty of virtue involves the free adoption of some end which pure practical reason directs. Duties of virtue arise from the Supreme Principle of the Doctrine of Virtue: "Act according to a maxim whose ends are such that it can be a universal law that everyone have these ends" (MPV 395).[25] Unlike the Universal Principle of Justice, this principle is synthetic: since it directs the adoption of ends and so concerns our motives, it must be established that it applies to the human will. It is deduced from the possibility of pure practical reason. It is a feature of human beings and probably all finite rational beings that we always act for an end (R 6n–8n; TP 279n–80n). And, "since sensible inclinations may misdirect us to ends (the matter of choice) which may be contrary to duty, legislative reason cannot guard against their influence other than, in turn, by means of an opposing moral end, which therefore must be given *a priori* independently of inclination" (MPV 381). Practical reason is a faculty of ends, so if there is pure practical reason there must be necessary ends. This means that there are duties to have these ends, duties of virtue (MPV 395).

The ends that reason sets are humanity in one's own person and that of every other, and, following from that, one's own perfection – moral and natural – and the happiness of others (MPV 385–88). Virtue also encompasses the duties of justice: rights are sacred to a person who values humanity, and acts of justice are transformed into acts of virtue when done for this reason. To achieve virtue we must adopt these ends freely. We cannot be coerced to adopt them, in two senses: it is impossible in fact to force someone to adopt an end, and it would in any case be illegitimate to do so. My lacking a good moral disposition cannot hinder your freedom, but only my performing wrong actions (MPV 381–82).

Duties of virtue are of broad obligation, while duties of justice are of strict obligation. Duties of justice require particular actions or omissions, and the obligation is strict because it can be discharged. If you perform a just action, it is not creditable, but just what you owe. If you do not, you have done something bad (MPV 389–94; but see R 22n–23n). Duties of virtue, by contrast, tell you to adopt and pursue certain ends. Such a duty cannot simply be discharged, for the ends in question cannot be completely achieved. So the obligation here is broad. To the extent that you pursue the end, as an end dictated by the law, you achieve moral worth. So, for example, the person who transgresses the rights of others is bad, the person who simply conforms to the law merely does what is owed, but the person who conforms to the law *because* he or she has made the rights of humanity his or her end is morally good (MPV 390–91).

The distinction between strict and broad obligations is sometimes confused with the distinction between perfect and imperfect duties. Kant himself does not use the four terms in a perspicuous way.[26] Perfect duties require definite actions or omissions, while in the case of imperfect duties inclination is allowed to play a role in determining exactly what and how much we will do to carry them out. Duties of justice are all perfect, but there are both imperfect and perfect duties of virtue. We have an imperfect duty of virtue when there is a positive end to promote, but the law does not say exactly how. For instance, you ought to develop your talents and powers, but you may choose those that are suitable to your occupation and tastes

(MPV 392). You ought to promote the happiness of others, but you may concentrate your efforts on the happiness of your friends (MPV 390). Perfect duties of virtue arise because we must refrain from particular actions *against* humanity in our own person or that of another. Suicide, physically destructive habits, and the failures of self-respect exhibited in self-deception and servility violate perfect duties to ourselves (MPV 421–44). Failures of respect, such as calumny, mockery and pride, violate perfect duties to others (MPV 462–68). And the general duty to *adopt* morally good ends – the duty of moral perfection – is perfect. Adopting an end is a definite, though internal, action. But making something your end and making that end the motive of your conduct is not something a human being can simply *decide* all at once to do. Our motives for the outward acts we do for these ends may be mixed with non-moral motives, and we cannot be certain that they are pure (MPV 392–93; 441–42; see also R 29–30). For instance, you may resolve, when tempted, not to commit suicide not only because you value humanity in your own person but because you are afraid; or your beneficence may require the support of your natural sympathies. So Kant says of the duty of moral perfection that it is "in quality strict and perfect, though in degree it is broad and imperfect" (MPV 446). The internal actions that are required are definite, but they are not dischargeable. Valuing humanity in the proper way must be worked at: it is an internal labor with which we are never simply done. So the obligations of virtue are always broad.

So there are four categories of duties of virtue: (1) perfect duties to oneself, to preserve and respect the humanity in one's own person; (2) imperfect duties to oneself, to develop one's humanity, intellectually and physically; (3) duties of love for others, to promote their happiness; and (4) duties of respect for others, including respect for their rights. The degree of one's virtue is measured by the extent to which one succeeds in doing all of these duties from the pure moral motive of regard for humanity. Complete virtue is unattainable (in this life), so our duty to achieve it is itself of broad obligation: it is a duty to progress towards it (MPV 409; C2 82–86; TP 284–85).

Kant explains all of our duties in terms of freedom. Duties of justice spring from the very idea of external freedom: a world in which everyone's rights are respected is a world in which complete external freedom is achieved. Virtue is the achievement of inner freedom, for the virtuous person acts from freely chosen ends rather than being governed by inclinations and desires. If both of these kinds of duties were universally practiced, human beings would be in every sense free.

AUTONOMY AND THE KINGDOM OF ENDS

The next step in the *Groundwork* argument is to relate the two formulas already given to one another and produce a third.

Objectively the ground of all practical legislation lies (according to the first principle) in the rule and in the form of universality, which makes it capable of being a law . . . subjectively, it lies in the end. But the subject of all ends is every rational being as an end in itself (by the second principle); from this there follows the third practical principle of the will as the supreme condition of its harmony with universal practical reason, viz., the idea of the will of every rational being as making universal law. (G 431)

Rational beings are the determiners of ends – the ones who set value on things. So a rational being must value rational nature as an end in itself; and it is with this end in view that we act only on maxims which could be universal laws. Since we are the ones who make rational nature our end, we are the ones who give ourselves this law. We are autonomous.

There are two ways of being motivated, autonomously and heteronomously. When you are motivated autonomously, you act on a law that you give to yourself; when you act heteronomously, the law is imposed on you by means of a sanction – you are provided with an interest in acting on it. Take a simple example: you might obey some positive law – for instance, you might pay your taxes – because you are afraid of being punished if you do not. This is heteronomy: your interest in avoiding punishment binds you to the law. On the other hand, you might pay your taxes even if you believe that you could avoid it, either because you think everyone should pay their share, or because you think that people should obey laws made by popular legislation. These would be, in an ordinary sense, examples of autonomy – of giving the law to yourself because of some commitment to it or belief in it as a law.

From what I have said so far, it looks as if you could adopt any principle autonomously, and the idea of autonomy does not determine the content of the principle that is autonomously adopted. But Kant claims that it does, and that the categorical imperative is in a special way *the* principle of autonomy. Heteronomous motivation can only be associated with hypothetical imperatives, for the hypothesis expresses the interest that binds you to the law. The main problem with most ethical theorists before Kant is that they have failed to see that moral motivation cannot be heteronomous. Duty is supposed to obligate us unconditionally. Any theory that tries to explain obligation by offering us an interest of some kind in doing our duty provides us with a principle that commands hypothetically, not categorically. When the imperative is hypothetical, we always have an option: either perform the action, or give up the interest. To explain obligation, we need an imperative that binds us unconditionally. But this means that moral motivation, if it exists, must be autonomous. There can only be one reason why human beings must obey the moral law, and that is that we give that law to ourselves (G 432–33).

The human will must be seen as universally legislative. Each of us has a will that makes laws for itself as if for everyone. Since human beings together legislate the moral law, we form a moral community: a Kingdom of Ends. The Kingdom of Ends is an ideal. It is "a systematic union of different rational beings through common laws," a republic of all rational beings. It is a community in which freedom is perfectly realized, for its citizens are free both in the sense that they have made their own laws and in the sense that the laws they have made are the laws of freedom – the juridical laws of external freedom and the ethical laws of internal freedom. The Kingdom of Ends is also "a whole of rational beings as ends in themselves as well as of the particular ends which each may set for himself," a system of all good ends (G 433). Each citizen takes his own perfection and the happiness of others as an end and treats every other as an end in itself. It is a community engaged in the harmonious and cooperative pursuit of the good.

The Kingdom of Ends provides us with a way of representing the sense in which moral laws are laws of autonomy. Suppose all rational beings were really to form a Kingdom of Ends, and held a constitutional convention to make its laws. What laws would we choose? Each of us would be eager to preserve his or her own freedom, so we would have to choose laws that preserved the freedom of each according to a universal law. Since we would will a world in which the assistance of others and the resources of human talents were available for use as the means of action, we would will that each person contribute something to the obligatory ends. The laws we would choose to be under, if it were ours to choose, would be moral laws. When we do obey moral laws, then, we are autonomous and free.[27] It is only because we are imperfectly rational, and subject to the importunities of desire, that morality appears to us as constraint – as *duty* (G 397).

This gives Kant another way of formulating the categorical impera-tive. We are always to act as if we were legislating for the Kingdom of Ends (G 434). Of course, this ideal is not actually brought about by the individual's living up to it. The accidents of nature, and the actions of other people, may distort the results of morally good con-duct, and lead to the unhappiness of the moral agent or others. But since the moral law commands categorically, we must nevertheless act as legislators in the Kingdom of Ends. Although this seems like a constraint when the results will be bad, there is a sense in which the agent's freedom is highlighted in such a case. The agent is not con-strained by external forces to act against the rational ideal that is the object of his/her will.

THE FOUNDATION OF MORALITY

If there is a categorical imperative, a law of pure reason applying to the will, then these three formulas tell us what it is. But to demon-strate that the categorical imperative is real, Kant needs to show something else – that the human will can be motivated by it. Other-wise morality is a "mere phantom of the mind" (G 445), a dogma of rationalist metaphysics which does not apply to the world. To estab-lish the moral law, we need a critique of practical reason.

The categorical imperative is synthetic. Morality is not contained in the concept of a rational will. When a proposition is synthetic, its two terms must be linked "through their union with a third in which both of them are to be found": it must be deduced (G 447). Kant's view is that this third term is provided by the positive concep-tion of the freedom of the will. His argument is that (1) a rational will must be regarded as a free will, and (2) a free will is a will under moral law. Therefore, a rational will is a will under moral law.

The second premise is proved first. The will is the causality of a rational being. If the will's actions – its choices and decisions – are determined by the laws of nature, it is not a free will. Suppose that all your choices could be traced to a psychological law of nature: say, "a person's will is always determined by the strength of his/her desires." Although you would always do what you "want most," your will would not be free. A free will is one that is not determined by any external force, even your own desires. This is the negative conception of freedom. But we also require a positive conception of freedom. The will is a causality, and the concept of a causality entails laws: a causality which functions randomly is a contradiction. To put it another way, the will is practical reason, and we cannot conceive a practical reason that chooses and acts for no reason. Since reasons are derived from principles, the will must have a principle. A free will must therefore have its own law or principle, which it gives to itself. It must be an autonomous will. But the moral law is the law of an autonomous will. Kant concludes that "a free will and a will under moral laws are identical" (G 447).[28]

Readers are often puzzled by this argument. If the will is free to choose its own principle, why should it be under the moral law? To see why, consider the problem from the perspective of a free rational will. Because it is a rational will, it must have a principle. Because it is free, it must choose this principle for itself. Nothing determines this choice: it is completely spontaneous. Since its principle determines what it counts as a reason, nothing yet counts as a reason for it. But if nothing yet counts as a reason for it, it appears to have no basis for choosing its principle. There is no constraint on its choice, except that it choose a law. But notice that this is just what the Formula of Universal Law says. The only constraint that it imposes on our choices is that they have the form of law. Nothing provides any content for that law; all that it has to be is a law. The moral law simply describes the position of a free will. When the will's choices are directed by the moral law, it expresses its spontaneity. The moral law is the law of spontaneity. The will that is governed by morality is free.

On the other hand, if the will allows its choices to be directed by an external force, it surrenders its freedom. In *Religion Within the Limits of Reason Alone*, Kant emphasizes that this is a *Fall*, perverse and inexplicable (R 34–35, 41–44, 78–79). Since the free will is not moved by desire unless it chooses to be, the will's surrender of its freedom cannot be explained by the pressures of temptation. Susceptibility to temptation is itself the product of the will's perverse choice to allow incentives of inclination to outweigh moral incentives (R 23–24, 30, 36–37).

But why should we believe that the human will is free? In the *Groundwork*, Kant begins this part of the argument by observing that as rational beings we must act under the idea of freedom. When we make rational choices and decisions, we must think of ourselves as free. A being which must regard itself as free really is "practically free" and so bound by the laws of freedom (G 448). But Kant then complains that this argument by itself is circular if offered as an account of how we can be morally motivated. A *purely* rational will is just a will under moral laws, but we are not purely rational. Morality demands we subordinate our happiness to our freedom. What is needed is an explanation of how we can be motivated to do this. This explanation is provided by the idea of the intelligible world.

Everyone, Kant claims, distinguishes between things as they appear and things as they are in themselves. And everyone can apply this distinction to himself as well as to other things. But in addition, human beings have reason, which is distinguished from everything else in that it is a pure spontaneous activity. Therefore, a human being must count himself as belonging to the intelligible world, as well as to the world of sense (G 450–53; C1 A538–41/B566–69). The intelligible world is the noumenal world, regarded as consisting of pure agencies which generate the world that appears to us. We know nothing of these agencies, except that we must think of them as the source of the appearances from which our knowledge is constructed. But our own capacity for pure activity places us among them. If we are among the intelligences, we are free and spontaneous, and so bound by morality.

In the *Critique of Practical Reason* the argument goes the other way.[29] The reality of moral obligation is known through what Kant calls a "Fact of Reason" (C2 31). This fact is our consciousness of the moral law and its capacity to motivate us whenever we construct maxims. We are conscious of the law not only in the sense that it tells us what to do, but in the sense that we know we *can* do what it tells us, no matter how strong the opposing motives (C2 30). The fact that we are able to act against our strongest desires reveals to us that we are free, and so are members of the intelligible world.

The intelligible world plays two roles in Kant's argument. First, the distinction between the intelligible and sensible worlds removes the fatal difficulty for morality that would otherwise come from the universal determinism that holds in the phenomenal world (G 455– 56). Just as importantly, the intelligible world explains "the interest attaching to the ideas of morality" (G 449). For we realize that ". . . the intelligible world contains the ground of the world of sense and hence of its laws" (G 453). The causal laws that determine everything that happens are part of the world of appearances, and are therefore part of what the intelligences produce. It is the intelligible world that generates the world as we know it. So if you are a member of the intelligible world, you are among the forces that make the world the way it is. If you will morally, you really are a co-legislator of the Kingdom of Ends. This is the motivating idea of morality.

. . . the idea of a pure intelligible world as a whole of all intelligences to which we ourselves belong as rational beings . . . is always a useful and permissible idea for the purpose of a rational faith. This is so even though all knowledge terminates at its boundary, for through the glorious ideal of a universal realm of ends in themselves (rational beings) a lively interest in the moral law can be awakened in us. (G 462)

THE RELIGION OF REASON

The positive conception of freedom shows us how a metaphysical concept can be defined and supported by practical reason. The moral law defines spontaneous causality. "In the entire faculty of reason only the practical can lift us above the world of sense and furnish cognitions of a supersensuous order . . . " (C2 106). In the Dialectic of the *Critique of Practical Reason* Kant extends this kind of account to the concepts of God and immortality. The moral law commits us to its complete object, the Highest Good: virtue and happiness proportional to it. Virtue is unconditionally good. But this does "not imply that virtue is the entire and perfect good as the object of the faculty of desire of finite rational beings. For this, happiness is also required" (C2 110). The Highest Good is the systematic totality of good ends to which the moral law directs us. Morality demands that we make this our end, but it seems to be impossible to achieve. Complete virtue cannot be realized in this life, and virtue would have to be necessarily connected to happiness for the Highest Good to be realized.[30] But no such connection obtains, for virtue does not inevitably lead to happiness, nor morally good intentions to good results. In fact, an empirical causal connection would be insufficient to solve the problem, for it would have to be between good actions and happiness, yet good actions may be done without a good will (C2 125–29). This apparent impossibility gives rise to an antinomy. We know through the Fact of Reason that the moral law commands categorically. But we cannot be categorically commanded to seek an end that is impossible for us to achieve. "If, therefore, the highest good is impossible according to practical rules, then the moral law which commands that it be furthered must be fantastic, directed to empty imaginary ends, and consequently inherently false" (C2 114).

It has seemed to critics that Kant here forsakes the purity of his position. The moral law is categorical and not conditioned by consistency with happiness. This criticism is a misunderstanding both of what Kant asserted earlier and what he claims here. As Kant himself points out in reply to criticisms by Christian Garve (1742–98), he never asserted, and nothing he says implies, that happiness is not of the utmost importance (TP 278–89). The unconditional character of morality means that the desire for your own happiness must not stop you from doing what is right; it does not mean that morality is the only good and important thing. Happiness is conditionally valuable, but when its condition is met, it is a genuine good. The moral law commits us to the realization of the good things that rational beings place value on. A world in which good people are miserable is morally defective.

The threat posed by the impossibility of achieving the Highest Good is best understood by considering the way the moral motive functions. You view yourself as a member of the intelligible world and so as a possible co-legislator in a Kingdom of Ends. You are among the world's first causes. But there are other first causes: other persons, and whatever else is responsible for the way things appear to us and so of the material content of the laws of nature. In the phenomenal world the results of our actions are determined not just by our own intentions, but by the forces of nature and the actions of other persons. Our attempts to realize the good are often diverted by these other forces. It is this that gives rise to the antinomy. Kant's description of the problem in the *Critique of Judgment* is better:

He [a righteous man] desires no advantage to himself from following [the moral law], either in this or in another world; he wishes, rather, disinterestedly to establish the good to which that holy law directs all his powers. But his effort is bounded; and from nature, although he may expect here and there a contingent accordance, he can never expect a regular harmony . . . with the purpose which he yet feels himself obliged and impelled to accomplish. Deceit, violence, and envy will always surround him, although he himself be honest, peaceable, and kindly; and the righteous men with whom he meets will, notwithstanding their worthiness of happiness, be yet subjected by nature, which regards not this, to all the evils of want, disease, and untimely death, just like the beasts of the earth. . . . The purpose, then, which this well-intentioned person had and ought to have before him in his pursuit of moral laws, he must certainly give up as impossible. (C3 452)

The motivating thought of morality is the thought that you can contribute to making the world a Kingdom of Ends. But if your attempts are always diverted by other forces, that thought is, as Kant says, false and fantastic.

The solution to this as to every antinomy is to appeal to the noumenal/phenomenal distinction. In the world of sense, there is no causal connection between a virtuous disposition and happiness, but there could be a connection between one's noumenal disposition and one's happiness in the world of sense. But this connection would be indirect: it would be mediated by an Author of Nature who had designed the laws of nature so that the connection holds (C2 114–15). In order to play the role envisaged, this Author would have to be omnipotent (to design the laws of nature), omniscient (to look into the hearts of rational beings and know their moral dispositions), and perfectly good. The Author of Nature would have the attributes traditionally ascribed to God (C2 140). If there were a God, then, the Highest Good would be possible, and morality would not direct us to impossible ends. Since we must obey the moral law, and therefore must adopt the Highest Good as our end, we need to believe that end is possible. So we need to believe in what will make it possible. This is not a contingent need, based on an arbitrary desire, but "a need of pure reason." This provides a pure practical reason for belief in God (C2 142–43).

A similar argument establishes the practical rationality of belief in immortality. The moral law commands you to seek your own moral perfection: the holiness of your will. This cannot be achieved in the course of your life, for no one with a sensuous as well as a rational nature has a morally perfect disposition. What a creature who exists in time, subject to causality and so to sensibility, can achieve is *progress* towards holiness of will. An endless progress is the same, in the eyes of God, as the achievement of holiness. "The Infinite Being, to whom the temporal condition is nothing, sees in this series, which is for us without end, a whole conformable to the moral law" (C2 123).[31]

A faith in God and in immortality of the soul thus based on practical reason – pure practical faith – is not just wishful thinking, because it springs from a rational demand. As Kant strikingly puts it:

Granted that the pure moral law inexorably binds every man as a command (not as a rule of prudence), the righteous man may say: I will that there be a God, that my existence in this world be also an existence in a pure world of the understanding, and finally that my duration be endless. (C2 143)

This does not mean that faith is commanded. The moral law demands that we think the highest good possible but "the manner in which we are to think of it as possible is subject to our own choice" since "reason cannot objectively decide whether it is by universal laws of nature without a wise Author presiding over nature or whether only on the assumption of such an Author" (C2 145). Faith springs from a need of the moral disposition and as such is voluntary. Salvation depends on moral character, not on what one believes.[32]

Our beliefs in God, immortality and freedom – that is, existence in an intelligible world – are "postulates of practical reason." A postulate of practical reason is theoretical in form, asserting something about what is the case, yet it cannot be shown theoretically to be either true or false. But we have an interest springing from the needs of morality in believing it.[33] Since practical reason supports belief in the postulates, its power is more extensive than that of theoretical reason. In establishing the postulates, practical reason takes up the metaphysical tasks that theoretical reason had to abandon. For if there is a God, who made the world in order to achieve the Highest Good, then the world does have an unconditionally good purpose. A teleological account of the sort that the metaphysician seeks – one according to which everything is made for the best in the Best of All Possible Worlds – would be true (C2 132–41).

But Kant insists that practical faith, although rational, does not in any way extend our *knowledge*. We cannot use the tenets of practical faith to explain the way things are, or for any theoretical purposes. This shows that our faculties are wisely adapted to our vocation. For the final purpose of the Best of All Possible Worlds is the achievement of moral goodness by human beings (C3 442–43). And if we had metaphysical knowledge:

> ... God and eternity in their awful majesty would stand unceasingly before our eyes. . . . Transgression of the law would indeed be shunned, and the commanded would be performed. But because the disposition from which actions should be done cannot be instilled by any command, and because the spur to action would in this case be always present and external, reason would have no need to endeavor to gather its strength to resist the inclination by a vivid idea of the dignity of the law. Thus most actions conforming to the law would be done from fear, few would be done from hope, none from duty. The moral worth of actions, on which alone the worth of the person and even of the world depends in the eyes of supreme wisdom, would not exist at all. (C2 147)

"I have therefore found it necessary to deny knowledge, in order to make room for faith" (C1 Bxxx).

REVOLUTION AND WORLD PEACE

Kant was an ardent champion of the American and French Revolutions. His support for the latter won him a reputation as a Jacobin, and at one point there was a widespread rumor that he was going to Paris as an advisor to the new government.[34] Jachmann writes of Kant's impatience for news from France, and his obsession with the subject in conversation.[35] His enthusiasm for the Revolution was not as idealizing as that of many of its admirers, and he did not turn against it when so many others did. According to one report "he said all the horrors in France were unimportant compared with the chronic evil of despotism from which France had suffered and the Jacobins were probably right in all they were doing."[36] Given the high value he places on freedom and human rights, it is not surprising that he regards a republic as the ideal form of government. But it is surprising to find this enthusiasm for its ruthless establishment in a man who believed that we must always act as citizens in the Kingdom of Ends regardless of consequences, and have faith in God to set things right. What makes it even more surprising is that Kant himself wrote that revolution is always wrong, and that "It is the people's duty to endure even the most intolerable abuse of supreme authority" (MPJ 320).[37]

Kant's political theory, like his ethics generally, owes a great deal to Rousseau. It is a social contract theory, in which people unite according to a General Will. I have explained above how property rights arise from the Juridical Postulate of Practical Reason. These rights exist in a state of nature, but they are "provisional." Since a right is an authorization to use coercion, anyone may defend his right against another. Disputes will inevitably arise, and there is no way to settle them, except by violence. In this way we present a threat to one another in the state of nature. This licenses us to use coercion against one another to establish a juridical state of affairs – a state in which rights are guaranteed rather than provisional. So we have a right and, indeed, a duty to coerce others to enter into political society with us (MPJ 255–313).

The point of political society is to protect rights and freedom. The ideal state – indeed, the "one and only legitimate constitution" (MPJ 340–42; PP 349–53) – is a republic (MPJ 340). But as things stand we must take the existing government to represent the general will of the people, and, consequently, must obey it. Oddly, we must do this even if the existing government is the result of a recent revolution. The government itself has a duty to promote its own gradual evolution to a republican form. And there should be complete freedom of speech, so that the citizens can discuss these matters. But no citizen is in a legitimate position to force the transition (MPJ 318–23; 370–72; TP 297–306).

The argument that shows that individuals should enter into juridical relations with one another also shows what nations should do. Freedom will only be realized when there is a world community guaranteeing perpetual peace. Only a cosmopolitan union of all the states of the world under common law, on the model of the union of the American states, will guarantee peace. This being an unattainable ideal, there should at least be a Congress or League of Nations, and an observation of the Laws of Nations (MPJ 350–51; IUH 24ff.;

PP; TP 307–13). Important among these will be laws for the conduct of war, for wars should be conducted according to laws that will make possible the eventual achievement of peace. In the *Metaphysical Principles of Justice* (MPJ 343–51) and in *Perpetual Peace* (PP 343–60) Kant attempts to spell out in detail what these laws should be, and expresses a hope that rulers will attend to what he says (PP 368–69).[38]

Peace is important not only because it is the end of violence and injustice. Peace will bring with it the entire achievement of the Kingdom of Ends on earth. It goes hand in hand with the state of affairs in which every nation is a republic. When the people, not the rulers, decide whether to go to war, war will come to an end, for the people will not go to war for trivial reasons (PP 351). When there is less war, social institutions will improve, for as things now stand, they are mostly designed for the sake of war. Public funds will be channelled into education rather than war debts, and culture will be improved (IUH 26, 28; CBHH 121). Enlightenment – the condition in which people think for themselves (WE 35) – will be fostered by freedom of speech and discussion. And, finally, morality itself will be achieved, as the ultimate product of culture and enlightenment. For a "good constitution is not to be expected from morality, but, conversely, a good moral condition of a people is to be expected only under a good constitution" (PP 366, OQ 92–93).

At the end of the *Metaphysical Principles of Justice* there is a suggestion that we may have an historical faith in the possibility of peace, on the same model as practical religious faith. No theoretical knowledge can be attained as to whether peace is possible or not. In such a case we may consider whether we have an interest in accepting the conjecture that it is. If the interest is based on morality – if the conjecture is one that must be true if moral ends are to be achieved – then we may accept it. "Even if the realization of this goal of abolishing war were always to remain just a pious wish, we still would not be deceiving ourselves by adopting the maxim of working for it with unrelenting perseverance" (MPJ 354). Indeed we have a duty to do this, and this gives rise to a need to believe it possible. The structure of the argument is exactly that of the argument for belief in God and immortality. Kant calls perpetual peace the "highest political good."

This faith in the possibility of peace is buttressed, in the historical writings, by a teleological interpretation of history in which nature is envisioned as working towards the moral condition of the human race, even using war and the selfishness of human nature as her tools. Every region of the globe supplies materials that humans can use to adapt to life there, and war has the function of ensuring that human beings eventually do spread everywhere. This brings about the cultivation and development of human powers and talents. As the populations of the various regions increase, these groups are again, inevitably, brought back into contact with one another. Differences of religion and language keep them at war for a time, but pressures to establish peace come from the need for commerce. Eventually this forces them to establish juridical relations with one another, and will lead to peace and justice all over the world.[39] This interpretation of history is offered, not as something knowable, and not as a reason for moral quiescence, but as a way those morally committed to peace can envision nature's cooperation with their efforts (PP 368).

This picture of history as leading to peace is strikingly deterministic. In it the moral disposition is seen as resulting from the republican constitutions and conditions of enlightenment that nature produces. Nature is seen as working through "the mechanism of human passions" (PP 368), through competition, the love of luxury, and war; as using methods that would work on "a race of devils" (PP 366). It is from a practical standpoint that we see ourselves as free; to the theorizing mind, everything is explicable in terms of causes. While theoretical reason explains, practical reason is wholly normative: actual examples of moral conduct cannot be identified with certainty, nor are they necessary to support the moral law's claims on us (G 407).

And yet Kant believes that history *has* provided us with one piece of evidence that the moral disposition is real in the human race, and may yet prevail. This piece of evidence is the enthusiasm of the spectators of the French Revolution. The French Revolution aims at a republican constitution. It therefore aims at justice, and "the condition whereby war (the source of all evil and corruption of morals) is deterred" (OQ 86). The enthusiasm of the spectators must be explained by the existence of a moral disposition, for "genuine enthusiasm always moves only towards what is ideal and, indeed, to what is purely moral, such as the concept of right, and it cannot be grafted onto self-interest" (OQ 86). So Kant concludes:

The revolution of a gifted people which we have seen unfolding in our day may succeed or miscarry; it may be filled with misery and atrocities to the point that a sensible man, were he boldly to hope to execute it successfully the second time, would never resolve to make the experiment at such cost – this revolution, I say, nonetheless finds in the hearts of all the spectators (who are not engaged in this game themselves) a wishful participation that borders closely on enthusiasm, the very expression of which is fraught with danger; this sympathy, therefore, can have no other cause than a moral predisposition in the human race. (OQ 85)

Kant began his critical work as the "All-destroyer," toppling the edifice of the Leibniz-Wolffian philosophy, along with its optimism that God has chosen everything for the best in the Best of All Possible Worlds. In its place he put a faith in human freedom, as the source of purely rational morality and the cornerstone of a metaphysics of practical reason. This freedom is not an object of knowledge, but of a rational aspiration: something for human beings to achieve, and thereby to realize the ideals of reason in the world. The remarks on the French Revolution quoted above are from the essay "On the Old Question: Is the Human Race Constantly Progressing?" In the French Revolution Kant found evidence that freedom is real in human nature, and may yet become real in the world.

I claim to be able to predict to the human race ... I predict its progress towards the better ... because it [the Revolution and its reception] has revealed a tendency and faculty in human nature for improvement ... which nature and freedom alone, united in the human race in conformity with inner principles of right, could have promised. (OQ 88)

Optimism is restored, but it is an optimism based on a moral faith in humanity.

NOTES

I would like to thank Ted Cohen, Manley Thompson, and the editors of *Ethics in the History of Western Philosophy* for comments on an earlier draft of this chapter.

1 Just as reason provides principles that determine what, given our circumstances, we ought to believe, it can provide principles that determine what in our circumstances we ought to do. The latter is "practical reason." Some of the British Empiricists appear to have believed that practical reason is merely applied theoretical reason: for instance, instrumental

practical reasoning is just "applied" causal reasoning. See, for example, David Hume, *A Treatise of Human Nature*, pp. 413–18. What this account leaves out is that if I am to act on the knowledge that something is a means to my end, I must still have a distinctively *practical* rational capacity: that of being *motivated* to take the means to my ends. This distinctly practically rational capacity may also move us to govern our actions by principles of *pure* practical reason which are not applications but analogues of theoretical principles. For discussions of this point see Thomas Nagel, *The Possibility of Altruism*, chapters V and VI; and my "Skepticism about Practical Reason," Chapter 11 in this volume.

2 Ernst Cassirer, *Kant's Life and Thought*, pp. 20–21.

3 Paul Schilpp, *Kant's Pre-Critical Ethics*, p. 6. See also the foreword to *Lectures on Ethics*, where Lewis White Beck quotes one of Kant's friends as saying:

> How often he moved us to tears, how often he agitated our hearts, how often he lifted our minds and feelings from the fetters of selfish eudaemonism to the high consciousness of freedom, to unconditional obedience to the law of reason, to the exhaltation of unselfish duty! The immortal philosopher seemed to us to be inspired with a heavenly power, and he inspired us, who listened to him in wonder. His hearers certainly never left a single lecture in his ethics without having become better men. (LE ix)

4 Cassirer, *Kant's Life and Thought*, p. 46.

5 That is, the principle that anything that exists or occurs must be explained by a reason which shows why the thing must exist or occur and cannot be otherwise than as it is.

6 Lewis White Beck, *Early German Philosophy: Kant and His Predecessors*, p. 274.

7 Beck, *Early German Philosophy: Kant and His Predecessors*, p. 274.

8 See below, pp. 9–10.

9 Eric A. Blackall, *The Emergence of German as a Literary Language, 1700–1755*, pp. 26–48.

10 Beck, *Early German Philosophy: Kant and His Predecessors*, p. 260.

11 Beck, *Early German Philosophy: Kant and His Predecessors*, pp. 441–42.

12 It is sometimes asserted that in his pre-critical period Kant was a moral sense theorist, or sentimentalist, but as the above discussion shows, he was at best an ambivalent one. (See also Schilpp, *Kant's Pre-Critical Ethics*, Chapter III.) Kant was a rationalist by training and perhaps by temperament, but there is no doubt he admired Francis Hutcheson (1694–1746) and Adam Smith (1723–90). Kant's admiration of Hutcheson is

clear from the frequent (though critical) discussions of Hutcheson in his work. For Kant's admiration of Smith see D. D. Raphael and A. L. Macfie's Introduction to Smith's *The Theory of Moral Sentiment*, p. 31. In this period among the British Moralists, the sentimentalists were incomparably better moral philosophers than rationalists such as Samuel Clarke (1675–1729) and his followers. One may see Kant as trying to respond to two of the main objections which the sentimentalists levelled at ethical rationalism. First, the sentimentalists had a functional account of what reason is, which enabled them to deny that reason can give rise to *a priori* concepts such as the rationalists believed "right" and "good" to be. The early rationalists by contrast had no competing account of what reason is that they could use to support their position. Only with Richard Price (1723–91) do we find a British rationalist attacking this problem head-on. Second, the early rationalists insisted that reason can directly determine the will, but they did not have an account of *how* it does so. With his rich account of what reason is in hand, Kant attempts to construct a rationalist ethical theory which will solve these problems.

13 So called because it was publicly defended on the occasion of Kant's appointment to the Chair of Professor of Logic and Metaphysics at Königsberg.

14 In the mid-1760s Kant wrote:

By inclination I am an inquirer. I feel a consuming thirst for knowledge, the unrest which goes with the desire to progress in it, and satisfaction at every advance in it. There was a time when I believed this constituted the honor of humanity, and I despised the people, who know nothing. Rousseau corrected me in this. . . . I learned to honor men, and I would find myself more useless than the common laborer if I did not believe that this view of mine can give a worth to all others in establishing the rights of humanity.

In rendering this passage I have drawn on the translations by Lewis White Beck in the introduction to *Immanuel Kant: Critique of Practical Reason and Other Writings in Moral Philosophy*, p. 7; and by Paul Schilpp in *Kant's Pre-Critical Ethics*, p. 48.

15 Beck, *Early German Philosophy: Kant and His Predecessors*, p. 337.

16 Beck, *Early German Philosophy: Kant and His Predecessors*, p. 400.

17 Lewis White Beck, *A Commentary on Kant's Critique of Practical Reason* pp. 3–18. For further treatment see pp. 26–27 and note 31 of this chapter.

18 Hume, in the *Treatise of Human Nature*, had argued that "regard for the virtue of [an] action" cannot be "the first virtuous motive, which bestows a merit on any action." For, he says:

Before we can have such a regard, the action must be really virtuous; and this virtue must be deriv'd from some virtuous motive: And consequently the virtuous motive must be different from regard to the virtue of the action. (p. 478)

This was, at the time, a potentially powerful point against his rationalist opponents. Because they argued that the sense of duty was the "first" motive of moral conduct, Hume's argument forbids them to say that its motive is what makes an action a duty. It forces them to take an intuitionist view about the content of morality. But Kant overcomes Hume's objection by distinguishing the formal and the material elements of motivation. If the "first virtuous motive" does not have to be given materially, the objection does not hold. Nevertheless, an argument similar to Hume's is used by W. D. Ross "against any theory which holds that motive of any kind is included in the content of duty." Interestingly, Ross uses the argument in support of intuitionism, since he thinks that "it would be paradoxical to hold that we ought to act from some other motive but never ought to act from a sense of duty, which is the highest motive." See The Right and the Good, pp. 5–6. For further discussion see Chapter 2 in this volume.

19 The reading of the contradiction test which I give here is not uncontroversial. There is disagreement both about Kant's intentions and about what form the contradiction test must take in order to work. For a defense of this interpretation against the major alternatives see my "Kant's Formula of Universal Law," Chapter 3 in this volume. As I point out there, my reading does not work for Kant's other example of this sort of contradiction, that of a man who considers suicide as an escape from future misery. I do not think that Kant was right in supposing that the duty not to commit suicide could be derived from the first contradiction test, for the universalization of suicide as a method of escaping misery is not self-defeating, nor can I see that it is in any way self-contradictory. No reading that I know of successfully deals with all of Kant's examples, but this need not mean that the test cannot be constructed. It may mean that Kant chose his examples badly.

20 Kant's claim that his contradiction test can serve as a criterion for determining what our specific duties are has generated a vast literature of criticism and defense. The criticism I mention here, one of the most influential, was made by Hegel and the Idealists (see, for instance, Hegel, Phenomenology of Spirit, trans. A. V. Miller, p. 262 and Philosophy of Right, trans. T. M. Knox, p. 90). Idealists also claimed that the test forbids too much: Bradley, for instance, in "Duty for Duty's Sake" in Ethical Studies, p. 155, claims that the test makes charity immoral,

since universal charity would eliminate its objects. Both objections overlook the role of the agent's intentions and purposes in generating the contradiction. The first overlooks the fact that the agent intends to avail himself of the institution which the universalization of his maxim would eliminate; for him, given his intentions, the institution is necessary. The second overlooks the fact that the agent's purpose in say, acts of charity, would be satisfied in a world where such were no longer called for. For a careful defense of Kant's view from these objections see Marcus Singer, *Generalization in Ethics*, pp. 279–95. See also Chapter 3 in this volume.

21 For a helpful discussion of Kant's account of this duty see Barbara Herman, "Mutual Aid and Respect for Persons," in *The Practice of Moral Judgment*, chapter 3.

22 For a more detailed explication of this argument, see my "Kant's Formula of Humanity," Chapter 4 in this volume.

23 On Kant's strictures against coercion and deception, see my "The Right to Lie: Kant on Dealing with Evil," Chapter 5 in this volume, and Onora O'Neill, "Between Consenting Adults," in *Constructions of Reason: Explorations of Kant's Practical Philosophy*, chapter 6.

24 The *Metaphysics of Morals* has only recently received much attention in Anglo-American criticism. For treatments of this work and accounts of the division of duties, see Mary Gregor, *Laws of Freedom: A study of Kant's Method of Applying the Categorical Imperative in the Metaphysik der Sitten*; Onora Nell (O'Neill), *Acting on Principle: An Essay on Kantian Ethics*; and Bruce Aune, *Kant's Theory of Morals*.

25 In the *Groundwork* Kant claims that in making moral decisions, the best formula to use is that of Universal Law (G 436–37). Interestingly, in the *Metaphysics of Morals* no direct use is made of the Formula of Universal Law: the Universal Principle of Justice and the Supreme Principle of Virtue are used instead. There are two possible reasons for this. One of course is that Kant changed his mind. A better reason is that the moral principles of the *Metaphysics of Morals* are at a general level, and Kant may still intend that one should use the universal law formulation at the level of particular decisions. The latter view has a certain plausibility, for the Formula of Universal Law is intended as a decision procedure. It is not a rule or a way of generating general rules, but a way of making decisions in concrete situations. This is why Kant holds the view, startling to many of his readers, that there can be no genuine conflicts of duty (MM 224). There is no room for conflict when decisions are made under the Formula of Universal Law, for the morally relevant features of the case are included in your maxim, and the maxim simply passes or fails the contradiction tests. Yet there are of course things to say about

what in general our duties are, and this is the territory that the *Metaphysics of Morals* covers.

26 For a good account of this distinction see Onora Nell (O'Neill), *Acting on Principle*, pp. 43–58.

27 The idea of legislation in a Kingdom of Ends provides the most accessible link between Kant's own writings and those of his contemporary "contractualist" successors, for here we find the thought that we may be autonomously bound by the laws we would choose under ideal circumstances. For the most notable example see John Rawls, *A Theory of Justice* (Cambridge, Mass.: Harvard University Press, 1971).

28 This idea that freedom, autonomy and morality are the same is suggested by Rousseau in *The Social Contract*. Rousseau wrote: "To the preceding acquisitions could be added the acquisition in the civil state of moral liberty, which alone makes man truly the master of himself. For to be driven by appetite alone is slavery, and obedience to the law one has prescribed for oneself is liberty" (p. 151). Possibly it was this suggestion that provided Kant with the solution to a problem he had worked on nearly all of his life – the problem of what freedom is.

29 There is critical controversy over whether this resulted from a change in Kant's views. Kant did not say explicitly that it did; but in the *Groundwork* he refers at the end of his argument to "this deduction" (G 454), whereas in the *Critique of Practical Reason* he says that "the reality of the moral law can be proved through no deduction" (C2 47). Additional external evidence is provided by the fact that writing the *Critique of Practical Reason* was a change of plan on Kant's part. (See Beck, *A Commentary on Kant's Critique of Practical Reason*, pp. 13 – 18.) For some recent discussions of this question, see Karl Ameriks, "Kant's Deduction of Freedom and Morality," pp. 53 – 79, and Dieter Henrich, "Die Deduktion des Sittengesetzes: Über die Gründe der Dunkelheit des letzten Abschnitte von Kants *Grundlegung zur Metaphysik der Sitten*."

30 It is not easy to understand why Kant holds that a perfect or holy will cannot be achieved in this life, either from what Kant says here or from the *Religion*, where he claims that there is "radical evil in human nature." In the *Religion* Kant squares the existence of evil with autonomy by showing how an evil will can be thought of as the result of our own choice. The incentives arising from our sensible nature do not compel us in any way: we act on them insofar as we make it our maxim to do so. But this makes it hard to understand why an imperfect will should be *inevitable* for a finite creature in the world of sense. Kant denies that the fact that we *have* non-moral incentives is an imperfection and, in any case, as he points out, the fact would not be imputable (R 28). For a

discussion of this problem and of Kant's theory of moral faith generally, see Allen W. Wood, *Kant's Moral Religion.*

31 It is not clear what exactly we are supposed to believe when we believe in immortality. Great difficulties lie here. If we are still to exist in time, the other life seems just to be a continuation of this one, perhaps with the same troubling conditions; if we are not, the notion of progress seems out of place. It also seems that it is in this other life that the virtuous are to be made happy. In fact in the earliest version of the theory, in the "Canon" of the *Critique of Pure Reason,* this is the reason for belief in immortality (C1 A810–11 B838–39). Kant is aware of the difficulties, and takes them up in "The End of All Things." In fact, the case illustrates Kant's thesis, explained below, that the postulates of practical faith cannot be taken to extend our theoretical knowledge in any way (END 333–34). If we try to think of the other life, we necessarily think of something temporal; when we try to think of eternity, we find ourselves thinking of nature as petrified, or monotonous (END 334–35). This is a condition of the way we think.

32 In *Religion Within the Limits of Reason Alone,* Kant spells out in some detail what a religion based on moral faith would be, and offers reinterpretations of scripture and traditional Christian doctrines in terms of it. This work got Kant into trouble with the authorities for the only time in his life. The liberal Frederick the Great died in 1786, and his more orthodox successor Friedrich Wilhelm II appointed Johann Christoff Wöllner as head of the state department of church and schools. Wöllner, a known opponent of the Enlightenment, began a campaign to stamp out religious enlightenment, and to enforce the authority of orthodox Protestant doctrine. Kant's prestige protected him from these repressive efforts for a time, but the *Religion* provoked Wöllner. Kant was forbidden to write on religious subjects by a direct order from the King, actually written by Wöllner. Notoriously, Kant complied "as Your Majesty's most faithful subject," and took this phrase as license to publish his views about religion once again after Frederick Wilhelm's death. See Beck, *Early German Philosophy: Kant and His Predecessors,* p. 435.

33 The concept of property is also established by a postulate, the Juridical Postulate of Practical Reason, which says that external objects can be property (MPJ 246). One can see the similarity: it is theoretical in form, metaphysical in content (Kant carefully distinguishes "property" properly speaking from mere empirical possession), and held valid because it is needed for the tasks of practical reason. Since the argument for the possibility of achieving world peace has the same structure as his argu-

ments for God and immortality, "Peace can be achieved" is also a postulate of practical reason. See below, pp. 33–34.

34 G. P. Gooch, *Germany and the French Revolution*, pp. 276–77.

35 Gooch, *Germany and the French Revolution*, p. 264.

36 Gooch, *Germany and the French Revolution*, p. 269.

37 See also the conclusion of Part II of "On the Common Saying: 'This may be true in Theory but it does not apply in Practice,' " where Kant comes out strongly against revolution – to the relief, according to Gooch (*Germany and the French Revolution*, p. 269), of many of Kant's admirers who by then opposed the French Revolution. For discussions of the paradoxical character of Kant's attitude to the French Revolution see Lewis White Beck, "Kant and the Right to Revolution," in his *Essays on Kant and Hume*, chapter 10; and Hans Reiss, "Kant and the Right of Rebellion."

38 The League or Congress of Nations is only a "negative surrogate" of a real World Republic, and the laws of war are in a sense only a negative surrogate of the laws of a world republic (PP 357). Instead of compelling us to act peacefully, they compel us to conduct ourselves in a way that will not make peace and international justice impossible (MPJ 347).

39 These remarks summarize things Kant says throughout his historical writings. See especially: *Idea for a Universal History from a Cosmopolitan Point of View; Conjectural Beginning of Human History;* and *Perpetual Peace*, First Supplement, "Of the Guarantee for Perpetual Peace."

2 Kant's analysis of obligation: The argument of *Groundwork I*

One of the debates of recent moral philosophy concerns the question whether moral judgments express "internal" or "external" reasons.[1] According to internalists, if someone knows or accepts a moral judgment then she must have a motive for acting on it. The motive is part of the content of the judgment: the reason why the action is right is a reason *for doing it*. According to externalists, this is not necessarily so: there could be a case in which I understand both that and why it is right for me to do something, and yet have no motive *for doing it*. Since most of us believe that an action's being right is a reason for doing it, internalism seems more plausible. It captures one element of our sense that moral judgments have *normative* force: they are *motivating*. But some philosophers believe that internalism, if correct, would also impose a restriction on moral reasons. If moral reasons are to motivate, they must spring from an agent's personal desires and commitments.[2] This is unappealing, for unless the desires and commitments that motivate moral conduct are universal and inescapable, it cannot be required of everyone. And this leaves out the other element of our sense that moral judgments have normative force: they are *binding*. Some internalists, however, have argued that the force of internalism cuts the other way. If moral reasons must motivate, and I show you that an action is morally right, I have *ipso facto* provided you with a motive for doing it. Moral reasons motivate *because* they are perceived as binding.[3] A good person, according to these internalists, does the right thing because it is the right thing, or acts from the motive of duty.

43

Many of the moves in the contemporary debate were anticipated in the debate between the rationalists and the sentimentalists of the eighteenth century. At the center of their dispute was the notion of *obligation*, a term they used primarily to refer to the *normativity* of duty. The term "obligation" is a source of confusion, because "an obligation" is sometimes used loosely as synonym for "a duty," a required action. But "obligation" refers not so much to the action as to the *requiredness* of the action, to its normative pull. We say that we *feel* obliged, or are *under* an obligation, to express our sense that the claims of morality are claims *on us*. The idea that moral conduct is obligatory, like the idea that moral judgments express internal reasons, is intended to capture both elements of the normativity of morality: its power both to motivate and to bind. And the eighteenth-century moralists, like contemporary internalists, ran into a difficulty when they tried to combine these two elements.

Rationalist moral philosophers criticized their opponents for not being able to explain how we are *bound* to do our duty. Samuel Clarke, for instance, levels this complaint against what he takes to be the view of Hobbes: that moral laws are the positive laws of a sovereign (possibly God) who has the power to enforce them. Either we are obliged to obey the sovereign, Clarke urges, in which case obligation is prior to positive law, or there is no real obligation at all.[4] According to later rationalists, sentimentalism is subject to the very same objection. The sentimentalist Francis Hutcheson, for example, believes that God has provided us with a moral sense which causes us to approve benevolence and deem it virtuous. But rationalists argue that providing us with a sense which endues certain motives with a moral quality is just a way for God to create morality by positive institution. Hutcheson admits as much, for he says that God could have given us a malice-approving moral sense had He so chosen. It is not because benevolence is obligatory in itself, but because God is benevolent, and approving benevolence is good for us, that God has caused us to approve it.[5] But the rationalist Richard Price complains that this makes morality a kind of illusion. We may indeed have moral "perceptions," but unless what we perceive is a rightness that is really *in* the action, the action is not really right, and so not really obligatory, after all. Price says that moral sense theory implies "That there being nothing intrinsically proper or im-

proper, just or unjust; there is nothing *obligatory*. . . ."[6] The rightness of an action cannot be something extrinsic to it, projected onto
it, like a secondary quality, by the operation of a sense. The action
must be *intrinsically* obligatory if it is obligatory at all.

But sentimentalists, in turn, criticized rationalists for not being
able to explain how we are *motivated* to do our duty. According to
rationalists, rightness is a real property of an action or of the relation
of an action to its situation, discerned by reason. But the bare grasp
of a rational truth seems to have no motivational power. Hume
famously complains:

> . . . men are often govern'd by their duties, and are deter'd from some actions
> by the opinion of injustice, and impell'd to others by that of obligation.
>
> Since morals, therefore, have an influence on the actions and affections, it
> follows, that they cannot be deriv'd from reason; and that because reason
> alone, as we have already prov'd, can never have any such influence.[7]

The problem was to find an account of obligation that combines the
two elements of normativity: motivation and bindingness.

This problem was inherited by Kant. A form of rationalism was the
dominant ethical theory in Germany, and Kant was a rationalist by
training as well as by temperament. But he was also a great admirer of
the British sentimentalists.[8] As early as the so-called Prize Essay,
Kant identifies obligation (*Verbindlichkeit*) as the "primary concept"
of ethics[9] (PE 298). There, he argues that the project of moral philosophy is to show how there can be obligations, understood as unconditional "oughts" which both bind and motivate. It is easy to see how an
action can be necessary to achieve a certain end, but for an unconditional "ought" the end itself must also be necessary (PE 298–99). At
this point in his career Kant endorses the Wolffian ethical principles
"Do the most perfect possible by you" and "Do not do that which
would hinder the greatest possible perfection realisable through you"
as the "primary *formal ground* of all obligation" (PE 299). But he
levels against these principles a charge later to be leveled against his
own view by Hegel: by themselves, they constitute an empty formalism, from which "no particularly definite obligation flows" (PE 299).
The content of morality, Kant speculates, must be determined by the
operation of unanalyzable feelings. He praises Hutcheson's idea of the
moral sense as a possible source for this content (PE 300). But the

Prize Essay's discussion of ethics ends inconclusively. Kant says, "... it has still to be discovered in the first place whether the faculty of knowledge or feeling ... exclusively decides the primary principles of practical philosophy" (PE 300).

By Kant's critical period this uneasy alliance between rationalism and sentimentalism is over, and rationalism has won the day. The problem of obligation, like any philosophical problem, must be solved in two stages. Since the concepts of morality are concepts of pure reason, we must start with a metaphysical account showing how pure reason generates these concepts and so what they (analytically) contain. But the claim that a concept of pure reason applies to the world is always synthetic. Kant cannot, like earlier rationalists, simply insist that a rational moral order is intuited in the nature of things. Dogmatic metaphysics has no more place in ethics than in theoretical philosophy. So we must turn to a critical synthesis to show that the concepts of morality apply to that part of the world to which they purport to apply: to us. The first step, and the one I am concerned with in this paper, shows what obligation is, that is to say, what the concept of obligation contains. The second, or synthetical, step shows that the concept has application, that is, that we have obligations.[10]

In *Groundwork II*, Kant appears to think there is no difficulty about analyzing the concept of obligation. An obligation would be prescribed by a categorical imperative, and analyzing that idea leads us immediately to the Formula of Universal Law. Kant says:

... we will first inquire whether *the mere concept* of a categorical imperative does not also furnish the formula containing the proposition which alone can be a categorical imperative....

... if I think of a categorical imperative, *I know immediately what it contains*. For since the imperative contains besides the law only the necessity that the maxim should accord with this law, while the law contains no condition to which it is restricted, there is nothing remaining in it except the universality of law as such to which the maxim of the action should conform....

There is, therefore, only one categorical imperative. It is: Act only according to that maxim by which you can at the same time will that it should become a universal law. (G 420–21, my emphases)

In fact, the analysis given in these cryptic passages is almost identical to the argument of *Groundwork I*.

In this paper my aim is to show how Kant's analysis of obligation, contained in the argument of *Groundwork I*, provides a solution to the problem of obligation that emerged from the controversy between rationalism and sentimentalism. In Section 2, I explain in more detail how the very concept of obligation generates a
dilemma which is central to that controversy. The argument of
Groundwork I, which I reconstruct in Section 3, shows the way out
of this dilemma, and in so doing shows what sort of thing an
obligation must be.

II   HUME'S DILEMMA

The argument of *Groundwork I* is an attempt to give what I shall
call a "motivational analysis" of the concept of a right action, in
order to discover what that concept applies to, that is, which actions
are right.[11] A motivational analysis is one that defines or identifies
right actions in terms of the motives from which they are done by a
morally good person.[12] The starting point of Kant's analysis is that a
morally good action is one done from the motive of duty, or, we
might say, a right action is one that is done by a morally good person
because it is right. If the analysis works, Kant's achievement is to
argue from this feature of right actions to a substantive moral principle which identifies which actions are right. In order to appreciate
the importance of this achievement, we must consider it in light of
an argument of Hume's which purports to show that exactly this
cannot be done. This argument gives rise to what I shall call
"Hume's Dilemma."

In opposition to the thesis that the sense of duty is the only moral
motive, Hume argues that "the first virtuous motive, which bestows
a merit on any action, can never be a regard to the virtue of that
action, but must be some other natural motive or principle."[13] He
points out that when we praise an action, and regard it as virtuous,
we do so because we suppose that it has a virtuous motive. And:

To suppose, that the mere regard to the virtue of the action, may be the first
motive, which produc'd the action, and render'd it virtuous, is to reason in a
circle. Before we can have such a regard, the action must be really virtuous;
and the virtue must be deriv'd from some virtuous motive: And consequently the virtuous motive must be different from the regard to the virtue
of the action. A virtuous motive is requisite to render an action virtuous. An

action must be virtuous, before we can have a regard to its virtue. Some virtuous motive, therefore, must be antecedent to that regard.[14]

This argument can be recast in terms of rightness. Suppose that a right action is essentially, or by definition, one prompted by a morally good motive. To know which actions are right we must know which motives are good. But if the only good motive is the sense of duty, then we do seem to get the kind of circle Hume describes here. I want to do what is right and ask you what that is. You tell me: right actions are those done just because they are right. How can I derive any content from this? The objection may be taken to be a version of the "empty formalism" objection, for the principle "do the right thing because it is the right thing" appears to be an empty formalism. According to Hume, I need prior information about which acts are virtuous or right before I can do them with regard to their virtue or rightness. This shows the need for a moral sense, which will enable us to pick out the virtuous motives which make actions right. And the moral sense must approve motives other than the motive of duty, in order to get some content into the system. This leaves us with a dilemma. If we retain the thesis that it is motives that essentially make actions right, it apparently must be motives other than a regard for rightness itself. On the other hand, if we are to retain the thesis that the primary motive of virtuous action is the motive of duty, we must have some way of identifying or defining right actions which does not depend on their motives.

Sentimentalists opted for the motivational analysis, but at a cost. On Hume and Hutcheson's view, what renders actions virtuous is our approval of the natural affections which motivate them, and these are, accordingly, the "first virtuous motives," in Hume's phrase, to morally right action. This leads to two problems, one concerning the fact of obligation, and the other concerning the sense of obligation or motive of duty. I have already mentioned the problem concerning the fact of obligation. The action is supposed to be right because we approve its motive. But we might, had we been given a differently constituted moral sense, have approved a different motive and so a different action. So the action is not *necessarily* right. But then it is hard to see how it can be obligatory. An obligatory action is one that is binding – one that it is necessary to do. But if the action is not necessarily right, how can it be necessary to do? Contemporary internalists make a similar objection to externalism. If the moral motive is simply a natural affection such as benevolence, we can really have no obligations. For how can there be an obligation to have the motive which gives us obligations? And how can we be obliged to perform the actions, unless we are obliged to have the motive that produces them? If it is not necessary to have the motive, it is not really necessary to perform the actions.[15] Behind both objections is the idea that the rightness of an action cannot be extrinsically conferred. If it is *necessary* for us to have a benevolence-approving moral sense or benevolent motives, this must be because benevolent action is intrinsically obligatory. If benevolent action is not intrinsically obligatory, then neither an arbitrarily implanted moral sense nor dispensable natural affections can make it so.

As these arguments suggest, the idea that we are in fact obliged is naturally associated with the idea that we should act from the motive of obligation. To be obliged to the performance of an action is to believe that it is a right action and to find *in that fact* a kind of motivational necessity: the action is called for or demanded by the situation, and that is the motive for doing it. And this brings us to the second problem. If the "first virtuous motives" are admirable natural motives, then the motive of obligation must play at best a secondary role.

Hutcheson, accordingly, dismisses most of what is said about obligation as "confused" and "obscure."[16] When we say someone is morally obliged to an action we mean only that the moral sense approves the action: that there is a *justifying* reason for it.[17] We are not talking about *exciting* or motivating reasons. The two parts of the normativity of morality, its power to bind, or justify, and its power to motivate, or excite, have separate sources. But, Hutcheson complains:

Some farther perplex this subject by asserting, 'that the same reasons determining approbation ought also to excite to election.'[18]

Obviously he disagrees. A good action need not be motivated by the agent's approval of it. This does not mean that there are no actions to which we are motivated by moral approval. Hutcheson says:

The prospect of the pleasure of self-approbation is indeed often a motive to choose one action rather than another; but this supposes the moral sense, or determination to approve, prior to the election.[19]

Hume's account of actions done from the motive of duty is similar:

> But may not the sense of morality or duty produce an action, without any other motive? I answer, It may: But this is no objection to the present doctrine. When any virtuous motive or principle is common in human nature, a person, who feels his heart devoid of that principle, may hate himself upon that account, and may perform the action without the motive, from a certain sense of duty, in order to acquire by practice, that virtuous principle, or at least, to disguise to himself, as much as possible, his want of it.[20]

In both accounts, the motive of obligation is reduced to a desire for self-approval. It is also reduced to a second-rate moral motive; action from spontaneous natural affection is more authentically virtuous.[21]

This is contrary to the widely-shared idea that obligation is central to moral experience, and that there are at least some actions which ought to be performed from the sense that they are obligatory. Now in our own century it has been argued that we should abandon these ideas about obligation. In her famous 1958 paper "Modern Moral Philosophy," Elizabeth Anscombe argued that the moral "ought" and "obligation" are specifically modern notions that classical philosophers like Aristotle did very well without. Anscombe claims that these ideas are naturally associated with a divine law conception of ethics, and, in the absence of that conception, lack sense.[22] Similar charges have been made more recently by Bernard Williams in the last chapter of his book *Ethics and the Limits of Philosophy*.[23] But Anscombe and, although to a lesser extent, also Williams, share an important assumption with their sentimentalist predecessors, for both tend to think that the primary force of saying that I am obliged to do something is that I will be judged, punished, blamed, or will blame myself, if I do not.[24] This emphasis is characteristic of sentimentalism, which constructs morality from the standpoint of the spectator or judge, taking the affections of approval and disapproval as the source of our most fundamental moral conceptions. For a sentimentalist, the idea of obligation can only arise by turning disapproval against the self.[25] For a rationalist, however, the focus on obligation comes from an agent-centered or deliberative perspective, not from that of the moral judge. The primary deliberative force of saying "I am obliged to do this" is not "I will blame myself if I do not" but "my judgment that it is right impels me to do this."[26] And this is at least related to an older thought, which *is* found in the classical philosophers. Aristotle's person of practical wisdom does the virtuous action for its own sake and *for the sake of the noble* (το καλον).[27] He is moved to act by an ethical quality, a moral beauty and nobility, which he apprehends in the action. He does not merely act on some spontaneous natural affection which sideline judges applaud.[28] And this element of moral action – this feature of how it looks from the agent's point of view – essentially drops out of sentimentalism.

This had a great deal to do, I believe, with keeping ethical rationalism alive in the eighteenth century. On many points, Hutcheson and Hume's attacks on early rationalism were effective, and later rationalists, such as John Balguy and Richard Price, particularly admired Hutcheson.[29] But the idea of obligation and its connection to motivation was captured better by Clarke's ethical system than by either sentimentalist or Hobbesian views. In describing right actions as "fit to be done," "reasonable," and "proportionate," Clarke tries to capture the sense that right actions are called for or demanded by their situations, that they have a kind of rational necessity comparable to the necessity of demonstrable truth.[30] He argues that "the original *Obligation* of all . . . is the eternal *Reason* of Things"[31] and that the moral motive is the sense of this obligation:

For the Judgment and Conscience of a Man's own Mind, concerning the Reasonableness and Fitness of the thing, that his Actions should be conformed to such or such a Rule or Law; is the truest and formallest *Obligation*; even more properly and strictly so, than any opinion whatsoever of the Authority of the Giver of a Law, or any Regard he may have to its Sanction by Rewards and Punishments.[32]

Increasingly, as the eighteenth century progresses, we find philosophers on both sides of the debate working to combine the best insights of sentimentalism with a more rationalistic account of obligation.[33]

But rationalism too has a cost, so long as Hume's argument is accepted. For Hume's argument makes it appear that the idea that the motive of duty is the primary motive to right action can be maintained only at the expense of the idea that right actions are defined essentially in terms of good motives. Instead, the rationalist must hold that rightness is in the nature of the actions required. As Price puts it:

... all actions, undoubtedly, have a *nature*. That is, *some character* certainly belongs to them, and somewhat there is to be *truly* affirmed of them. This may be, that some of them are right, others wrong. But if this is not allowed; if no actions are, *in themselves*, either right or wrong, ... it follows, that, in themselves, they are all indifferent.[34]

Since that is unacceptable, we must conclude that "right and wrong are real characters of *actions*."[35] This, of course, removes any difficulty about doing actions with regard to their rightness. If the rightness is in the action, we can certainly do it for the sake of that rightness. But now the rationalist is saddled with the view that rightness is (to speak anachronistically) a non-natural property, inherent in the actions, and intuited by reason. In this way, rationalism seems to entangle us in a metaphysical moral realism, as well as an epistemological intuitionism, which are both unpalatable. This will in particular be an objection for Kant, since his project forbids the uncritical assumption that necessary principles may be found, by rational intuition, to hold in the nature of things. And, although the rationalists rejected the empiricist theory of reason from which it follows that reason cannot motivate, they had no account of *how* we can be motivated by rational truths to put in its place. The rationalists saw that obligation is only possible in one way: the perception of the bindingness of the right action must be what moves us. But instead of explaining how this is possible, they simply insisted that it is.

   In England things got worse instead of better. In our own century, W. D. Ross defended intuitionism by an argument similar to Hume's. In the opening pages of *The Right and the Good*, Ross attacks the possibility of a motivational analysis of rightness. When we say that an act proceeds from a good motive, we are saying that it is morally good. So to say that rightness admits of a motivational analysis is to say that "right" means "morally good."[36] But Ross says that he can show that this is wrong, or, as he startlingly puts it: "that nothing that ought to be done is ever morally good."[37] One of his arguments goes this way. Those who "hold that our duty is to act from a certain motive" usually hold that the motive in question is the sense of duty. But:

... if the sense of duty is to be my motive for doing a certain act, it must be the sense that it is my duty to do that act. If, therefore, we say 'it is my duty to do act *A* from the sense of duty', this means 'it is my duty to do act *A* from the sense that it is my duty to do act *A*'. And here the whole expression is in contradiction with a part of itself. The whole sentence says 'it is my duty to-do-act-*A*-from-the-sense-that-it-is-my-duty-to-do-act-*A*.' But the latter part of the sentence implies that what I think is that it is my duty to-do-act-*A* simply.[38]

Probably feeling that this is not perspicuous, Ross reiterates:

Again, suppose that I say to you 'it is your duty to do act *A* from the sense of duty'; that means 'it is your duty to do act *A* from the sense that it is your duty to do act *A*.' Then I think that it is your duty to act from a certain motive, but I suggest that you should act under the supposition that it is your duty to do a certain thing, irrespective of motive, i.e. under a supposition which I must think false since it contradicts my own.

The only conclusion that can be drawn is that our duty is to do certain things, not to do them from the sense of duty.[39]

This argument, like Hume's, turns on the idea that you cannot do your duty from the motive of duty until you know, independently, what your duty is. So far, like Hume's, it leaves it open that it could have been our duty to act from certain motives other than the motive of duty. But Ross has another argument which he thinks disallows any moral requirement on motives. This argument turns on the principle that "ought implies can," which Ross endorses. He says:

It is not the case that I can by choice produce a certain motive (whether this be an ordinary desire or the sense of obligation) in myself at a moment's notice, still less that I can at a moment's notice make it effective in stimulating me to act.[40]

Therefore, Ross concludes, it cannot be the case that what I ought to do is act from certain motives.

Like earlier rationalists, Ross concludes that rightness must simply be a property of certain actions. But Ross has a much more difficult time explaining the normative force of rightness than his predecessors. For Clarke, Price, and Balguy were all what we should now call internalists.[41] They believed that the perception of an action as right, or, what they took to be the same thing, obligatory, *is* a motive to do it. So the problem Ross notices in this last argument, that we cannot muster the sense of obligation at a moment's notice, does not arise for them. As Price says:

When we are conscious that an action is *fit* to be done, or that it *ought* to be done, it is not conceivable that we can remain *uninfluenced*, or want a *motive* to action. It would be to little purpose to argue much with a person, who would deny this; or who would maintain that the *becomingness* or *reasonableness* of an action is no reason *for* doing it; and the *immorality* or *unreasonableness* of an action, no reason *against* doing it. An affection or inclination to rectitude cannot be separated from the view of it.[42]

Whereas Ross, following Prichard, is an externalist.[43] Like some internalists, Ross and Prichard think that a good person does the right thing "because it is the right thing." But Ross and Prichard think of the motive of duty as something like a desire that takes right action for its object, not as something that is involved in the very grasp of the fact that the action is right. So like Hutcheson, Ross in effect separates the justifying reason – the fact that the action is right – from the motivating reason – the desire to do what is right. And since this "desire" might simply fail to be present, it cannot be our duty to act from it. All we can say is that acting from it is morally good. This means that for Ross, the fact that something is right only becomes a reason *for action*, in the sense of a motive, when the desire to do what is right happens to be on the scene to interest us in it. Furthermore, Ross denies that a right action need be in any way good. For, he argues, if someone does a right action from a bad or indifferent motive, that can at best be instrumentally good.[44] There is no guarantee that it will even be that, for "right" neither means "productive of good consequences" (since "right" is unanalyzable) nor has it ever been shown to be coincident with that property.[45] So a right action is not necessarily instrumentally good, and according to Ross, it has no intrinsic value. What has value, says Ross, "is the doing of the right act because it is right."[46] But rightness by itself "is not a form of value at all."[47] By itself, then, rightness has no normative force. This makes it clear why Ross must be an externalist. Since rightness is not a value, the desire to do what is right is not a response to a value. Nor does it seem, therefore, to be an especially rational motive. Like the natural affections favored by sentimentalists, it is merely a motive we happen to have. So rightness by itself neither motivates nor binds, nor are we bound to the desire to do what is right by any tie of reason or duty. Thus it turns out that, for Ross, the whole normative force of rightness springs from the supposed intrinsic value of acting from a certain motive, which we simply happen to have.

In the Preface to the *Groundwork*, Kant says that his method in the first part of the book will be "to proceed analytically from common knowledge to the determination of its supreme principle" (G 392). Specifically, *Groundwork I* seeks the principle behind "common rational knowledge of morals" (G 393). Because he is analyzing common knowledge, Kant starts from an idea which he expects the reader, once he recognizes it, to accept: that nothing is unconditionally valuable except a good will. Whenever we believe we have witnessed the exercise of such a will, we think we have seen an action that has a special kind of value: value that is independent of "what it effects or accomplishes," and so, unconditional (G 394). In order to discover the principle of morality, or of unconditionally good action, we need to discover what principle a good will acts on.

The notion of duty includes that of a good will, since the notion of duty is the notion of a good will operating under "certain subjective restrictions and hindrances" (G 397). Therefore, Kant proposes to look at cases in which we should say that a person acted "from duty" in order to discover the principle of action which characterizes a good will. He proceeds to distinguish three kinds of motivation. One may act from duty (do the right thing because it is the right thing), from direct inclination (perform an action because one enjoys it), or from indirect inclination (perform an action as a means to a further end). The first of Kant's four examples concerns a merchant who refrains from overcharging hapless customers because a good reputation helps business. This is an example of *indirect* inclination. We are unlikely to confuse such an action with an action from duty, Kant says,

For it is easily decided whether an action in accordance with duty is performed from duty or for some selfish purpose. It is far more difficult to note this difference when the action is in accordance with duty and, in addition, the subject has a direct inclination to do it. (G 397)[48]

The other three examples are meant to illustrate this point: in each of them, we consider an action that one ought to do from duty, but that one may also be naturally inclined to do. For instance, Kant says, there are persons

... so sympathetically constituted that without any motive of vanity or selfishness they find an inner satisfaction in spreading joy, and rejoice in the contentment of others which they have made possible. (G 398)

Actions done on this basis are "dutiful and amiable" and "deserve praise and encouragement," yet they do not evince the moral worth of the action done from duty (G 398). To find the essence of duty and the good will, we must find the basis on which we distinguish these actions from those done from duty.

It is essential not to confuse the point of these examples with that of the honest merchant, who acts "neither from duty nor from direct inclination, but only for a selfish purpose" (G 397). According to a familiar but misguided reading of these passages, Kant holds a crudely hedonistic theory about all motives other than moral ones: he thinks that all actions except moral ones are done for the sake of one's own pleasure, and so are all equally selfish and without moral worth. So understood, Kant means to emphasize the *similarity* of actions done from direct inclination to those done from indirect inclination: their purpose, like the honest merchant's, is fundamentally selfish. But what Kant clearly emphasizes here is the *difference* between direct and indirect inclination, and he says explicitly that the sympathetic person is "without any motive of vanity or selfishness" (G 398). He praises such actions as amiable and even "dutiful" (*pflichtmäßig*), and compares them to actions arising from the inclination to honor, which he elsewhere describes as a "simulacrum" of morality (IUH 26).[49] In fact, if we suppose that Kant holds a hedonistic theory of the *purpose* of all actions done from inclination, neither the distinction between direct and indirect inclination, nor (as I will show in a moment) the general argument of *Groundwork I*, makes much sense. Instead, Kant envisions the act of the sympathetic person as one done for its own sake. The pleasure a sympathetic person takes in helping is not an ulterior purpose, but is rather the reason why he makes *helping* his purpose.[50] Pleasure is not the purpose of his action, but the ground of the adoption of his purpose.

And the person who helps others from duty *also* does so for its own sake. The duty in question, as Kant makes clear elsewhere, is the duty to make the happiness of others one's *end* (G 430; MPV 385; 388). It is because of this similarity of purpose that the sympathetic person's actions are characterized as "dutiful" despite their lack of moral worth. We may say, going beyond Kant, that sympathy is a simulacrum of morality because it is an impulse inspired by the humanity in others, just as honor is a simulacrum of morality because it is a motive to obey certain strict laws of conduct for their own sake.[51] So the difference between the sympathetically helpful person and the dutifully helpful person does not rest in their purpose, but must lie elsewhere. This leads Kant to his "second proposition," namely, "An action performed from duty does not have its moral worth in the purpose which is to be achieved through it but in the maxim by which it is determined" (G 399).

To say that the worth of an action does not lie in its purpose, but in its maxim, is to say that its worth lies in the grounds on which the action along with its purpose has been chosen. Unfortunately, at this point in the argument Kant introduces the idea of a maxim with no preparation whatever – he simply says, in a footnote clumsily attached to its fifth usage, that a maxim is a "subjective principle of volition" (G 400). In fact, the idea of a maxim is essential to Kant's solution of the problem of obligation.

According to Kant it follows from the fact that a rational being acts "under the idea of freedom" (G 448) that she acts for a reason or on a principle which she must regard as voluntarily adopted. The point here has to do with the way a rational being must think of her actions when she is engaged in deliberation and choice. When you make a choice, you do not view yourself as simply impelled into it by desire or impulse. Instead, it is as if there were something over and above all of your desires, something that is *you*, and that decides which if any of your desires to gratify. You may of course *choose* to act on a desire, but that does not mean that you are impelled by it. It means you take this desire as a reason, or, in Kant's language, you make it your maxim to satisfy this desire. You may even choose to act on your strongest desire, but still that does not mean its strength is impelling you. It means that you are taking strength as a reason for choosing to satisfy one desire rather than another, making it your maxim to act on your strongest desire. Your maxim thus expresses what you take to be a reason for action; since reasons are derived from principles, or laws, it expresses your conception of a law.

Kant believes that all human action is purposive, and so that every maxim of action contains an end (See G 427; MPV 381; 384–85; R 4). A maxim of action will therefore usually have the form "I will do Action-A in order to achieve Purpose-P." You will only act on that maxim if you also make it your maxim "to achieve Purpose-P." Since this maxim too must be adopted for a reason there are reasons for having purposes, which are again expressed in maxims. Although Kant does not emphasize this, it is perhaps easiest to think of maxims as hierarchically organized: "I will do Action-A to achieve Purpose-P" is adopted on the basis of "I will achieve Purpose-P" (plus a relevant hypothetical imperative); "I will achieve Purpose-P" is in turn adopted on the basis of a further maxim that "I will make it my purpose to have the things that I desire" or whatever it might be.

Therefore, when Kant says that the difference between the sympathetic person and the dutiful person rests in their maxims, the contrast he has in mind is this: although the sympathetic person and the dutiful person both have the purpose of helping others, they have adopted this purpose on different grounds. The sympathetic person sees helping as something pleasant, and that is why he makes it his end. The morally worthy person sees helping as something called for, or necessary, and this is what motivates him to make it his end.[52]

A common complaint is that this suggests that a person who helps reluctantly and with a stiff upper lip is morally better than one who does so gladly and from spontaneous benevolence, and that this is both unintuitive and unattractive. This complaint, however, is based on a misunderstanding of Kant's point. There are three important things to remember. First, Kant makes it clear that the reason he contrasts cases of natural affection with cases where the motive of duty operates in the absence of natural affection is that the operation of the motive of duty is especially obvious in the latter kind of case. Despite the misunderstandings to which this strategy gives rise, the essential difference between the two people contrasted does not rest in whether the helping action is enjoyed. It rests in whether one helps only because of this enjoyment or because help is perceived as something it is necessary to give. Nothing prevents an action from being done from the motive of duty by someone in whom sympathy is also present. Actually, we must distinguish two cases here. There might be a person in whom sympathy serves as a supplementary or cooperating motive that provides needed support for the motive of duty. This person's motives are impure, in the sense developed in *Religion Within the Limits of Reason Alone*, and he would not, or not always, do the helping action when required if sympathy did not serve as a prop to duty (R 24). This *does* decrease the person's moral worth. But another person in whom sympathy is present might be motivated entirely, or at least sufficiently, by the motive of duty, so that she would do the helping action even if sympathy were not present. This person has moral worth, yet her native sympathy will contribute to her enjoyment of the action.

However, a second point is even more important. Kant is talking here about the grounds on which a purpose is adopted and held. We must distinguish between the emotions, feelings, and desires which prompt us to *adopt* a purpose and those that *result from* the adoption of a purpose. Once you have adopted a purpose and become settled in its pursuit, certain emotions and feelings will naturally result. In particular, in ordinary circumstances the advancement of achievement of the purpose will make you happy, regardless of whether you adopted it originally from natural inclination or from duty. So a dutiful person, who after all really does value the happiness of others, will *therefore* take pleasure in making others happy.[53]

This is a point that Kant makes explicitly in his later ethical writings. For instance, in *The Metaphysical Principles of Virtue*, when Kant is explaining the duty of beneficence, he says:

Beneficence is a duty. Whoever often exercises this and sees his beneficent purpose succeed comes at last really to love him whom he has benefited. When therefore it is said, "Thou shalt love thy neighbor as thyself," this does not mean you should directly (at first) love and through this love (subsequently) benefit him; but rather, "Do good to your neighbor," and this beneficence will produce in you the love of mankind (as a readiness of inclination toward beneficence in general). (MPV 402)

Of course you may wonder why then the dutiful person in Kant's *Groundwork* example does not enjoy the helping action. Kant suggests two scenarios. In one, the action is done by someone whose mind "is clouded by a sorrow of his own which extinguished all sympathy with the lot of others" (G 398). In the other, the person is "by temperament cold and indifferent to the sufferings of others, perhaps because he is provided with special gifts of patience and fortitude" (G 398). The conditions of these persons make them incapable of deriving enjoyment from their helping actions. These are cases in which the motive of duty shines, according to Kant, because the advancement of the happiness of others is so clearly conceived as necessary rather than merely pleasant. But neither case suggests that in ordinary conditions a dutiful person will not have the emotions normally consequent upon the adoption of a purpose, including enjoyment of its successful pursuit, and joy in its realization.

Once this is accepted, the intuition behind the common complaint should collapse, and this is the third important point. The complaint is based on the usual misreading of the examples, in which the person who acts from duty is envisioned as someone who does not really have the happiness of others as his end. This is simply a mistake. Duty is not a different purpose, but a different ground for the adoption of a purpose. So Kant's idea here is captured better by saying that the sympathetic person's motive is *shallower* than the morally worthy person's: both want to help, but there is available a *further* stretch of motivating thought about helping which the merely sympathetic person has not engaged in.[54] This further stretch of thought concerns the sort of world which this would be if no one helped – or better, if no one perceived the need for help as a *reason* to help, or a *claim* on help. Such a world would be unacceptable because we regard our own needs as reasons why *we* should be helped (G 423; MPV 453). Regarding my needs as normative for others, or, as Kant puts it, making myself an end for others, I must regard the needs of others as normative for me (MPV 393).[55] And this is to say that the needs of others are a law to me. So the morally worthy person helps because she believes that the needs of others make a claim on her and so that there is a normative demand, or a law, that she ought to help. This characterization of the point of the example brings us to Kant's third proposition, which is that "Duty is the necessity of an action executed from respect for law" (G 400).

Now at this point it is essential to remember that what Kant is doing is a *motivational analysis* of the notion of duty or rightness. Kant is analyzing the good will, characterized as one that does what is right because it is right, in order to discover the principle of unconditionally good action.[56] The assumption behind such an analysis is that *the reason why a good-willed person does an action, and the reason why the action is right, are the same.* The good-willed person does the right thing because it is the right thing, so if we can discover why the good-willed person does it, we will have *ipso facto* discovered why it is the right thing. What the analysis reveals is that the reason why the good-willed person does the action is not merely because it serves this or that purpose, but because it is necessary – that is, it is a law – to perform such an action or to have such a purpose. The maxim of the action, or the maxim of the purpose, has what I shall call a "legal character": that is, it is normative, it has the capacity to express a demand made on us. Since the legal character of the maxim is what motivates the good-willed person, it is that, and nothing else, that makes the action or the purpose right. Kant's analysis identifies the rightness of the action *essentially* with the legal character of its maxim.

Now comes the critical step. It follows that the maxim must not get its legal character from anything outside of itself. For, if there were an outside source of legal character, then that source, rather than legal character itself, would be what makes the action right. Instead, the maxim's legal character must be intrinsic: it must have what I shall call a "lawlike form." This is why legal character, or *universality*, must be understood as lawlike form, that is, as a requirement of *universalizability*. Kant draws this conclusion this way:

Since I have robbed the will of all impulses which could come to it from obedience to any law, nothing remains to serve as a principle of the will except universal conformity of its action to law as such. That is, I should never act in such a way that I could not also will that my maxim should be a universal law. Mere conformity to law as such (without assuming any particular law applicable to certain actions) serves as the principle of the will, and it must serve as such a principle if duty is not to be a vain delusion and chimerical concept. (G 402)

The point is a delicate one. You might suppose, at first, that the legal character by which the good-willed person is motivated could come from something other than lawlike form of the maxim. For instance, you might suppose that the action is prescribed by some law whose grounds are independent of everything Kant has said here, and that the maxim could be "legal" in the sense that it conforms to this independent law. This is the possibility which Kant means to *block* in the above quotation when he adds the words "without assuming any particular law applicable to certain actions," and it is important to see why it is disallowed. Suppose that there were such a law, prescribing certain actions. I will call this the External Law. And suppose we say that the maxim gets its legal character not from its intrinsic lawlike form, but from the extrinsic fact that the action is prescribed by the External Law. Then we will have to ask why the External Law is a law before we have found the real reason why the action is right. That is to say, we will have to ask why the External Law is in force, why it is normative. Because obviously, the mere *grammatical* form of universality cannot make anything a law: a law must be normative. A law does not make a claim on me merely because it is addressed to me, or to some group that includes me. It must get its grip or hold on me, its capacity to bind me, from some intelligible source. But then the source of the External Law's normativity, rather than legal character of the maxim, will be what motivates the good-willed person. The reason why the External Law is in force, rather than the fact that the maxim has legal character, will be the good-willed person's motive, for it will be the real reason why the action is right. And this is contrary to Kant's analysis of the motive of duty.

An example will make this point clearer: Suppose that right actions were those commanded in laws laid down by God. According to Kant's analysis, the good-willed person does these actions because it is a law to do so. But why is it a law to do so? The answer is: because God so commands. Now, which of these two reasons is the reason why the good-willed person does the action, which is also the reason why the action is right? If the action is right because God commands it, it is not right because its maxim is intrinsically legal; and the reason why the good-willed person does it will not be grasp of its legal character, but response to divine command. This is contrary to Kant's analysis. The maxim of the action must be legal in itself, and this can only be because it has a lawlike form. The religious moralist may want to reply that the maxim's legal character, and the action's being divinely commanded, are the same thing. But its conformity to divine law can only make a maxim extrinsically, not intrinsically, legal. So the dilemma remains: If the person is moved by divine command, then legal character is not the motive, and the motive of duty is not at work. Since the legal character of a maxim and the divine commandedness of an action are not analytically the same thing, rightness must essentially lie in one of them or the other, and, according to the analysis, it must be the legal character of the maxim. And so this must be its intrinsic lawlike *form*. This argument will apply to any attempt to derive the legal character of a maxim from anything other than its intrinsic lawlike form: only legal character and lawlike form are *analytically* or essentially the same thing.[57]

Now that last argument may make it clear why the legal character of a maxim cannot come from an External Law. But the conclusion – that it must therefore come from lawlike form, as specified by the universalizability test – may seem much less obvious. Why, then, does Kant conclude that a maxim has *intrinsic* legal character only if it has what the universalizability test identifies as lawlike form?[58] To understand this, we must keep in mind two points. The first I have already noticed. In order to be a law, it is not enough that a principle be grammatically universal. It must also be normative for the person who is to follow it: there must be some intelligible reason why it binds *that person*. The second point concerns the way the universalizability requirement functions. The requirement tells us that we must act in such a way that we can at the same time will our maxims as universal laws. If a maxim passes this test, the action is right in the broad sense – it is all right, permissible, not wrong. It is only if a maxim fails the test that we get a duty – the duty of doing the opposite of what the failed maxim says, or, more precisely, of adopting the opposite of what the maxim says as law. So a maxim of *duty* is not merely one that you *can* will as universal law, but one that you *must* will as universal law. And this means that the maxim is a law to which your own will commits you. But a maxim to which your own will commits you is *normative for you*. And this, to return to the first point, is what a principle must be in order to be a law for you – it must be *normative for you*.

Again an example will clarify the point. I will take Kant's easiest example, that of the lying promise (G 422). A man in financial difficulties considers getting ready money on the strength of a lying promise that he will repay. His maxim is "I will make a lying promise, in order to get some ready money." He asks himself whether he could will his maxim to be at the same time a universal law. This means that he imagines a world in which everyone who needs money makes a lying promise and he imagines that, at the same time, he is part of this world, willing his maxim. His question is whether he can will this whole state of affairs. Now his maxim is derived from a hypothetical imperative: "If you will to get some ready money, then make a lying promise." This hypothetical imperative, in turn, is derived from the rational principle that whoever wills an end wills the necessary means, together with the "causal" law that lying promises are a means to, or will cause, the possession of ready money (G 417). However, in the world in which this maxim is universalized, this "causal" law does not hold. For if everyone in want of ready cash tried to make a lying promise, Kant says, "no one would believe what was promised to him but would only laugh at any such assertion as vain pretense" (G 422). The man in the example cannot, at the same time, rationally will both acting on his maxim and a state of affairs which undermines the causal law from which the rationality of acting on his maxim is derived. A man who wills to use the institution of promising in pursuit of his end must will that the institution should work. And it does not work unless promises are generally made in good faith. So he *himself* is committed to willing the law that people should make their promises in good faith, so long as he wills this particular maxim. Therefore, he cannot rationally will to act on this maxim at the same time as he wills it as a law.[59]

The important thing to see here is that it is the man's own will that commits him to the law that promises should be made in good faith, if they are to be made at all. The argument is not that promising is generally a useful institution or that the rightness of keeping promises is written into the nature of things. The man is committed to the institution of promising by his own maxim because he wills to employ it as a means to his end. It is his own will, and nothing else, that makes it impossible for him to will the universality of lying promises. In this way the universalizability test shows us what principles our own maxims commit us to willing as laws. As Kant says, if the man does will the maxim, he cannot also be willing it as a law, but rather must be regarding himself as an exception (G 424).[60]

Let me digress a moment. It is at this point in the argument that the objection Kant leveled against Wolff – the "empty formalism" objection – enters the picture as an objection against Kant himself. According to the objection, the Formula of Universal Law lacks content, since there are no restrictions on what we *can* will as a universal law, and therefore no implications about what we *must* so will. Now I hope that the example that I have just given will suggest that this objection is mistaken, and that there are laws to which our own wills do commit us. But it is also important to see what is wrong with one proposal for solving the emptiness problem sometimes made by those who, like Hegel, approve Kant's account of moral motivation but think that the Formula of Universal Law is empty. This proposal is that some external law or normative consideration can be imported into the system to solve the supposed emptiness problem and give content to our duties.[61]

This was Kant's own solution in the Prize Essay, where the judgments of the moral sense were brought in to give content to the obligations of which the principle "do that which is perfect" is the form. A variant of Kant's own argument in *Groundwork I* shows why this solution is disallowed. Either the action has its perfection in itself, or we are not doing it on account of its perfection, but on account of what gives it its perfection – in this case, the approval of the moral sense. The reason why the action is perfect, and the reason why a good person does it, must be exactly the same. The action's perfection cannot be extrinsically conferred by the moral sense, but must be intrinsic to the action itself. Content brought in from external normative sources violates Kant's analysis in the way we have seen.

We can now see a rather simpler way of making the argument against the External Law. Suppose, again, that the External Law is in force because it is the law of God's will. This is supposed to be what makes it normative. But how? God's will is only normative for me if it is the law of my own will to obey God's will. This is an old Hobbesian thought – that nothing can be a law for me unless I am bound to obey it, and nothing can bind me to obey it unless I have a motive for obeying it.[62] But Kant goes a step further than Hobbes. *Nothing* except my own will can make a law normative *for me*. Even the imposition of a sanction cannot bypass my will, for a reward or punishment only binds my will if I will to get the reward or avoid the punishment – that is, if I make it my maxim that my interest or preservation should be a law to me. Only those maxims shown to be necessary by the universalizability test – only those to which my own will commits me – are *intrinsically* normative. And this, as the rationalists had argued all along, is what an obligation must be. Autonomy is the only possible source of intrinsic normativity, and so of obligation.

One result of this is that it shows that the British rationalists to some extent mistook their target. They opposed Hobbesianism, moral sense theory, and divine command theory, all on the grounds, as they thought, that these make morality a matter of positive law. But Kant's analysis shows that positivity is not the problem. A law in the nature of things, if it is understood as a theoretical or metaphysical principle that is external to the will, gives rise to exactly the same problem that divine law does.[63] Laws in the nature of things can only make our maxims extrinsically, not intrinsically, normative. The problem with these theories is not that their laws are positive, but that their laws are not willed autonomously, and so are not intrinsically normative. But the Kantian laws of autonomy are positive laws: moral laws exist because *we* legislate them.

Another mistaken target, this time of British moral philosophy more generally, is the analyzability of moral concepts. Price and Hutcheson agree that moral ideas are fundamentally "simple," and can only be defined trivially by synonyms.[64] This idea is echoed in G. E. Moore's concern with the "naturalistic fallacy": because "pleasure" and "good", for instance, cannot be taken to mean the same thing, Moore concludes that "good" is a simple idea.[65] Ross, following Moore, makes a similar claim about "right."[66] The truth in these arguments is this: claims about, say, pleasure, or what maximizes pleasure, are not intrinsically normative, the way claims about the right and the good are. The normativity of an ethical concept cannot be derived from any non-ethical concept, so no ethical concept can be completely analyzed in terms of a natural or factual one. All of these philosophers conclude that normative concepts are unanalyzable. As a result, they think that our understanding of the normative concept does not enable us to pick out its objects, and that we must therefore have recourse to a sense or to a faculty of intuition that functions like a sense.

But Kant's analysis does not reduce the normative concept to a non-normative one; instead, it reduces normative content to normative form. What the analysis yields is that right actions are those whose maxims have lawlike form, which is the form of normativity itself. Provided that the categorical imperative procedure can be made to work, Kant's analysis does enable us to pick out the objects of the concept; that is, it enables us to identify our duties. We discover the content of morality by seeing which maxims have normative form.

But perhaps the most fundamental mistake of the British moralists of both the eighteenth and twentieth centuries has been the acceptance of Hume's dilemma. For Hume's dilemma leaves us with an unfortunate choice. If the virtue of an action is conferred by its motive, then that motive cannot be the motive of obligation. The rationalists found this objectionable, both because it seems as if at least some actions really ought to be done from the motive of obligation, and because the fact of obligation seems to be dependent on the possibility of the motive. The rationalist saved obligation, but at the cost of locating morality in the metaphysical properties of actions, rather than in the motivational properties of people.

The argument of *Groundwork I* shows us we do not have to accept Hume's dilemma. For Kant shows that the premise of Hume's argument – that doing your duty from the motive of duty is an empty formalism – is false. An obligation, or an action done from the motive of duty, is one that the agent herself must will as a universal law. It is, in its very nature and essence, an action autonomously willed. To complete the argument, and show that obligations really exist, Kant needs only to show that human beings are capable of autonomous motivation: that is, that we can be motivated by those laws that we must will. If we are capable of giving laws to ourselves, then we have obligations.

NOTES

I would like to thank Charlotte Brown and Manley Thompson for their valuable assistance with this paper.

1 The contemporary debate began with W. D. Falk's " 'Ought' and Motivation" in his *Ought, Reasons, and Morality: The Collected Papers of W. D. Falk*, chapter 1. Among other important discussions are William Frankena, "Obligation and Motivation in Recent Moral Philosophy" in his *Perspectives on Morality: Essays of William K. Frankena*, chapter 6; Part I of Thomas Nagel's *The Possibility of Altruism*; Bernard Williams, "Internal and External Reasons" in his *Moral Luck*, chapter 8; and Stephen Darwall, *Impartial Reason*. I discuss the subject in "Skepticism About Practical Reason," Chapter 11 in this volume.

2 See for instance Frankena, "Obligation and Motivation in Recent Moral Philosophy" and Williams, "Internal and External Reasons."

3 See for instance Nagel, *The Possibility of Altruism* and my "Skepticism about Practical Reason."

4 Samuel Clarke, *A Discourse Concerning the Unalterable Obligations of Natural Religion and the Truth and Certainty of the Christian Revelation: The Boyle Lectures 1705* in *The Works of Samuel Clarke*, pp. 609–10. Selections from the Boyle Lectures can be found in D. D. Raphael, ed., *The British Moralists 1650–1800* vol. I; the passages cited are at pp. 194–96. Hereinafter this work will be cited as "Clarke" with page numbers from the Garland edition followed by those from the Raphael selections where available.

5 Francis Hutcheson, *Illustrations on the Moral Sense*. This work is the second part of *An Essay on the Nature and Conduct of the Passions and Affections. With Illustrations on the Moral Sense*. Hereinafter this work will be cited as "Hutcheson's *Illustrations*."

6 Richard Price, *A Review of the Principal Questions in Morals*, ed. D. D. Raphael, p. 49. The *Review* was the first published in London in 1758 under the title *A Review of the Principal Questions and Difficulties in Morals*. Raphael's edition, which I have cited, is reprinted from the third edition of 1787. Selections from the *Review* can be found in D. D. Raphael, ed., *The British Moralists 1650–1800* vol. II, pp. 131–98; the passage cited is at p. 147. Hereinafter this work will be cited as "Price" with page numbers from Raphael's edition of the book followed by those from the selections in *British Moralists*.

7 David Hume, *A Treatise of Human Nature*, p. 457. Hereinafter cited as "Hume's *Treatise*."

8 For discussion see Paul Schilpp, *Kant's Pre-Critical Ethics*, ch. 3. Kant praises Hutcheson in the Prize Essay (see below), and in later works treats Hutcheson's view as representative of attempts to base morality on feeling. In his Introduction to Adam Smith's *Theory of Moral Sentiments*, D. D. Raphael describes a letter of 1771 from Markus Herz to Kant in which Herz refers to Smith as "your favorite" (p. 31).

9 "So-called" because it was written for a prize offered in 1763 by the Berlin Academy. Kant did not actually win the prize, which went to Moses Mendelssohn. See Lewis White Beck, *Early German Philosophy: Kant and His Predecessors*, pp. 441–42.

10 The two steps described correspond approximately to the metaphysical and transcendental deductions of the categories in the *Critique of Pure Reason*; although the relation between a metaphysical deduction of an *a priori* concept and its analysis is not perfectly clear. In any case the analysis of the concept of obligation, with which I am concerned here, will show that it is logically possible – that the idea contains no contradiction – while the synthesis will show how it is really possible, how it can apply to us. For the distinction between logical and real possibility, see C1 A243–44/B301–02 and A596n/B624n. The account of

real possibility in these passages is given in terms of the possibility of experience and therefore does not apply to ethical concepts, but there must still be an analogue of it for ethical concepts if dogmatic rationalism in ethics is to be avoided.

11 For the most part, I will use "right" and "obligatory" to denote any action that is morally called for. The term "right" may be used more broadly, to include permissible actions, and Kant's analysis also explicates this notion, but my focus will be on required actions. Both "right" and "obligatory" can also be used more specifically, to refer actions called for by so-called perfect duties, or still more specifically to actions called for by justice. Some philosophers, for example Hume and Bernard Williams, believe that "right" and "obligatory" should only be used for one of these latter two classes of actions, and at various points would find in this view grounds for objecting to the argument of this paper. I do not try to deal with the issue, but I do try to notice the points where it comes up. See nn13, 21, and 23.

12 Rightness is strictly speaking a property of acts, and any given act can be done from a variety of motives, good, bad, or indifferent. But right acts can be defined or identified in terms of motives even if they are not always done from those motives; they can be defined as the ones a person with good motives would do, or ones that good motives would prompt. The strategy is thought to be characteristic of virtue-centered ethical theories, but as I will show it is also Kant's.

13 Hume's *Treatise*, p. 478. This argument occurs at the beginning of the section in which justice is identified as an artificial virtue, and it is important to point out that its conclusion in a certain way only applies to the natural virtues. The "first motive" to justice turns out to be self-interest (492; 495), but this is neither an especially virtuous motive (492) nor is it the motive usually at work in agents performing just actions. Particular acts of justice taken separately are not necessarily in our interest (497). We approve of justice because sympathy makes us approve whatever is in the collective interest (499–500); we perform just actions, or restrain ourselves from unjust ones, because we approve of justice: that is, because justice is virtuous, and we value our own character (500–01; see also the *Enquiry Concerning the Principles of Morals*, ed. L. A. Selby-Bigge and P. H. Nidditch [Oxford; Clarendon Press, 1975], pp. 282–83). This is one sense in which justice is an "artificial" virtue. This point becomes important later in the argument; see n21.

14 Hume's *Treatise*, p. 478.

15 See for instance Nagel, *The Possibility of Altruism*, pp. 4–5.

16 Hutcheson's *Illustrations*, p. 130.

17 Hutcheson's *Illustrations*, pp. 121, 130.

18 Hutcheson's *Illustrations*, p. 139.

19 Hutcheson's *Illustrations*, p. 140. See also Hutcheson's *Inquiry Concerning the Original of Our Ideas of Virtue or Moral Good*, in D. D. Raphael, ed. *The British Moralists 1650–1800* vol. I, p. 293.

20 Hume's *Treatise*, p. 479.

21 However, as I point out in n13, the motive of obligation *is* the usual motive at work in the case of *just* actions (and, when we are tempted, abstentions), and this is an important point in Hume's favor. Our belief that obligation should be the motive of just actions is much firmer than our belief that it should be the motive of those actions springing from what Hume would call the natural virtues, which we may regard as meritorious rather than required (See n11). It should be observed that in the passage in which he complains that rationalists cannot account for morality's power to motivate us, which I have quoted on p. 315, Hume is careful about this: he speaks specifically about just actions. Thus Hume could argue, against the point I am making here, that his system favors the operation of the motive of duty in exactly those cases in which we feel most sure that it should operate.

22 Reprinted in her *Ethics, Religion, and Politics: Collected Philosophical Papers of G. E. M. Anscombe, Volume III*, pp. 26–42.

23 Williams wants us to recognize that obligations "form just one type of ethical consideration" (p. 196). Some actions are not obligatory but more or less than obligatory: admirable, or heroic, or simply what a person of good character would do (p. 179). Williams's view is similar to Hume's view that the motive of obligation is appropriate for one kind of moral consideration (that of justice) but not all (See n11, 14, 21). Williams regards attempts to treat all ethical claims as forms of obligation (by means of such devices as Ross's *prima facie* obligations, or imperfect duties, or general duties, or duties to oneself) as fundamentally misguided (pp. 178–92). The point of such attempts, I believe, is not merely to impose an artificial orderliness on the moral terrain, nor to license blaming people who ignore certain ethical claims, but to explain how these claims have normative force for the agents who act on them. Williams does see that this is part of the motive for the idea of general or imperfect or *prima facie* obligations, but thinks that it is an error to suppose that all practical necessity, or normative force, springs from obligations (p. 196). Even if he is right, some account of the normative force of these claims is needed, as he would agree. See n26.

24 Anscombe says that the terms "should" and "ought" "have now acquired a special so-called 'moral' sense – i.e., a sense in which they imply some absolute verdict (like one of guilty/not guilty on a man) on what is described in the 'ought' sentences" ("Modern Moral Philosophy," p. 29; see

also p. 32.) Williams says: "... once I am under the obligation, there is no escaping it, and the fact that a given agent would prefer not to be in this system [the morality system] or bound by its rules will not excuse him; nor will blaming him to be based on a misunderstanding. *Blame is the characteristic reaction of the morality system*" (*Ethics and the Limits of Philosophy*, p. 177; my emphasis). This seems to me wrong; the morality system Williams describes in the text is distinctly rationalistic, but the emphasis on blame, and on the general ideas of merit and demerit, is more characteristic of sentimentalist theories, for reasons I mention in the text. Kant notices the ways the duties of respect *restrict* our practices of blaming: he says that "the reproach of vice ... must never burst out in complete contempt or deny the wrongdoer all moral worth, because on that hypothesis he could never be improved either – and this is incompatible with the idea of man, who as ... a moral being can never lose all predisposition to good" (MPV 463). I discuss this attitude to blame in "Morality as Freedom," Chapter 6 in this volume.

25 This is most explicit in the theory of Adam Smith, who has more to say about moral motivation than Hume or Hutcheson, and who gives a more positive account of the role of the motive of duty. Smith says: "When our passive feelings are almost always so sordid and selfish, how comes it that our active principles should often be so generous and so noble? ... It is not the soft power of humanity, it is not that feeble spark of benevolence which Nature has lighted up in the human heart, that is thus capable of counteracting the strongest impulses of self-love. It is a stronger power, a more forcible motive, which exerts itself upon such occasions. It is reason, principle, conscience, the inhabitant of the breast, *the man within, the great judge and arbiter of our conduct*" (*The Theory of Moral Sentiments*, p. 137; my emphasis). The "man within," Smith's impartial spectator, develops by a process of internalization that begins with our judgment of the conduct of others. Sympathizing with others who in a similar way judge us turns our attention to our own conduct, and by this process we are led to the idea of an internal spectator whose judgment is the motive of duty (*The Theory of Moral Sentiments*, pp. 109–78).

26 To be fair, Williams also discusses this side of the idea of obligation, in the chapter cited and in "Practical Necessity" in his *Moral Luck*.

27 See for instance *Nicomachean Ethics* III.7 1115b11–14; III.12 1119b15; IV.1 1120a23; X.9 1179b30; and X.9 1180a6–8.

28 I discuss this in my "Aristotle on Function and Virtue." See especially 269–72. The point is related to the fact that "... it is not merely the state in accordance with the right rule, but the state that implies the *presence* of the right rule, that is virtue" (*Nicomachean Ethics* VI. 13

1144b27). There *is* a sense in which Aristotle's virtuous person acts *from* the right rule, although it is not the same sense that the rationalists had in mind.

29 Both Price's *Review* and John Balguy's *The Foundation of Moral Goodness: Or a Further Inquiry into the Original of Our Idea of Virtue* were written directly in response to Hutcheson's theory.

30 Clarke, pp. 596–97; 608–12/192–99.

31 Clarke, pp. 614/202.

32 Clarke, pp. 614/202. These passages are quoted with approval by Price (118) and Frankena ("Obligation and Motivation," p. 59).

33 On the one side, Price incorporated Hutcheson's idea of a moral sense into his rationalist theory (see Price, pp. 57–68/148–52). On the other side, Adam Smith developed an account of the genesis of the motive of duty, and gave it a prominent role, in a sentimentalist context (see n25, above). And Joseph Butler, while aspiring like the sentimentalists to explain morality in terms of human nature, argued that conscience is intrinsically authoritative and no sanction is needed for obeying it. See Joseph Butler, *Five Sermons Preached at the Rolls Chapel*, hereinafter cited as "Butler," pp. 11, 43.

34 Price, pp. 47–48, 146–47.

35 Price, pp. 15, 133.

36 W. D. Ross, *The Right and the Good*, p. 3 (hereinafter referred to as "Ross"). I have already mentioned that a motivational analysis does not require this: "right act" can mean an act that a person with a certain sort of motive would do, without any implication that every such act is done from that motive and so is morally good (see n12, above). But this does not affect Ross's argument and so is not to the point here. Notice that Hume's use of the term 'virtuous' in the original statement of the dilemma does carry both the implication of 'right' and of 'morally good'.

37 Ross, p. 4.

38 Ross, p. 5.

39 Ross, pp. 5–6.

40 Ross, p. 5.

41 See the quotation from Clarke on p. 51 and the one from Price below, p. 54.

Balguy says "What is the Reason exciting a Man to the Choice of a Virtuous Action? I answer, his very Approbation of it. . . ." Balguy, p. 45; see also pp. 56, 61.

42 Price, pp. 186–87, 194.

43 See H. A. Prichard, "Duty and Interest" in his *Moral Obligation and Duty and Interest: Essays and Lectures by H. A. Prichard.* Falk's paper " 'Ought' and Motivation," which introduced the internalism/

externalism distinction, is addressed to Prichard and Ross on just this point.

44 Ross, pp. 132–33.

45 Ross, pp. 7–11 and 34–39.

46 Ross, p. 122n.

47 Ross, p. 122.

48 Kant must mean that there is room for conceptual confusion in the case of direct inclination. If you perform a dutiful act that is also, for some people, pleasant in itself, we cannot tell whether you acted from duty or only from pleasure. But no one gives correct change just for the pleasure of it, so here we know that the action was either from duty or self-interest. But there is surely no way to tell about an actual honest action that happens to be in someone's interest that she *did it* from interest rather than duty.

49 In the passage cited Kant sounds negative about honor; he says that "The ideal of morality belongs to culture; its use for some simulacrum of morality in the love of honor and outward decorum constitutes mere civilization" and that "Everything good that is not based on a morally good disposition . . . is nothing but pretense and glittering misery." But in another passage Kant speaks more leniently of honor. He is discussing the question whether the government has the right to punish two kinds of murderers: young officers who kill in duels, and unmarried mothers who kill their children to avoid disgrace. Rather surprisingly, Kant thinks there is reason to doubt whether these murderers may be punished, for he says that honor "is no delusion in these cases" and that "legislation itself . . . is responsible for the fact that incentives of honor among the people do not accord (subjectively) with the standards that are (objectively) appropriate to their purpose" (MPJ 336–37). Kant is generally characterized as believing that duty and inclination are the only two kinds of motivation, but both of these passages suggest that he regards honor as something in between – a sort of proto-moral motive that precedes the genuine motive of duty in the education of the human species. I speculate that Kant means that the motive of honor approximates the motive of moral autonomy insofar as the person governed by it follows, for its own sake, a strict law of conduct which represents an ideal of character. Yet motives of honor fall short of the full-fledged moral motive because the laws of honor are not derived from autonomy itself. See n51, below.

50 See Andrews Reath, "Hedonism and Heteronomy."

51 Kant calls the sympathetic person a *"Menschenfreundes"* (G 398): a friend to humanity. And sentimentalist moral philosophers thought of sympathy as a response we have to human beings as such (not just to

those to whom we are particularly attached) in virtue of the universal human characteristics which make them similar to ourselves. Thus sympathy makes an end of humanity and so serves as a simulacrum of the Formula of Humanity just as honor serves as a simulacrum of the Formula of Universal Law.

52 After Butler wrote his famous Sermon XI on the consistency of benevolence with self-love, it was not uncommon for eighteenth-century philosophers to treat the principle of self-love as providing a method of choosing among various ends, all of which are valued for their own sakes. Butler argued that the pleasure we get from satisfying a desire presupposes, rather than explains, the desire: it is because we have the desire that we enjoy achieving its object (Butler, pp. 46–54). The principle of self-love selects among things, all of which we desire for their own sakes, on the basis of how much pleasure we will get from achieving them. Kant apparently did not read Butler, but Butler's picture of the operation of self-love was adopted both by Hume in the *Enquiry Concerning the Principles of Morals* (pp. 281–82; 301–02), and to some extent by Hutcheson in *Illustrations Upon the Moral Sense*. Kant uses the principle of self-love in this sense – as one way of choosing among things we desire for their own sakes – but sets the principle of duty up as rival to it – as another way of choosing our purposes.

53 It may seem as if I am guilty of a commonplace error in making these remarks: confusing pleasure with satisfaction or gratification. Once I've made up my mind to do or achieve something, I am of course gratified to see it done. But that point applies even to actions undertaken for the most purely instrumental reasons, actions that are only means to other ends. The point I am making here is a different one, having to do with what it *means* to say that you have made something your purpose. My claim is that if you really succeed in making something your purpose, and so value it as an end, you will come to take pleasure in its successful pursuit. I explain this further in "Morality as Freedom," Chapter 6 in this volume.

54 The same point is made by other rationalists. Price distinguishes rational from instinctive benevolence, and, like Kant, claims that instinctive benevolence is lovable but falls short of virtue (Price, pp. 190–91, 196–97). Balguy makes a similar comparison (Balguy, pp. 59–60). Ross says, "The conscientious attitude is one which *involves* the thought either of good or of pleasure for some one else, but it is *a more reflective attitude* than that in which we aim directly at the production of some good or some pleasure for another, since . . . we stop to think whether in all the circumstances the bringing of that good or pleasure into existence is what is really incumbent upon us. . . . " (Ross, pp. 162–63; my emphasis).

55 Nagel employs a similar argument in *The Possibility of Altruism*, pp. 82–84.

56 I say this in spite of the fact that in the third section of the *Groundwork*, Kant says that the principle that "an absolutely good will is one whose maxim can always include itself as a universal law" is synthetic because "by analysis of the concept of an absolutely good will that property of the maxim cannot be found" (G 447). I believe that this is a misstatement, or at least a poor way of putting the point. What is synthetic is that the moral law holds *for us* – that we are capable of having absolutely good wills. The statement that a good will is one whose maxim is universalizable is synthetic only if "good" is being used in a fully normative sense – to signify a demand on us.

57 I formulated an earlier version of this argument in a comment on David Cummiskey's paper "Kant's Refutation of Consequentialism" at the American Philosophical Association meetings in April 1988, and I would like to thank Cummiskey for prompting me to do so.

58 Perhaps it is worth saying a word about what it means to claim that a maxim has a "form." The "form" of a thing is ordinarily thought to rest in the relations among its parts, and the parts of a maxim of action (to take the simplest case) are the action to be performed and the purpose to be realized. The plausibility of Kant's thought that the rightness of a particular action rests in the form of its maxim can be seen intuitively by considering the following triples of maxims:

(A) I will knock Alex down, in order to remove him from the path of an oncoming bullet.

(B) I will knock Alex down, in order to relieve my temper.

(C) I will punch a punching bag, in order to relieve my temper.

Or:

(A) I will avoid visiting my grandmother in the hospital, in order to avoid a contagion to which I am especially susceptible.

(B) I will avoid visiting my grandmother in the hospital, in order to spare myself unpleasantness.

(C) I will avoid watching prime-time television, in order to spare myself unpleasantness.

In each set, maxims A and B concern the same act or omission, yet adopting maxim A is permissible or even good, while B is wrong. But this is not simply because of the purpose in maxim B, for maxim C contains the same purpose, yet it, once again, is permissible. What is wrong with the action whose maxim is B, then, does not rest either in the action that is performed or in the purpose for which it is performed, but in the relation between the two. And the relation between the two parts of the maxim is its form.

59 I explain my views about how the Formula of Universal Law should be applied more fully in "Kant's Formula of Universal Law," Chapter 3 in this volume.

60 It is essential to keep in mind that these considerations by themselves do not show why the action is irrational. All that this argument shows is why the maxim cannot be willed as a law – not why a rational being must only will maxims that can be willed as laws. For that part of the argument we need to take the further step described in the conclusion of this paper.

61 For instance, after praising and affirming Kant's conception of the autonomy of the will Hegel says ". . . still to adhere to the exclusively moral position, without making the transition to the conception of ethics, is to reduce this gain to an empty formalism . . . of course, material may be brought in from the outside and particular duties may be arrived at accordingly. . . ." *The Philosophy of Right*, trans. T. M. Knox, pp. 89–90. I owe the reference to Daniel Brudney.

62 See especially *Leviathan*, Part I, ch. 14.

63 This may be especially hard to see, because the arguments that British rationalists use to show that moral laws are indeed laws of reason are similar to those that Kant uses to show that moral laws are laws we must rationally will. Strictly speaking, rationalists should not give arguments *for* moral laws, since they think these laws are self-evident. But Clarke, in particular, tries to impress this self-evidence upon his audience by appeal to arguments from the "Golden Rule," and arguments from this principle are similar to those from the categorical imperative. For instance, Clarke says that if we were not corrupt, "It would be as impossible that a Man, contrary to the eternal Reason of things, should desire to gain some small profit to Himself, by doing violence and damage to his Neighbor; as that he should be willing to be deprived of necessaries himself, to satisfy the unreasonable Covetousness or Ambition of another" (Clarke, pp. 619–20/208).

64 Price, p. 41/141; Hutcheson, *Inquiry Concerning the Original of Our Ideas of Virtue or Moral Good*, p. 305.

65 G. E. Moore, *Principia Ethica*, pp. 5–17.

66 Ross, pp. 7–12.

3 Kant's Formula of Universal Law

Kant's first formulation of the categorical imperative, the Formula of Universal Law, runs:

Act only according to that maxim by which you can at the same time will that it should become a universal law. (G 421)

A few lines later, Kant says that this is equivalent to acting as though your maxim were by your will to become a law of nature, and he uses this latter formulation in his examples of how the imperative is to be applied. Elsewhere, Kant specifies that the test is whether you could will the universalization for a system of nature "of which you yourself were a part" (C2 69); and in one place he characterizes the moral agent as asking "what sort of world he would create under the guidance of practical reason, . . . a world into which, moreover, he would place himself as a member" (R 5). But how do you determine whether or not you can will a given maxim as a law of nature? Since the will is practical reason, and since everyone must arrive at the same conclusions in matters of duty, it cannot be the case that what you are able to will is a matter of personal taste, or relative to your individual desires. Rather, the question of what you can will is a question of what you can will *without contradiction*.

According to Kant, willing universalized maxims may give rise to contradictions in two ways:

Some actions are of such a nature that their maxim cannot even be *thought* as a universal law of nature without contradiction, far from it being possible that one could will that it should be such. In others this internal impossibility is not found, though it is still impossible to *will* that their maxim should be raised to the universality of a law of nature, because such a will would contradict itself. We easily see that the former maxim conflicts with the

77

stricter or narrower (imprescriptible) duty, the latter with broader (meritorious) duty. (G 424)

The first sort of contradiction is usually called a contradiction in conception, and the second a contradiction in the will.

In this paper I am concerned with identifying the sense in which there is a "contradiction" in willing the universalization of an immoral maxim, and especially with the sense in which the universalization of such a maxim can be said to have a contradiction *in* it — that is, with the idea of a contradiction in conception. There are three different interpretations of the kind of contradiction Kant has (or ought to have) in mind found in the literature.[1] They are:

i) The Logical Contradiction Interpretation. On this interpretation, there is something like a logical impossibility in the universalization of the maxim, or in the system of nature in which the maxim is a natural law: if the maxim were universalized, the action or policy that it proposes would be inconceivable.

ii) The Teleological Contradiction Interpretation. On this interpretation, it would be contradictory to will your maxim as a law for a system of nature teleologically conceived: either you are acting against some natural purpose, or your maxim could not be a teleological law. The maxim is inconsistent with a systematic harmony of purposes, or with the principle that any organ, instinct, or action-type has a natural purpose for which it must be the one best suited.

iii) The Practical Contradiction Interpretation. On this interpretation, the contradiction is that your maxim would be self-defeating if universalized: your action would become ineffectual for the achievement of your purpose if everyone (tried to) use it for that purpose. Since you propose to use that action for that purpose at the same time as you propose to universalize the maxim, you in effect will the thwarting of your own purpose.

In trying to determine which of these views is correct, it is important to remember that it is not just because of the contradiction in the universalized maxim that immoral action is irrational. Kant is not claiming that immoral conduct is contradictory — if he were, the moral law would be analytic rather than synthetic. In any event, a contradiction in the universalization of your maxim would not prove that there is a contradiction in your maxim, for these are different.

The Formula of Universal Law is a test of the sufficiency of the reasons for action and choice which are embodied in our maxims. The idea that universalizability is a test for sufficiency ("what if everybody did that?") is a familiar one, and shows in an intuitive way why it is rational to attend to a universalizability requirement. But the claim that universalizability is a test for a reason sufficient to motivate a rational being cannot be fully defended at this stage of the argument, for the full defense requires the connection to autonomy. Kant's critical ethical project is to prove that perfect rationality includes conformity to the categorical imperative: but in the *Groundwork* this project is not directly taken up until the Third Section.[2] The Second Section, where the Formula of Universal Law appears, is devoted to showing us what the content of the categorical imperative will be *if there is one*. The question of contradictions arises not in the context of determining *why* you must conform your conduct to the categorical imperative, but of *how* you do so.

Yet in trying to come to an understanding of how the Formula of Universal Law is to be applied, we must not lose sight of this further goal. Any view of how the Formula of Universal Law is applied must presuppose some view of what rational willing is. The problem is most obviously pressing for the case of contradictions in the will, for it seems impossible to say what contradicts a rational will until we know what a rational will is, or what it necessarily contains. There is a contradiction in one's beliefs if one believes both x and not-x, or things that imply both x and not-x. There is a contradiction in one's will if one wills both x and not-x, or things that imply both x and not-x. But until one knows what things are involved in or implied by "willing x," one will not know how to discover these contradictions. So in determining which maxims can be willed as universal law without contradiction, we will have to employ some notion of what rational willing is. Some of the interpretations of the contradiction in conception test also rely on particular views of what rational willing is. This is why we must keep in view Kant's eventual aim of showing that moral conduct is rational conduct. Whatever view of the nature of rational willing is used in determining how the formula is to be applied must also be used in determining why it is rational to act as the formula prescribes.

One constraint this places on interpretations of the test is this: it must not employ a notion of rational willing that already has moral content. An example will show what I mean. John Stuart Mill says of Kant:

But when he begins to deduce from this precept any of the actual duties of morality, he fails, almost grotesquely, to show that there would be any contradiction, any logical (not to say physical) impossibility, in the adoption by all rational beings of the most outrageously immoral rules of conduct. All he shows is that the consequences of their universal adoption would be such as no one would choose to incur.[3]

Mill thinks that Kant's view really amounts to an appeal to utility, to what we would now call rule-utilitarianism. A rule-utilitarian interpretation of the Formula of Universal Law gives, as Mill points out, no sense to Kant's use of the word "contradiction" in this context. Yet, we could give it sense by claiming that a rational being is *by definition* opposed to undesirable consequences, and therefore cannot, without contradiction, will the universalization of any maxim if that universalization would have undesirable consequences. But roughly this kind of connection between a rational will and a moral will is what Kant is trying to *establish*, and therefore to use such a definition in explaining the contradiction test would make the Kantian argument circular. For if we use this definition we are already presupposing a morality-laden conception of what it is to be rational: we are assuming the sort of connection between moral goodness and rationality that Kant is preparing to demonstrate. So although the contradiction tests by themselves do not show us why immoral action is irrational, the notion of rational willing which they presuppose must be one that can be used at the later stage of the argument.

My question is which of the three "kinds" of contradiction we should expect to find in the universalized version of an immoral maxim, and my aim is to defend the third answer, that it is a practical contradiction. I should say from the outset that although there is one important piece of textual evidence for this answer, it is my view that no interpretation can be based on textual considerations alone. Language supporting all of them can be found in Kant's texts, and it seems possible that he was not aware of the differences among them. My defense of the practical contradiction interpretation will therefore be based primarily on philosophical considerations. For each interpretation I will ask (i) what kinds of cases it can handle, (ii) whether it can meet some standard objections, (iii) what sort of distinction between the contradiction in conception test and the contradiction in the will test is implied by it, and, most importantly, (iv) what presuppositions about rationality it makes and so what kind of case it will allow Kant to make when he turns to the critical project of showing that morality *is* pure rationality.

I THE LOGICAL CONTRADICTION INTERPRETATION

Some of Kant's defenders have tried to identify a contradiction of just the sort Mill denies can be found. Versions of a Logical Contradiction Interpretation have been defended by Dietrichson, Kemp, and Wood,[4] among others. I suppose hardly any of this interpretation's proponents have held it in the pure form that Mill describes: what they have looked for is something very like a logical or physical impossibility. Part of the reason for this is that it is clear that nothing like a logical contradiction can be found for the contradiction in the will test, since we are explicitly told that maxims that fail that test are conceivable. But there is no question that much of Kant's language favors a Logical Contradiction Interpretation for the contradiction in conception test. He says that universalizations of immoral maxims destroy themselves (G 403), annihilate themselves (C2 27), are inconceivable or cannot be thought, and so on. The example that fits this view best is the false promising example. A man in financial difficulties considers "borrowing" money which he knows he can never repay. Kant explains how this fails the contradiction in conception test this way:

... the universality of a law which says that anyone who believes himself to be in need could promise what he pleased with the intention of not fulfilling it would make the promise itself and the end to be accomplished by it impossible; no one would believe what was promised to him but would only laugh at any such assertion as vain pretense. (G 422)

Proponents of the Logical Contradiction Interpretation tend to focus on the remark that the promise itself would be impossible, as this seems to be where a logical inconceivability would lie. Kant tells us that promises would be impossible if this maxim were universalized because no one would believe them. There are various ways to find a contradiction here. One could say that the contradiction is that we are trying to conceive a world in which the agent (and everyone with his purpose) is making a certain sort of false promise, but at the same time we are necessarily conceiving a world in which no one can be making this sort of promise, since you cannot make a promise (of this sort) to someone who will not accept it. Perhaps the clearest way to bring out a logical contradiction is to say that there would be no such thing as a promise (or anyway a repayment-promise) in the world of the universalized maxim. The practice of offering and accepting promises would have died out under stress of too many violations. Thus we are imagining a world in which the agent and everyone with his purpose is making a certain sort of promise, but also a world in which there is no such thing. And this is logically inconceivable. If universalizing a maxim makes the action proposed inconceivable, then, we can get a logical contradiction.

A problem about violence

The difficulty in taking this line shows up in a problem that Dietrichson describes in "Kant's Criteria of Universalizability." He considers the case of a woman who has decided to consider the maxim "if I give birth to a baby weighing less than six pounds, I shall do everything in my power to kill it."[5] Dietrichson points out that it is certainly possible to conceive the idea of every mother behaving according to this rule. In my view, Dietrichson's example is not a properly formulated maxim, since it does not mention the mother's reason for killing the child. The child's weighing less than six pounds is not by itself recognizable as a *prima facie* reason for killing it. Since the Formula of Universal Law is a test of the sufficiency of reasons, the maxim must include them. But this is not the problem brought out by Dietrichson's example. We can make the maxim one of killing children that tend to cry at night more than average, in order to get enough sleep. Either Dietrichson's maxim or mine could clearly be a universal law without a logical contradiction. There could in fact be worlds where these things happen. They could happen in our world.

Dietrichson's solution is to appeal to the second contradiction test, and to place this among the maxims whose universalizations cannot be willed although they can be conceived. But this will not work. Different ways of deriving duties lead to different kinds of duty, with different moral and legal consequences. In the *Groundwork*, Kant associates the contradiction in the will test with wide, meritorious duties (G 424), and the duty not to kill a child is obviously not of that kind.

Since Kant's account of the division of duties changes it is worth noting that even the later views will not permit Dietrichson's solution. The examples in the *Groundwork* are divided in the text into perfect duties to self, perfect duties to others, imperfect duties to self, and imperfect duties to others. A footnote warns us, however, that Kant will make his own division of duties in the *Metaphysics of Morals* (G 421). That work is divided into duties of justice and of virtue. Now it might seem tempting to simply identify duties of justice, narrow duties, perfect duties, and negative duties with one another and similarly to suppose that duties of virtue, wide duties, imperfect duties, and positive duties are the same. But this would be an oversimplification: Kant's categorizations are more intricate than that.[6] For although the duties of virtue are said to be broad or wide duties, there are perfect and negative duties that appear in this category: the duty not to commit suicide (one of Kant's *Groundwork* examples) being an important instance. The perfect duties of virtue are the duties not to abuse your own moral and physical person and duties of respect (as opposed to those of love) to others (MPV 464, §41).

There is room for controversy about exactly what effect this complex categorization has on the derivation of the relevant duties. In the *Groundwork*, Kant's view seems to be that all perfect duties, whether of virtue or justice, are to be derived from the contradiction in conception test. At least, this is how he tries to derive the duty not to commit suicide. Later, I will explain why I think that the derivation of this duty given by Kant under the Formula of Universal Law in the *Groundwork* does not work. My own opinion is that this is because the perfect duties of virtue require a more complex derivation than Kant gives them in the *Groundwork*. Perfect duties of virtue spring from the fact that there are ends against which we must not act, and ends cannot be assigned to us by the contradiction in the conception test, although they can by the contradiction in the will test. Kant's own texts do not give us direct guidance here, for in spelling out the duties of virtue in the *Metaphysics of Morals* he for the most part uses the concepts and casuistical methods of the Formula of Humanity rather than that of Universal Law. But if one holds that all duties of virtue, perfect or imperfect, depend on obligatory ends, one might be tempted to use the contradiction in the will test, which now can identify some perfect duties, for cases like Dietrichson's.

But this move could not solve the problem because even if this is a way to derive some perfect duties they are still only duties of virtue if they are arrived at in this way. Like the imperfect duties of virtue that assign ends we are to promote, they are externally unenforceable because the law cannot make us hold an end (MPV 379–85). Imperfect duties of virtue are wide duties because the law does not prescribe exactly what and how much you must do to promote the obligatory ends. Perfect duties of virtue are wide for the somewhat different reason that acting for the sake of these ends is something we must work towards – we cannot, in our "phenomenal" lives, just decide to act for the sake of these ends (MPV 392 and §22, 446). You can decide to treat someone with outward respect, but you cannot *just* decide to treat them so out of real respect. The attitudes involved are ones that you must cultivate, a sort of internal labor that ethics assigns to us, and how much and what you can do may depend on the circumstances of your life and perhaps the temperamental obstacles you have to overcome. But the murder of a child does not merely show the mother's failure to value it as an end in itself (although it does do that). This means only that the mother lacks virtues that she ought to have. The murder is also an injustice, a violation of right, and the duty not to commit murder is – as duties of virtue are not – rightfully enforceable (MM 218–21; MPV 383–84). This puts it into the category of duties of justice, which are enforceable. We need the contradiction in conception test to identify this *kind* of immorality.[7]

Natural and conventional actions

The problem that is demonstrated by Dietrichson's example springs from the fact that the action contemplated is one of natural violence. In the promising case we were able to generate a logical contradiction because the practice of promising was, under stress of universal violation, ushered off the scene. There would no longer be such a thing as promising. No such analysis is available here, because killing cannot be ushered off the scene by the way it is employed. The reason is obvious. Promising is, in the sense developed by Rawls in "Two Concepts of Rules,"[8] a practice. Both the possibility and the efficacy of actions performed within a convention such as promising – such as making, accepting, and keeping promises – depend on the existence, by conventional establishment, of the practice. The practice is comprised of certain rules, and its existence (where it is not embodied in an institution with sanctions) consists in the general acknowledgement and following of those rules. Now it is perhaps difficult to say exactly under what conditions a practice exists. We know that practices can exist if their rules are violated sometimes, for they do. But they cannot exist if their rules are universally violated. One may generate the contradiction by saying that when this happens the practice has new rules and becomes a different practice, but this is somewhat obscure. The clearer thing to say is this: a practice has a standard purpose, and if its rules are universally violated it ceases to be efficacious for this purpose, and so ceases to exist. People find some other way to achieve it, and the practice simply goes out of business. This is what happens in Kant's false promising example. Repayment promises, because they are never accepted, become nonexistent. People either make no loans or find another way to ensure repayment. For this reason, all actions which could not intelligibly exist or would not be efficacious without the existence of practices, and yet violate the rules of those practices, are easily handled by both the Logical and the Practical Interpretations of the contradiction test. Willing universal violation creates an inconsistency by making the action-type that it universalizes a nonexistent one, and *ipso facto*, ineffectual.

But in Dietrichson's case there is no practice. The action is killing, and no amount or kind of use of the action of killing is going to make it impossible. And this is because the existence of this kind of action and its efficacy depend only on the laws of nature, not on any conventional practice. For shorthand, I am going to call actions like promising "conventional actions" and actions like killing "natural actions." The Logical Contradiction interpretation works well for immoral conventional actions, but it is not very clear how it can handle immoral natural actions. When an action's possibility depends only on the laws of nature it cannot become inconceivable through universal practice.

Two Hegelian objections

In my view, it is the difficulty about natural actions which is most damaging to the Logical Contradiction Interpretation. Before I turn to the other views, however, I should mention some objections that are usually taken to be its most serious problem. I will call these the Hegelian objections, since they were originally put forward by Hegel and promulgated by Bradley and others.[9] One of the Hegelian objections is that the universal law test is empty. I will borrow the formulation used by H. B. Acton, discussing Kant's *Critique of Practical Reason* example of a man who is considering not returning a deposit (C2 27–28):

> In an essay entitled *On the Scientific Treatment of Natural Law* (1803), Hegel says that all Kant's argument shows is that a system without deposits is contradicted by a system with deposits, but not that there is any contradiction in a system without deposits. Kant makes there seem to be a contradiction in a system without deposits because he assumes that everyone would want there to be deposits, and this, says Hegel, shows that Kant was assuming the system of property and was arguing that if everyone kept what belongs to others then there would be no system of property. The interesting question, Hegel goes on, is just why there should be property, and about this Kant says nothing.[10]

This objection as it stands does not hold. On the Logical Contradiction Interpretation, the contradiction lies not in envisioning a society in which there are no deposits, but in envisioning a society in which the agent and others with his purpose are making use of the deposit system even though there is no such thing. The contradiction is generated when the agent tries to will his maxim and the universalization of his maxim *at the same time*, or tries to will it for a system of which he is to be a part. The non-existence of the practice that results from universalization is contradicted by the existence of it presupposed in the individual maxim.

The other Hegelian objection pulls in the opposite direction: instead of showing the test to be empty, it shows it to be too strong. Bradley describes it this way:

> 'Steal property' is a contradiction, for it destroys property, and with it possibility of theft.

We have no need here to push further a metaphysical argument against this view, for it supplies us at once with a crushing instance against itself. The essence of morality was a similar contradiction. . . . Morality is . . . as inconsistent as theft. 'Succor the poor' both negates and presupposes (hence posits) poverty: as Blake comically says:

> Pity would be no more,
> If we did not make somebody poor.

If you are to love your enemies, you must never be without them; and yet you try to get rid of them. Is that consistent? In short, every duty which presupposes something to be negated is no duty; it is an immoral rule, because self-contradictory.[11]

It is true that we cannot imagine a world in which people give to the poor and there are no poor. Since there is no one to give to, it is an impossible state of affairs. But the advocate of Logical Contradiction Interpretation can handle the objection. He can say that Bradley has misstated the maxim. The maxim is to succor those who need it, and this maxim can be consistently held (and in a degenerate sense acted on) in a world where no one needs help. The policy of succoring those who need it when no one does is not inconceivable. It merely gives one nothing to do.

II THE TELEOLOGICAL CONTRADICTION INTERPRETATION

According to the Teleological Contradiction interpretation, when we test our maxim by the two contradiction tests under the Formula of the Law of Nature, we are to consider whether we could will the universalized maxim as a possible law in a teleologically organized system of nature. There are two versions of this view. The first, which I will call the simple view, is usually understood this way: the contradiction emerges when an action or instinct is used in a way that is inconsistent with its natural purpose, or is not used in a way that its natural purpose calls for. A problem with this view as I have just stated it is that it makes no real use of universalization. Yet, there is some textual support for this interpretation: Kant does not scruple to use teleological language, and there are five arguments in the published ethical writings in which Kant's reasoning is explicitly teleological. One is the argument about the function of practical reasoning in the first section of the Groundwork (G 395–96). That argument is certainly teleological – Kant indeed carefully sets forth its teleological basis – but it is not a derivation of duty. Of the other four, two appear in the *Groundwork*, in connection with the first set of examples: in deriving the duty not to commit suicide (G 421–22) and in deriving the duty of self-cultivation (G 423). The other two are in the *Metaphysics of Morals*, where lying is said to violate the natural purpose of the power of communication (MPV 429) and carnal self-defilement is denounced by appeal to the natural purpose of the sexual instincts (MPV 424–25).

The second version of this view is that of H. J. Paton, spelled out in Chapter XV of *The Categorical Imperative*.[12] Paton is the major proponent of the Teleological Contradiction Interpretation and Beck partly endorses Paton's view. Aune also believes that Kant relies on a teleological conception in applying the Law of Nature formulation.[13] Paton thinks that it is clear that the laws of nature Kant had in mind were teleological rather than causal, and that the test is whether "a will which aimed at a systematic harmony of purposes in human nature could consistently will this particular maxim as a law of human nature."[14] Paton's view differs from the simple view in that he thinks that a teleological system serves as the *type* of the moral law, rather than thinking that our actions must not contradict actual natural purposes. However, in his account of the examples he takes Kant's explicitly teleological language as evidence for his interpretation, although that language suits the simple view.[15] The difference matters more than Paton seems to realize, for the presuppositions about rationality are different. On his own view the claim must be that a rational being as such values a systematic harmony of human purposes, whereas on the simple view we must claim that a rational being as such values natural purposes. In what follows I will consider both versions.

As I mentioned, the usual understanding of the teleological view is that we find some way to assign natural purposes to various instincts and types of actions and then find the contradiction when universalized maxims involve uses of those instincts and actions that defeat the natural purpose or perhaps are merely deviant. The best evidence that Kant understood the contradiction test this way is the suicide example,[16] and it can be made to fit this pattern.

In the first teleological argument in the *Groundwork*, Kant offers this as a general principle of teleological judgment: "we assume as an axiom that no organ will be found for any purpose which is not the fittest and best adapted to that purpose" (G 395). We can use this regulative principle to assign natural purposes to action-types as well as to organs, instincts, and other organic arrangements. Kant uses it to establish that the attainment of happiness is not the natural purpose of practical reason – the argument being that since instinct would be a better guide to happiness than reason is, reason is not the fittest and best adapted thing for that purpose. So let us say that there is a teleological contradiction if we propose as a universal law that a certain organ, instinct, or action-type be used in a way that makes it less than the fittest and best device for achieving its natural purpose. For example, we will say that the "natural purpose" of promising is to establish trust and confidence and the cooperation which they make possible. False promising on a universal scale makes promising less than the best device for this natural purpose. The suicide case will work this way: self-love is for the natural purpose of self-preservation; in the system of nature that results from universalizing the maxim of committing suicide out of self-love, self-love would not be the instinct fittest and best adapted to the purpose of self-preservation. As Kant says, "One sees immediately a contradiction in a system of nature whose law would be to destroy life by the feeling whose special office is to impel the improvement of life" (G 422). So the standard set by the regulative principle of teleological judgment is not met.

An attraction of the Teleological Contradiction Interpretation is that it looks at first as if it is going to resolve the most difficult problem faced by the Logical Contradiction Interpretation, that of natural actions. Suicide, after all, is such an action. The reason that it is not hard to find a contradiction in willing the universal violation of a practice is that the practice has a standard purpose: universal violation causes people to find some other way to carry out this purpose, and that is why the practice is abandoned. The Teleological view promises to allow us to treat natural actions in a similar way, for it assigns these actions or the instincts that prompt them standard purposes like the ones practices have – namely natural purposes. Of course it is true that a natural action or instinct, unlike a practice, will survive its universal abuse. But this is not a problem for the Teleological Contradiction Interpretation, for the defender of this view can say that the action or instinct will not, if universally misused, be best fitted for its purpose. That, not the existence of the action-type or instinct, is his criterion for establishing the contradiction.

But there is a difficulty with this solution to the problem of natural actions and with the proposed reading of the suicide case generally. It is that the suicide *himself* is not supposed to be able to will the teleological system based on the universalization of his maxim. Now it may be said that the suicide certainly cannot will the teleological system resulting from the universalization of his maxim, since, *qua* teleological system, it has a contradiction in it (an instinct not best adapted to its purpose). But this is a curiously abstract way to make a case against suicide. The contradiction in the teleological system is, after all, that a mechanism designed for the protection of life is mal-functioning. But the suicide doesn't want the mechanism to function well in his own case, and he may be indifferent about other cases. So neither his own purpose nor anything else commits him to the pur-pose. So if Kant's point were that the suicide cannot will the teleologi-cal system in question because *qua* teleological system it has a contra-diction in it, Kant would simply be committed to the view that a rational being as such wills a well-functioning teleological system, regardless of whether he wills the purposes that it serves. But then it is hard to see how the argument can go through. This instinct would be malfunctioning with regard to *this* purpose, but nothing prevents the suicide from willing that both the instinct and its purpose be scrapped. The problem is that of the first Hegelian objection: just in the same way that Hegel says that there is no contradiction in willing away deposits because the world does not require them, so the suicide will say that the world does not require a self-preservation instinct (or any other teleological device) to make people go on living unless one supposes that it is better that people go on living. But this is what a suicide undertakes not to suppose. And we cannot use the answer to that objection that we used before. In the false promising case we said, using the Logical Contradiction view, that the man who is unable to will the universalization of the maxim of false promising does envi-sion promising going on. *He* is going to make a promise. But the suicide's intention does not require him either to will or to envision the well-functioning of the self-preservation instincts. He does not plan to use them, or care whether they exist.

This objection does not apply in the same way to Paton's view. On

Paton's view, the order of nature is a typic for the systematic harmony of human purposes. He supposes that a rational agent is committed to *this* harmony. One might object that this has the same problem as the utilitarian view: it presupposes a morality-laden view of reason. But Paton can counter this objection. He cites as evidence Kant's argument in the *Critique of Practical Reason* that self-love cannot be the basis of morality because it does not produce a harmony of purposes (C2 28).[17] And he might also cite as evidence the *Critique of Pure Reason* view that a harmony of purposes is the highest formal unity of pure reason (C1 A686–87/B714–15). These things may be taken to imply that Kant thinks that rationality commits us to a harmony of purposes. Of course, this conclusion does not necessarily imply that when we reason morally we reason *from* such a harmony – it might instead be that this is a harmony that morality teaches us how to achieve. However that may be, the idea that a rational being is committed to a harmony of purposes will only help us with the Formula of Universal Law if we can somehow establish that the proposed natural purpose of the action-type is one needed for the systematic harmony of all human purposes and therefore is one that the agent must will.

The problem shows up in Paton's analysis of the false promising case. He reads the Teleological Contradiction Interpretation into the promising case by suggesting that the purpose of promises is to produce trust and mutual confidence; false promises destroy trust and therefore universalization makes the purpose of promising impossible. Paton comments:

What Kant says is true enough so far as it goes, but it does not offer a satisfactory basis for moral judgment unless we make the further assumption that the keeping of such promises and the mutual confidence thereby aroused are essential factors in the systematic harmony of human purposes.[18]

That is, we have to presuppose that the teleological system needs promises. Again, we get a problem like that of the first Hegelian objection.

On either Paton's or the simple view, the teleological analysis requires a commitment to specific purposes: either purposes of nature (like the preservation of life in the suicide example) or purposes required for the systematic harmony of human purposes. The trouble with bringing in teleological considerations in order to assign these purposes to natural as well as conventional actions is that such purposes may have nothing to do with what the agent wants or ought rationally to want, or even with what any human being wants. Unless we can show that the agent is committed to the purpose, it is possible to say that the system can do without the teleological arrangement because it can do without the purpose.

The Practical Contradiction Interpretation, which appeals to thwarting of the agent's *own* purpose in formulating the maxim in the first place, will solve this problem.

III   THE PRACTICAL CONTRADICTION INTERPRETATION

According to the Practical Contradiction Interpretation[19] of the contradiction in conception test, the contradiction that is involved in the universalization of an immoral maxim is that the agent would be unable to act on the maxim in a world in which it were universalized so as to achieve his own purpose – that is, the purpose that is specified in the maxim. Since he wills to act on his maxim, this means that his purpose will be frustrated. If this interpretation is correct, then it is essential that in testing maxims of actions the purpose always be included in the formulation of the maxim. It is what happens to the purpose that is the key to the contradiction.

The test is carried out by imagining, in effect, that the action you propose to perform in order to carry out your purpose is the standard procedure for carrying out that purpose.[20] What the test shows to be forbidden are just those actions whose efficacy in achieving their purposes depends upon their being exceptional. If the action no longer works as a way of achieving the purpose in question when it is universalized, then it is an action of this kind. Intuitively speaking, the test reveals unfairness, deception, and cheating. For instance, in the false promising case, the difficulty is that the man's end – getting the money – cannot be achieved by his means – making a false promise – in the world of the universalized maxim. The efficacy of the false promise as a means of securing the money depends on the fact that not everyone uses promises this way. Promises are efficacious in securing loans only because they are believed, and they are believed only if they are normally true. Since promising is the means he proposes to use, his end would not be achieved at all, but frustrated. In willing the world of the universalized maxim and – as Kant says – *at the same time* – willing the maxim itself, the man wills the frustration of his own end. As Kant says, the man "would make the promise itself and the end to be accomplished by it impossible" (G 422). This way of looking at the test also shows us one sense in which violations of the universal law test imply that you are using others as mere means. If you do something that only works because most people do not do it, their actions are making your action work. In the false promising case, other people's honesty makes your deceit effective.

Practical contradictions

Even proponents of this view, or versions of it, sometimes describe a practical contradiction as being a contradiction in a weaker sense than a theoretical one.[21] This is not correct. Kant's ethics is based on the idea that there is a specifically practical employment of reason, which is not the same as an application of theoretical reason. It includes a specifically practical sense of "contradiction." The argument that shows this seems to me to be an almost decisive one in favor of this interpretation.

After laying out the three kinds of imperatives, Kant tells us that hypothetical imperatives are analytic. This means, ordinarily, two things: the relation expressed is one of conceptual containment, and the opposite or denial is a flat contradiction. Intuitively, we can see why failing to conform your conduct to relevant hypothetical imperatives, and thus frustrating your own purposes, is contradictory. Someone who wills an end, knows that it will be brought about by a certain necessary and available means, has no extraneous reason not to use that means, and yet is utterly unmoved to take it, is irrational in a way that does seem to amount to contradiction.[22] We might capture the sense that there is a contradiction here by saying that such a person is acting as if she both did and didn't will the end. But Kant can do better than that, for he also explains the containment relation that makes the hypothetical imperative analytic:

Whoever wills the end, so far as reason has decisive influence on his action, wills also the indispensably necessary means to it that lie in his power. This proposition, in what concerns the will, is analytical; for, in willing the object as my effect, my causality as an acting cause, i.e., the use of means, is already thought, and the imperative derives the concept of necessary actions to this end from the concept of willing this end. (G 417)

The argument is based on an idea that plays a central role in Kant's ethics generally, namely that willing is regarding yourself as a cause: that the will is, as Kant says in the opening argument of *Groundwork III*, "a causality of living beings insofar as they are rational" (G 446). It is because we must regard ourselves not only as a cause but as a free cause or a first cause that it turns out rationality requires autonomy, and this is the basis of moral obligation. In the argument above, Kant's point is this: willing is regarding yourself as the cause of the end in question – as the one who will bring it about. This distinguishes willing from mere wanting or wishing or desiring. Conceiving yourself as a cause of the end is conceiving yourself as setting off a causal chain that will result in the production of the end. It is conceiving yourself as using the available causal connections. But the available causal connections are, by definition, "means." So, willing the end contains, or insofar as you are rational is already, willing the means. It is because this is a "containment" relation – in the logic of practical reason – that acting against the hypothetical imperative is contradictory. This gives us a sense of practical contradiction – of contradiction in the will – which is different from but not weaker than "theoretical" contradiction.

Since this is the sort of contradiction implied by the analyticity of hypothetical imperatives, it is reasonable to think that this will be the sort of contradiction employed in the categorical imperative tests. On the Practical Contradiction Interpretation, such a contradiction in the universalization of an immoral maxim is exactly what the test shows. In the world of the universalized maxim, the *hypothetical* imperative from which the false promiser constructs his maxim is no longer true. It was "if you want some ready cash, you ought to make a false promise." But at the same time that he employs this hypothetical imperative in constructing his maxim, he wills its falsification, by willing a state of affairs (the world of the universalized maxim) in which it will be false. In that world, false promising is not a means to getting ready cash. Kant, therefore, not only has a specifically practical sense of "contradiction," but should be seen as employing it in his contradiction tests.

The Hegelian objections

Like the Logical Contradiction Interpretation, the Practical Contradiction Interpretation enables us to answer the Hegelian objections, and it shows even more clearly why those objections miss the *moral* point of a universalization test. The first Hegelian objection is that the universalization test is empty. There is no contradiction in a system without such practices as deposits or promises. The proponent of the Logical Contradiction view replies that the contradiction is not merely in a system without these practices but in an agent engaging in these practices in a system without them. On the Practical Contradiction Interpretation the answer we shall give is still better. The person who tries to will the universalization of this maxim is not only thereby willing a situation in which practices like deposits and promises do not exist. He is also willing that they do exist, precisely because he is willing to *use* them to achieve his ends. The man who wills the universalization of the false promise, for example, is also willing to use a false promise to get the money. But he cannot rationally will to use a promise to achieve his end at the same time he wills a situation in which promises will not be accepted, because if his promise is not accepted it is not a means to achieving his end. Thus the Practical Contradiction Interpretation's answer to this Hegelian objection is that Kant need not be assuming that everyone wants there to be deposits. The man in the example wants there to be a system of deposits, because he proposes to use that system as the means to his end. In a clear sense he is unfair.

The second objection was that the test is too strong. You cannot universalize "succor the poor," since if everyone did this poverty would be eliminated and there would be no one to succor. The Practical Contradiction Interpretation answers this objection both readily and, in an obvious way, correctly. One's purpose in succoring the poor is to give them relief. The world of the universalized maxim only contradicts one's will if it thwarts one's purpose. A world without poverty does not contradict this purpose, but rather satisfies it another (better) way, and no contradiction arises.[23]

Contradictions in conception and in the will

Another advantage of this view is that it should enable us to employ the same sense of contradiction in interpreting the two contradiction tests, and yet still to distinguish between them. Consider what the other two interpretations say about this question. The Logical Contradiction Interpretation forces us to look for a different sort of contradiction altogether for the contradiction in the will test, since Kant is explicit about the fact that no logical inconceivability is involved there. The Logical Contradiction Interpretation seems initially to have the virtue that it involves no presuppositions about rationality that are not completely uncontroversial. The contradiction it identifies in universalizing immoral maxims is of a familiar kind. But this advantage is lost if we must use different presuppositions in order to understand the contradiction in the will test. Often, proponents of the Logical Contradiction Interpretation for the contradictions in conception end up with something like a utilitarian or a teleological view about contradictions in the will. But the utilitarian reading has the same problem for the second test as it does for the first: it presupposes a morality-laden conception of rationality. The Teleological Contradiction Interpretation, on the other hand, does not seem to allow for a very well-defined distinction between the two tests. I suppose one may say that in the case of a contradiction in conception, some specific instinct or action is found not to be best adapted to its particular purpose; and in the case of a contradiction in the will, we lose some positive good needed for a teleological system, or for the systematic harmony of human purposes. But it is not really obvious that these are distinct. Recall that Paton could not find a contradiction in the false promising case without assuming that promises are needed for the harmony of human purposes. This problem tends to collapse the two tests.

→ Now consider the Practical Contradiction Interpretation. If a thwarted purpose is a practical contradiction, we must understand the contradiction in the will test this way: we must find some purpose or purposes which belong essentially to the will, and in the world where maxims that fail these tests are universal law, these essential purposes will be thwarted, because the means of achieving them will be unavailable. Examples of purposes that might be thought to be essential to the will are its general effectiveness in the pursuit of its ends, and its freedom to adopt and pursue new ends. The arguments for self-development and mutual aid will then be that without the development of human talents and powers and the resources of mutual cooperation, the will's effectiveness and free-

dom would be thwarted. This is of course just a sketch. Exactly
which purposes are essential to the will and how they can be shown
to be so is a topic in its own right, which I will not pursue further
here. The point is that the Practical Contradiction Interpretation
gives a better account of the relation between the two tests than
either of the others. The difference between the two tests will not lie
in the use of a different kind of contradiction, as it does in the
Logical Contradiction Interpretation. And yet there will be a difference. The purpose thwarted in the case of a maxim that fails the
contradiction in the conception test is *the one in the maxim itself*,
and so the contradiction can be said to be *in* the universalized
maxim. The purpose thwarted in the case of the contradiction in the
will test is not one that is in the maxim,[24] but one that is essential to
the will.

The problem of natural actions

The Practical Contradiction Interpretation, like the Logical, works
especially well with respect to wrong actions which are conventional. But the reason why it works is slightly different. On the
Logical Contradiction Interpretation, the contradiction arises because the agent wills to engage in a conventional action, but he also
wills a state of affairs in which that kind of action will no longer
exist. On the Practical Contradiction Interpretation, the contradiction arises because the agent wills to engage in a conventional action, but he also wills a state of affairs in which the action will no
longer *work*. When we are dealing with an action that falls under a
practice, the two views are readily confused, because the reason the
action no longer works is *because* it no longer exists. But on the
Practical Contradiction Interpretation it is the failure of efficacy, not
the non-existence, that really matters.

   This gives rise to the possibility that with the Practical Contradiction Interpretation we will be able to derive at least some of our duties
of omission with respect to natural actions. Natural actions are not
going to cease to exist if used wrongly, but their efficacy for some
purposes may depend on their exceptional use. A great deal depends
here on what the purpose is taken to be and how it is described. One
case that is borderline between natural and conventional is stealing.
That might seem wholly conventional, since property is a practice,

but it is difficult to imagine an economic system in which the means
of production and action were not guaranteed to the use of particular
persons at particular times.²⁵ And any violation of these guaranteed
assignments would be "stealing." Now if the purpose of stealing is to
acquire something for your personal use or possession – to get something you want when you want it – and you imagine that anyone in
your situation – anyone who wants something not assigned to him –
steals it, as a standard procedure – then you see that under these
conditions it is quite impossible to acquire something for your use or
possession, to have it when you want it. The idea here is that what the
thief really wants is to make something his property, to have some
guarantee that he will have it when he wants it. His purpose is therefore thwarted if his maxim is universalized.

That case is borderline, but a similar analysis might apply to
wholly natural acts. Here is a silly example. Suppose you are second
in line for a job, and are considering murder as a way of dealing with
your more successful rival. Can this be universalized? Killing is a
natural act, not a conventional one. We cannot say that if this sort of
action is abused the practice will die out, for that makes no sense
whatever. Nor can we say that any amount or kind of use of killing
will destroy its efficacy in achieving its purpose *if* we specify that
purpose simply as that of getting someone dead. So here the test will
only work if the purpose is specified differently. We must say that
the purpose is that of securing a job, and we must emphasize the fact
that if anyone else wants this job, or any job you hold, universalization makes you the victim. Now, it may seem that the purpose that
is thwarted by universalization – that of staying alive – is not the
same as the purpose in your maxim – that of securing the job. This
would be bad. It is the fact that it is the purpose in the maxim that
gets thwarted in the world of the universalized maxim that enables
us to carry out the test without any extraneous information about
the agent's desires and purposes. If it is some other, contingent,
purpose that gets thwarted, then it looks as if the test (i) requires
empirical information about what other purposes people have and
(ii) functions idiosyncratically, giving different results to people with
different desires. These are both conclusions the Kantian wants to
avoid. We shall avoid them here by pointing out that this is not a
case of an extraneous end being thwarted. Staying alive matters in
this example because it is a necessary condition of having the job.

That might seem like a silly thing to say in this case, but it is an application of a point which is not in general silly at all. In *Utilitarianism*, Mill argues that justice is specifically concerned with a special object of human interest – that of security. Security is not merely one good thing among others, but to put it in Kantian language, a condition of the goodness of anything else:

> . . . but security no human being can possibly do without; on it we depend for all our immunity from evil, and for the whole value of all and every good, beyond the passing moment, since nothing but the gratification of the instant could be of any worth to us, if we could be deprived of anything the next instant by whoever was momentarily stronger than ourselves.[26]

The Kantian may avail himself of this insight. To want something is to want to be secure in the possession of it. The use of violent natural means for achieving ends cannot be universalized because that would leave us insecure in the possession of these goods, and without that security these goods are no good to us at all. So, if we include as part of the purpose that the agent wants to be secure in the possession of the end, we can get a practical contradiction in the universalization of violent methods. And in fact, Kant's argument in the *Metaphysical Principles of Justice* about why there must be proprietary rights is not very different from Mill's: it is that we need to be secure in the possession of certain sorts of goods in order to successfully make use of them (MPJ 246ff.).

The method of dealing with natural acts which I have just suggested focuses on the question whether you could really achieve your purpose – with everything that purpose involves (i.e., security in its possession) in a world where your action was the universal method of achieving that purpose. Another way to approach this problem is to consider whether the social conditions that allow violence to work as a method of achieving this purpose would exist if it were the universal method. It is true that natural laws are all that is needed to make violent methods yield their natural effects, but more is needed to make them yield their social effects. For example, the simplest way of making the argument against cheating on an entrance examination is to point out that if everyone did this the entrance examination would cease to be used as a criterion for selection. Since a lot of incompetent people would get in, it would be found impracticable and some other method would be chosen.

("Everyone would laugh at entrance examinations as vain pre-
tenses.") Placing people in jobs is like this: it is something for which
there must be a method, and if one method were universally abused,
another, not liable to that abuse, would be found. Now if murder to
get a job were universally practiced, the best candidates would not
get the jobs. So whatever it is about the old selection process that
makes this possible would be changed. Perhaps no one would be told
who the candidates were, or people would even keep it a secret what
jobs they held. Again, the argument sounds silly in this case but is
meant to bring out something that is not silly. Cheating could not be
the first or standard procedure for getting into an educational pro-
gram. It is essentially parasitic on the existence of another method.
Violence, in many cases, also has this parasitic nature when it is a
way of achieving a purpose in society.

The Practical Contradiction Interpretation can therefore handle
some cases of natural actions. A harder kind of case would be something like killing for revenge, or out of hatred. In these cases it is not
some enduring condition that the agent wants to achieve – he wants
the immediate result – so the security consideration will not help us
here.[27] These grim kinds of cases are managed without difficulty
when using the Formula of Humanity, but it will be difficult to find
any contradiction of the sort needed here. And this problem applies
to the suicide case as well. On the Practical Contradiction Interpretation we cannot get an analysis of that case, for the suicide's purpose,
if it is release from his own misery, will not be thwarted by universal
practice. There is an important parallel to this problem. Kant's
theory is least helpful and least plausible when one is dealing with a
case where other people around the agent have already introduced
evil into the situation. His debate with Benjamin Constant about
whether you may lie to the murderer whose victim is hidden in your
house, and his insistence that there is never a right to revolution, are
infamous examples of cases in which his view seems to forbid us to
try to prevent or to set right the wrongs committed by others. I
believe that there is a similar sort of difficulty in making out what
Kant is to say about cases where something has gone wrong inside,
where the problem is not the selfish pursuit of an ordinary purpose,
but a diseased purpose. I do not say that Kant is unable to give us an
account of these cases. But the kind of case around which the view is
framed, and which it handles best, is the temptation to make oneself

an exception: selfishness, meanness, advantage-taking, and disregard for the rights of others. It is this sort of thing, not violent crimes born of despair or illness, that serves as Kant's model of immoral conduct. I do not think we can fault him on this, for this and not the other is the sort of evil that most people are tempted by in their everyday lives.

CONCLUSION

It is conceivable that Kant did not perceive the differences among these three readings, and that this is why language supporting all of them can be found in his texts. In a certain kind of case, the three readings are very close. Where the immoral action involves the abuse of a practice, the Logical Contradiction Interpretation says you cannot universalize because the practice will not exist and the action will be inconceivable; the Teleological Contradiction Interpretation says you cannot universalize because the practice will then not be best suited for what in a teleological system would be its natural purpose; and the Practical Contradiction Interpretation says you cannot universalize because if the practice disappears it will of course no longer be efficacious in producing your purpose. These three analyses are very close, and for this kind of case the differences are insignificant. It is only when we begin to consider the problems created by natural actions, the Hegelian objections, and the need to extend our analysis in the right way to the contradiction in the will test that differences emerge. In my view, the Practical Contradiction Interpretation deals with these problems better than the other two, although not always with complete success.

The best argument for it, however, is that it employs the sense of contradiction which Kant identifies in his analysis of the hypothetical imperative. Each interpretation must presuppose some notion of rationality in determining whether a rational being can will the universalization of a maxim at the same time as that maxim without contradiction. The Logical Contradiction view works with a notion of contradiction indistinguishable from that of theoretical rationality and this is a great advantage. But this advantage is lost when we turn to contradictions in the will, which then require another interpretation. The Teleological Contradiction view works with a rather rich notion of rationality as aiming at a harmony of purposes. I think on

Kant's view pure reason does aim at a harmony of purposes, but that only morality tells us how that is to be achieved. We cannot reason morally from that idea. The Practical Contradiction view uses a specifically practical notion of rationality and of contradiction which springs from the notion of the will as a causality. This is not a morality-laden notion of rationality, for on Kant's view this notion is needed to explain *instrumental* rationality.

Yet the same notion will also be employed in explaining why the moral law applies to us. The Practical Contradiction Interpretation allows us to sketch an explanation, in terms of autonomy, of why conformity to the Formula of Universal Law is a requirement of reason. Start with a parallel to theoretical reasoning: as a rational being, you may take the connection between two events to be a causal one. But this connection must always hold – must hold universally – if the cause you have identified is indeed *sufficient* to produce that effect. Only in this case is what you have identified a law. The rational will, regarding itself as a causality, models its conception of a law on a causal law. As a rational being you may take the connection between a purpose you hold and an action that would promote it to be a reason for you to perform the action. But this connection must be universalizable *if the reason is sufficient*. Only in this case have you identified a law. If universalization would destroy the connection between action and purpose, the purpose is not a sufficient reason for the action. This is how, on the Practical Contradiction Interpretation, the contradiction in conception test shows an immoral maxim to be unfit to be an objective practical law. As an autonomous rational being, you must act on your conception of a law. This is why autonomy requires comformity to the Formula of Universal Law.[28]

NOTES

I would like to thank Barbara Herman for comments which have enabled me to make this paper much clearer.

1 Of course, these are general categories and fitting everyone's views into them would involve distortion; there are many slight differences in interpretation. I think, however, that they represent the main kinds of reading, and will indicate how I am classifying some important commentators as I present the views.

2 See the last paragraph of Section Two, G 444–45; also the last full paragraph on G 420.

3 John Stuart Mill, *Utilitarianism*, p. 4.

4 Paul Dietrichson, "Kant's Criteria of Universalizability." For Kemp's views, see J. Kemp, "Kant's Examples of the Categorical Imperative." I attribute this view to Allen Wood on the basis of his paper "Kant on False Promises."

5 Dietrichson, "Kant's Criteria of Universalizability," p. 188.

6 For a good discussion of this issue, see Onora Nell (O'Neill), *Acting on Principle: An Essay on Kantian Ethics.* Although I do not agree with this work on every point, it will be obvious to anyone who knows the book that I owe a great deal to it.

7 Kant does not use the Formula of Universal Law to derive the duties of justice in the *Metaphysics of Morals.* Instead he uses the Universal Principle of Justice, which tells us that our actions should be consistent with universalizable external freedom (MPJ 230–31). But in the *Groundwork*, Kant suggests that violations of right are wrong in the same way as false promising (G 430), and this suggests that they should be derivable from the contradiction in conception test. Furthermore, it is reasonable to think that if injustices are by definition inconsistent with universalizable external freedom, their universalizations should display contradictions in conception if anything does.

8 John Rawls, "Two Concepts of Rules."

9 Obviously, this discussion is not intended as a complete treatment of Hegel's criticisms of Kant's ethical philosophy. I mean only to cover some objections that recur in the literature and are usually referred to Hegel.

10 H. B. Acton, *Kant's Moral Philosophy*, pp. 24–25.

11 F. H. Bradley, "Duty for Duty's Sake," Essay IV in *Ethical Studies*, p. 55.

12 H. J. Paton, *The Categorical Imperative*, pp. 146–157.

13 See Lewis White Beck, *A Commentary on Kant's Critique of Practical Reason*, pp. 159–63; and Bruce Aune, *Kant's Theory of Morals*, pp. 59ff.

14 Paton, *The Categorical Imperative*, p. 151.

15 This emerges when Paton, in discussing one of Kant's direct uses of teleological language, says that in this case "... Kant is on stronger ground. Here his teleology is more explicit...." See *The Categorical Imperative*, p. 155.

16 This is contrary to the view of Paton, who thinks this example is the best evidence that Kant intended the typic to be ordinary causal laws, and also that it is not a good example. See *The Categorical Imperative*, p. 148.

17 Paton, *The Categorical Imperative*, p. 140.

18 Paton, *The Categorical Imperative*, p. 153.

19 This view is supported by Marcus Singer in *Generalization in Ethics* and a version of it is supported in Onora Nell (O'Neill), *Acting on Principle: An Essay on Kantian Ethics.*

20 The test works most smoothly where the hypothetical reasoning behind the maxim to be tested is purely instrumental. The problem of universalizing maxims like that of becoming a doctor in order to make one's living (the objection being that not everyone could do this) arises because the reasoning is constitutive. Being a doctor is an *instance* of a profession with certain features which the agent wants. The more we can specify these features, the closer we will come to the testable reasons that should be embodied in the maxim.

21 See for instance Singer, *Generalization in Ethics*, p. 259. Although O'Neill's version of the test is like the Practical Contradiction Interpretation in that she emphasizes the impossibility of acting on the maxim in the world of the universalized maxim, she supposes that Kant appeals to the Law of Nature formulation because applying the notions of self-defeat or self-frustration is not as clear as applying that of contradiction. See *Acting on Principle*, p. 63. Although she notes that Kant thinks that hypothetical imperatives are analytic, she thinks this is in a loose sense (p. 70n).

22 Perhaps you will be tempted to say that this case does not occur. There would always be some extraneous reason for such a person not to take the means. This temptation is one to be resisted. Kant thinks that we are imperfectly rational: and one thing this means is that we will not always have *reasons* for being uninfluenced by reasons. It may be that there is always a cause of irrationality. Perhaps someone does not take the means to an end because she is depressed. This can be forced into the mold of a reason ("I feel so tired it would not be worth it to me right now"), and the agent herself will feel inclined to treat it that way. But it may not be the best way to describe what is really going on to say she has a reason not to take the means. If we think she would be better off taking the means even though she feels lethargic, we will find it better to say the depression is a cause of irrationality rather than that it changes the structure of the available reasons.

23 See the discussion in Singer, *Generalization in Ethics*, pp. 279–92.

24 In Kant's first set of examples of the contradiction in the will test in the *Groundwork*, there is no purpose given in the maxim. But even if we assigned purposes to the agents who adopt these maxims the point will hold. The man who does not develop his talents and powers presumably has the purpose of taking his ease. But the purpose that is thwarted is the development of his rational nature.

25 I do not mean that there has to be property in the thick Lockean sense of complete control of an object and absolute right to do anything with it. I only mean that there could not be a society in which persons did not have rights of use with respect to objects for certain durations – say the way you "own" the furniture in your office. Barbara Herman has pointed out to me that a system without something like promises may be just as hard to imagine, in which case that too will be a borderline case.

26 Mill, *Utilitarianism*, p. 53.

27 Here is something we cannot do. We cannot get something like the security condition by saying that the vengeful killer wants to kill and get away with it – he wants not to be killed in turn himself, so he cannot universalize his vengeful maxim. We cannot say this because we don't know it. The security argument works only if we can say that security in the possession of a good or the continuance of a situation is really a condition of achieving that good or situation at all. It must not be a separate end. But wanting to get away with it is a separate end; getting away with it is not a condition of getting revenge. For notice that if we tried to make this our argument a vengeful killer would be morally all right if he did not mind paying the price.

4 Kant's Formula of Humanity

I INTRODUCTION

The Second Section of the *Groundwork of the Metaphysics of Morals* contains three arguments that have the form: if there were a categorical imperative, this is what it would have to be like.[1] Each of these arguments leads to a new set of terms in which the categorical imperative can be formulated. In summarizing these arguments, Kant tells us that universality gives us the form of the moral law; rational nature or humanity as an end in itself gives us the material of the law; and autonomous legislation in a kingdom of ends represents a complete determination of maxims and a totality of ends. The Formula of the Universal Law is to be used in actual decision making, we are told; the other two, which bring the moral law "closer to intuition" and "nearer to feeling" can be used to "gain a hearing for the moral law" (G 436).

Attention to these remarks about the relations among the three formulas has perhaps obscured the fact that the three formulas represent a progression in the argument that leads from "popular moral philosophy" into "the metaphysics of morals." I think that it is sometimes supposed that Kant's claim that the categorical imperative is a principle of reason rests squarely on the Formula of Universal Law – i.e., on that formula's "formality." The claims of the other two formulas to be rational principles are then taken to be based upon their presumed equivalence to the Formula of Universal Law. Those who make such a supposition err not only by ignoring the fact that the Categorical Imperative is not "deduced" in the *Groundwork* until the Third Section, but also by ignoring the fact that each formulation is intended to represent some characteristic feature of

106

rational principles. In particular, "humanity" is argued to be the appropriate material for a rational principle, just as universality is its appropriate form. Furthermore, the addition of each new feature represents a step further into the metaphysics of morals, with the idea of autonomy providing the stepping-stone that will make the transition to a critique of practical reason possible. In this paper, I am concerned with the argument for the Formula of Humanity. Specifically, I want to consider what characteristic feature of "humanity" as Kant thinks of it makes humanity the appropriate material for a principle of practical reason.

At the end of the discussion of the Formula of Universal Law and the examples of its application, Kant claims to have shown that duty must be expressed in categorical imperatives and to have "clearly exhibited the content of the categorical imperative," if there is one (G 425). Having established that a categorical imperative would say that we should act only on such maxims as we can will to be universal laws, Kant raises a new question: "Is it a necessary law for all rational beings that they should always judge their actions by such maxims as they themselves could will to serve as universal laws?" (G 426). To answer this question we must discover an *a priori* connection between the law and the will of a rational being, and in order to discover this connection we will be driven into metaphysics (G 426). That is, we have to investigate the possibility of "reason thus determining conduct" (G 427). This investigation is a motivational one.

Kant proceeds to tell us that what "serves the will as the objective ground of its self-determination" is an end. Ends may be either objective or subjective, depending on whether they are determined by reason or not. A formal principle is one that disregards all subjective ends; not one that disregards ends altogether (G 427). It is Kant's view throughout his moral philosophy that every action "contains" an end; there is no action done without some end in view. The difference between morally worthy action and morally indifferent action is that in the first case the end is adopted because it is dictated by reason and in the second case the end is adopted in response to an inclination for it. For instance, in the *Groundwork I* example of the comparison between morally worthy beneficence and morally indifferent beneficence, the difference is found to rest in the different grounds on which each of the two men have adopted the welfare of others as his end. It is a mistake to suppose that Kant is contrasting a man who helps others as a mere means to his own pleasure with a man who does so from duty. Kant says explicitly that the man of sympathetic temperament is "without any motive of vanity of selfishness" (G 398). Each of these characters genuinely has the welfare of others as his end – that is, each values it for its own sake.² The difference is that the morally worthy man has adopted this end because it is a duty to have such an end. Of course, in the case of action that promotes the obligatory ends it is obvious that the morally motivated person has an end in view. But is there an end in view in the sort of moral action that is required as strict duty, and does not involve one of the two obligatory ends? Kant's answer is that there is – the end in view is humanity. The difference between the person who acts merely in accordance with duty and the person who acts *from* duty is described, in the *Metaphysical Principles of Virtue*, in terms of this end:

> Although the conformity of actions to right (i.e., being an upright man) is nothing meritorious, yet the conformity to right of the maxim of such actions regarded as duties, i.e., *respect* for right, is meritorious. For by this latter conformity a man makes the right of humanity or of men his end. (MPV 390)

It is important here to keep in mind that there are two different roles an end can play in the determination of conduct; it can serve as a purpose pursued, or it can play a negative role and serve as something one must not act against. To take an ordinary example: we do not often get into situations where self-preservation serves as a positive incentive to any action, but it might quite frequently keep us from taking undue risks in the pursuit of our other ends: without much thought and in an everyday way, one might, under the influence of this end, avoid a dangerous area or going out at night. Kant thinks that the end of humanity functions in this negative way: "the end here is not conceived as one to be effected but as an independent end, and thus merely negatively. It is that which must never be acted against . . . " (G 437). In the *Metaphysical Principles of Virtue* Kant explains the constraining role of humanity as an end this way:

> The doctrine of right had to do merely with the formal condition of external freedom. . . . Ethics, on the other hand, supplies in addition a matter (an object of free choice), namely, an *end* of pure reason which is at the same time represented as an objectively necessary end, i.e., as a duty for

man. For since sensible inclinations may misdirect us to ends (the matter of choice) which may be contrary to duty, legislative reason cannot guard against their influence other than, in turn, by means of an opposing moral end, which therefore must be given a priori independently of inclination. (MPV 380–81)

The role that Kant here assigns to this end stands in a specific relation to *human* reason, for it is human reason that has the obstacles provided by sensuous inclination to overcome. The sensuous inclinations present themselves falsely as sufficient reasons for action, because of a tendency in human nature which is described in *Religion Within the Limits of Reason Alone* as a "propensity to evil" (R 34–36), and in the *Critique of Practical Reason* as "self-conceit" (C2 73–74). These obstacles to goodness are controlled by making humanity an unconditional end which must never be acted against; and it is in this that human virtue consists (C2 84–89). There is no contradiction between this view and the many passages where Kant insists that morality needs no end as an incentive. Having humanity as an end is not an incentive for adopting the moral law; rather, the moral law commands that humanity be treated as an end. Although the role of this end in checking the inclinations is specific to human reason, it has a metaphysical point. Human *freedom* is realized in the adoption of humanity as an end in itself, for the one thing that no one can be compelled to do by another is to adopt a particular end (MPV 381), and this end, freely adopted, checks the power of the inclinations. In the *Groundwork*, the argument for the Formula of Humanity is preceded by warnings that the motive we are seeking not only must not be an empirical or subjective feeling or propensity, but also must not be derived from "a particular tendency of the human reason which might not hold necessarily for the will of every rational being" (G 425). Therefore, it must turn out that freely acting *from* duty and adopting humanity as one's unconditioned end are one and the same thing.

The argument for the Formula of Humanity as an End in Itself has two parts: Kant first argues that there must be an unconditional end; second, that the end must be humanity. The first part of this argument is simple; one can make it in either direction. If there is a necessary end, then there is a categorical imperative, for this end would be "a ground of definite laws" (G 428). If there is a categorical imperative, then there must be some necessary end or ends, for if there is a categorical imperative there are necessary actions, and every action contains an end (MPV 385). In the *Metaphysical Principles of Virtue* this consideration also serves as the basis for what Kant calls a deduction of the duties of virtue from pure practical reason:

For practical reason to be indifferent to ends, i.e., to take no interest in them, would be a contradiction; for then it would not determine the maxims of actions (and the actions always contain an end) and, consequently, would not be practical reason. (MPV 395)

This shows that if there is a categorical imperative, it must have as its material a necessary end or ends. This end, Kant argues, must be "humanity."

II HUMANITY

Before looking at Kant's argument that the necessary end must be humanity, I want to review the available evidence about what Kant means by that term. The argument itself will show us what Kant has in mind, but preliminary evidence will pave the way for the argument. In the *Groundwork*, Kant interchanges the terms "humanity" and "rational nature." And he tells us that

Rational nature is distinguished from others in that it proposes an end to itself. (G 437)

The fullest statement of his notion of humanity is found in the *Metaphysical Principles of Virtue*:

The capacity to propose an end to oneself is the characteristic of humanity (as distinguished from animality). The rational will is therefore bound up with the end of the humanity in our own person, as is also, consequently, the duty to deserve well of humanity by means of culture in general, and to acquire or promote the capacity of carrying out all sorts of ends, as far as this capacity is to be found in man. (MPV 392)

In clarifying the idea of cultivation he has referred to "humanity, by which he alone is capable of setting himself ends" (MPV 387).

As these passages indicate, Kant takes the characteristic feature of humanity, or rational nature, to be the capacity for setting an end. Ends are "set" by practical reason; human beings are distinguished from animals by the fact that practical reason rather than instinct is the determinant of our actions. An end is an object of free choice (MPV 384). A rational being, as possessor of a will, acts on maxims of his or her own choosing; but every maxim contains an end, and in choosing the maxim one also chooses an end. In the case of morally worthy actions, the end is chosen because of the necessity of the principle embodied in the maxim; but it is not only the morally obligatory ends that are freely chosen under the agency of practical reason. All maxims are freely adopted and so all ends are so chosen.

While it will be obvious that Kant thinks that the obligatory ends are objects of reason, the idea that all human ends are in some sense set by reason requires a little more explanation. It might seem to some that it is more natural to say of ends other than the obligatory ends that they are "set" by inclination or "passion," and that reason's only role with respect to these is that of determining the means by which they are to be realized. To see that this is not Kant's view is important for an understanding of the Formula of Humanity: it is the capacity for the rational determination of ends in general, not just the capacity for adopting morally obligatory ends, that the Formula of Humanity orders us to cherish unconditionally. I would therefore like to cite some additional evidence for this point.

First, there are the remarks about reason and happiness in the *Groundwork*. In the teleological argument concerning the purpose of practical reason in Section One, Kant argues that if happiness were nature's end for us, instinct would have been a better guide; nature would have allowed us theoretical reason with which to contemplate out happy state, but

would have taken care that reason did not break forth into practical use nor have the presumption, with its weak insight, to think out for itself the plan of happiness and the means of attaining it. Nature would have taken over not only the choice of ends but also that of the means, and with wise foresight she would have entrusted both to instinct alone. (G 395)

This remark could be read either as suggesting that nature has the choice of ends but would also have taken over the means as well, or as suggesting that in us nature has relinquished the control of both ends and means (and would not have done so if happiness had been her purpose). The remark that practical reason tries to think out the plan of happiness as well as the means to it, however, suggests the latter reading. The latter remarks to the effect that happiness is an indefinite "ideal of the imagination" support this reading (G 418). If happiness were some plain and obvious thing – for example pleasure as Bentham thought of it – the problem of determining the means to it could be no more serious than the problem of determining the means to anything whatever. The difficulty Kant points to is that in constructing the imperative of prudence reason must specify the end before it can determine the means; but there is no possible rule for specifying "the plan of happiness."³

The second and best piece of evidence for the role of reason in the selection of ends in general comes from the essay *Conjectural Beginning of Human History*. In this essay, Kant uses Genesis as the basis for a speculative reconstruction of the steps taken by humanity in its transformation from a creature governed by instinct to a rational being. The first object of free choice is the apple and Kant explains how it comes about. Humans are guided by instinct through the sense of smell and taste to their natural food. But by means of comparison they notice that other foods are visually similar to the things they eat. This operation of comparison is assigned to reason, and it leads to new desires; not only desires that go beyond instinct, but desires that are positively contrary to it (CBHH 111). The result of this event is described by Kant:

> The original occasion for deserting natural instinct may have been trifling. But this was man's first attempt to become conscious of his reason as a power which can extend itself beyond the limits to which all animals are confined . . . this was a sufficient occasion for reason to do violence to the voice of nature (3:1) and, its protest notwithstanding, to make the first attempt at a free choice . . . He discovered in himself a power of choosing for himself a way of life, of not being bound without alternative to a single way, like the animals . . . He stood, as it were, at the brink of an abyss. Until that moment instinct had directed him toward specific objects of desire. But from these now opened up an infinity of such objects, and he did not yet know how to choose between them. (CBHH 111–12)

Kant goes on to trace further steps by which the powers of reason are developed. Reason not only directs the human being to objects around it for which there is no instinctual desire, but leads to the development of specifically human desires, such as love and the taste for beauty, and later concern for the future (CBHH 112–15). Morality comes only at the end of this development. But the development represents a logical or rational completion as well as a genesis. The possession of practical reason, through such operations as comparison and foresight, directs our desires to an ever-increasing range of objects, but so far it does not teach us how to choose among them. Reason makes it possible to set new ends, but its guidance at this stage is only partial. This is a crucial point, for it is because of this fact that these ends are still "subjective" and not yet "objective" ends. Reason plays a role in determining our interest in them, but they are not dictated by reason. Human reason, by directing us to "an infinity" of new possible objects of desire without determining more definitely which are worthy of choice, sets up a problem. The *Groundwork* argument suggests that the idea of making a plan for happiness will not solve this problem. Rather, it is only through the development of morality that reason can give us *complete* guidance in choosing ends. In any case, there can be no question that in this essay Kant thinks of all human ends as being partially "set" by the operations of reason. They may be objects of desire or inclination, but it is reason that is responsible for the unique human characteristic of having non-instinctual desires.

The third piece of evidence for Kant's views about the specific nature of "humanity" comes from *Religion Within the Limits of Reason Alone*. In a discussion of the question whether human beings are good or evil by nature, Kant describes an "Original Predisposition to Good in Human Nature," divided into three parts: predispositions to animality, humanity, and personality (R 26–27). Of these three predispositions the first is associated with the instinctual desires and the last with respect for the moral law as sufficient incentive of the will. In between them comes the predisposition to humanity which

can be brought under the general title of self-love which is physical and yet *compares* (for which reason is required); that is to say, we judge ourselves happy or unhappy only by making comparison with others. (R 27)

Kant adds that

The first requires no reason, the second is based on practical reason, but a reason thereby subservient to other incentives, while the third alone is rooted in reason which is practical of itself, that is, reason which dictates laws unconditionally. (R 28)

It might be possible to read "practical reason . . . subservient to other incentives" as referring to a "hypothetical" use of practical reason – that is, a discovery of means – except that the role actually assigned to practical reason here is not the discovery of means but "comparison." This is the role of reason in *Conjectural History* as well, although in the *Religion* the comparison is not among possible objects of desire but a comparison of one's own lot with another's. Again, however, the result must be the acquisition of new, specifically human ends, for Kant claims that "nature, indeed, wanted to use the idea of such rivalry . . . only as a spur to culture" (R 27).

Throughout the historical writings, culture represents the development towards the perfect freedom or rule of reason that will only be achieved by morality.

When Kant says that the characteristic of humanity is the power to set an end, then, he is not merely referring to personality, which would encompass the power to adopt an end for moral or sufficient reasons. Rather, he is referring to a more general capacity for choosing, desiring, or valuing ends; ends different from the ones that instinct lays down for us, and to which our interest is directed by the operations of reason. At the same time, of course, it is important to emphasize that this capacity is only completed and perfected when our ends are fully determined by reason, and this occurs only when we respond to moral incentives. Humanity, completed and perfected, becomes personality, so that in treating the first as an end in itself we will inevitably be led to realize the second. Thus, in the *Critique of Practical Reason*, humanity in one's own person and personality are spoken of as if they were the same thing (C2 87). But the distinctive feature of humanity, *as such*, is simply the capacity to take a rational interest in something: to decide, under the influence of reason, that something is desirable, that it is worthy of pursuit or realization, that it is to be deemed important or valuable, not because it contributes to survival or instinctual satisfaction, but as an end – for its own sake. It is this capacity that the Formula of Humanity commands us never to treat as a mere means, but always as an end in itself.

III   THE BASIS OF THE ARGUMENT

But suppose that there were something the existence of which in itself had absolute worth, something which, as an end in itself, could be a ground of definite laws. In it and only in it could lie the ground of a possible categorical imperative, i.e., of a practical law (G 428).

With these words, Kant, in the *Groundwork*, establishes the connection between the existence of a categorical imperative and the existence of an unconditionally valuable end. Immediately after, he asserts, and then argues, that this end must be "man and, in general, every rational being." In the next section, I want to reconstruct that argument in order to show why humanity must be this unconditional end and the material of a rational principle. In this section I want to say something about the theory of rational action upon which that argument is based.

In the discussion of good and evil in the *Critique of Practical Reason* (57–71), Kant discusses what he refers to as an old formula of the schools: *Nihil appetimus, nisi sub ratione boni; nihil aversamur, nisi sub ratione mali.* If this is taken to mean that "we desire nothing except with a view to our weal or woe" it is "at least very doubtful." But if it is read as saying "we desire nothing, under the direction of reason, except in so far as we hold it to be good or bad" it is "indubitably certain" (C2 59–60). Similarly, in the *Groundwork* Kant says that "the will is a faculty of choosing only that which reason, independently of inclination, recognizes as practically necessary, i.e., as good" (G 412–29). Insofar as we are rational agents we will choose what is good – or take what we choose to be chosen as good.

As the identification of "good" with "practically necessary" in the *Groundwork* quotation suggests, Kant takes "good" to be a rational concept. This means two related things. First, reason must determine what is good. On this basis Kant argues in the *Critique of Practical Reason* that if the end were set by inclination and reason determined only the means, then only the means could be called "good" (C2 62). Thus, if an end is good, it must be set by reason; and if an action is done under the full direction of reason, then the end must be good. Second, and correlatively, if an end is deemed good it provides reasons for action that apply to every rational being:

> What we call good must be, in the judgment of every reasonable man, an object of the faculty of desire, and the evil must be, in everyone's eyes, an object of aversion. Thus, in addition to sense, this judgment requires reason. (C2 60–61)

It is this that gives rise to the *Groundwork* requirement, associated with the Formula of Humanity, that others "must be able to contain in themselves the end of the very same action" (G 430). If one's end cannot be shared, and so cannot be an object of the faculty of desire for everyone, it cannot be good, and the action cannot be rational.

From these considerations it follows that if there are perfectly rational actions, there must be good ends, and that when we act under the direction of reason, we pursue an end that is objectively good. But human beings, who act on their conception of laws, take themselves to act under the direction of reason. In the argument for the Formula of Humanity, as I understand it, Kant uses the premise that when we act we take ourselves to be acting reasonably and so we suppose that our end is, in his sense, objectively good. Perhaps it will at first seem odd that he uses that premise in an argument leading to a formula of the categorical imperative, since only if there is a categorical imperative will anything be in his sense objectively good. Here it is crucial to remember that the arguments leading to the formulations of the categorical imperative all tell us what the imperative will be like *if it exists*. Only *if* there is a categorical imperative will there be perfectly rational action; but if there is perfectly rational action there will be ends that are good.

Since good is a rational concept, a good end will be one for which there is reason – an end whose existence can be *justified*. But this by itself is not enough to establish a categorical imperative, for reasons can be relative: means for example can be called good, but only relatively to a given end (C2 62). If the goodness of an end is only relative, it will not have that claim upon all rational beings that Kant associates with the rationality of the concept "good," and cannot provide the basis for a categorical imperative:

> The ends which a rational being arbitrarily proposes to himself as the consequences of his action are material ends and are without exception only relative, for only their relation to a particularly constituted faculty of desire in the subject gives them their worth. And this worth cannot, therefore, afford any universal principles for all rational beings or valid and necessary principles for every volition. (G 427–28)

What is required for a categorical imperative, therefore, is an end for which there is sufficient reason – an end whose existence can be completely justified, and which therefore has a claim on every rational will. This is why Kant seeks "something the existence of which in itself has absolute worth" or an "end in itself" (G 428). Justification – the giving of practical reasons for ends and actions – is in one sense subject to the same fate as explanation – the giving of theoretical reasons for events. Reason seeks the "unconditioned," as the basis for an account (justification or explanation) that provides a sufficient reason.

As these comparisons suggest, the argument for the Formula of Humanity depends upon the application of the unconditioned/conditioned distinction to the concept of goodness. This follows from the fact that good is a rational concept. In any case where anything is conditioned in any way, reason seeks out its conditions, not resting until the "unconditioned condition" is discovered (if possible). An inquiry in the "analytic" or as Kant in one passage more helpfully calls it the "regressive" style (PFM 276n) is an argument in which something is taken as given or actual and the conditions of its possibility are explored. The arguments of the *Groundwork*, at least in the first two sections, like the arguments of the *Prolegomena*, are "regressive." If there is a categorical imperative, then there is fully rational action. If there is fully rational action, how is it possible? In the case of the Formula of Humanity the material of the law is sought through an investigation of the question: what is capable of fully justifying an end? What is unconditionally good?

In one sense, this question has already been answered in the first section of the book. There, Kant asserts that the only thing that can be conceived to be unconditionally good is a good will. The location of this claim shows us that Kant attributes it to "common rational knowledge of morals." It is used as a starting point for his analysis. In the remarks that follow, Kant elucidates the claim by explaining that the good will is the only thing that has its "full worth in itself" (G 394); and is the only thing whose value is in no way relative to its circumstances or results. Its value is independent of "what it effects or accomplishes" (G 394); it is in the strictest sense *intrinsically* good.

The good will is also said to be the condition of all our other purposes (G 396). This follows from its being the only unconditionally good thing. The value of anything else whatever is dependent upon certain conditions being met. Kant mentions talents of the mind, qualities of temperament, gifts of fortune such as power, wealth, and health, and happiness among the things whose value is conditional. If the value of something is conditional, however, an inquiry into the conditions of its value should lead us eventually to what is unconditioned. This is partly affirmed in these early passages, for Kant tells us that the talents and temperamental qualities must be directed, the advantages used, and the happiness possessed by one with a good will in order that they be good. The good will is, in all cases, the unconditioned condition of the goodness of other things.

As the inclusion of happiness among the conditional goods shows, although Kant is claiming that the good will is the only thing whose value is intrinsic, he is not claiming that the good will is the only thing that is valuable as an end.⁴ Means are obviously conditional goods, for their goodness depends upon the goodness of the ends to which they are instrumental. But happiness, although clearly an end, and an end under which Kant thinks all of our other ends are subsumed, is also a conditional good whose value depends upon the good will. So Kant tells us that the good will is not the sole or complete good but "the condition of all others, even of the desire for happiness" (G 396). It is for this reason that "an impartial observer" disapproves "the sight of a being adorned with no feature of a pure and good will, yet enjoying uninterrupted prosperity" (G 393). But the impartial observer is equally dismayed by the idea that the virtuous person be without happiness:

That virtue (as the worthiness to be happy) is the supreme condition of whatever appears to us to be desirable and thus of all our pursuit of happiness and, consequently, that it is the supreme good have been proved in the Analytic. But these truths do not imply that virtue is the entire and perfect good as the object of the faculty of desire of rational finite beings. For this, happiness is also required, and indeed not merely in the partial eyes of a person who makes himself his end but even in the judgment of an impartial reason, which impartially regards persons in the world as ends-in-themselves. (C2 110)

A thing, then, can be said to be objectively good, either if it is unconditionally good or if it is conditionally good and the condition under which it is good is met. The happiness of the virtuous, for this reason, forms the other part of the "highest good": virtue, and happiness in proportion to virtue, together comprise all that is objectively good. A conditionally good thing, like happiness, is objectively good when its condition is met in the sense that it is fully justified and the reasons for it are sufficient. Every rational being has a reason to bring it about, and it is this that makes it a duty both to pursue the happiness of others and, in general, to make the highest good one's end.

Since all objective value must come from unconditioned value, the good will is the source of all the good in the world. The highest good, as virtue and happiness in proportion to virtue; or the Kingdom of Ends, as "a whole of rational beings as ends in themselves as well as of the particular ends which each may set for himself" (G 433) are representations of a system of ends which can be said to be "synthesized" by the categorical imperative. This system is the totality of all that is objectively good under the unconditioned good; it is the systematic whole or unity formed by practical reason.

> As pure practical reason it likewise seeks the unconditioned for the practically conditioned (which rests on inclinations and natural need); and this unconditioned is not only sought as the determining ground of the will but, even when this is given (in the moral law), is also sought as the unconditioned totality of the object of pure practical reason, under the name of the *highest good*. (C2 108)

I have said that practical reason shares the "fate" of theoretical reason insofar as it, too, is driven to "seek the unconditioned." In an important sense, however, the fate of practical reason is different from that of theoretical reason; this is one of the most central tenets of Kant's philosophy. Theoretical reason, in its quest for the unconditioned, produces antinomies; in the end, the kind of unconditional explanation that would fully satisfy reason is unavailable. Practical reason in its quest for justification is subject to no such limitation.[5] This is part of Kant's doctrine of the primacy of practical reason. The argument for the Formula of Humanity provides an initial access to that doctrine, by showing that Humanity can be regarded as an unconditionally good thing, and a source of justification for things that are only conditionally good.

IV   THE ARGUMENT FOR THE FORMULA OF HUMANITY

Having established that if there is a categorical imperative there must be something that is unconditionally valuable, Kant proceeds to argue that it must be humanity. Here is what he says:

All objects of inclinations have only a conditional worth, for if the inclination and the needs founded on them did not exist, their objects would be without worth. The inclinations themselves as sources of needs, however, are so lacking in absolute worth that the universal wish of every rational being must be indeed to free himself completely from them. Therefore, the worth of any objects to be obtained by our actions is at all times conditional. Beings whose existence does not depend on our will but on nature, if they are not rational beings, have only a relative worth as means and are therefore called "things"; on the other hand, rational beings are designated "persons" because their nature indicates that they are ends in themselves, i.e. things which may not be used merely as means. Such a being is thus an object of respect and, so far, restricts all [arbitrary] choice. . . . For, without them, nothing of absolute worth could be found, and if all worth is conditional and thus contingent, no supreme practical principle for reason could be found anywhere. (G 428–29)

In one sense, it seems as if Kant is just reviewing the available options in his search for something unconditionally good: considering objects of inclinations, inclinations, natural beings or "things", and finally persons, that being the one that will serve. But it is also possible to read this passage as at least suggesting a regress towards the unconditioned: moving from the objects of our inclinations, to the inclinations themselves, finally (later) back to ourselves, our rational nature. The final step, that rational nature is itself the objective end, is reinforced by this consideration:

The ground of this principle is: rational nature exists as an end in itself. Man necessarily thinks of his own existence in this way; thus far it is a subjective principle of human actions. Also every other rational being thinks of his existence by means of the same rational ground which holds also for myself; thus it is at the same time an objective principle from which, as a supreme practical ground, it must be possible to derive all laws of the will. (G 429)

I have quoted these rather long passages because my aim in what follows is to give a reconstruction along these lines – that is, on the assumption that the argument is intended as a regress upon the conditions. The reconstruction depends upon the ideas set forth in the previous sections. A rational action must be done with reference to an end that is good, and a good end is one for which there is a sufficient reason. It must be the object of every rational will, and it must be fully justified. If it is only conditionally good, the unconditioned condition for its goodness must be sought. Although we know already that the good will is this condition, the argument helps to show us what the good will must be, by showing us what will serve as such a condition.

Suppose that you make a choice, and you believe what you have opted for is a good thing. How can you justify it or account for its goodness? In an ordinary case it will be something for which you have an inclination, something that you like or want. Yet it looks as if the things that you want, if they are good at all, are good because you want them – rather than your wanting them because they are good. For "all objects of inclinations have only a conditional worth, for if the inclinations and the needs founded on them did not exist, their objects would be without worth" (G 428). The objects of inclination are in themselves neutral: we are not attracted to them by their goodness; rather their goodness consists in their being the objects of human inclinations.

This, however, makes it sound as if it were our inclinations that made things good. This cannot be right, for "the inclinations themselves, as sources of needs, however, are so lacking in absolute worth that the universal wish of every rational being must be indeed to free himself completely from them" (G 428). Now even without fully endorsing what Kant says here, we can easily agree that there are some inclinations of which we want to be free: namely those whose existence is disruptive to our happiness. Take the case of a bad habit associated with an habitual craving – it would not be right to say that the object craved was good simply because of the existence of the craving when the craving itself is one that you would rather be rid of. So it will not be just any inclination, but one that we choose to act on, that renders its object good.

Even consistency with our own happiness does not make the objects of inclination good, however. (Now I am, admittedly, departing from the passage I am interpreting – for Kant leaves it at the undesirability of having inclinations at all.) This is partly because we are not certain what our happiness consists in, but more because of a claim that has already been made in the opening lines of the *Groundwork*: we do not believe that happiness is good in the possession of one who does not have a good will. This is, of course, our great temptation – to believe that our own happiness is unconditionally good. But it is not really a tenable attitude. For either one must have the attitude that just one's own happiness is unconditionally good, which is rather a remarkable feat of egocentricism,[6] or one has to have the attitude that each person's happiness is unconditionally good. But since "good" is a rational concept and "what we call good must be, in the judgment of every reasonable man, an object of the faculty of desire" (C2 60–61), we cannot rest with the position that everyone's happiness, whatever it might be, is absolutely good. For:

> Though elsewhere natural laws make everything harmonious, if one here attributed the universality of law to this maxim, there would be the extreme opposite of harmony, the most arrant conflict, and the complete annihilation of the maxim itself and its purpose. For the wills of all do not have one and the same object, but each person has his own. . . . In this way a harmony may result resembling that depicted in a certain satirical poem as existing between a married couple bent on going to ruin, "Oh, marvelous harmony, what he wants is what she wants"; or like the pledge which is said to have been given by Francis I to the Emperor Charles V, "What my brother wants (Milan), that I want too." (C2 28)

Given that the good must be a consistent, harmonious object of rational desire and an object of the faculty of desire for every rational being, one can take neither everyone's happiness nor just one's own happiness to be good without qualification: the former does not form a consistent harmonious object; and the latter cannot plausibly be taken to be the object of every rational will if the former is not. Thus happiness cannot in either form be the "unconditioned condition" of the goodness of the object of your inclination, and the regress upon the conditions cannot rest here. We have not yet discovered what if anything makes the object of your choice good and so your choice rational.

Now comes the crucial step. Kant's answer, as I understand him, is that what makes the object of your rational choice good is that it *is* the object of a rational choice. That is, since we still *do* make choices and have the attitude that what we choose is good in spite of our incapacity to find the unconditioned condition of the object's goodness in this (empirical) regress upon the conditions, it must be that we are supposing that rational choice itself *makes* its object good. His idea is that rational choice has what I will call a value-conferring status. When Kant says: "rational nature exists as an end in itself. Man necessarily thinks of his own existence in this way; thus far it is a subjective principle of human actions" (G 429), I read him as claiming that in our private rational choices and in general in our actions we view ourselves as having a value-conferring status in virtue of our rational nature. We act as if our own choice were the sufficient condition of the goodness of its object: this attitude is built into (a subjective principle of) rational action. When Kant goes on to say: "Also every other rational being thinks of his existence by means of the same rational ground which holds also for myself; thus, it is at the same time an objective principle from which, as a supreme practical ground, it must be possible to derive all laws of the will" (G 429), I read him as making the following argument. If you view yourself as having a value-conferring status in virtue of your power of rational choice, you must view anyone who has the power of rational choice as having, in virtue of that power, a value-conferring status. This will mean that what you make good by means of your rational choice must be harmonious with what another can make good by means of her rational choice – for the good is a consistent, harmonious object shared by all rational beings. Thus it must always be possible for others "to contain in themselves the end of the very same action" (G 430).[7]

Thus, regressing upon the conditions, we find that the unconditioned condition of the goodness of anything is rational nature, or the power of rational choice. To play this role, however, rational nature must itself be something of unconditional value – an end in itself. This means, however, that you must treat rational nature wherever you find it (in your own person or in that of another) as an end. This in turn means that no choice is rational which violates the status of rational nature as an end: rational nature becomes a limiting condition (G 437–38) of the rationality of choice and action. It is an unconditional end, so you can never act against it without contradiction. If you overturn the *source* of the goodness of your end, neither your end nor the action which aims at it can possibly be good, and your action will not be fully rational.

To say that humanity is of unconditional value might seem, at first sight, somewhat different from the claim with which the *Groundwork* opens: that the good will is of unconditional value. What enables Kant to make both claims without any problem is this: humanity is the power of rational choice, but only when the choice is fully rational is humanity fully realized. Humanity, as I argued in Section III, is completed and perfected only in the realization of "personality," which is the good will. But the possession of humanity and the capacity for the good will, whether or not that capacity is realized, is enough to establish a claim on being treated as an unconditional end.

V   TREATING HUMANITY AS AN END IN ITSELF

Readers have often been puzzled by the prescription "treat human-ity as an end." Kant's claims that the Humanity formula is closer to intuition (G 436), that the Formula of Universal Law gives the con-tent the categorical imperative (G 420–21; 425), and that the latter ought to be used in actual decision making (G 437), might make it seem as if Kant does not intend this formulation to give definite directions for application, independently of its equivalence with the Formula of Universal Law. In opposition to this is the fact that Kant re-explains his *Groundwork* examples in terms of this formulation; in one case – the suicide example – providing a rather better account in terms of this formulation than he does in terms of universal law. Even more important, however, is the fact that all of the duties described in the *Metaphysical Principles of Virtue* are derived from the idea that humanity must always be treated as unconditionally valuable.

In fact, the argument that reveals the unconditional value of hu-manity also teaches us how to apply the Formula of Humanity. In order to know what is meant by "treating humanity as an end," we need only consider this argument, and see how humanity got to be an end in itself. What was in question was the source of the goodness of an end – the goodness say, of some ordinary object of inclination. This source was traced to the power of rationally choosing ends, exercised in this case on this end. So when Kant says rational nature or humanity is an end in itself, it is the power of rational choice that he is referring to, and in particular, the power to set an end (to make something an end by conferring the status of goodness on it) and pursue it by rational means.

The question is then: what is involved in treating your own and every other human being's capacity for the rational choice of ends – that is to say, for conferring value – as an end in itself? There are several things that are important to keep in mind. First, Kant thinks that this end functions in our deliberations negatively – as some-

thing that is not to be acted against. The capacity for rational choice
is not a purpose that we can realize or something for us to bring into
existence. Second, it is an unconditional end, and that has two important implications. The first is that as an unconditional end it
must *never* be acted against. It is not one end among others, to be
weighed along with the rest. The second implication in a sense gives
the reason for the first: as an unconditional end it is the condition of
the goodness of all our other ends. If humanity is not regarded and
treated as unconditionally good then nothing else can be objectively
good. As Kant puts it in the *Groundwork*: "the subject of a possible
will which is absolutely good . . . cannot be made secondary to any
other object without contradiction" (G 437). No relative end can be
pursued as if it were better or more important than humanity itself
without a kind of contradiction.

While it would not be feasible to go through all of the many cases
Kant gives of duties derived from the Formula of Humanity, I want
to say something about the two major kinds of derivations from this
formula that exist, and how each is supposed to work. In order to do
this, I will concentrate on the *Groundwork* examples.

The first treatment of the examples, used to illustrate the work-
ings of the Formula of Universal Law, divides them into two groups.
The duty not to commit suicide because of the prospect of wretched-
ness, and the duty not to make a false promise because of a financial
emergency, illustrate cases in which the maxim cannot be thought
as a universal law without contradiction. Under the Formula of Humanity, these are classified as cases in which humanity, in your own
person or another, is treated as a mere means. The duties of developing your talents and powers, and of helping others, are classified
under Universal Law as cases where the maxim, though thinkable as
a universal law, cannot be willed as such. Under the Formula of
Humanity, these are classified as cases in which the action is not in
conflict with humanity, but fails to "harmonize" with it (G 430). In
both cases, what is involved is a failure to properly acknowledge in
your conduct the value-conferring status either of another or of yourself. We can make this plausible, and also see why Kant takes the
two formulas to be identical, by considering the examples and the
way Kant explains them.

In the suicide case, Kant says that "if, in order to escape from
burdensome circumstances, he destroys himself, he uses a person

merely as a means to maintain a tolerable condition up to the end of life" (G 429). As mentioned before, Kant takes it to be a consequence of his argument that humanity cannot be made secondary to any relative end without contradiction. This is what happens in the case of suicide: the end, in the example, is "a tolerable condition" and the means is the destruction of a rational being – hence a rational being is being used as a mere means to a relative or conditional end. The reason why this is said to be a contradiction rather than merely a case of misordered values is that the relative end must get its value from the thing that is being destroyed for its sake. However obvious it may seem that a "tolerable condition" is a good thing, it is good only because of the value conferred upon it by the choice of a rational being. Destroy the rational being, and you cut off the source of the goodness of this end – it is no longer really an end at all, and it is no longer rational to pursue it.

The false promising case is slightly more complicated, and easier to explain if we use the result of applying the Formula of Universal Law. Because we know from that test that the maxim of false promising in order to escape a financial emergency could not be universalized, we know that false promising could not be the universal method of escaping financial emergencies. From this it follows, because reasons must be universal, that the desire to escape a financial emergency cannot justify (be a sufficient reason for) making a false promise. If you make a false promise, then, you accord to your value-conferring capacity a greater power, so to speak, than you do that of others. You act as if your desire to avoid financial trouble has a justifying power that someone else's exactly similar desire would not have. But this cannot be right: if your desire gets its justifying power from your humanity, then any other person's similar desire would have the same justifying power. If the end of your action is not good because of your humanity, on the other hand, it cannot be good at all, and your action is not rational. There is another way to describe this kind of case that is perhaps even better for bringing out the violation of humanity that is involved. Whenever you violate the first contradiction test under the Formula of Universal Law, and act on a maxim that cannot be universalized, you must be using some method to achieve your end that not everyone could use to achieve that end. The efficacy of your action depends upon the fact that others do not act as you do, and that in a sense means that others are making your method work. This is characteristic of the kind of violation of duty that is most amenable to treatment under the first contradiction test. For example, when you tell a lie for a certain purpose, the lie works to achieve the purpose only because most people tell the truth. That is why you are believed, and so why the lie achieves its purpose. In such a case it is not just the person to whom you lie that you treat as a means but all of those who tell the truth. This is because you allow their actions to fuel your method, and that is explicitly treating their rational nature as a mere means: indeed it is making a tool of other people's good wills. Whenever you use a method that works only because others do not use it – which is the first contradiction test reveals – you make an instrument of the rational nature of others, and treat them as mere means.

The third and fourth examples, of the duty of self-perfection and the duty to promote the happiness of others, admit of very clear accounts in terms of the idea of acknowledging the value-conferring power of rational beings as ends in themselves. In the case of the duty of self-perfection, it is a question of developing and realizing the capacities which enable you to exercise your power of rational choice – the talents and powers that make it possible for you to set and pursue ends. It is your powers as an agent that are to be promoted. This, indeed, is as close as Kant comes to assigning a positive function to humanity as an end. What makes this possible is the fact that rational nature is a sort of capacity. It is, as Kant says, not an end to be effected (G 437), for rational nature is not something that we can create; nevertheless, we can realize our rational capacities more or less fully, and this is what generates the various positive duties of self-perfecting. In the case of the duty to promote the happiness of others, Kant says:

> For the ends of any person, who is an end in himself, must as far as possible also be my end[s][8] if that conception of an end in itself is to have its full effect on me. (G 430)

This is because the full realization and acknowledgment of the fact that another is an end in itself involves viewing the end upon which this person confers value as *good* – and when one acknowledges that something is good, one acknowledges it to be "in the judgment of every reasonable man, an object of the faculty of desire." To treat another as an end in itself is to treat his or her ends as

objectively good, as you do your own. To treat anyone as an end in
itself is to regard that person as one who confers value on the objects
of his or her choice.

VI CONFERRING VALUE

In this last section I want to bring in as a final piece of support for
the reading I have given a set of passages from the *Critique of Judgment*. These passages seem to me to support in a very forceful way
the idea that it is our power to confer objective value that Kant
thinks of as having unconditional worth.

In the "Methodology of Teleological Judgment," Kant is concerned with the question of what might appropriately play the role
of final purpose of creation. He has established the idea of a natural
purpose, which provides the basis for a teleological interpretation of
nature; but in order to view nature as a teleological *system*, we must
discover its final purpose: we must discover, that is, a reason for the
existence of nature itself. This will not be a purpose internal to
nature, but one outside or independent of it: "an objective supreme
purpose, such as the highest reason would require for creation" (C3
436). In carrying out his inquiry, Kant undertakes a familiar sort of
regress argument. In this case, the condition of a given thing is its
purpose, and the regress must end with something which is in itself
a final purpose, "that purpose which needs no other as the condition
of its possibility"; something about which "it can no longer be asked
why" it exists (C3 434–35). Starting with the idea of a natural purpose, the argument proceeds to what Kant calls an ultimate purpose:
this will be that which we judge to be the purpose *within* nature
towards which all nature is organized. This ultimate purpose, being
as it were nature's contribution to the final purpose, will give us an
idea of what the final purpose is.

Beginning with consideration of vegetable nature, we can reason
back to the ultimate purpose as follows:

a more intimate knowledge of its indescribably wise organization does not
permit us to hold to this thought (that it is a mere mechanism), but prompts
the question: What are these things created for? If it is answered: For the
animal kingdom, which is thereby nourished and has thus been able to
spread over the earth in genera so various, then the further question comes:

What are these plant-devouring animals for? The answer would be something like this: For beasts of prey, which can only be nourished by that which has life. Finally we have the question: What are these last, as well as the first-mentioned natural kingdoms, good for? For man in reference to the manifold use which his understanding teaches him to make of all these creatures. He is the ultimate purpose of creation here on earth, because he is the only being who can form a concept of purposes and who can, by his reason, make out of an aggregate of purposively formed things a system of purposes. (C3 426–27)

Kant then goes on to inquire for the more specific feature of human life that is the purpose of nature – that is to say, for something "found in man himself which is to be furthered as a purpose by means of his connection with nature" (C3 429). This Kant supposes must be either human happiness or human culture (C3 429–30). At this point Kant takes up an argument that is repeated throughout the teleological historical writings and also appears in the teleological argument at the beginning of the *Groundwork*. Happiness does not seem to be something that nature can achieve or aims at achieving: the evidence favors culture. But furthermore, the argument requires that the ultimate purpose of human beings within nature teaches us what the final purpose of nature itself is. And happiness cannot be the final purpose of nature, for the same reasons that we found, in the argument for the Formula of Humanity, that happiness could not be the unconditioned good.

Happiness, on the contrary, as has been shown in the preceding paragraphs by the testimony of experience, is not even a *purpose of nature* in respect of man in preference to other creatures, much less a *final purpose of creation*. Men may of course make it their ultimate subjective purpose. But if I ask, in reference to the final purpose of creation, Why must men exist? then we are speaking of an objective supreme purpose, such as the highest reason would require for creation. If we answer: These beings exist to afford objects for the benevolence of that supreme cause, then we contradict the condition to which the reason of man subjects even his own inmost wish for happiness (viz. the harmony with his own internal moral legislation). (C3 436n)

The answer then will be that the ultimate purpose in nature is "culture" in the specific sense of the development of humanity:

The production of the aptitude of a rational being for arbitrary purposes in general (consequently in his freedom) is *culture*. (C3 431)

Culture, according to Kant, is an appropriate ultimate purpose in nature, for the development of culture is something that "nature can do in regard to the final purpose that lies outside it" (C3 431).

The final purpose of nature, Kant argues, is morality itself. It is in morality that the aptitude of setting purposes before ourselves finds its completion, for an end or purpose must be objectively good, and only in morality do we find the unconditioned condition of its goodness:

> Only in man, and only in him as subject of morality, do we meet with unconditioned legislation in respect of purposes, which therefore alone renders him capable of being a final purpose, to which the whole of nature is teleologically subordinated. (C3 435–36)

It is our capacity to set ends – to freely choose what shall be an end by means of reason, that not only makes every rational being an end in itself, but which forms the only possible final purpose of nature, teleologically conceived. It is only this capacity that has its value completely in itself; so that this not only forms the basis of a possible categorical imperative, but also the only possible basis for a complete teleological view of creation.

> Without men the whole creation would be a mere waste, in vain, and without final purpose. But it is not in reference to man's cognitive faculty (theoretical reason) that the being of everything else in the world gets its worth; he is not there merely that there may be someone to *contemplate* the world . . . we must presuppose for it a final purpose, in reference to which its contemplation itself has worth. Again it is not in reference to the feeling of pleasure or to the sum of pleasures that we think a final purpose of creation as given; . . . or, in a word, by happiness. For the fact that man, if he exists, takes this for his final design gives us no concept as to why in general he should exist and as to what worth he has in himself. . . . But it is that worth which he alone can give to himself and which consists in what he does, how and according to what principles he acts, and that not as a link in nature's chain but in the *freedom* of his faculty of desire. That is, a good will is that whereby alone his being can have an absolute worth and in reference to which the being of the world can have a *final purpose*. (C3 442–43)

Or as Kant puts it in an earlier footnote:

> There remains, then, nothing but the value which we ourselves give our life, . . . in such independence of nature that the existence of nature itself can only be a purpose under this condition. (C3 434n)

On Kant's view it is human beings, with our capacity for valuing things, that bring to the world such value as it has. Even the justification of nature is up to us.

NOTES

1 The three arguments mentioned here are in the *Groundwork* at 420–21; 427–29; 431–32.

2 In fact, the example is explicitly given as one in which the agent has a "direct inclination" to the action and its purpose as opposed to the kind of case (like that of the "honest" grocer) in which the agent has no direct inclination but is "impelled to do [the action] by another inclination." That is, the action with its purpose is an end and not a means (G 397). Admittedly, Kant's discussion of happiness in the *Critique of Practical Reason* (C2 23) suggests a hedonistic view of the inclinations. But though the sympathetic character may value the beneficent action because it is pleasant, this *may* still be taken as an explanation of why he values it rather than a reduction of it to a mere means. (This is the way Mill, as I understand him, proposes to interpret hedonism in Chapter IV of *Utilitarianism*.) However, Kant's language in the *Critique of Practical Reason* is that of the more conventional sort of hedonism which makes pleasure and the avoidance of pain ends to which everything else desired must be regarded as means.

3 If Kant's view of the inclinations in the *Critique of Practical Reason* is understood to be a conventional hedonistic view (see note 2), then the account of happiness given there must count either against my reading of these remarks in the *Groundwork* or against the *Groundwork's* "Ideal of the Imagination" view itself. Beck thinks that the difficulty is in Kant's psychological views. See *A Commentary on Kant's Critique of Practical Reason*, p. 101. I would like to thank a reader for *Kant-Studien* for this reference, as well as for other useful references and comments.

4 A more extended version of some of the arguments of this section appears in my paper *Two Distinctions in Goodness*, Chapter 9 in this volume. In that paper I compare G. E. Moore's conception of intrinsic value as something possessed by all ends that ought to be valued for their own sakes and Kant's conception of unconditional value as possessed only by the good will.

5 Practical reason does of course also have its antinomy, but it results not from a failure to locate the unconditioned as the "determining ground of the will" (the original source of all justification), but rather from the apparent failure of the unconditioned principle to produce the associated

unconditioned totality, the highest good, in the natural world (C2 108; 113–14).

6 Some of the standard arguments against the rationality of egoism might be useful in supporting this point: for example, that of G. E. Moore in *Principia Ethica*, Sections 59–61. See also the discussions by Thomas Nagel in *The Possibility of Altruism*, especially Chapter X.

7 The idea that choice in accordance with the moral law is the basis of the concept of "good" (and not the reverse) is also argued in the *Critique of Practical Reason*, in the chapter on "The Concept of an Object of Pure Practical Reason" (57–67).

8 Beck translates this passage "as far as possible also be my end." On my reading, the plural fits the sense of the passage better.

5 The right to lie: Kant on dealing with evil

One of the great difficulties with Kant's moral philosophy is that it seems to imply that our moral obligations leave us powerless in the face of evil. Kant's theory sets a high ideal of conduct and tells us to live up to that ideal regardless of what other persons are doing. The results may be very bad. But Kant says that the law "remains in full force, because it commands categorically" (G 438–39). The most well-known example of this "rigorism," as it is sometimes called, concerns Kant's views on our duty to tell the truth.

In two passages in his ethical writings, Kant seems to endorse the following pair of claims about this duty: first, one must never under any circumstances or for any purpose tell a lie; second, if one does tell a lie one is responsible for all the consequences that ensue, even if they were completely unforeseeable.

One of the two passages appears in the *Metaphysical Principles of Virtue*. There Kant classifies lying as a violation of a perfect duty to oneself. In one of the casuistical questions, a servant, under instructions, tells a visitor the lie that his master is not at home. His master, meanwhile, sneaks off and commits a crime, which would have been prevented by the watchman sent to arrest him. Kant says:

Upon whom . . . does the blame fall? To be sure, also upon the servant, who here violated a duty to himself by lying, the consequence of which will now be imputed to him by his own conscience. (MPV 431)

The other passage is the infamous one about the murderer at the door from the essay, "On a Supposed Right to Lie from Altruistic Motives." Here Kant's claims are more extreme, for he says that the liar may be held legally as well as ethically responsible for the conse-

133

quences, and the series of coincidences he imagines is even more fantastic:

After you have honestly answered the murderer's question as to whether his intended victim is at home, it may be that he has slipped out so that he does not come in the way of the murderer, and thus that the murder may not be committed. But if you had lied and said he was not at home when he had really gone out without your knowing it, and if the murderer had then met him as he went away and murdered him, you might justly be accused as the cause of his death. For if you had told the truth as far as you knew it, perhaps the murderer might have been apprehended by the neighbors while he searched the house and thus the deed might have been prevented. (SRL 427)

Kant's readers differ about whether Kant's moral philosophy commits him to the claims he makes in these passages. Unsympathetic readers are inclined to take them as evidence of the horrifying conclusions to which Kant was led by his notion that the necessity in duty is rational necessity – as if Kant were clinging to a logical point in the teeth of moral decency. Such readers take these conclusions as a defeat for Kant's ethics, or for ethical rationalism generally; or they take Kant to have confused principles which are merely general in their application and *prima facie* in their truth with absolute and universal laws. Sympathetic readers are likely to argue that Kant here mistook the implications of his own theory, and to try to show that, by careful construction and accurate testing of the maxim on which this liar acts, Kant's conclusions can be blocked by his own procedures.

Sympathetic and unsympathetic readers alike have focused their attention on the implications of the first formulation of the categorical imperative, the Formula of Universal Law. The *Groundwork of the Metaphysics of Morals* contains two other sets of terms in which the categorical imperative is formulated: the treatment of humanity as an end in itself, and autonomy, or legislative membership in a Kingdom of Ends. My treatment of the issue falls into three parts. First, I want to argue that Kant's defenders are right in thinking that, when the case is treated under the Formula of Universal Law, this particular lie can be shown to be permissible. Second, I want to argue that when the case is treated from the perspective provided by the Formulas of Humanity and the Kingdom of Ends, it becomes clear why Kant *is* committed to the view that lying is wrong in every case. But from this perspective we see that Kant's rigorism about lying is not the result of a misplaced love of consistency or legalistic thinking. Instead, it comes from an attractive ideal of human relations which is the basis of his ethical system. If Kant is wrong in his conclusion about lying to the murderer at the door, it is for the interesting and important reason that morality itself sometimes allows or even requires us to do something that from an ideal perspective is wrong. The case does not impugn Kant's ethics as an *ideal* system. Instead, it shows that we need special principles for dealing with evil. My third aim is to discuss the structure that an ethical system must have in order to accommodate such special principles.

UNIVERSAL LAW

The Formula of Universal Law tells us never to act on a maxim that we could not at the same time will to be a universal law. A maxim which cannot even be conceived as a universal law without contradiction is in violation of a strict and perfect duty, one which assigns us a particular action or omission. A maxim which cannot be willed as universal law without contradicting the will is in violation of a broad and imperfect duty, one which assigns us an end, but does not tell us what or how much we should do towards it. Maxims of lying are violations of perfect duty, and so are supposed to be the kind that cannot be conceived without contradiction when universalized.

The sense in which the universalization of an immoral maxim is supposed to "contradict" itself is a matter of controversy. On my reading, which I will not defend here, the contradiction in question is a "practical" one: the universalized maxim contradicts itself when the efficacy of the action as a method of achieving its purpose would be undermined by its universal practice.[1] So, to use Kant's example, the point against false promising as a method of getting ready cash is that if everyone attempted to use false promising as a method of getting ready cash, false promising would no longer *work* as a method of getting ready cash, since, as Kant says, "no one would believe what was promised to him but would only laugh at any such assertion as vain pretense" (G 422).

Thus the test question will be: could this action be the universal method of achieving this purpose? Now when we consider lying in general, it looks as if it could not be the universal method of doing anything. For lies are usually efficacious in achieving their purposes because they deceive, but if they were universally practiced they would not deceive. We believe what is said to us in a given context because most of the time people in that context say what they really think or intend. In contexts in which people usually say false things – for example, when telling stories that are jokes – we are not deceived. If a story that is a joke and is false counts as a lie, we can say that a lie in this case in not wrong, because the universal practice of lying in the context of jokes does not interfere with the *purpose* of jokes, which is to amuse and does not depend on deception. But in most cases lying falls squarely into the category of the sort of action Kant considers wrong: actions whose efficacy depends upon the fact that most people do not engage in them, and which therefore can only be performed by someone who makes an exception of himself (G 424).

When we try to apply this test to the case of the murderer at the door, however, we run into a difficulty. The difficulty derives from the fact that there is probably already deception in the case. If murderers standardly came to the door and said: "I wish to murder your friend – is he here in your house?" then perhaps the universal practice of lying in order to keep a murderer from his victim would not work. If everyone lied in these circumstances the murderer would be aware of that fact and would not be deceived by your answer. But the murderer is not likely to do this, or, in any event, this is not how I shall imagine the case. A murderer who expects to conduct his business by asking questions must suppose that you do not know who he is and what he has in mind.[2] If these are the circumstances, and we try to ascertain whether there could be a universal practice of lying in these circumstances, the answer appears to be yes. The lie will be efficacious even if universally practiced. But the reason it will be efficacious is rather odd: it is because the murderer supposes you do not know what circumstances you are in – that is, that you do not know you are addressing a murderer – and so does not conclude from the fact that people in those circumstances always lie that *you* will lie.

The same point can be made readily using Kant's publicity criterion (PP 381–83). Can we announce in advance our intention of lying to murderers without, as Kant says, vitiating our own purposes by publishing our maxims (PP 383)? Again the answer is yes. It does not matter if you say publicly that you will lie in such a situation, for the murderer supposes that you do not know you are in that situation.[3]

These reflections might lead us to believe, then, that Kant was wrong in thinking that it is never all right to lie. It is permissible to lie to deceivers in order to counteract the intended results of their deceptions, for the maxim of lying to a deceiver is universalizable. The deceiver has, so to speak, placed himself in a morally unprotected position by his own deception. He has created a situation which universalization cannot reach.

HUMANITY

When we apply the Formula of Humanity, however, the argument against lying that results applies to any lie whatever. The formula runs:

Act so that you treat humanity, whether in your own person or in that of another, always as an end and never as a means only. (G 429)

In order to use this formula for casuistical purposes, we need to specify what counts as treating humanity as an end. "Humanity" is used by Kant specifically to refer to the capacity to determine ends through rational choice (G 437; MPV 392). Imperfect duties arise from the obligation to make the exercise, preservation, and development of this capacity itself an end. The perfect duties – that is, the duties of justice, and, in the realm of ethics, the duties of respect – arise from the obligation to make each human being's capacity for autonomous choice the condition of the value of every other end.

In his treatment of the lying promise case under the Formula of Humanity, Kant makes the following comments:

For he whom I want to use for my own purposes by means of such a promise cannot possibly assent to my mode of acting against him and cannot contain the end of this action in himself . . . he who transgresses the rights of men intends to make use of the persons of others merely as means, without considering that as rational beings, they must always be esteemed at the same time as ends, i.e., only as beings who must be able to contain in themselves the end of the very same action. (G 429–30)

In these passages, Kant uses two expressions that are the key to understanding the derivation of perfect duties to others from the Formula of Humanity. One is that the other person "cannot possibly assent to my mode of acting toward him" and the second is that the other person cannot "contain the end of this action in himself." These phrases provide us with a test for perfect duties to others: an action is contrary to perfect duty if it is not possible for the other to assent to it or to hold its end.

It is important to see that these phrases do not mean simply that the other person *does not* or *would not* assent to the transaction or that she does not happen to have the same end I do, but strictly that she *cannot* do so: that something makes it impossible. If what we cannot assent to means merely what we are likely to be annoyed by, the test will be subjective and the claim that the person does not assent to being used as a means will sometimes be false. The object you steal from me may be the gift I intended for you, and we may both have been motivated by the desire that you should have it. And I may care about you too much or too little to be annoyed by the theft. For all that, this must be a clear case of your using me as a mere means.[4]

So it must not be merely that your victim will not like the way you propose to act, that this is psychologically unlikely, but that something makes it impossible for her to assent to it. Similarly, it must be argued that something makes it impossible for her to hold the end of the very same action. Kant never spells out why it is impossible, but it is not difficult to see what he has in mind.

People cannot *assent* to a way of acting when they are given no chance to do so. The most obvious instance of this is when coercion is used. But it is also true of deception: the victim of the false promise cannot assent to it because he doesn't know it is what he is being offered. But even when the victim of such conduct does happen to know what is going on, there is a sense in which he cannot assent to it. Suppose, for example, that you come to me and ask to borrow some money, falsely promising to pay it back next week, and suppose that by some chance I know perfectly well that your promise is a lie. Suppose also that I have the same end you do, in the sense that I want you to have the money, so that I turn the money over to you anyway. Now here I have the same end that you do, and I tolerate your attempts to deceive me to the extent that they do not prevent my giving you the money. Even in this case I cannot really assent to the transaction *you* propose. We can imagine the case in a number of different ways. If I call your bluff openly and say "never mind that nonsense, just take this money" then what I am doing is not accepting a false promise, but giving you a handout, and scorning your promise. The nature of the transaction is changed: now it is not a promise but a handout. If I don't call you on it, but keep my own counsel, it is still the same. I am not accepting a false promise. In this case what I am doing is *pretending* to accept your false promise. But there is all the difference in the world between actually doing something and pretending to do it. In neither of these cases can I be described as accepting a false promise, for in both cases I fix it so that it is something else that is happening. My knowledge of what is going on makes it *impossible* for me to accept the deceitful promise in the ordinary way.

The question whether another can assent to your way of acting can serve as a criterion for judging whether you are treating her as a mere means. We will say that knowledge of what is going on and some power over the proceedings are the conditions of possible assent; without these, the concept of assent does not apply. This gives us another way to formulate the test for treating someone as a mere means: suppose it is the case that if the other person knows what you are trying to do and has the power to stop you, then what you are trying to do cannot be what is really happening. If this is the case, the action is one that by its very nature is impossible for the other to assent to. You cannot wrest from me what I freely give to you; and if I have the power to stop you from wresting something from me and do not use it, I am in a sense freely giving it to you. This is of course not intended as a legal point: the point is that any action which depends for its nature and efficacy on the other's ignorance or powerlessness fails this test. Lying clearly falls into this category of action: it only deceives when the other does not know that it is a lie.[5]

A similar analysis can be given of the possibility of holding the end of the very same action. In cases of violation of perfect duty, lying included, the other person is unable to hold the end of the very same action because the way that you act prevents her from *choosing* whether to contribute to the realization of that end or not. Again, this is obviously true when someone is forced to contribute to an end, but it is also true in cases of deception. If you give a lying

promise to get some money, the other person is invited to think that
the end she is contributing to is your temporary possession of the
money: in fact, it is your permanent possession of it. It doesn't
matter whether that would be all right with her if she knew about it.
What matters is that she never gets a chance to choose the end, not
knowing that it is to be the consequence of her action.[6]

According to the Formula of Humanity, coercion and deception
are the most fundamental forms of wrongdoing to others – the roots
of all evil. Coercion and deception violate the conditions of possible
assent, and all actions which depend for their nature and efficacy on
their coercive or deceptive character are ones that others cannot
assent to. Coercion and deception also make it impossible for others
to choose to contribute to our ends. This in turn makes it impossible, according to Kant's value theory, for the ends of such actions to
be good. For on Kant's view "what we call good must be, in the
judgment of every reasonable man, an object of the faculty of desire"
(C2 60). If your end is one that others cannot choose – not because of
what they want, but because they are not in a position to choose – it
cannot, as the end of that action, be good. This means that in any
cooperative project – whenever you need the decisions and actions
of others in order to bring about your end – everyone who is to
contribute must be in a position to *choose* to contribute to the end.

The sense in which a good end is an object for everyone is that a
good end is in effect one that everyone, in principle, and especially
everyone who contributes to it, gets to cast a vote on. This voting, or
legislation, is the prerogative of rational beings; and the ideal of a
world in which this prerogative is realized is the Kingdom of Ends.

THE KINGDOM OF ENDS

The Kingdom of Ends is represented by the kingdom of nature; we
determine moral laws by considering their viability as natural laws.
On Kant's view, the will is a kind of causality (G 446). A person, an
end in itself, is a free cause, which is to say a first cause. By contrast,
a thing, a means, is a merely mediate cause, a link in the chain. A
first cause is, obviously, the initiator of a causal chain, hence a real
determiner of what will happen. The idea of deciding for yourself
whether you will contribute to a given end can be represented as a

decision whether to initiate that causal chain which constitutes your contribution. Any action which prevents or diverts you from making this initiating decision is one that treats you as a mediate rather than a first cause; hence as a mere means, a thing, a tool. Coercion and deception both do this. And deception treats you as a mediate cause in a specific way: it treats your reason as a mediate cause. The false promiser thinks: if I tell her I will pay her back next week, then she will choose to give me the money. Your reason is worked, like a machine: the deceiver tries to determine what levers to pull to get the desired results from you. Physical coercion treats someone's person as a tool; lying treats someone's *reason* as a tool. This is why Kant finds it so horrifying; it is a direct violation of autonomy.

We may say that a tool has two essential characteristics: it is there to be used, and it does not control itself – its nature is to be directed by something else. To treat someone as a mere means is to treat her as if these things were true of her. Kant's treatment of our duties to others in the *Metaphysical Principles of Virtue* is sensitive to *both* characteristics. We are not only forbidden to use another as a mere means to our private purposes. We are also forbidden to take attitudes toward her which involve regarding her as not in control of herself, which is to say, as not using her reason.

This latter is the basis of the duties of respect. Respect is violated by the vices of calumny and mockery (MPV 466–68): we owe to others not only a practical generosity toward their plans and projects – a duty of aid – but also a generosity of attitude toward their thoughts and motives. To treat another with respect is to treat him as if he were using his reason and as far as possible as if he were using it well. Even in a case where someone evidently *is* wrong or mistaken, we ought to suppose he must have what he takes to be good reasons for what he believes or what he does. This is not because, as a matter of fact, he probably does have good reasons. Rather, this attitude is something that we *owe* to him, something that is his right. And he cannot forfeit it. Kant is explicit about this:

Hereupon is founded a duty to respect man even in the logical use of his reason: not to censure someone's error under the name of absurdity, inept judgment, and the like, but rather to suppose that in such an inept judgment there must be something true, and to seek it out. . . . Thus it is also with the reproach of vice, which must never burst out in complete contempt or deny the wrongdoer all moral worth, because on that hypothesis he could never be improved either – and this latter is incompatible with the idea of man, who as such (as a moral being) can never lose all predisposition to good. (MPV 463–64)

To treat others as ends in themselves is always to address and deal with them as rational beings. Every rational being gets to reason out, for herself, what she is to think, choose, or do. So if you need someone's contribution to your end, you must put the facts before her and ask for her contribution. If you think she is doing something wrong, you may try to convince her by argument but you may not resort to tricks or force. The Kingdom of Ends is a democratic ideal, and poor judgment does not disqualify anyone for citizenship. In the *Critique of Pure Reason*, Kant says:

Reason depends on this freedom for its very existence. For reason has no dictatorial authority; its verdict is always simply the agreement of free citizens, of whom each one must be permitted to express, without let or hindrance, his objections or even his veto. (C1 A738–39/B 766–67)

This means that there cannot be a good reason for taking a decision out of someone else's hands. It is a rational being's prerogative, as a first cause, to have a share in determining the destiny of things.

This shows us in another way why lying is for Kant a paradigm case of treating someone as a mere means. Any attempt to control the actions and reactions of another by any means except an appeal to reason treats her as a mere means, because it attempts to reduce her to a mediate cause. This includes much more than the utterance of falsehoods. In the *Lectures on Ethics*, Kant says "whatever militates against frankness lowers the dignity of man" (LE 231).[7] It is an everyday temptation, even (or perhaps especially) in our dealings with those close to us, to withhold something, or to tidy up an anecdote, or to embellish a story, or even just to place a certain emphasis, in order to be sure of getting the reaction we want.[8] Kant holds the Socratic view that any sort of persuasion that is aimed at distracting its listener's attention from either the reasons that she ought to use or the reasons the speaker thinks she will use is wrong.[9]

In light of this account it is possible to explain why Kant says what he does about the liar's responsibility. In a Kantian theory our responsibility has definite boundaries: each person as a first cause exerts some influence on what happens, and it is your part that is up to you. If you make a straightforward appeal to the reason of another person, your responsibility ends there and the other's responsibility begins. But the liar tries to take the consequences out of the hands of others; he, and not they, will determine what form their contribution to destiny will take. By refusing to share with others the determination of events, the liar takes the world into his own hands, and makes the events his own. The results, good or bad, are imputable to him, at least in his own conscience. It does not follow from *this*, of course, that this is a risk one will never want to take.

If the foregoing casuistical analyses are correct, then applying the Formula of Universal Law and the Formula of Humanity leads to different answers in the case of lying to the murderer at the door. The former seems to say that this lie is permissible, but the latter says that coercion and deception are the most fundamental forms of wrongdoing. In a Kingdom of Ends coercive and deceptive methods can never be used.

This result impugns Kant's belief that the formulas are equivalent. But it is not necessary to conclude that the formulas flatly say different things, and are unrelated except for a wide range of coincidence in their results. For one thing, lying to the murderer at the door was not shown to be permissible in a straightforward manner: the maxim did not so much pass as evade universalization. For another, the two formulas can be shown to be expressions of the same basic theory of justification. Suppose that your maxim is in violation of the Formula of Universal Law. You are making an exception of yourself, doing something that everyone in your circumstances could not do. What this means is that you are treating the reason *you* have for the action as if it were stronger, had more justifying force, than anyone else's exactly similar reason. You are then acting as if the fact that it was in particular *your* reason, and not just the reason of a human being, gave it special weight and force. This is an obvious violation of the idea that it is your humanity – your power of rational choice – which is the condition of all value and which therefore gives your needs and desires the justifying force of *reasons*. Thus, any violation of the Formula of Universal Law is also a violation of the Formula of Humanity. This argument, of course, only goes in one direction: it does not show that the two formulas are equivalent. The Formula of Humanity is stricter than the Formula of Universal Law – but both are expressions of the same basic theory of value: that your rational nature is the source of the justifying power of your reasons, and so of the goodness of your ends.

And although the Formula of Humanity gives us reason to think that all lies are wrong, we can still give an account in the terms it provides of what vindicates lying to a liar. The liar tries to use your reason as a means – your honesty as a tool. You do not have to passively submit to being used as a means. In the *Lectures on Ethics*, this is the line that Kant takes. He says:

> If we were to be at all times punctiliously truthful we might often become victims of the wickedness of others who were ready to abuse our truthfulness. If all men were well-intentioned it would not only be a duty not to lie, but no one would do so because there would be no point in it. But as men are malicious, it cannot be denied that to be punctiliously truthful is often dangerous . . . if I cannot save myself by maintaining silence, then my lie is a weapon of defense. (LE 228)

The common thought that lying to a liar is a form of self-defense, that you can resist lies with lies as you can resist force with force, is according to this analysis correct.[10] This should not be surprising, for we have seen that deception and coercion are parallel. Lying and the use of force are attempts to undercut the two conditions of possible assent to actions and of autonomous choice of ends, namely, knowledge and power. So, although the Formula of Universal Law and the Formula of Humanity give us different results, this does not show that they simply express different moral outlooks. The relation between them is more complex than that.

TWO CASUISTICAL PROBLEMS

Before I discuss this relation, however, I must take up two casuistical problems arising from the view I have presented so far. First, I have argued that we *may* lie to the murderer at the door. But most people think something stronger: that we ought to lie to the murderer – that we will have done something wrong if we do not. Second, I have argued that it is permissible to lie to a deceiver in order to counter the deception. But what if someone lies to you for a good end, and, as it happens, you know about it? The fact that the murderer's *end* is evil has played no direct role in the arguments I have given so far. We have a right to resist liars and those who try to use force because of their methods, not because of their purposes. In one respect this is a virtue of my argument. It does not license us to lie to or use violence against persons *just* because we think their purposes are bad. But it looks as if it may license us to lie to liars whose purposes are good. Here is a case: suppose someone comes to your door and pretends to be taking a survey of some sort.[11] In fact, this person is a philanthropist who wants to give his money to people who meet certain criteria, and this is his way of discovering appropriate objects for his beneficence. As it happens, you know what is up. By lying, you could get some money, although you do not in fact meet his criteria. The argument that I derived from the Formula of Universal Law about lying to the murderer applies here. Universalizing the lie to the philanthropist will not destroy its efficacy. Even if it is a universal law that everyone will lie in these circumstances, the philanthropist thinks you do not know you are in these circumstances. By my argument, it is permissible to lie in this case. The philanthropist, like the murderer, has placed himself in a morally unprotected position by his own deception.

Start with the first casuistical problem. There are two reasons to lie to the murderer at the door. First, we have a duty of mutual aid. This is an imperfect duty of virtue, since the law does not say exactly what or how much we must do along these lines. This duty gives us *a* reason to tell the lie. Whether it makes the lie imperative depends on how one understands the duty of mutual aid, on how one understands the "wideness" of imperfect duties.[12] It may be that on such an urgent occasion, the lie is imperative. Notice that if the lie were impermissible, this duty would have no force. Imperfect duties are always secondary to perfect ones. But if the lie is permissible, this duty will provide a reason, whether or not an imperative one, to tell the lie.

The second reason is one of self-respect. The murderer wants to make you a tool of evil; he regards your integrity as a useful sort of predictability. He is trying to use you, and your good will, as a means to an evil end. You owe it to humanity in your own person not to allow your honesty to be used as a resource for evil. I think this would be a perfect duty of virtue: Kant does not say this specifically, but in his discussion of servility (the avoidance of which is a perfect duty of virtue) he says "Do not suffer your rights to be trampled underfoot by others with impunity" (MPV 436).

Both of these reasons spring from duties of virtue. A person with a good character will tell the lie. Not to tell it is morally bad. But there is no duty of justice to tell the lie. If we do not tell it, we cannot be punished, or, say, treated as an accessory to the murder. Kant would insist that even if the lie ought to be told this does not mean that the punctiliously truthful person who does not tell it is somehow implicated in the murder. It is the murderer, not the truthful person, who commits this crime. Telling the truth cannot be part of the crime. On Kant's view, persons are not supposed to be responsible for managing each other's conduct. If the lie were a duty of justice, we would be responsible for that.

These reflections will help us to think about the second casuistical problem, the lie to the philanthropist. I think it does follow from the line of argument I have taken that the lie cannot be shown to be impermissible. Although the philanthropist can hardly be called evil, he is doing something tricky and underhanded, which on Kant's view is wrong. He should not use this method of getting the information he wants. This is especially true if the reason he does not use a more straightforward method is that he assumes that if he does, people will lie to him. We are not supposed to base our actions on the assumption that other people will behave badly. Assuming this does not occur in an institutional context, and you have not sworn that your remarks were true, the philanthropist will have no recourse to justice if you lie to him.[13] But the reasons that favor telling the lie that exist in the first case do not exist here. According to Kant, you do not have a duty to promote your own happiness. Nor would anyone perform such an action out of self-respect. This is, in a very trivial way, a case of dealing with evil. But you can best deal with it by telling the philanthropist that you know what he is up to, perhaps even that you find it sneaky. This is *because* the ideal that makes his action a bad one is an ideal of straightforwardness in human relations. This would also be the best way to deal with the murderer, if it *were* a way to deal with a murderer. But of course it is not.

IDEAL AND NONIDEAL THEORY

I now turn to the question of what structure an ethical theory must have in order to accommodate this way of thinking. In *A Theory of Justice*, John Rawls proposes a division of moral philosophy into ideal and nonideal theory.[14] In that work, the task of ideal theory is to determine "what a perfectly just society would be like" while nonideal theory deals with punishment, war, opposition to unjust regimes, and compensatory justice (Sec. 2, pp. 8–9). Since I wish to use this feature of Rawls's theory for a model, I am going to sketch his strategy for what I will call a double-level theory.

Rawls identifies two conceptions of justice, which he calls the general conception and the special conception (Secs. 11, 26, 39, 46). The general conception tells us that all goods distributed by society, including liberty and opportunity, are to be distributed equally unless an unequal distribution is to the advantage of everyone, and especially those who fall on the low side of the inequality (Sec. 13). Injustice, according to the general conception, occurs whenever there are inequalities that are not to the benefit of everyone (Sec. 11, p. 62). The special conception in its most developed form removes liberty and opportunity from the scope of this principle and says they must be distributed equally, forbidding tradeoffs of these goods for economic gains. It also introduces a number of priority rules, for example, the priority of liberty over all other considerations, and the priority of equal opportunity over economic considerations (Secs. 11, 46, 82).

Ideal theory is worked out under certain assumptions. One is strict compliance: it is assumed that everyone will act justly. The other, a little harder to specify, is that historical, economic, and natural conditions are such that realization of the ideal is feasible. Our conduct toward those who do not comply, or in circumstances which make the immediate realization of a just state of affairs impossible, is governed by the principles of nonideal theory. Certain ongoing natural conditions which may always prevent the full realization of the ideal state of affairs also belong to nonideal theory: the problems of dealing with the seriously ill or mentally disturbed, for instance, belong in this category. For purposes of constructing ideal theory, we assume that everyone is "rational and able to manage

their own affairs" (Sec. 39, p. 248). We also assume in ideal theory
that there are no massive historic injustices, such as the oppression
of blacks and women, to be corrected. The point is to work out our
ideal view of justice on the assumption that people, nature, and
history will behave themselves so that the ideal can be realized, and
then to determine – in light of that ideal – what is to be done in
actual circumstances when they do not. The special conception is
not applied without regard to circumstances. Special principles will
be used in nonideal conditions.

Nonideal conditions exist when, or to the extent that, the special
conception of justice cannot be realized effectively. In these circumstances our conduct is to be determined in the following way: the
special conception becomes a goal, rather than an ideal to live up to;
we are to work toward the conditions in which it is feasible. For
instance, suppose there is a case like this: widespread poverty or
ignorance due to the level of economic development is such that the
legal establishment of equal liberties makes no real difference to the
lot of the disadvantaged members of society. It is an empty formality. On the other hand, some inequality, temporarily instituted,
would actually tend to foster conditions in which equal liberty could
become a reality for everyone. In these circumstances, Rawls's
double-level theory allows for the temporary inequality (Secs. 11,
39). The priority rules give us guidance as to which features of the
special conception are most urgent. These are the ones that we
should be striving to achieve as soon as possible. For example, if
formal equal opportunity for blacks and women is ineffective, affirmative action measures may be in order. If some people claim that
this causes inefficiency at first, it is neither here nor there, since
equality of opportunity has priority over efficiency. The special conception may also tell us which of our nonideal options is least bad,
closest to ideal conduct. For instance, civil disobedience is better
than resorting to violence not only because violence is bad in itself,
but because of the way in which civil disobedience expresses the
democratic principles of the just society it aspires to bring about
(Sec. 59). Finally, the general conception of justice commands categorically. In sufficiently bad circumstances none of the characteristic features of the special conception may be realizable. But there is
no excuse *ever* for violation of the general conception. If inequalities
are not benefiting those on the lower end of them in some way, they

are simply oppression. The general conception, then, represents the point at which justice becomes uncompromising.[15]

A double-level theory can be contrasted to two types of single-level theory, both of which in a sense fail to distinguish the way we should behave in ideal and nonideal conditions, but which are at opposite extremes. A consequentialist theory such as utilitarianism does not really distinguish ideal from nonideal conditions. Of course, the utilitarian can see the difference between a state of affairs in which everyone can be made reasonably happy and a state of affairs in which the utilitarian choice must be for the "lesser of evils," but it is still really a matter of degree. In principle we do not know what counts as a state in which everyone is "as happy as possible" absolutely. Instead, the utilitarian wants to make everyone as happy as possible relative to the circumstances, and pursues this goal regardless of how friendly the circumstances are to human happiness. The difference is not between ideal and nonideal states of affairs but simply between better and worse states of affairs.

Kant's theory as he understood it represents the other extreme of single-level theory. The standard of conduct he sets for us is designed for an ideal state of affairs: we are always to act as if we were living in a Kingdom of Ends, regardless of possible disastrous results. Kant is by no means dismissive toward the distressing problems caused by the evil conduct of other human beings and the unfriendliness of nature to human ideals, but his solution to these problems is different. He finds in them grounds for a morally motivated religious faith in God.[16] Our rational motive for belief in a moral author of the world derives from our rational need for grounds for hope that these problems will be resolved. Such an author would have designed the laws of nature so that, in ways that are not apparent to us, our moral actions and efforts do tend to further the realization of an actual Kingdom of Ends. With faith in God, we can trust that a Kingdom of Ends will be the consequence of our actions as well as the ideal that guides them.

In his *Critique of Utilitarianism*, Bernard Williams spells out some of the unfortunate consequences of what I am calling single-level theories.[17] According to Williams, the consequentialist's commitment to doing whatever is necessary to secure the best outcome may lead to violations of what we would ordinarily think of as integrity. There is no kind of action that is so mean or so savage that it can *never* lead to a better outcome than the alternatives. A commitment to always securing the best outcome never allows you to say "bad consequences or not, this is not the sort of thing I do; I am not that sort of person." And no matter how mean or how savage the act required to secure the best outcome is, the utilitarian thinks that you will be irrational to regret that you did it, for you will have done what is in the straightforward sense the right thing.[18] A Kantian approach, by defining a determinate *ideal* of conduct to live up to rather than setting a *goal* of action to strive for, solves the problem about integrity, but with a high price. The advantage of the Kantian approach is the definite sphere of responsibility. Your share of the responsibility for the way the world is is well-defined and limited, and if you act as you ought, bad outcomes are not your responsibility. The trouble is that in cases such as that of the murderer at the door it seems grotesque simply to say that I have done my part by telling the truth and the bad results are not my responsibility.

The point of a double-level theory is to give us both a definite and well-defined sphere of responsibility for everyday life and some guidance, at least, about when we may or must take the responsibility of violating ideal standards. The common-sense approach to this problem uses an intuitive quantitative measure: we depart from our ordinary rules and standards of conduct when the consequences of following them would be "very bad." This is unhelpful for two reasons. First, it leaves us on our own about determining *how* bad. Second, the attempt to justify it leads down a familiar consequentialist slippery slope: if very bad consequences justify a departure from ordinary norms, why do not slightly bad consequences justify such a departure? A double-level theory substitutes something better than this rough quantitative measure. In Rawls's theory, for example, a departure from equal liberty cannot be justified by the fact that the consequences of liberty are "very bad" in terms of mere efficiency. This does not mean that an endless amount of inefficiency will be tolerated, because presumably at some point the inefficiency may interfere with the effectiveness of liberty. One might put the point this way: the measure of "very bad" is not entirely intuitive but, rather, bad enough to interfere with the reality of liberty. Of course this is not an algorithmic criterion and cannot be applied without judgment, but it is not as

inexact as a wholly intuitive quantitative measure, and, importantly, does not lead to a consequentialist slippery slope.

Another advantage of a double-level theory is the explanation it
offers of the other phenomenon Williams is concerned about: that of
regret for doing a certain kind of action even if in the circumstances
it was the "right" thing. A double-level theory offers an account of at
least some of the occasions for this kind of regret. We will regret
having to depart from the ideal standard of conduct, for we identify
with this standard and think of our autonomy in terms of it. Regret
for an action we would not do under ideal circumstances seems
appropriate even if we have done what is clearly the right thing.[19]

KANTIAN NONIDEAL THEORY

Rawls's special conception of justice is a stricter version of the egali-
tarian idea embodied in his general conception. In the same way, it
can be argued that the Formula of Universal Law and the Formula of
Humanity are expressions of the same idea – that humanity is the
source of value, and of the justifying force of reason. But the Formula
of Humanity is stricter, and gives implausible answers when we are
dealing with the misconduct of others and the recalcitrance of nature.
This comparison gives rise to the idea of using the two formulas and
the relation between them to construct a Kantian double-level theory
of individual morality, with the advantages of that sort of account.
The Formulas of Humanity and the Kingdom of Ends will provide the
ideal which governs our daily conduct. When dealing with evil circumstances we may depart from this ideal. In such cases, we can say
that the Formula of Humanity is inapplicable because it is not designed for use when dealing with evil. But it can still guide our conduct. It defines the goal toward which we are working, and if we can
generate priority rules we will know which features of it are most
important. It gives us guidance about which of the measures we may
take is the least objectionable.

Lying to deceivers is not the only case in which the Formula of Humanity seems to set a more ideal standard than the Formula of Universal Law. The arguments made about lying can all be made about
the use of coercion to deal with evildoers. Another very difficult case
in which the two formulas give different results, as I think, is suicide.

Kant gives an argument against suicide under the Formula of Universal Law, but that argument does not work.[20] Yet under the Formula of Humanity we can give a clear and compelling argument against suicide: nothing is of any value unless the human person is so, and it is a great crime, as well as a kind of incoherence, to act in a way that denies and eradicates the source of all value. Thus it might be possible to say that suicide is wrong from an ideal point of view, though justifiable in circumstances of very great natural or moral evil.

There is also another, rather different sense of "rigorism" in which the Formula of Humanity seems to be more rigorous than that of Universal Law. It concerns the question whether Kant's theory allows for the category of merely permissible ends and actions, or whether we must always be doing something that is morally worthy: that is, whether we should *always* pursue the obligatory ends of our own perfection and the happiness of others, when no other duty is in the case.

The Formula of Universal Law clearly allows for the category of the permissible. Indeed, the first contradiction test is a test for permissibility. But in the *Metaphysical Principles of Virtue*, there are passages which have sometimes been taken to imply that Kant holds the view that our conduct should always be informed by morally worthy ends (MPV 390). The textual evidence is not decisive. But the tendency in Kant's thought is certainly there. For complete moral worth is only realized when our actions are not merely in accordance with duty but from duty, or, to say the same thing a different way, perfect autonomy is only realized when our actions and ends are completely determined by reason, and this seems to be the case only when our ends are chosen as instantiations of the obligatory ends.

Using the Formula of Humanity it is possible to argue for the more "rigorous" interpretation. First, the obligatory ends can be derived more straightforwardly from Humanity than from Universal Law. Kant does derive the obligatory ends from the Formula of Universal Law, but he does it by a curiously roundabout procedure in which someone is imagined formulating a maxim of rejecting them and then finding it to be impermissible. This argument does not show that there would be a moral failing if the agent merely unthinkingly neglected rather than rejected these ends. The point about the pervasiveness of these ends in the moral life is a more complicated one,

one that follows from their adoption by this route: among the obligatory ends is our own moral perfection. Pursuing ends that are determined by reason, rather than merely acceptable to it, cultivates
one's moral perfection in the required way (MPV 380–81; 444–47).

It is important to point out that even if this is the correct way to
understand Kant's ideal theory, it does not imply that Kantian ethics
commands a life of conventional moral "good deeds." The obligatory ends are one's own perfection and the happiness of others; to be
governed by them is to choose instantiations of these larger categories as the aim of your vocation and other everyday activities. It is
worth keeping in mind that natural perfection is a large category,
including all the activities that cultivate body and mind. Kant's
point is not to introduce a strenuous moralism but to find a place for
the values of perfectionism in his theory. But this perfectionism will
be a part of ideal theory if the argument for it is based on the Formula of Humanity and cannot be derived from that of Universal
Law. This seems to be a desirable outcome. People in stultifying
economic or educational conditions cannot really be expected to
devote all their spare time to the cultivation of perfectionist values.
But they can be expected not to do what is impermissible, not to
violate the Formula of Universal Law. Here again, the Formula of
Humanity sheds light on the situation even if it is not directly applied: it tells us why it is morally as well as in other ways regrettable
that people should be in such conditions.

CONCLUSION

If the account I have given is correct, the resources of a double-level
theory may be available to the Kantian. The Formula of Humanity
and its corollary, the vision of a Kingdom of Ends, provide an ideal
to live up to in daily life as well as a long-term political and moral
goal for humanity. But it is not feasible always to live up to this
ideal, and where the attempt to live up to it would make you a tool
of evil, you should not do so. In evil circumstances, but only then,
the Kingdom of Ends can become a goal to seek rather than an ideal
to live up to, and this will provide us with some guidance. The
Kantian priorities – of justice over the pursuit of obligatory ends,
and of respect over benevolence – still help us to see what matters
most. And even in the worst circumstances, there is always the

Formula of Universal Law, telling us what we must not in any case do. For whatever bad circumstances may drive us to do, we cannot possibly be justified in doing something which others in those same circumstances could not also do. The Formula of Universal Law provides the point at which morality becomes uncompromising.

Let me close with some reflections about the extent to which Kant himself might have agreed with this modification of his views. Throughout this essay, I have portrayed Kant as an uncompromising idealist, and there is much to support this view. But in the historical and political writings, as well as in the *Lectures on Ethics*, we find a somewhat different attitude. This seems to me to be especially important: Kant believes that the Kingdom of Ends on earth, the highest political good, can only be realized in a condition of peace (MPJ 354–55). But he does not think that this commits a nation to a simple pacifism that would make it the easy victim of its enemies. Instead, he draws up laws of war in which peace functions not as an uncompromising ideal to be lived up to in the present, but as a long-range goal which guides our conduct even when war is necessary (PP 343–48; MPJ 343–51). If a Kantian can hold such a view for the conduct of nations, why not for that of individuals? If this is right, the task of Kantian moral philosophy is to draw up for individuals something analogous to Kant's laws of war: special principles to use when dealing with evil.

NOTES

This paper was delivered as the Randall Harris Lecture at Harvard University in October 1985. Versions of the paper have been presented at the University of Illinois at Urbana-Champaign, the University of Wisconsin at Milwaukee, the University of Michigan, and to the Seminar on Contemporary Social and Political Theory in Chicago. I owe a great deal to the discussions on these occasions. I want to thank the following people for their comments: Margaret Atherton, Charles Chastain, David Copp, Stephen Darwall, Michael Davis, Gerald Dworkin, Alan Gewirth, David Greenstone, John Koethe, Richard Kraut, Richard Strier, and Manley Thompson. And I owe special thanks to Peter Hylton and Andrews Reath for extensive and useful comments on the early written versions of the paper.

1 I defend it in "Kant's Formula of Universal Law," Chapter 3 in this volume.

2 I am relying here on the assumption that when people ask us questions, they give us some account of themselves and of the context in which the questions are asked. Or, if they don't, it is because they are relying on a context that is assumed. If someone comes to your door looking for someone, you assume that there is a family emergency or some such thing. I am prepared to count such reliance as deception if the questioner knows about it and uses it, thinking that we would refuse to answer his questions if we knew the real context to be otherwise. Sometimes people ask me, "Suppose the murderer just asks whether his friend is in your house, without saying anything about why he wants to know?" I think that, in our culture anyway, people do not *just ask* questions of each other about anything except the time of day and directions for getting places. After all, the reason why refusal to answer is an unsatisfactory way of dealing with this case is that it will almost inevitably give rise to suspicion of the truth, and this is because people normally answer such questions. Perhaps if we did live in a culture in which people regularly *just asked* questions in the way suggested, refusal to answer would be commonplace and would not give rise to suspicion: it would not even be considered odd or rude. Otherwise there would be no way to maintain privacy.

3 In fact, it will now be the case that if the murderer supposes that you suspect him, he is not going to ask you, knowing that you will answer so as to deceive him. Since we must avoid the silly problem about the murderer being able to deduce the truth from his knowledge that you will speak falsely, what you announce is that you will say whatever is necessary in order to conceal the truth. There is no reason to suppose that you will be mechanical about this. You are not going to be a reliable source of information. The murderer will therefore seek some other way to locate his victim.

On the other hand, suppose that the murderer does, contrary to my supposition, announce his real intentions. Then the arguments that I have given do not apply. In this case, I believe your only recourse is refusal to answer (whether or not the victim is in your house, or you know his whereabouts). If an answer is extorted from you by force you may lie, according to the argument I will give later in this chapter.

4 Kant himself takes notice of this sort of problem in a footnote to this passage in which he criticizes Golden-Rule type principles for, among other things, the sort of subjectivity in question: such principles cannot establish the duty of beneficence, for instance, because "many a man would gladly consent that others should not benefit him, provided only that he might be excused from showing benevolence to them" (G 430n.).

5 Sometimes it is objected that someone could assent to being lied to in

advance of the actual occasion of the lie, and that in such a case the deception might still succeed. One can therefore agree to be deceived. I think it depends what circumstances are envisioned. I can certainly agree to remain uninformed about something, but this is not the same as agreeing to be deceived. For example, I could say to my doctor: "Don't tell me if I am fatally ill, even if I ask." But if I then do ask the doctor whether I am fatally ill, I cannot be certain whether she will answer me truthfully. Perhaps what's being envisioned is that I simply agree to be lied to, but not about anything in particular. Will I then trust the person with whom I have made this odd agreement?

6 A similar conclusion about the way in which the Formula of Humanity makes coercion and deception wrong is reached by Onora O'Neill in "Between Consenting Adults," in her *Constructions of Reason: Explorations of Kant's Practical Philosophy*, chapter 6.

7 It is perhaps also relevant that in Kant's discussion of perfect moral friendship the emphasis is not on good will toward one another, but on complete confidence and openness. See MPV 471–72.

8 Some evidence that Kant is concerned with this sort of thing may be found in the fact that he identifies two meanings of the word "prudence" (*Klugheit*); "The former sense means the skill of a man in having an influence on others so as to use them for his own purposes. The latter is the ability to unite all these purposes to his own lasting advantage" (G 416n.). A similar remark is found in *Anthropology from a Pragmatic Point of View*. See ANTH 322.

9 I call this view Socratic because of Socrates' concern with the differences between reason and persuasion and, in particular, because in the *Apology*, he makes a case for the categorical duty of straightforwardness. Socrates and Plato are also concerned with a troublesome feature of this moral view that Kant neglects. An argument must come packaged in some sort of presentation, and one may well object that it is impossible to make a straightforward presentation of a case to someone who is close to or admires you, without emphasis, without style, without taking some sort of advantage of whatever it is about you that has your listener's attention in the first place. So how can we avoid the nonrational influence of others? I take it that most obviously in the *Symposium*, but also in other dialogues concerned with the relation of love and teaching such as the *Phaedrus*, Plato is at work on the question whether you can use your sex appeal to draw another's attention to the reasons he has for believing or doing things, rather than as a distraction that aids your case illicitly.

10 Of course you may also resist force with lies, if resisting it with force is not an option for you. This gives rise to a question about whether these

options are on a footing with each other. In many cases, lying will be the better option. This is because when you use coercion you risk doing injury to the person you coerce. Injuring people unnecessarily is wrong, a wrong that should be distinguished from the use of coercion. When you lie you do not risk doing this extra wrong. But Kant thinks that lying is in itself worse than coercion, because of the peculiarly direct way in which it violates autonomy. So it should follow that if you can deal with the murderer by coercion, this is a *better* option than lying. Others seem to share this intuition. Cardinal John Henry Newman, responding to Samuel Johnson's claim that he would lie to a murderer who asked which way his victim had gone, suggests that the appropriate thing to do is "to knock the man down, and to call out for the police" (*Apologia Pro Vita Sua: Being a History of His Religious Opinions*, p. 361. I am quoting from Sissela Bok, *Lying*, p. 42). If you can do it without seriously hurting the murderer, it is, so to speak, cleaner just to kick him off the front porch than to lie. This treats the *murderer himself* more like a human being than lying to him does.

11 I owe this example to John Koethe.

12 For a discussion of this question see Barbara Herman, "Mutual Aid and Respect for Persons," in her *The Practice of Moral Judgment*, chapter 3.

13 In the *Lectures on Ethics*, Kant takes the position that you may lie to someone who lies to or bullies you as long as you don't say specifically that your words will be true. He claims this is not lying, because such a person should not expect you to tell the truth (LE 227, 229).

14 John Rawls, *A Theory of Justice*. Section and page numbers referring to this work will appear in the text.

15 In a nonideal case, one's actions may be guided by a more instrumental style of reasoning than in ideal theory. But nonideal theory is not a form of consequentialism. There are two reasons for this. One is that the goal set by the ideal is not just one of good consequences, but of a just state of affairs. If a consequentialist view is one that defines right action entirely in terms of good consequences (which are not themselves defined in terms of considerations of rightness or justice), then nonideal theory is not consequentialist. The second reason is that the ideal will also guide our choice among nonideal alternatives, importing criteria for this choice other than effectiveness. I would like to thank Alan Gewirth for prompting me to clarify my thoughts on this matter, and David Greenstone for helping me to do so.

16 See the "Dialectic of Pure Practical Reason" of the *Critique of Practical Reason* and the *Critique of Teleological Judgment*, Sec. 87.

17 Bernard Williams, in *Utilitarianism For and Against*, by J.J.C. Smart and Bernard Williams, pp. 75–150.

18 Williams also takes this issue up in "Ethical Consistency," in his *Problems of the Self*, pp. 166–86.

19 It is important here to distinguish two kinds of exceptions. As Rawls points out in "Two Concepts of Rules," a practice such as promising may have certain exceptions built into it. Everyone who has learned the practice understands that the obligation to keep the promise is canceled if one of these obtains. When one breaks a promise because this sort of exception obtains, regret would be inappropriate and obsessive. And these sorts of exceptions may occur even in "ideal" circumstances. The kind of exception one makes when dealing with evil should be distinguished from exceptions built into practices.

20 Kant's argument depends on a teleological claim: that the instinct whose office is to impel the improvement of life cannot universally be used to destroy life without contradiction (G 422). But as I understand the contradiction in conception test, teleological claims have no real place in it. What matters is not whether nature assigns a certain purpose to a certain motive or instinct, but whether everyone with the same motive or instinct could act in the way proposed and still achieve their purpose. There is simply no argument to show that everyone suffering from acute misery could not commit suicide and still achieve their purpose: ending that misery.

6   Morality as freedom

Elevating though man's privilege is, of being capable of such an idea as freedom of choice – [those who are accustomed only to physiological explanations] are stirred up by the proud claims of speculative reason, which feels its power so strongly in other fields. They are stirred up just as if they were allies, leagued in defense of the omnipotence of theoretical reason and roused by a general call to arms to resist the idea of freedom of choice and thus at present, and perhaps for a long time to come (though ultimately in vain), to attack the moral concept of freedom and, if possible, render it suspect.

Immanuel Kant (MPV 378)

Kantian ethical philosophy has often been criticized for its dependence on an untenable conception of the freedom of the will. Kant is supposed to have asserted that we are morally responsible for all of our actions because we have free will, and that we have free will because we exist in a noumenal world in which we are uninfluenced by the temptations of desire and inclination. If we existed *only* in the noumenal world, we would invariably act as the categorical imperative requires, but because we are also phenomenal beings we sometimes go wrong. The view so understood gives rise to several problems. First, the claim that purely noumenal persons would act as the categorical imperative requires may be questioned. It is not obvious why persons uninfluenced by causality should act morally rather than any other way. Secondly, if it *can* be established that insofar as we are noumena we obey the moral law, then the account of moral imputability becomes unintelligible. If we are only responsible because we are noumena and if insofar as we are noumena we only do what is right, then we cannot be responsible for our evil actions. Or, if we are responsible, it is so radically that no room is left for excuses. For how can we take into account the terrible temptations to which the wrongdoer was subjected, when the choosing noumenon was uninfluenced by those temptations? Finally, the view seems to require an unappealing ontological commitment to the existence of "two worlds," and to give rise to a variety of puzzles about how what occurs in the one can influence the other.

In this paper my aim is to address these problems. In the first part of the paper, I show why Kant thinks that the moral law is the law of a free will, and why he thinks we must regard ourselves as free. I then argue that the supposed problems about responsibility and ontology arise from a common source: a failure to appreciate the radical nature of Kant's separation of theoretical and practical reason, and of their respective domains of explanation and deliberation. When these domains are separated in the way that Kant's philosophy requires, the problems about responsibility disappear, and we see that Kant's theory of freedom does not commit him to an ontological dualism.[1] In the second part of the paper I show what it does commit him to: a certain conception of the moral virtues.

I   LAW AS FREEDOM

1. Freedom enters Kant's moral philosophy as the solution to a problem. The categorical imperative is not analytic, and disregarding its claims is therefore not inconsistent. Yet it is supposed to present us with a rational necessity. In order to show that morality is not a "mere phantom of the mind" (G 445), Kant seeks to provide a deduction of (or a credential for)[2] the moral law: he must link being rational to acting on the moral law. The third idea through which rationality and morality are linked is the positive conception of freedom. By showing, first, that a free person as such follows the moral law, and, second, that a rational person has grounds for regarding herself as free, Kant tries to show that insofar as we are rational, we will obey the moral law.

It was making the second of these two connections that troubled Kant – the connection between rationality and freedom. The arguments intended to demonstrate this connection in the *Ground-*

work of the Metaphysics of Morals and in the *Critique of Practical Reason* are obscure and appear to be different from one another. In *Groundwork III*, Kant calls his argument a "deduction" of the moral law (G 454), and connects freedom and reason through the capacity of reason for pure spontaneous activity which is exhibited in its production of ideas. This spontaneous activity shows we are members of the intelligible world and therefore free (G 452). In the *Critique of Practical Reason*, we are instead offered what Kant calls a "credential" for morality (C2 48) and told that "the objective reality of the moral law can be proved through no deduction" (C2 47). The credential is provided by the fact that freedom can be deduced *from* morality. Kant does not comment on the difference between these two arguments, and his readers do not agree about whether they come to the same thing, or are different arguments serving different purposes, or are incompatible arguments resulting from a change of mind.[3]

But Kant was not in doubt about his success in making the first connection, between morality and freedom. Kant was confident that "if freedom of the will is presupposed, morality together with its principle follows from it by the mere analysis of its concept" (G 447). In *Groundwork III*, the argument for this point takes about a page; in the second *Critique*, it is a mere paragraph, posed as

Problem II

Granted that a will is free, find the law which alone is competent to determine it necessarily.

Since the material of the practical law, i.e., an object of the maxim, cannot be given except empirically, and since a free will must be independent of all empirical conditions (i.e., those belonging to the world of sense) and yet be determinable, a free will must find its ground of determination in the law, but independently of the material of the law. But besides the latter there is nothing in a law except the legislative form. Therefore, the legislative form, in so far as it is contained in the maxim, is the only thing which can constitute a determining ground of the [free] will. (C2 29)

Not everyone has found this connection so perspicuous. In his well-known appendix to *The Methods of Ethics*,[4] Sidgwick complains that Kant's whole moral philosophy is vitiated by a confusion between two senses of "freedom." "Moral or neutral" freedom is the freedom we exercise when we choose between good and evil. "Good or rational" freedom is the freedom we exercise when we act morally, and so are not "enslaved" by our passions and desires. Sidgwick accuses Kant of being unaware of the distinction. This accusation is unfair, for the distinction Sidgwick makes is closely related to Kant's own distinction between negative and positive freedom. As we shall see, Kant rejects moral or neutral freedom as a conception of freedom; but it is a consequence of negative freedom, or the absence of all determination.

We may put Kant's reply to Sidgwick in these terms. Following John Rawls, we may distinguish the *concept* of X, formally or functionally defined, from a *conception* of X, materially and substantively defined.[5] The Kantian *concept* of free will would be "a will which makes choices independently of all alien influences," that is, a will which is negatively free. A positive *conception* of freedom would be a material account of what such a will would in fact choose. Kant's reply to Sidgwick will then be that there is a single concept of freedom, of which the moral law is the unique positive conception. My aim in the next section is to explain Kant's claim that the moral law is the unique positive conception of freedom.

2 Kant argues that when you make a choice you must act "under the idea of freedom" (G 448). He explains that "we cannot conceive of a reason which consciously responds to a bidding from the outside with respect to its judgments" (G 448). You may of course *choose* to act on a desire, but insofar as you take the act to be *yours*, you think you have made it your maxim to act on this desire. If you feel that the desire impelled you into the act, you do not regard the act as a product of your will, but as involuntary. The point is not that you must *believe* that you are free, but that you must choose *as if* you were free. It is important to see that this is quite consistent with believing yourself to be fully determined. To make it vivid, imagine that you are participating in a scientific experiment, and you know that today your every move is programmed by an electronic device implanted in your brain. The device is not going to bypass your thought processes, however, and make you move mechanically, but rather to work through them: it will determine what you think. Perhaps you get up and decide to spend the morning working. You no sooner make the decision than it occurs to you that it must have

been programmed. We may imagine that in a spirit of rebellion you then decide to skip work and go shopping. And then it occurs to you that *that* must have been programmed. The important point here is that efforts to second guess the device cannot help you decide what to do. They can only prevent you from making any decision. In order to *do* anything, you must simply ignore the fact that you are programmed, and decide what to do – just as if you were free. You will believe that your decision is a sham, but it makes no difference.[6] Kant's point, then, is not about a theoretical assumption necessary to decision, but about a fundamental feature of the standpoint from which decisions are made.[7] It follows from this feature that we must regard our decisions as springing ultimately from principles that we have chosen, and justifiable by those principles. We must regard ourselves as having free will.

Kant defines a free will as a rational causality that is effective without being determined by an alien cause. Anything outside of the will counts as an alien cause, including the desires and inclinations of the person. The free will must be entirely self-determining. Yet, because it is a causality, it must act on some law or other. "Since the concept of a causality entails that of laws . . . it follows that freedom is by no means lawless" (G 446). The free will therefore must have its own law. Alternatively, we may say that since the will is practical reason, it cannot be conceived as acting and choosing for no reason. Since reasons are derived from principles, the free will must have its own principle. Kant thinks that the categorical imperative is the free will's law or principle. But it may seem unclear why this more than anything else should be the free will's principle. If it is free to make its own law, why can't it make any law whatever?

To see why, imagine an attempt to discover the freely adopted principle on which some action is based. I ask to know why you are doing some ordinary thing, and you give me your proximate reason, your immediate end. I then ask why you want that, and most likely you mention some larger end or project. I can press on, demanding your reason at every step, until we reach the moment when you are out of answers. You have shown that your action is calculated to assist you in achieving what you think is desirable on the whole, what you have determined that you want most.

The reasons that you have given can be cast in the form of maxims derived from imperatives. From a string of hypothetical imperatives, technical and pragmatic (G 416–17), you have derived a maxim to which we can give the abbreviated formulation:

> I will do this action, in order to get what I desire.

According to Kant, this maxim only determines your will if you have adopted another maxim that makes it your end to get what you desire. This maxim is:

> I will make it my end to have the things that I desire.

Now suppose that I want to know why you have adopted this maxim. Why should you try to satisfy your desires?

There are two answers which we can dismiss immediately. First, suppose you appeal to a psychological law of nature that runs something like "a human being necessarily pursues the things he or she desires."[8] To appeal to this causal law as an answer would be to deny your freedom and to deny that you are acting under the idea of freedom. The answer does not have the structure of reason-giving: it is a way of saying "I can't help it." Second, suppose you claim that you have adopted this maxim randomly. There is nothing further to say. You think you could have adopted some other maxim, since you regard your will as free, but as it happened you picked this one. As we know, Kant rejects this, as being inconsistent with the very idea of a will, which does what it does according to a law, or for a reason. It seems as if the will must choose its principle for a reason and so always on the basis of some more ultimate principle.

We are here confronted with a deep problem of a familiar kind. If you can give a reason, you have derived it from some more fundamental maxim, and I can ask why you have adopted that one. If you cannot, it looks as if your principle was randomly selected. Obviously, to put an end to a regress like this we need a principle about which it is impossible, unnecessary, or incoherent to ask why a free person would have chosen it. Kant's argument must show that the categorical imperative has this status.

Although Kant does not think that a free will exists in time, we may imagine that there is a "moment" when the free will is called upon to choose its most fundamental principle. In order to be a will, it must have a principle from which it will derive its reasons. The principle it chooses will determine what it counts as a reason. But precisely because at this "moment" the will has not yet determined what it will count as a reason, it seems as if there could be no reason for it to choose one principle rather than another. Kant calls this feature of the will its "spontaneity."[9]

As the argument stands now, it looks as if the will could adopt any maxim we can construct. If you have a free will you could adopt a maxim of pursuing only those things to which you have an aversion, or perhaps all and only the things your next-door neighbor enjoys. For us human beings, however, these are not serious options, for reasons that come out most clearly in *Religion Within the Limits of Reason Alone*. Kant uses the term "incentive" (*Triebfeder*) to describe the relation of the free person to the candidate reasons among which she chooses. An incentive is something that makes an action interesting to you, that makes it a live option. Desires and inclinations are incentives; so is respect for the moral law. An inclination by itself is *merely* an incentive, and does not become a reason for action until the person has adopted it freely into her maxim (R 23–24; 44). Although incentives do not yet provide reasons for the spontaneous will, they do determine what the options are – which things, so to speak, are candidates for reasons. And having an aversion to something is not, for us human beings, an incentive for pursuing it, and so will not become a reason. In the *Religion*, Kant claims that it is impossible for a human being not to be moved at all by incentives; our freedom, rather, is exercised in choosing the order of precedence among the different kinds of incentives to which we are subject (R 30; 36). So the real choice will be between a maxim of self-love, which subordinates the incentives of morality to those of inclination, and the moral maxim, which subordinates incentives of inclination to moral ones. The maxim of self-love says something like:

> I will do what I desire, and what is morally
> required if it doesn't interfere with my self-love.

and the moral maxim says something like:

> I will do what is morally required, and what
> I desire if it doesn't interfere with my duty.

More specifically stated, of course, the moral maxim is the maxim derived from the categorical imperative:

> I will act only on a maxim that I can will as a universal law.

It looks at first as if the problem here is to show that there is some reason for the spontaneous will to choose the moral maxim rather than the maxim of self-love. Yet this seems impossible, since the spontaneous will by hypothesis has not yet determined what it counts as a reason. But on reflection we shall see that this problem can be circumvented. We need only consider the *standpoint* of the spontaneous will, and the *content* of the categorical imperative.

At the standpoint of spontaneity, the will must, in order so to speak to commence operations, choose a principle or a law for itself. Nothing provides any content for that law. *All that it has to be is a law.*

Suppose that it chooses the categorical imperative, as represented by the Formula of Universal Law. This formula merely tells us to choose a law. Its only constraint on our choice is that it have the form of a law. Nothing provides any content for that law. *All that it has to be is a law.*

By making the Formula of Universal Law its principle, the free will retains the position of spontaneity. Or, to put it a better way, the argument shows that the free will need do nothing to make the Formula of Universal Law its principle: it is already its principle. The categorical imperative is thus shown to be the law of spontaneity. In a sense, the Formula of Universal Law simply describes the function or task of an autonomous will. The moral law does not impose a constraint on the will; it merely says what it has to do in order to be an autonomous will at all. It has to choose a law.

On the other hand, suppose the will chooses the maxim of self-love. In that case, it departs from its position of spontaneity and puts itself in the service of inclination. A constraint on its choice is acquired. The important thing to see is that there is no incentive for the spontaneous will to do this. Since we are just talking about the will itself right now, and not the whole person, the incentives of inclination cannot provide a temptation to adopt the maxim of self-love. Incentives of inclination cannot move the will to abandon its position of spontaneity, since they cannot move the will at all until it has already abandoned that position by resolving to be moved by them.

This argument, which I will call the Argument from Spontaneity, shows that there are not really two choices, morality and self-love, on an equal footing. The will that makes the categorical imperative its law merely reaffirms its independence of everything except law

Will comes before inclination?
Is the will conscious. I find myself
on some decisions acting out

in general. Its dependence on law in general is not a constraint, for
that is just a consequence of the fact that it is a will. Making the
categorical imperative its principle does not require the spontaneous
will to take an action – it is already its principle. Adopting the
maxim of self-love is surrendering the position of spontaneity, and
does require an action (R 31–32). And it is an action for which there
could be no reason. Thus, not only are the two options not on a
footing, but the choice of the maxim of self-love over that of morality is unintelligible. Morality is the natural condition of a free will.
The free will that puts inclination above morality sacrifices its freedom for nothing.

3. A crucial point in the Argument from Spontaneity is that the
spontaneous will is not tempted by incentives of inclination. Now,
we human beings are not so situated with respect to the incentives
of inclination, because we are imperfectly rational beings. Or rather,
this is what makes us imperfectly rational beings. Our inclinations
may be alien to our purely rational wills, but they are not alien to us,
and they do tempt us. Letting our wills serve our happiness therefore
does not seem pointless to us. So although the Argument from Spontaneity explains why a purely rational will would have the moral
law as its first principle, it does not show us exactly why we should
do so. In Kant's language, it does not explain "the interest attaching
to the ideas of morality" (G 448).

Without an account of moral interest, Kant complains, there will
be a circle in our explanation of moral obligation (G 449–50). Now,
what exactly this circle is is rather difficult to see. Kant has already
claimed that, as creatures who must act under the idea of freedom,
we are bound by the laws of freedom (G 448). But he thinks this does
not yet explain how "the worth we ascribe" to moral actions (G 449)
can so completely outweigh the worth of our condition – that is, our
happiness or unhappiness. We are willing to grant the importance of
the autonomy we express in moral conduct only because we already
think that morality is supremely important. But it is still unclear
why we think so. What is needed is an incentive for us to identify
with the free and rational side of our nature. To provide this, Kant
introduces the distinction between the intelligible and sensible
worlds, or noumena and phenomena.[10] This distinction introduces
two new elements into the argument.

of moral character & in others merely
acting out of personality.

The first element is the emphasis on complete causal determination in the phenomenal world. Up until now, I have spoken of the will that adopts the maxim of self-love as adopting an unnecessary constraint. But the addition of the two-worlds picture makes the consequence of adopting the maxim of self-love look even worse. The will that adopts self-love as its maxim is determined by inclinations, and inclinations, in the world of phenomena, are completely determined by natural forces, by the nexus of causal laws. So such a will becomes a mere conduit for natural forces. The person who acts from self-love is in a sense not actively willing at all, but simply allowing herself to be controlled by the passive part of her nature, which in turn is controlled by all of nature. From the perspective of the noumenal world, ends we adopt under the influence of inclination rather than morality do not even seem to be our own.

The other element is introduced with the claim that *"the intelligible world contains the ground of the sensible world and hence of its laws"* (G 453).[11] Although we can *know* nothing of the noumenal world, it is what we conceive as lying behind the phenomenal world and giving that world its character. To conceive yourself as a member of the noumenal world is therefore to conceive yourself as among the grounds of the world as we know it.[12] And if you hold this position in so far as you have a will, then that means that the actions of your will make a real difference to the way the phenomenal world is.

Combining these two new elements we can generate a very stark contrast between choosing the maxim of morality and choosing that of self-love. We can think of the noumenal world as containing our own wills and whatever else forms part of "the ground of the sensible world and its laws." In particular, the noumenal world contains the ground, whatever it might be, of the laws of nature (for these are not objects of our wills).[13] We can influence the phenomenal world, and these other forces do so as well. Of course, nothing can be known about the nature of this influence or its mechanisms, or of how these various agencies together generate the world of appearances. But we can still say this: if by choosing the maxim of self-love you allow the laws of nature to determine your actions, then you are in effect surrendering your place among "the grounds of the sensible world and its laws." The existence of your will in the noumenal world makes no difference to the character of the phenomenal world. For your will is determined by the laws of nature, and those in turn can be accounted for by other forces in the noumenal world. Although you are free, you could just as well not have been. Your freedom makes no difference. But if you will in accordance with the moral law, you do make a difference. You actually contribute – we might say to the rational, as opposed to the merely natural, ordering of the sensible world. The choice of the moral maxim over the maxim of self-love may then be seen as a choice of genuine activity over passivity; a choice to use your active powers to make a difference in the world.

Recall that all of this is supposed to solve the problem of moral interest. Kant thinks of the idea of our intelligible existence as being, roughly speaking, the motivating thought of morality, and so what makes morality possible. In the *Religion*, Kant tells us that one who honors the moral law cannot avoid thinking about what sort of world he would create under the guidance of practical reason, and that the answer is determined by the moral idea of the Highest Good (R 5). In the second *Critique*, Kant says in one place that our intelligible existence gives us a "higher vocation" (C2 98). This vocation is to help to make the world a rational place, by contributing to the production of the Highest Good.[14]

This argument also explains why Kant thinks that unless the Highest Good is possible the moral law is "fantastic, directed to empty imaginary ends, and consequently inherently false" (C2 114). The difficulty arises in this way. We have explained moral interest in terms of a stark contrast between being a mere conduit for natural forces on the one hand and making a real difference in the world through one's intentions on the other. But in between these two possibilities we discover a third – that our intentions and actions will make a real difference in the world, but that we will have no control over what sort of difference they make – because the consequences of our actions will not be what we intend. This can happen because we are not the only elements of the noumenal world and the various forces it contains combine, in ways we cannot comprehend, to generate the world of appearances. The forces of nature and the actions of other persons mediate between our intentions and the actual results of our actions, often distorting or perverting those results. This possibility then makes the appeal of freedom seem like a fraud. If the motivating thought of morality is that freedom means that we can make a difference in the world, but we then find that we have no control over the form this difference ultimately takes, then the motivating thought is genuinely threatened. Postulating God as the author of the laws of nature is a way of guaranteeing that other noumenal forces will cooperate with our good intentions, and leaves our moral interest in place. In the *Groundwork*, Kant says:

the idea of a pure intelligible world as a whole of all intelligences to which we ourselves belong as rational beings . . . is always a useful and permissible idea for the purpose of a rational faith. This is so even though all knowledge terminates at its boundary, for through the glorious idea of a universal realm of end-in-themselves (rational beings) a lively interest in the moral law can be awakened in us. (G 462)

The Two-Worlds Argument is worked out better in the *Critique of Practical Reason* than in *Groundwork III*. In *Groundwork III*, Kant wants to argue that the idea of our existence in the intelligible world suggests our freedom to us: our capacity for pure spontaneous activity, which reveals itself in reason's production of ideas, makes us members of the intelligible world. As such we may regard ourselves as free. In the second *Critique*, Kant develops the reverse argument that freedom leads us to the conception of our existence in the intelligible world. It is morality, in turn, that teaches us that we are free. So morality itself "points" us to the intelligible world (C2 44). The argument of the *Critique of Practical Reason* is superior because freedom requires not just that we exist in the intelligible world, but that we exist there insofar as we have wills – that we can be motivated from there, so to speak. The *Groundwork* argument places our theoretical capacity to formulate pure ideas in the intelligible world, but that by itself does not imply that we can be moved by them.[15] And the latter is what the argument must show. The second *Critique* argument starts firmly from the fact that we can be motivated by pure ideas. That we can be so motivated is what Kant calls the Fact of Reason.

But the function of the idea of our intelligible existence as an incentive is essentially the same in both books. The famous address to Duty in the *Critique of Practical Reason*, like *Groundwork III*, demands to know the source of the special worth we assign to morality (C2 86–87). And the answer is again that respect for the moral law is produced by the thought of our intelligible nature. Kant says that the incentive of pure practical reason is nothing else than the pure moral law itself, so far as it lets us perceive the sublimity of our own supersensuous existence. (C2 89)[16]

The Argument from Spontaneity shows why a free and spontaneous will, uninfluenced by anything, makes the moral law its principle. The Argument from the Two Worlds shows us why we imperfectly rational beings, influenced by sensibility as well as morality, should do so as well. If we are free we are members of the intelligible world, the ground of the sensible world and its laws. This gives us a "higher vocation" than the satisfaction of our own desires. We can help to bring about the Highest Good in the world. The thought of that higher vocation is the motive of morality.

4. But the result of the Argument from Spontaneity may seem too strong. If the will *is* free, moral evil is unintelligible, for if this argument is correct, moral evil is the pure will's wholly unmotivated abandonment of its freedom. However, this is exactly Kant's view: evil is unintelligible. Neither a good will nor an evil will admits of explanation, for both must be regarded as grounded in the person's own free and spontaneous choice. If these choices could be explained, they would be derived from something else, and then they would not be the spontaneous choices that they purport to be (R 21). Yet it is evil that is unintelligible, for it is in the evil choice that the will falls away from its freedom. Kant says:

Evil could have sprung only from the morally-evil (not from mere limitations in our nature); and yet the original predisposition is a predisposition to good; there is then for us no conceivable ground from which the moral evil in us could originally have come. (R 43)

Moral evil is a Fall, in the Biblical sense, and it is exactly as hard to understand as the Fall in the Bible (R 19; 41ff.).

In fact, Kant goes so far as to deny that what Sidgwick calls moral or neutral freedom, the freedom to choose between good and evil, is really a conception of freedom at all:

freedom can never be located in the fact that the rational subject is able to make a choice in opposition to his (legislative) reason, even though experience proves often enough that this does happen (though we cannot comprehend how this is possible). . . . Only freedom in relation to the internal legislation of reason is properly a capacity; the possibility of deviating from it is an incapacity. (MM 226–27)

Many readers, among them Sidgwick,[17] have complained that so strong an identification of freedom and morality should force Kant to give up his account of moral imputability. If the moral law is the unique positive conception of freedom, then it seems as if only morally good actions are really free. Kant does say that if we were solely members of the intelligible world we would always act in accordance with the moral law. How then are we to account for the imputability of bad actions and characters? Your noumenal self would not have chosen them. Your phenomenal self, being wholly determined, cannot be held responsible.

But these complaints ignore the status of the positive conception of freedom, and its corollary, intelligible existence, in the Kantian system. The positive conception of freedom, understood as noumenal causality, is a postulate of practical reason, in the sense developed in the *Dialectic* of the *Critique of Practical Reason.* Kant explains the basis of such postulates this way:

The postulates of pure practical reason all proceed from the principle of morality, which is not a postulate but a law by which reason directly determines the will. This will . . . requires these necessary conditions for obedience to its precept. These postulates are not theoretical dogmas but presuppositions of necessarily practical import; thus, while they do not extend speculative knowledge, they give objective reality to the ideas of speculative reason in general (by means of their relation to the practical sphere), and they justify it in holding to concepts even the possibility of which it could not otherwise venture to affirm.

These postulates are those of immortality, of freedom affirmatively regarded (as the causality of a being so far as he belongs to the intelligible world), and of the existence of God. (C2 132)

A postulate of practical reason is an object of rational belief, but the reasons for the belief are practical and moral. The person needs the belief as a condition for obedience to the moral law, and it is this, combined with the categorical nature of that law, that justifies the belief. Although the beliefs are theoretical in form – the will is free, there is a God – their basis and their function are practical. As Kant says in the passage quoted above, and as he constantly emphasizes in the second *Critique,* the postulates play no theoretical or explanatory role whatsoever. They provide us with concepts that define the intelligible world, but we have no intuitions to which we may apply those concepts, and consequently no theoretical knowledge of their objects (e.g. C2 54–56; 133; 136).

The fact that the postulates of practical reason play no theoretical role has two important implications. One is that we cannot conclude from the Argument from Spontaneity that evil is impossible, or that a person who does something evil has not done it freely. A free but evil will is shown to be unintelligible *from the standpoint of pure practical reason,* but not to be theoretically impossible. It cannot be explained, but no act of freedom can be explained. And we are whole persons, not just pure spontaneous wills. Unlike the pure will in the Argument from Spontaneity, we are imperfectly rational, because we *are* subject to temptation from inclinations. There is no problem about explaining how *we* go wrong.

A central feature of Kant's philosophy as a whole is brought out here. The deliberating agent, employing reason practically, views the world as it were from a noumenal standpoint, as an expression of the wills of God and other rational agents. This is the philosophical consequence of the fact that we act under the idea of freedom, and of the way in which freedom leads to the other practical postulates: the ethical world replaces the world of speculative metaphysics. Kant tells us that "a moral principle is nothing but a dimly conceived metaphysics, which is inherent in every man's rational constitution" (MPV 376). The theorizing spectator, on the other hand, views the world as phenomena, mechanistic and fully determined. The interests of morality demand a different conceptual organization of the world than those of theoretical explanation (MM 217; 221; 225). Both interests are rational and legitimate. And it is important that neither standpoint is privileged over the other – each has its own territory. Or, if either is privileged, it is the practical, because, according to Kant, "every interest is ultimately practical" (C2 121).[18] From the explanatory standpoint of theoretical reason, nothing is easier to understand than that a human being might evade duty when it is in conflict with her heart's desire. From the normative standpoint of practical reason her sacrifice of her freedom for some mere object of inclination is completely unintelligible. These two standpoints give us two very different views of the world. To suppose that the Argument from Spontaneity shows anything at all about what can *happen* is to mix the theoretical and explanatory standpoint with the practical and normative one in an illegitimate way.

The second implication follows from the first. The standpoint from which you adopt the belief in freedom is that of the deliberating agent. You are licensed to believe in the practical postulates because they are necessary conditions of obeying the moral law. Thus it is primarily your own freedom that you are licensed to believe in, and, as a consequence, it is primarily yourself that you hold imputable. The result is that the business of praising and blaming others occupies a somewhat unstable position in Kantian ethics. It is true that you are supposed to regard others as free, and to treat them accordingly. But the necessity of doing so comes from the moral law, which commands the attribution of freedom to persons, and not from theoretical reasoning about how their wills actually function.[19] The moral sentiments of approval and disapproval, praise and blame, are, when directed to others, governed by the duties associated with the virtues of love and respect. And these duties, as Kant understands them, may actually demand attitudes of us that exclude or curtail theoretical reasoning about the motives of others. To the extent that we respect others and regard them as free, we must admit that we do not know the ultimate ground of their motives. And not knowing it, we are obligated wherever possible to take a generous attitude. Even when dealing with an actual wrongdoer, Kant says we must

not deny the wrongdoer all moral worth, because on that hypothesis he could never be improved either – and this latter is incompatible with the idea of man, who as such (as a moral being) can never lose all predisposition to good. (MPV 463–64)[20]

And Kant urges us to "cast the veil of philanthropy over the faults of others, not merely by softening but also by silencing our judgments" (MPV 466).[21]

The positive conception of freedom, then, is not to be given a theoretical employment. The idea of positive freedom is not supposed to show that moral evil is so irrational that it is impossible. Indeed, Kant does not propose that we should explain actions theoretically by referring them to the free choice of maxims in an intelligible world. The role of the idea of freedom and the intelligible world is, rather, a practical one. It provides a conception of ourselves which motivates us to obey the moral law.

In Kant's philosophy, freedom of the will *cannot* be theoretically

established. To establish it would be to achieve knowledge of the
noumenal world, and this is something that we cannot have. The
freedom of the will is asserted, but as a practical postulate, and so
only from a practical point of view. But surely, one is tempted to say,
it cannot simply *fail to matter* to the moral agent who is to be
motivated by this conception whether she is in point of actual fact
free or mechanistically determined.

In one sense Kant's response to this worry is contained in the idea
of the Fact of Reason. The Fact of Reason is our consciousness of the
moral law as a determining ground of the will (C2 31). Kant says:
"We can come to know pure practical principles in the same way we
know pure theoretical principles, by attending to the necessity with
which reason prescribes them to us and to the elimination from
them of all empirical conditions, which reason directs" (C2 30). The
moral law is thus presented to us by reason "as soon as we construct
maxims for the will" (C2 29) and it reveals our freedom to us. It does
this by showing us that we are able to act against even our strongest
inclinations, because there are cases in which we ought to. Kant says
that a person considering such a case:

judges . . . that he can do something because he knows that he ought, and he
recognizes that he is free – a fact that, without the moral law, would have
remained unknown to him. (C2 30)

Putting this together with the argument from the *Groundwork* about
acting under the idea of freedom, we arrive at an account of the possibility of morality with a rather complicated structure. (i) We must act
under the idea of (at least negative) freedom; (ii) we must therefore act
on maxims we regard ourselves as having chosen; (iii) by the Argument from Spontaneity (or, as Kant puts it here, by eliminating all
empirical conditions, as reason directs) we are led to the moral law
(the positive conception of freedom); (iv) our ability to act on the
moral law teaches us that we *are* (negatively) free; (v) if so, we are
members of the intelligible world, and have a higher vocation than
the satisfaction of our desires; and (vi) this provides us with the incentive to be positively free – that is, moral.

But all of this still remains at the level of the practical postulate.
For the sense in which our ability to act on the moral law teaches us
that we are free (step iv) and so are members of an intelligible world
(step v) is that we must believe these things in order to obey the

categorical imperative. And articles of belief we hold because they are necessary conditions of obedience to the moral law are practical postulates, with no theoretical employment.

And, in a sense, Kant's answer to the question whether it matters if we are in fact (theoretically) free *is* that it does not matter. Kant's deduction of freedom from the moral law in the *Critique of Practical Reason* concludes:

Thus reason, which with its ideas always became transcendent when proceeding in a speculative manner, can be given for the first time an objective, *although still only practical*, reality; its transcendent use is changed into an immanent use, whereby reason becomes, in the field of experience, an efficient cause through ideas. (C2 48; my emphasis)

Reason becomes an efficient cause by telling us how a free person would act and by providing the conception of our higher vocation that motivates us to act that way. For if the moral law does indeed provide the positive conception of freedom, then we know how a person with a completely free will would act. Motivated by the idea of the higher vocation freedom gives us, we can act that way ourselves. But if we are able to act exactly as we would if we were free, under the influence of the idea of freedom, then we are free. Nothing is missing: the will in the Argument from Spontaneity, when making its original choice of a principle, could not do more. It chooses to act on the moral law for the sake of maintaining its freedom; and we can do the same. *By acting morally, we can make ourselves free.*

II   VIRTUE AS FREEDOM

5. At this point a natural objection arises. The proposed solution to the free will problem depends on our being able to act according to the moral law for the sake of our freedom. I have claimed that what interests us in our freedom is the higher vocation of contributing to the Highest Good. But if this interest *determines* our moral actions, how can we be free? To answer this question, we must turn to Kant's theory of virtue, or "internal freedom."

It is Kant's view that all human action is purposive. A human being always acts for the sake of an end. Kant speaks of this as being the result of our finite and sensible nature. In a footnote in *Religion* I Kant says:

All men could have sufficient incentive if (as they should) they adhered solely to the dictation of pure reason in the law. What need have they to know the outcome of their moral actions and abstentions . . . ? Yet it is one of the inescapable limitations of man and of his faculty of practical reason (a limitation, perhaps, of all other worldly beings as well) to have regard, in every action, to the consequence thereof – which consequence, though last in practice . . . is yet first in representation and intention. . . . In this end, if directly presented to him by reason alone, man seeks something that he can *love*; therefore the law, which merely arouses his respect, even though it does not acknowledge this object of love as a necessity, does yet extend itself on its behalf by including the moral goal of reason among its determining grounds. (R 6–7n)

The objective necessity in the law ought to motivate us directly, but a human being always acts for the sake of an end. This is why, in the *Groundwork*, it is *after* explaining the Formula of Universal Law that Kant embarks on the project of showing the possibility of reason determining conduct a priori, and launches into a discussion of ends (G 427). The Formula of Universal Law explains the objective necessity of moral conduct, but it does not explain the subjective necessity: that is, it does not explain how pure reason secures "access to the human mind" (C2 151). Pure practical reason itself must gain access to us through ends. Thus it is necessary to introduce the Formula of Humanity, which directs that we make humanity, and other aims which may be derived from it, our ends. The *Religion* footnote continues:

This extension is possible because of the moral law's being taken in relation to the natural characteristic of man, that for all his actions he must conceive of an end over and above the law (a characteristic which makes man an object of experience). (R 7n)[22]

Kant also says that it is because of our susceptibility to temptation that ethics extends to ends.

For since sensible inclinations may misdirect us to ends (the matter of choice) which may be contrary to duty, legislative reason cannot guard against their influence other than, in turn, by means of an opposing moral end, which therefore must be given a priori independently of inclination. (MPV 381)

This sounds like a different account of the need for ends, but I believe it is not. The same element in our nature – the passive, sensible, representational element that makes us require an end, is also what makes us susceptible to temptation.[23]

What this implies is that for human beings, freedom must take the form of virtue: the adoption and pursuit of moral ends. Kant explains why, in *The Metaphysical Principles of Virtue*, by setting up a problem (MPV 388–89). Every action has an end, and choice is always determined by an end (G 427; MPV 381, 384–85; R4). So a maxim of action, or of the means to an end, is adopted freely only when you have adopted the maxim of holding that end. But the moral law only says that the maxim we adopt must have a certain form, not that we must have certain maxims. How can it be necessary to have certain maxims? The answer is that if there are ends that are duties, there will be maxims that it is a duty to have: maxims of actions that promote those ends. Since we must believe that we are morally obligated (that is, that there are maxims we ought to have), we must believe that there are such obligatory ends. For example, Kant says that the (external) duties of justice can be done from a moral motive and so done freely by one who makes the rights of humanity one's end (MPV 390). The possibility of internal freedom is secured by the "Supreme Principle of the Doctrine of Virtue" which runs "Act according to a maxim whose ends are such that there can be a universal law that everyone have these ends" (MPV 395). This principle is deduced from pure practical reason by the following argument:

For practical reason to be indifferent to ends, i.e., to take no interest in them, would be a contradiction; for then it would not determine the maxims of actions (and the actions always contain an end) and, consequently, would not be practical reason. Pure reason, however, cannot a priori command any ends unless it declares these ends to be at the same time duties; such duties are then called duties of virtue. (MPV 395)

In the introduction to *The Metaphysical Principles of Virtue*, Kant says that the obligatory ends are one's own perfection and the happiness of others. But in fact, a number of different ends appear in this text and elsewhere in the ethical writings. One's own perfection includes moral perfection and so subsumes the whole of morality, as well as natural perfection, which involves the development of our physical and intellectual capacities. The duties of respect make the rational autonomy of others an end. Securing the rights of humanity is an end (MPV 390). In the political writings, the development of

republican forms of government is made a necessary end for sover-
eigns (MPJ 340), and peace is an end for everyone (MPJ 354–55). The
Highest Good, the whole object of practical reason, is a necessary
end, as we have already seen (C2 108–14; R 3–6). It is because there
are various ends, Kant says, that there are various virtues, even
though virtue is essentially one thing (MPV 395; 406). All of these
ends are determined by the moral law and so are necessary ends
(ends of reason); and all of them can be derived from the unconditional value of humanity. When we act for the sake of these ends, we
act from the moral law, for it determines them. It is because the law
determines ends that creatures like ourselves, who always act for
ends, can be free.[24]

6. But this may not seem to resolve the problem. Clearly it is not
enough that we act for moral ends; we must also do so *because* they
are moral ends. We must adopt the ends themselves freely, as ends
determined by the moral law. But if we must be free in order to adopt
moral ends, then adopting moral ends cannot be what makes us free.

The answer to this objection lies in the special nature of internal
freedom. To explain the answer, we must take a detour through
another problem about the adoption of moral ends. Kant argues that
the duties of virtue are all of broad obligation; they do not require
definite acts which may simply be discharged (MPV 390).[25] The duty
to *advance* a moral end is one of broad obligation because it is an
imperfect duty; the law does not say exactly what or how much we
should do to advance the end. But what about the duty to *adopt* a
moral end? Kant thinks that the adoption of an end is necessarily a
free act, for he says:

Another may indeed force me to do something which is not my end (but is
only the means to some other's end); but he cannot force me to make it my
own end, for I can have no end except of my own making. (MPV 381–82)

Making something your end is a kind of internal action, and it is
these internal actions that are commanded by the Supreme Principle
of the Doctrine of Virtue. The duty to adopt these ends (and so also
the duty not to act against them) is a perfect duty. The law does say
exactly what we must do. So why does Kant count such duties as
creating only broad obligations which may not be discharged?

One of the things we expect of a person who has an end is that she will notice facts that are associated with that end in a certain way, and things that bear on the promotion of the end will occur to her. This is a general point about ends, and does not apply only to moral ends. To see this, imagine that I claim that I am Charlotte's friend, and that I have her happiness as my end. But imagine also that it seldom or never occurs to me to do anything in particular to make Charlotte happy. When I see something in a shop window that suits her taste exactly, I do not think, "now that is something Charlotte would really like," and go in to purchase it. When I look at the calendar on what happens to be her birthday, it does not occur to me that it is her birthday, and I should telephone. When I hear of some catastrophe happening in her neighborhood, I do not wonder about the possible bearing of this event on her safety and comfort. These things just do not come to me. Under these circumstances, surely Charlotte would be entitled to complain that there is no real sense in which I have her happiness as my end.[26] It would not be pertinent for me to reply that I have no direct control over what occurs to me. To find certain features of the world salient is part of our notion of what it is to have an end. To have an end is to see the world in a certain way. But what determines salience most directly lies in our sensory and representational capacities – and so in the passive part of our nature. To adopt an end is to perform an internal action. But it is also to undergo certain changes, changes in your representational capacities. It is to come to perceive the world in the way that having the end requires.

When the end is one that is suggested by natural inclination, we are already inclined to perceive the world in the relevant way. Indeed, that you are inclined to perceive the world that way is the form that the incentive takes. Our sensible nature here helps us out. But when the end is one prompted by reason this may not be the case. Here, you are imposing a change on your sensible nature, and your sensible nature may, and probably will, be recalcitrant. Although adopting an end is a volitional act, it is one that you can only do gradually and perhaps incompletely.

This is why the duty to adopt an end is of broad obligation. You cannot, just by making a resolution, acquire a virtue or recover from a vice. Or better still, we will say that you can, because you are free, but then we must say that only what happens in the future establishes whether you have really made the resolution or not. I do not mean that only the future will produce the evidence: I mean that only what you do in the future will enable us to correctly attribute a resolution to you. There is a kind of backwards determination in the construction of one's character. Whether you have made it your maxim to be more just, helpful, respectful, or honest depends on what you do in the future – on whether you make progress towards being the sort of person you have (presumably) resolved to be. Because the materials we have to work with in these cases are recalcitrant, it is in the progress, not in the success, that Kant places virtue (MPV 409). But the work must show up in progress. Suppose, for instance, that I am selfish, but resolve to be more attentive to the needs of others. As a selfish person I will also be self-absorbed, and fail to notice when others are in trouble and to be perceptive about what they need. At first, others may have to draw my attention to the cases where I can help. But if I continue indefinitely to *fail to notice* when others are in need and I can help, then I just did not resolve. On the other hand, if I do progress, I will count as having resolved, even if I am not consistently unselfish all of the time.

This is Kant's explicit view in *Religion Within the Limits of Reason Alone*. According to Kant, we must think of our free actions and choices as being unconditioned by time. If they were conditioned by time they would be subject to causality and so not free (R 40). Still, time is a condition of our thinking, and this means that for us, temporally unconditioned choice must be represented as choice that either is before or in a certain way follows from the events of our lives. For purposes of holding ourselves responsible, we think of the free adoption of our most fundamental maxim as if it were before our phenomenal choices: the evil in us is present from birth, Kant says, as if it were innate (R 21–22, 41; see also C2 100). But if our maxims were innate, we could not change for the better, for our most fundamental reasons would be self-interested ones. So, for purposes of regarding ourselves as free to change, we see the free choice of our character as something to which the whole conduct of our life adds up. Kant explains:

duty demands nothing of us which we cannot do. There is no reconciliation possible here except by saying that man is under the necessity of, and is therefore capable of, a revolution in his cast of mind, but only of a gradual reform in his sensuous nature (which places obstacles in the way of the former). That is, if a man reverses, by a single unchangeable decision, that highest ground of his maxims whereby he was an evil man (and thus puts on the new man), he is, so far as his principle and cast of mind are concerned, a subject susceptible of goodness, but only in continuous labor and growth is he a good man. That is, he can hope . . . to find himself upon the good (though strait) path of continual *progress* from bad to better. For Him who penetrates to the intelligible ground of the heart (the ground of all maxims of the will [*Willkür*]) and for whom this unending progress is a unity, i.e., for God, that amounts to his being actually a good man (pleasing to Him); and, thus viewed, this change can be regarded as a revolution. (R 47–48)[27]

The appearance of freedom in the phenomenal world, then, is virtue – a constant struggle to love and respect the humanity in oneself and others, and to defeat the claims inclination tries to make against that humanity. So far from committing him to a mysterious dualism, Kant's theory of the atemporal nature of freedom permits him to harmonize freedom with a temporal account of the acquisition of virtue. One achieves virtue through a gradual habituation, and, as in Aristotle's ethics, the sign of success is gladness in its practice. In the *Religion*, Kant says:

This resolve, then, encouraged by good progress, must needs beget a joyous frame of mind, without which man is never certain of having really *attained a love* for the good, i.e., of having incorporated it into his maxim. (R 21n)

To the extent to which moral ends have really become our ends, we will take pleasure in the pursuit of them. Indeed we have all of the emotions appropriate to having an end. In the *Metaphysical Principles of Virtue*, Kant speaks of gratitude (MPV 454–56) and even sympathetic feeling (MPV 456–58) as being required. He is quick to qualify these remarks, for we have no direct control over our feelings. Yet it is his view that one who does adopt an end will normally come to have the feelings that are natural to a person who has this end. If the end were suggested by sensibility, we would already have had the feelings, but though the end is adopted on moral grounds we should still come to have them eventually.[28] When explaining the relation between inclination and morality in the duty of beneficence, for example, Kant says:

Beneficence is a duty. Whoever often exercises this and sees his beneficent purpose succeed comes at last really to love him whom he has benefited. When therefore it is said, "Thou shalt love thy neighbor as thyself," this does not mean you should directly (at first) love and through this love (subsequently) benefit him; but rather, "Do good to your neighbor," and this beneficence will produce in you the love of mankind (as a readiness of inclination toward beneficence in general). (MPV 402)

Kant does not mean that we will come to act solely from the inclination, but rather that the inclination will be in harmony with reason and so will no longer be an impediment. As long as we do not act from inclination, but because the ends are dictated by the law, this is no detriment to our moral character. On the contrary, it shows that we have advanced toward the complete control over our sensuous nature that is implied by freedom.

So we do not exactly need to adopt moral ends freely in order to be free. If we come, over time, to act purely for the sake of moral ends, it will come to be true that we are, timelessly, free.

7. Kant's theory of the freedom of the will involves neither extravagant ontological claims nor the unyielding theory of responsibility which seems to follow from those claims.[29] These problems arise only from a misunderstanding of a fundamental feature of the Kantian philosophy – the radical split between the theoretical and practical points of view. The idea of intelligible causality is a practical conception, and our belief in it is an article of practical faith. It is not supposed to be theoretically employed, and it cannot be used to explain anything that happens. It is true that the positive conception of freedom makes practical freedom possible – but not because it explains how it is possible. It makes practical freedom possible because we can act on it.

Kant sees positive freedom as pointing to a higher vocation, the thought of which moves us to moral conduct, and explains how we can take an interest in such conduct. This interest leads us to adopt moral ends, and so to struggle against the temptations that beset us. If we reach the point where we are indeed moved wholly by ends determined by the law, we are in fact free – practically free. Nothing in this development requires any ontological claims, or requires that we be radically different sorts of creatures than the mundane rational animals we suppose ourselves to be. All that Kant needs is the conclusion that the moral law does indeed represent the positive conception of freedom. The idea of freedom motivates us to cultivate the virtues, and, in turn, virtue makes us free.

NOTES

I would like to thank Manley Thompson, Andrews Reath, Stephen Engstrom, and Onora O'Neill for valuable comments on earlier drafts of this paper.

1 For another treatment of some of these same difficulties, but centered more on Kant's views in the *Critique of Pure Reason*, see Henry E. Allison, "Empirical and Intelligible Character in the *Critique of Pure Reason*."

2 The alternative language is used because of the difference in Kant's own two accounts of what he is doing. I discuss this below.

3 For some important discussions of this question see the following works: H.J. Paton, *The Categorical Imperative: A Study in Kant's Moral Philosophy* (1947), Book IV; W.D. Ross, *Kant's Ethical Theory*; Karl Ameriks, "Kant's Deduction of Freedom and Morality"; Dieter Henrich, "Die Deduktion des Sittengesetzes: über die Gründe der Dunkleheit des letzen Abschnittes von Kants Grundlegung zur Metaphysik der Sitten." My own view on the matter is explained in Section 3.

4 The appendix, "The Kantian Conception of Free Will [Reprinted with some omissions, from *Mind*, 1888, Vol. 13, no 51]" was first attached to the sixth edition in 1901.

5 John Rawls, *A Theory of Justice*, p. 5. Rawls is in turn drawing upon H.L.H. Hart, *The Concept of Law*, pp. 155–59. Rawls uses the distinction in separating the concept of justice, "a characteristic set of principles for assigning basic rights and duties and for determining . . . the proper distribution of the benefits and burdens of social cooperation," from conceptions of justice, that is, various substantive accounts of what those principles are.

6 You may take the belief into account in other ways, like other beliefs. For instance, you may decide to warn your friends that you may do something uncharacteristic today, and that if so they should not be upset, since you are, as we say, "not yourself."

7 This is brought out well by Thomas Hill, Jr., in "Kant's Argument for the Rationality of Moral Conduct," and in "Kant's Theory of Practical Reason" both in his *Dignity and Practical Reason in Kant's Moral Theory*, chapters 6 and 7.

8 To understand this as a law of nature, rather than as a tautology, we must of course understand a "desire" not merely as something we ascribe to a person on the basis of her actions, but as a psychological phenomenon of some sort. This view of desire is also implied by Kant's account of desire as an incentive, which I explain below.

9 More specifically, Kant associates the will's spontaneity with the fact

that it does not exist under temporal conditions and so is uninfluenced by causality, but the important point here is just being uninfluenced – by anything. I discuss the relation between freedom and time in Section 6.

10 "World" (*Welt*) is Kant's term, and it is in some respects unfortunate, since it has lent credence to the interpretation of the distinction as an ontological dualism. Actually these two worlds are two standpoints, or ways we have of looking at things; as I will argue in the next section, they represent a practical and a theoretical viewpoint. I have continued to use the terminology of two worlds, since it is convenient and suits Kant's own usage. I would like to thank Onora O'Neill for urging me to be clearer on this point.

11 The remark is not italicized in Beck's translation, although it is in the Akademie Textausgabe and the Paton and Abbott translations.

12 For a different reading than mine of the idea that the intelligible world contains the grounds of the sensible world and its laws, and of why we must conceive ourselves as among those grounds, see Onora O'Neill's "Agency and Anthropology in Kant's *Groundwork*."

13 That our noumenal choices are in some way the ground of the laws of nature is a possibility that remains open; it is enough for the argument that we do not conceive ourselves as choosing these laws.

14 In a footnote in "On the Common Saying: 'This may be True in Theory, but it does not Apply in Practice' " Kant speaks directly of the moral incentive as provided by the idea of the highest possible earthly good, as "attainable through his [man's] collaboration [*Mitwirkung*]" (TP 280n).

15 For a different and perhaps more sympathetic account of the argument of *Groundwork III*, see Onora O'Neill, "Agency and Anthropology in Kant's *Groundwork*," especially Section 6.

16 The view that the idea of the intelligible world plays a motivational role can also be supported by appeal to Kant's writings on moral education, especially in the Methodologies of the second *Critique* and *The Metaphysical Principles of Virtue*. In both, there is an emphasis on awakening the child to the sublimity of the intelligible existence which freedom reveals.

17 Sidgwick, *The Methods of Ethics*, p. 516.

18 The metaphysical conception of the world also provides the regulative principles used in the theoretical sphere – but what those do is regulate the *practice* of science.

19 In Kantian ethics moral concepts are ideals of practical reason that are imposed on the world, by the command of the moral law, and for practical and moral purposes only. When we praise and blame we are, so to speak, applying the concept of "freedom" to another. The moral law both commands and regulates the application of this concept. I discuss

this way of regarding moral concepts in "Two Arguments against Lying," Chapter 12 in this volume.

20 I give a fuller explanation of the attitude Kant thinks is required and the moral basis for it in my "The Right to Lie: Kant on Dealing with Evil," Chapter 5 in this volume.

21 In these respects Kant's views stand in sharp contrast to the British sentimentalists whom he admired: Hutcheson, Hume, and Adam Smith. All developed their ethical theories from the point of view of the spectator of the moral conduct of others, and took approbation and disapprobation as the central concepts of ethics, from which the other concepts of moral thought are developed. Hutcheson and Hume believe that the best moral agent is not thinking about morality at all, but acting from admirable natural affections. Smith comes closer to an agent-centered theory, for he takes the agent to act from specifically moral thoughts, but they are generated from an *internal spectator*.

22 The mysterious-sounding parenthetical phrase is *"welche Eigenschaft desselben ihn zum Gegenstande der Erfahrung macht."* I take the point to be to equate sensibility and the need for an end.

23 In the Introduction to the *Metaphysics of Morals*, the faculty of desire is "the capacity to be by means of one's representations the cause of the objects of these representations" and the capacity to act in accordance with representations is identified as "life" (MM 211).

24 It might seem to be a problem that the Highest Good is supposed to be conceived as a divine end. How can God have an end if that is a need of sensibility? Kant explains: "For while the divinity has no subjective need of any external object, it cannot be conceived as closed up within itself, but only as compelled by the very awareness of its own all-sufficiency to produce the highest good outside itself. In the case of the supreme being, this necessity (which corresponds to duty in man) can be envisaged by us only as a moral need" (TP 280n).

25 The question of the relation between the two distinctions, perfect/imperfect, and broad/strict, is a very difficult one. These have sometimes been thought to be simply alternative terms for the same distinction, but Kant explicitly asserts that all duties of virtue are of broad obligation, while mentioning many that are perfect. He does not explain himself, and his own use of the terms does not provide clear guidance. Two important discussions of this problem are in Mary Gregor, *The Laws of Freedom: A Study of Kant's Method of Applying the Categorical Imperative in the Metaphysik der Sitten*, pp. 95–127, and in Onora (O'Neill) Nell, *Acting on Principle: An Essay on Kantian Ethics*, pp. 43–58. The main justification I have to offer for the way I use these terms in the text is that they enable me to make the explanation that follows.

26 In one sense I may still claim to have her happiness as my end. I may hold
    an end merely negatively, as something I will endeavor not to act against.
    The Formula of Humanity says that we must never use another merely as
    a means, and Kant says in the *Groundwork* that humanity is conceived
    negatively, as "that which must never be acted against" (G 437). But Kant
    makes it clear that *virtue* is going to require a more positive pursuit of the
    end. He says: "It is not enough that he is not authorized to use either
    himself or others merely as means (this latter including also the case of
    his being indifferent to others)" (MPV 395).

27 See also this passage from the *Religion*: "we may also think of this endless
    progress of our goodness towards conformity to the law, even if this prog-
    ress is conceived in terms of actual deeds, or life-conduct, as being judged
    by Him who knows the heart, through a purely intellectual intuition, as a
    completed whole, because of the *disposition*, supersensible in its nature,
    from which this progress itself is derived" (R 67–68), and from the *Cri-
    tique of Practical Reason*: "Only endless progress from lower to higher
    stages of moral perfection is possible to a rational but finite being. The
    Infinite Being, to whom the temporal condition is nothing, sees in this
    series, which is for us without end, a whole comfortable to the moral
    law" (C2 123). This is why Kant thinks that ethics leads to a view of the
    "immortality" of the soul, which gives us a prospect of an *endless* prog-
    ress toward the better. Only an endless progress is adequate to the achieve-
    ment of freedom, and to wiping out the original evil in our nature (R 72;
    C2 122–24).

28 This is not guaranteed. The *Groundwork* contains a well-known discus-
    sion of the worth of a man who is helpful although "by temperament
    cold and indifferent to the sufferings of others, perhaps because he is
    provided with special gifts of patience and fortitude" (G 398), which
    shows that Kant thinks moral worth may be combined with a recalci-
    trant temperament. The discussion has unfortunately often been taken
    to suggest that Kant thinks moral worth *must* be combined with a
    recalcitrant temperament.

29 Kant's theory of free will is sometimes described as "compatibilist"
    because both freedom and determinism are affirmed. This description
    seems to me to be potentially misleading. Most compatibilists, I believe,
    want to assert both freedom and determinism (or, both responsibility
    and determinism) from the same point of view – a theoretical and ex-
    planatory point of view. Kant does not do this, and could not do it
    without something his view forbids – describing the relation between
    the noumenal and phenomenal worlds.

7   Creating the Kingdom of Ends: Reciprocity and responsibility in personal relations

As the virtuous man is to himself, he is to his friend also, for his friend is another self.

Aristotle[1]

When we hold a person responsible, we regard her as answerable for her actions, reactions, and attitudes. We use the concept of responsibility in two contexts, the legal and the personal. We use it in the legal context when we must determine whether to punish someone for a crime or make him liable for another's losses. We use it in the context of everyday personal interaction, when we are pressed to decide what attitude we will take toward another, or toward some action or reaction of another. It is frequently assumed that these two uses are the same or at least continuous. Because I have doubts about this, and some worries about the appropriateness of using the notion in the legal context, I want to lay that use aside.[2] In this paper, my focus will be on our practice of holding people responsible in the context of personal relations.

I begin by offering an account of personal relations, derived from Kant and Aristotle, along with an explanation of why they require us to hold one another responsible. I then distinguish two views about what holding someone responsible involves. Specifically, I argue that to hold someone responsible is to adopt an attitude towards him rather than to have a belief about him or about the conditions under which he acts. This view gives rise to a problem: if holding someone responsible is something that we *do*, why and how do we decide to do it? In the rest of the paper, I argue that Kant's theory of personal and moral relations provides some answers to this question.

In the British Empiricist tradition, the concept of responsibility has been closely associated with the ideas of praise and blame, and these in turn have played a central role in its moral philosophy. In the theories of Hutcheson, Hume, and Smith, the approval and disapproval of others is the fundamental moral phenomenon, from which all our moral ideas spring.[3] There is something obviously unattractive about taking the assessment of others as the starting point in moral philosophy. One of the appealing things about Kant's ethics, by contrast, is that in it moral thought is seen as arising from the perspective of the agent who is deciding what to do. Responsibility is in the first instance something taken rather than something assigned. And this fact about the structure of his view is complemented by a fact about its content. Kant is not very interested in praise and blame and seldom mentions them. And when he does discuss issues of moral assessment, much of what he says favors taking a generous attitude. His metaphysical view that we cannot know even our own most fundamental maxims (G 407) combines with a set of moral injunctions – to respect others, avoid scandal, and "never to deny the wrongdoer all moral worth" (MPV 462–64) – to give philosophical foundations to the Biblical injunction "Judge not."[4]

But in a broader sense it is not possible for us to avoid holding one another responsible.[5] For holding one another responsible is the distinctive element in the relation of adult human beings. To hold someone responsible is to regard her as a *person* – that is to say, as a free and equal person, capable of acting both rationally and morally. It is therefore to regard her as someone with whom you can enter the kind of relation that is possible only among free and equal rational people: a relation of reciprocity. When you hold someone responsible, you are prepared to exchange lawless individual activity for reciprocity in some or all of its forms. You are prepared to accept promises, offer confidences, exchange vows, cooperate on a project, enter a social contract, have a conversation, make love, be friends, or get married. You are willing to deal with her on the basis of the expectation that each of you will act from a certain view of the other: that you each have your reasons which are to be respected, and your ends which are to be valued. Abandoning the state of nature and so relinquishing force and guile, you are ready to share, to trust, and generally speaking to risk your happiness or success on the hope that she will turn out to be human.

I borrow the idea that personal relations are characterized by reciprocity from both Kant and Aristotle, two of the very few philosophers in our tradition who have written about this topic. And it will be important to my argument that I hold along with them that the territory of personal relations is continuous with moral territory. That is to say, I accept their view that the forms of friendship, at their best at least, are forms of the basic moral relation among human beings – particular forms of that relation which have been rendered perfect of their kind. Aristotle holds that the most perfect human relation is the friendship of virtue, in which two people of good character share their lives and activities, and in particular, share those virtuous activities that make their lives worth living (NE IX.9 1169b28ff.). And Kant holds that the ideal of friendship is that of "the union of two persons through equal mutual love and respect," a relation in which the two basic attitudes we owe to one other as moral beings are realized in spontaneous natural sentiment (MPV 469). Characteristically, Aristotle holds that achieving such a relationship is a virtue, and Kant, that striving to achieve it is a duty. For friendship, Aristotle tells us, it is "not only necessary but noble" (NE VIII.2 1155a29–31); and Kant echoes the thought: "friendship . . . is no ordinary duty but rather an honorable one proposed by reason." (MPV 469).

Both define this perfect relation, as well as the less perfect variants of it, in terms of reciprocity, and both cite reciprocity as the reason why friendship is found above all among people who are good. For Aristotle, friendship is characterized by acknowledged reciprocal good will, in which each person loves the other for his own (the other's) sake (NE VIII.2 1155b28–1156a5). This requires trust in the other's goodness, for as Aristotle says "it is among good men that trust and the feeling that 'he would never wrong me' and all the other things that are demanded in true friendship are found" (NE VIII.4 1157a22–24). Kant characterizes friendship in the *Lectures on Ethics* as "the maximum reciprocity of love" (LE 202). There he argues that friends exchange their private projects of pursuing their own happiness, each undertaking to care for the other's happiness instead of his own. "I, from generosity, look after his happiness and he similarly looks after mine; I do not throw away my happiness, but surrender it to his keeping, and he in turn surrenders into my hands" (LE 203). This requires the maximum reciprocity of love because "if I am to love him as I love myself I must be sure that he will love me as he loves himself, in which case he restores to me that with which I part and I come back to myself again" (LE 202). The later account in *The Metaphysics of Morals* adds another element. Friendship in its perfection involves what Kant calls "the most intimate union of love with respect" (MPV 469). While love moves you to pursue the ends of another, respect reminds you that she must determine what those ends are; while love moves you to care for the happiness of another, respect demands that you care for her character too. Kant means here the *feelings* of love and respect, for he is defining the friendship of sentiment, but this does not sever the tie to morality. Love and respect are the primary duties of virtue we owe to others. Although only the outward practices can be required of us, Kant makes it clear in many passages that he believes that in the state of realized virtue these feelings will be present. In one place he even defines love and respect as the feelings which accompany the exercise of our duties towards others (MPV 448; see also R 23–24n). Feelings of sympathy, gratitude, and delight in the happiness of others are not directly incumbent upon us, but they are the natural result of making the ends of others our own, as duty demands. The feeling of respect, a still higher achievement, is the natural result of keeping the humanity of others and so their capacity for good will always before our eyes. So this kind of friendship really is in Kant's eyes the friendship of *virtue*, the moral relation in a perfected form.

"When men are friends they have no need of justice," says Aristotle, and there are two ways to understand what he means (NE VIII.1 1155a25–26). The wrong way is to suppose that he is referring to an idea like Hume's of the "circumstances of justice": justice is only useful and so is only required when moderate scarcity holds among people who are only moderately benevolent.[6] Friends, because they are endlessly benevolent to each other, are not in the circumstances of justice and have no use for it. Now this clearly cannot be Aristotle's meaning, for he thinks that "the truest form of justice is thought to be a friendly quality" (NE VIII.1 1155a27–28) and that "friendship and justice . . . seem to be concerned with the same objects and exhibited between the same persons" (NE VIII.9 1159b25–27). Justice is, at its best, a kind of civic friendship. And indeed, friendship, like justice, is not primarily a matter of doing things *for* one another, but of doing things together. "Those in the prime of life it stimulates to noble actions – 'two going together' – for with friends men are more able to think and to act" (NE VIII.1 1155a14–16). Aristotle sums up his account with these words:

And whatever existence means for each class of men, whatever it is for whose sake they value life, in *that* they wish to occupy themselves with their friends; and so some drink together, others dice together, others join in athletic exercises and hunting, and in the study of philosophy, each class spending their days together in whatever they love most in life; for since they wish to live with their friends, they do and share in those things which give them the sense of living together. (NE IX.12 1172a2–9)

Justice isn't necessary between friends because the reciprocity (NE V.5–6) and unanimity (NE VIII.1; NE IX.6) characteristic of justice are already present. And this is because they want above all to act together. Kant would again agree. Kant thinks that justice is reciprocal coercion under a general will, made necessary by geographical and economic association (MPJ 232; 256). When we share a territory we may have a dispute about rights. But I may enforce my rights against you only on the understanding that you may enforce your rights against me, and in this way we make a social contract and constitute ourselves a state (MPJ 315–16). Friendship is a free and uninstitutionalized form of justice, where the association is created by love rather than geographical necessity, and regulated by mutual respect rather than reciprocal coercion.

But it is not merely the narrow relation of political justice, but rather the moral relation generally, that friendship mirrors. For to join with others as citizens in the Kingdom of Ends is to extend to our inner attitudes and personal choices the kind of reciprocity that characterizes our outer actions in the political state. This is seen best in the way Kant uses the Formula of Humanity to explain our duties to others.[7] In the positive sense, to treat another as an end in itself is to make her ends your own: "For the ends of any person, who is an end in himself, must as far as possible also be my end, if that conception of an end in itself is to have its full effect on me" (G 430). In the negative sense, to treat another as an end in itself is to respect her autonomy – to leave her actions, decisions, and ends to her own choice. But this respect gets its most positive and characteristic expression at precisely the moments when we must act together. Then another's right to choose becomes the "limiting condition" of my own (G 431). If my end requires your act for its achievement, then I must let you make it your end too. Both what I choose and the way I choose it must reflect this constraint. You must be free to choose whether you will contribute to the success of my project or not. Kant says anyone engaged in a transaction with me must be able to agree with my way of acting towards him and to share in the end of my action (G 430). If I force you to contribute to an end you have had no opportunity to decide for or against, or if I trick you into contributing to one end under the guise of soliciting your help with another, then I have used you as a mere means. Kant illustrates this with the example of the lying promise. If I ask you to lend me money, knowing I shall not be able to pay you back, I trick you into contributing to an end you have had no opportunity to choose. I make you think that the end produced by our transaction is my temporary use of your money, when in fact it is my permanent possession of it. Neither my way of acting nor the end produced by it are things that you are in a position to accept or reject, and this renders them morally wrong. Thus I must make your ends and reasons mine, and I must choose mine in such a way that they can be yours. But this just is reciprocity. Generalized to the Kingdom of Ends, my own ends must be the possible objects of universal legislation, subject to the vote of all. And this is how I realize my autonomy. Paradoxically if you like, my ends and actions are most truly my own when they are chosen under the restrictions of a possible reciprocal relation – a kind of friendship – with everyone.

I do not say this to join forces with those who believe that there could be no room in a Kantian life for personal as opposed to moral relations.[8] Nor, certainly, do I mean to suggest that being friends is just a matter of being good. My point is only that moral and personal relations are not different in kind. The difference between them is the difference between the degree of reciprocity that is *required* of us as one human being relating to another, and the degree of reciprocity that we are capable of when our relations are at their best. Anyone must tell the truth when the circumstances call for it, but between friends there is a presumption of intimacy, frankness, and confidence. Anyone must help another in need or emergency, but friends promote each other's projects as routinely as they do their own. Anyone must refrain from leading others into temptation; but friends help each other to be good. The difference is the difference between the absolute moral requirements we must meet if human relations are to be decent at all, and the further reaches of positive virtue, where our relations with one another become morally worthy. Friendships are human moral achievements that are lovely in themselves and testify to the virtue of those who sustain them. To become friends is to create a neighborhood where the Kingdom of Ends is real.[9]

Kant's faith in the moral force of reciprocity shows up best when he believes that the basic moral relation is at risk. In both the *Lectures on Ethics* and the *Metaphysics of Morals* Kant gives inarticulate voice to the view that there is something morally troublesome, even potentially degrading, about sexual relations. It is important to understand that what bothers him is *not* the idea that one is using another person as a means to one's own pleasure. That would be an incorrect view of sexual relations, and in any case any difficulty about it, would, by Kant's own theory, be alleviated by the other's simple act of free consent. What bothers Kant is rather that sexual desire takes a *person* for its object.[10] He says: "They themselves, and not their work and services, are its Objects of enjoyment" (LE 162). And he continues:

Man can, of course, use another human being as an instrument for his service; he can use his hands, his feet, and even all his powers; he can use him for his own purposes with the other's consent. But there is no way in which a human being can be made an Object of indulgence for another except through sexual impulse . . . it is an appetite for another human being. (LE 163)

Regarding someone as a sexual object is not like regarding him as an instrument or a tool, but more like regarding him as an aesthetic object. But in this case the attitude is not just appreciation but desire (MPV 426).[11] Viewed through the eyes of sexual desire another person is seen as something wantable, desirable, and, therefore, inevitably, possessable.[12] To yield to *that* desire, to the extent it is really *that* desire you yield to, is to allow yourself to be possessed. The problem is how you can do that in a way that is consistent with respect for your own humanity.[13] And the solution rests in reciprocity:

> If, then, one yields one's person, body and soul, for good and ill in every respect, so that the other has complete rights over it, and if the other does not similarly yield himself in return and does not extend in return the same rights and privileges, the arrangement is one-sided. But if I yield myself completely to another and obtain the person of the other in return, I win myself back; I have given myself up as the property of another, but in turn I take that other as my property, and so win myself back again in winning the person whose property I have become. In this way the two persons become a unity of will. (LE 167)

The language of self-surrender and retrieval here is strikingly similar to that Kant uses elsewhere for both friendship and justice. In making the social contract, Kant says, we do not sacrifice part of our freedom for a particular purpose, but rather sacrifice all of our lawless freedom in order to regain our freedom again, undiminished, under law (MPJ 316). In the case of friendship Kant says I surrender my happiness completely into the hands of my friend, but that in loving me as he loves himself "he restores to me that with which I part and I come back to myself again" (LE 202).[14] This perfect reciprocity is the only condition under which the sexual relation is morally legitimate; and Kant thinks this condition is only possible in marriage, where the reciprocity of surrender has been pledged. Extramarital sex is forbidden only because the woman, as Kant supposes, does not then have the same rights over the man that he has over her. Of course marriage as it has usually existed has hardly been a solution to *this* problem. The equality necessary for reciprocity is far more likely to be distanced even further by marriage, which has usually given the husband rights over his wife *additional* to those that accrue from the superior social position he has held as a man. Kant admits as much in the *Metaphysical Principles of Justice*, asserting that an unequal marriage is not a marriage in his sense at all. Thus marriage as it has been practiced in most societies has not sanctified but rather degraded sexual relations (MPJ 278–79).[15] But perhaps the most startling ramification of Kant's view emerges in what he says about incest. As strong as our natural aversion to it may be, and however risky and therefore *conditionally* wrong it is from a reproductive point of view, incest is only morally wrong in itself, *unconditionally*, in one case: the case of parent and child. And this is because, according to Kant, the equality of respect required for reciprocity cannot and should not be achieved in that relation (LE 168).

Which brings me back to my topic. The relations of reciprocity are relations that obtain between free and equal persons. As such, they call for mutual responsibility for two important reasons. In order to make the ends and reasons of another your own, you must regard her as a source of value, someone whose choices confer worth upon their objects, and who has the right to decide on her own actions. In order to entrust your own ends and reasons to another's care, you must suppose that she regards you that way, and is prepared to act accordingly. People who enter into relations of reciprocity must be prepared to share their ends and reasons; to hold them jointly; and to act together. Reciprocity is the sharing of reasons, and you will enter into it only with someone you expect to deal with reasons in a rational way. In this sense, reciprocity requires that you hold the other responsible.

It is certainly a concomitant of holding someone responsible that you are prepared for blame, resentment, and the other reactive attitudes.[16] If my friend fails me in a serious way and I do not blame her, shrugging it off as I would the misdemeanors of a child or a pet, then I was not holding her responsible after all, and probably I was holding myself back. But it is a mistake to make these reactions central. Blame is important, not as a tool of training or the enforcement of social norms, but as an expression of the tenacity of disappointed respect. At its best, it declares to its object a greater faith than she has in herself. Yet still it is not central. The willingness to take a chance on some form of reciprocity is the essence of holding someone responsible.

I mean in these words both to acknowledge the affinity of my position with P.F. Strawson's in "Freedom and Resentment" and to notice one point of difference. Strawson also emphasizes the employment of the concept of responsibility in everyday personal relations. But he tends to focus more on the effect of attributions of responsibility on our sentiments than their effect on our practices. His topic, as he describes it, is "the non-detached attitudes and reactions of people directly involved in transactions with each other; ... the attitudes and reactions of offended parties and beneficiaries; of such things as gratitude, resentment, forgiveness, love, and hurt feelings."[17] I want to focus less upon the exchange of benefits and harms, and the feelings that result from that exchange, and more upon the willingness to act in concert. But my point is similar to his. In everyday personal interaction, we cannot get on without the concept of responsibility. And therefore we cannot rest with the view that agents take responsibility for their own actions but can refrain from judging others. For a Kantian, this means it is necessary to say more than Kant himself did about what, on his view, is involved in determining when and whether to hold people responsible.

II   THEORETICAL AND PRACTICAL CONCEPTIONS OF RESPONSIBILITY

Attributions of responsibility may be understood in either of two ways, which I will call theoretical and practical. Construed theoretically, responsibility is a characteristic of persons. Construed practically, holding one another responsible is something that we do, the more or less deliberate adoption of an attitude. In what follows I will distinguish these two ways of understanding attributions of responsibility, and show that according to Kant we must understand attributions of responsibility in a practical way. I believe that this view of responsibility is implicit in our actual practices, and therefore that, on this point at least, Kant's account can make us more transparent to ourselves.

Responsibility is construed theoretically by those who think that it is a fact about a person that she is responsible for a particular action, or that there is some fact about her condition either at the time of action or during the events which led up to it which fully determines whether it is correct to hold her responsible. It is a fact, say, that she could have done otherwise, or that she could have avoided the condition which made it impossible for her to do otherwise. Similar although somewhat more complicated claims would be made about the person's reactions and attitudes: facts about the person settle the question whether she is accountable for them. Deciding whether to hold someone responsible is a matter of assessing the facts; it is a matter of arriving at a belief about her. It seems probable that we arrive at this model by a certain route: we think about legal responsibility first, and we suppose that in that case we *must* find facts which can settle the matter, and then we imagine that personal responsibility is an extension of this.

Responsibility is construed practically by those who think that holding someone responsible is adopting an attitude towards her, or, much better, placing yourself in a relationship with her. While of course facts about the agent and about her condition at the time of the action *guide* your decision whether to hold her responsible, they do not fully *determine* it. It is important to see that the facts still do provide guidance, for a practical conception need not be envisioned as completely voluntaristic. On either a theoretical or a practical conception, we will, when deciding whether to hold someone responsible, say such things as "he is very nervous about the interview he has tomorrow" or "he's been hurt so often that now he can never trust a woman." But in a practical conception these considerations appear in the role of practical reasons for not holding the person responsible rather than as evidence that he could not have helped what he did. When responsibility is viewed this way, we need not suppose that there is a *fixed degree* of nervousness or past heartbreak beyond which someone is *in fact* no longer responsible for the way he acts and reacts; deciding whether to hold him responsible is therefore not a matter of determining whether this fixed degree has been reached. A resulting feature of the practical conception which I take to be one of its virtues is that it distances the question whether to hold someone responsible from the question whether he acted voluntarily. I do not believe there is a stable relationship between the voluntariness of an action or attitude and the appropriateness of holding someone responsible for it. If a bad action is found to have been involuntary in some straightforward way, we will withdraw blame; we may also do this if the person is under severe emotional stress. But there is neither need nor reason to reduce the second kind of excusing condition to the first and say that people under severe emotional stress *cannot* control themselves. We do not need to understand a form of debilitation as a form of impossibility in order to make allowances for it; we need only to know what it is like. Conversely, we may well blame people for involuntary attitudes or expressions, because we blame people for lack of control itself. If you cannot repress a victorious grin on learning that your rival has met with a gruesome accident, you ought to be blamed, precisely on that account. The impulse to reduce all excusing conditions to claims about the voluntary comes from the theoretical conception of responsibility, which demands an answer to the question whether one could have done otherwise or not. On the practical conception excuses need not completely determine our decisions about whether to hold people responsible. If the decision to attribute responsibility is practical, it may be reasonable to make it partly on the basis of other kinds of considerations: in particular, which reciprocal relations you already stand in or plan to stand in or hope to stand in to the person in question.

Construing responsibility practically opens up possibilities that would not make sense if responsibility were a fact about the person. It is because we both accept and avail ourselves of these possibilities that I claim that we implicitly understand attributions of responsibility practically in everyday life. For instance, it may be perfectly reasonable for me to hold someone responsible for an attitude or an action, while at the same time acknowledging that it is just as reasonable for someone else not to hold the same person responsible for the very same attitude or action. Perhaps it is reasonable for *you* to forgive or overlook our friend's distrustful behavior on the grounds that he has suffered so much heartbreak, but not for me, *not* because I fail to appreciate how hurt he has been, but because I am the woman whose loving conduct is always met with distrust.[18] Again, if deciding whether to hold someone responsible is something that we do, it is something that we may in turn be held responsible for. Holding someone responsible can be insensitive or merciless; failing to hold someone responsible can be disrespectful or patronizing. Moral requirements will apply to our attributions of responsibility, just as Kant believes they do.

Consider, for instance, the appropriate reaction to a case where one is disappointed in friendship. Kant thinks the perfect friendship I described earlier, characterized by *feelings* of equal mutual love and respect, is impossible to achieve. But he does think we can achieve what he calls "moral friendship" (MPV 471–73). The form of reciprocity central to this relation is the frank conversation, the sharing of sentiments, of which Kant believes we all stand in need. Like other reciprocal relations it calls for good character on the part of the participants, because it is hedged with dangers – ranging from the crude risk that you will tell your secrets to an unreliable person who will publish them, to the more subtle risk that your confidences will be met with disrespectful attitudes.[19] I do not want to share my ambitions with someone who is inwardly amused by my vanity, nor whisper my temptations to someone who will place a harsh construction on them. One who consents to receive my confidences is committed to avoiding the vices of mockery and calumny, serious failures of respect in the Kantian catalogue (MPV 466–67). And I will blame her if she fails in these ways, without regard to the available evidence of her character or of the circumstances in which it was formed. Her circumstances must have been very bad indeed, or her failures very frequent, before I may decide it was simply *my* error to trust her. For in deciding this I write her off as a person, and I do this at my own moral peril.

I suppose that most of us have at one time or another had the experience of being tempted to "write somebody off." The extent to which we do this is a matter of degree, and hopefully we do not go so far as to give up treating the person with the most basic forms of moral decency. But we may avoid interaction, as far as possible; we may choose to execute our projects in the company of others; where interaction is necessary, we may come to treat the person as an obstacle to be worked around. In an extreme case we may cease to have reactive attitudes altogether, or at least we may scold ourselves, as for irrational feelings, when we have them. "You know that she always ends up infuriating you. Why don't you just stay out of her way?" Taking such attitudes towards others seems disrespectful, but it can certainly sometimes be tempting all the same. How do we decide what to do in such a case? On a theoretical construal of responsibility, we simply ask whether the person is in fact responsible for the offensive behavior, and treat her accordingly. On a practical construal, we must discover moral and practical reasons that will guide us to the right attitude. Kant's theory of moral and personal relations, I believe, can show us where these reasons are to be found.

III   KANT'S TWO STANDPOINTS

I will approach these issues in a roundabout way, however. I begin by discussing the way Kant reconciles free will and determinism, and by showing how his reconciliation gives rise to some apparent problems about holding people responsible. Kant's theory of moral and personal relations shows us how he might have resolved one of these issues, and how we might resolve the other.

Kant's solution to the problem of freedom and determinism is clear enough in outline, however much philosophers may disagree about what it means. We must view ourselves from two standpoints, from which we appear as members of two different "worlds" (G 452). Complete causal determinism holds in the phenomenal or sensible world, the world of things as they appear to us; but we cannot know that it holds in the noumenal world, the world of things as they are in themselves. Indeed, since we must suppose that there are some undetermined first causes, or free agencies, which generate the appearances, we must suppose that things which exist in the noumenal world are free.[20] Insofar as we regard ourselves as "intelligences," the spontaneity of reason induces us to attribute a noumenal existence to ourselves (G 452; C2 42–43). Insofar as we consider ourselves to be intelligent *agents*, then, we must regard ourselves as free: indeed, completely and transcendentally so. Yet at the same time we must view our actions, like all phenomena, as fully determined.[21]

Despite Kant's strictures against trying to envision what occurs on the boundary between the two worlds, it is natural to want a picture that reconciles these two views of ourselves. At one point in the *Critique of Practical Reason*, Kant supplies the beginning of such a picture. He proposes that we should think of ourselves, and also that we do think of ourselves, as if we created our own characters. Although a person may know that his actions are determined in the phenomenal world, Kant says:

... the same subject ... is conscious also of his existence as a thing-in-itself ... determinable only by laws which he gives to himself through reason. In this existence nothing is antecedent to the determination of his will; every action, and ... even the entire history of his existence as a sensuous being, is seen ... only as a consequence ... of his causality as a noumenon. From this point of view, a rational being can rightly say of any unlawful action which he has done that he could have left it undone, even if as an appearance it ... was inescapably necessary. For this action and everything in the past which determined it belong to a single phenomenon of his character, which he himself creates.... (C2 97–98)

Kant then applies this picture to our attributions of responsibility:

> From this point of view . . . judgments may be justified which . . . seem at
> first glance to conflict with equity. There are cases in which men . . . have
> shown from childhood such depravity . . . that they are held to be born
> villains and incapable of any improvement of character; yet they are judged
> by their acts, they are reproached as guilty of their crimes; and, indeed, they
> themselves find these reproaches as well grounded as if they . . . were just as
> responsible as any other men. This could not happen if we did not suppose
> that whatever arises from man's choice . . . has a free causality as its
> ground . . . the vicious quality of the will . . . is . . . the consequence of . . .
> freely assumed evil and unchangeable principles. (C2 99–100)

Here one's life is regarded as the phenomenal representation or expression of a single choice, the choice of one's character or fundamental principle. This choice must be understood as occurring outside of time, in the noumenal world. The choice is the one described
in the first book of *Religion Within the Limits of Reason Alone*: the
choice of how incentives are to be ordered in one's most fundamental maxim, the choice between morality and self-love (R 36). As Kant
sees it, human beings are subject to certain incentives – impulses
which present themselves to us as candidates, so to speak, to be
reasons for action. Among these are our desires and inclinations, as
well as respect for the moral law. Kant believes that we are not free
to ignore such incentives altogether. Instead, our freedom consists in
our ability to rank the incentives, to choose whether our self-love
shall be governed by morality or morality shall be subordinated to
self-love. This fundamental choice then governs our choice of lower-
order maxims. The fundamental choice is an act – in the *Religion*
Kant calls it an intelligible act – and it is ultimately this intelligible
act that is imputable to us, and makes our phenomenal actions
imputable to us (R 31–32).

When first exposed to Kant's view, one may be tempted to try to
picture how and where the choice of one's character enters the processes which ultimately issue in action. Suppose, with violent oversimplification, that it is a law of nature that children raised in certain
conditions of poverty and insecurity tend to become somewhat selfish as adults, and suppose that such a childhood has had this effect on
Marilyn. Are we to say to her: "Your childhood insecurity gave you an
incentive to be selfish, but it is still your own fault if you elevate that

incentive into a reason"? Then we are thinking that Marilyn's freedom inserts itself in between the causes in her background and their ultimate effect.[22] Or are we supposed to think that, in her noumenal existence, Marilyn *wills to be* a selfish person? Or, to get even fancier, should we think that in her noumenal existence Marilyn wills the law of nature that deprived children become selfish adults? Obviously, if we try to picture *how* Marilyn's freedom is related to the forces that determine her, we must imagine it either inserting itself somewhere into the historical process, or standing behind the laws of nature from which this historical process necessarily follows. And both of these pictures seem crazy.[23]

And of course they are crazy. Kant's response to this problem is to maintain that the question should not be asked. To ask how freedom and determinism are related is to inquire into the relation between the noumenal and phenomenal worlds, a relation about which it is in principle impossible to know anything. But our understanding of what this response amounts to will depend on how we understand the distinction between the noumenal and phenomenal worlds, and the related distinction between the two standpoints from which Kant says we may view ourselves and our actions.

This is a large issue which I cannot treat here in a satisfactory way; I shall simply declare my allegiance. On a familiar but as I think misguided interpretation, the distinction between the two worlds is an ontological one; as if behind the beings of this world were another set of beings, which have an active and controlling relation to the beings of this world, but which are inaccessible to us because of the limits of experience. According to this view, we occupy both worlds, and viewing ourselves from the two standpoints we discover two different sets of laws which describe and explain our conduct in the two different worlds. We act on the moral law in the noumenal world, the law of self-love in the phenomenal world. This view gives rise to familiar paradoxes about how evil actions are even possible, and how we could ever be held responsible for them if they were.[24]

On what I take to be the correct interpretation, the distinction is not between two kinds of beings, but between the beings of this world insofar as they are authentically active and the same beings insofar as we are passively receptive to them. The "gap" in our knowledge exists not because of the *limits* of experience but because of its essential *nature*: to experience something is (in part) to be passively receptive to it, and therefore we cannot have experiences of activity as such.[25] As thinkers and choosers we must regard ourselves as active beings, even though we cannot *experience* ourselves as active beings, and so we place ourselves among the noumena, necessarily, whenever we think and act. According to this interpretation, the laws of the phenomenal world are laws that describe and explain our behavior. But the laws of the noumenal world are laws which are *addressed to us* as active beings; their business is not to describe and explain at all, but to govern what we do.[26] Reason has two employments, theoretical and practical. We view ourselves as phenomena when we take on the theoretical task of describing and explaining our behavior; we view ourselves as noumena when our practical task is one of deciding what to do.[27] The two standpoints cannot be mixed because these two enterprises – explanation and decision – are mutually exclusive.[28]

These two ways of understanding the noumenal/phenomenal distinction yield very different interpretations of Kant's strictures against trying to picture the relation between the noumenal and phenomenal worlds. On the ontological view, the question how the two worlds are related is one which, frustratingly, cannot be answered. On the active/passive view, it is one which cannot coherently be *asked*. There is no question that is answered by my descriptions of how Marilyn's freedom interacts with the causal forces that determine her. For freedom is a concept with a practical employment, used in the choice and justification of action, not in explanation or prediction; while causality is a concept of theory, used to explain and predict actions but not to justify them.[29] There is no standpoint from which we are doing both of these things at once, and so there is no place from which to ask a question that includes both concepts in its answer.

So, if I am myself Marilyn, and I am trying to decide whether to do something selfish, reflections on the disadvantages of my background are irrelevant. I must act under the idea of freedom, and so I must act on what I regard as reasons. Being underprivileged may sometimes be a cause of selfish behavior, but it is not a reason that can be offered in support of it by a person engaged in it. So although we do not necessarily say of Marilyn: "her background gave her some tough incentives to deal with, but still it is up to her whether she treats them as reasons," that is what she must say to herself. I say that we do not *necessarily* say this, because, as I am about to argue, whether we say it depends on whether we have decided to enter into reciprocal relations with her and so to hold her responsible. But in that case, it is better regarded as something we say not *about* her but *to* her. The second-person grammatical form, so rarely privileged in philosophy, is exactly right here, for if anyone besides Marilyn has the right to make this judgment, it is her friends, those with whom she interacts. On the other hand, if I am not Marilyn's friend, but a social scientist who is trying to understand and explain her behavior, then my business is not to try to justify her conduct, and for my purposes the causal explanation which makes her selfish actions seem inevitable is the right one to pursue.

The two worlds, or the two views of the world we get from the two standpoints, may seem strangely incongruent, but it is important to see that there is no contradiction. The incongruity simply follows from the fact that we stand in two very different relations to our actions: we must try to understand them, but we must also decide which ones to do.

IV   PRACTICAL GROUNDS FOR HOLDING PEOPLE RESPONSIBLE

But we cannot just leave the matter there. For there are contexts in which we have to mix considerations derived from the two standpoints, and make a moral assessment of someone's action, on the basis of a theoretical explanation of what she did. This occurs when we are making judgments about responsibility: when we must decide whether, for instance, someone is to be exonerated, excused, forgiven, blamed, or not held responsible for a bad action at all.

There are really two problems here. First, given that we can view people and their actions either way, or from either standpoint, what reason do we have for settling on the practical point of view, and holding people responsible, at all?[30] Second, even if we can discover such a reason, won't Kant's view be intransigent? For if we do regard people as free agents, fellow citizens in the Kingdom of Ends, then it seems as if we must treat them as transcendentally free and so as completely responsible for each and every action, no matter what sorts of pressures they may be under. Yet the obvious fact is that we

live in neighborhoods which are at different distances from the Kingdom of Ends, and it seems merciless to give this obvious fact no
weight. But it also seems as if the only option Kant provides is to
switch to the theoretical standpoint and regard candidates for forgiveness as if they were no more responsible for their actions than
small children and animals. The very idea of an action's being excusable or forgivable or understandable seems, to bring together explanatory and justificatory thoughts. The doctrine of the two standpoints
seems to keep such thoughts resolutely apart.

In response to the first problem, why we hold people responsible
at all, it is important initially to separate two issues. One is the issue
of holding yourself responsible for your own actions in the context
of deliberative choice, and the other is the issue of holding other
people and yourself at other times responsible. On Kant's view, we
first encounter the idea of freedom when we are deciding what to do.
We encounter it in the necessity of acting under the idea of freedom,
and in the commands of the moral law.[31] At the moment of decision,
you must regard yourself as the author of your action, and so you
inevitably hold yourself responsible for what you do. It is only when
you think about the actions of other people, and when you think
about your own actions at other times, that you can view them from
either standpoint. You can take up the position of the social scientist, and regard actions as psycho-social phenomena that need to be
explained. Or you can put yourself in the other person's shoes as a
decision-maker, and think about what it is like to *choose* or to *do* an
action of that kind.

Now it seems clear that you cannot restrict the concepts of freedom and responsibility to yourself in the context of deliberative
choice. If you did, you would think that the only free agent in the
world is me-right-now. But the moral law, which according to Kant
presents itself to you in exactly these moments, commands that you
treat everyone as an end in himself (C2 29–30). Unless you hold
others responsible for the ends that they choose and the actions that
they do, you cannot regard them as moral and rational agents, and so
you will not treat them as ends in themselves. Indeed, unless you
regard others and your future self as moral agents, there will be no
content to your duties at all, for all duties (according to Kant) are
owed either to other persons or to the enduring self (MPJ 241; MPV
442–44). The moral law, announcing itself as the law of your will,

would be without content or application. Your relations to other people, and to yourself at other times, would be, at best, like your relations to small children and the other animals. But there is more at stake here than just whether you have any duties, for you cannot enter into *any* reciprocal relations with people whom you do not hold responsible. Nor can you do this if you do not take responsibility for your own actions at other times, since relationships after all are enduring things.

This is why our reaction to Derek Parfit's nineteenth-century Russian nobleman is that he's wrong, and in particular, that he wrongs his wife. The story goes like this. Parfit's Russian nobleman is now, in his youth, a socialist, and plans to distribute large portions of his inheritance, when he comes into it, to the poor. But he also anticipates that his attitudes will become more conservative as he grows older, and so that he may not think this is the right thing to do, when the inheritance is actually his own. So he asks his wife to hold him to the promise he makes *now*, to distribute the land, even if he tells her *then* that he has changed his mind.[32] Parfit makes it clear that the case is not like that of Ulysses binding himself to the mast to resist the Sirens' song. The young nobleman does not anticipate that he is going to become irrational, that his judgment will be clouded, or that he will be out of control. He merely believes that he is going to think differently than he does now. This case illustrates my point well. The young nobleman's attitude towards his own future attitudes is essentially a *predictive* and theoretical one, and, because it is so, he abdicates the kind of responsibility that is necessary for reciprocity: the kind of responsibility that enables people to act in concert. His way of making himself do the right thing is not to take responsibility for doing so, but to give the responsibility to his wife. This may be one way to form the "united will" that Kant says is necessary in marriage, but it is not the right way. The Russian nobleman leaves his wife alone in the standpoint of practical reason, where people who are married must stand together. Her decision is not, as Parfit says, which of these two men, older and younger, is her real husband, the man she loves, the man she has married. Nor, for that matter, would *that* be just a question about how she feels about them or what she thinks of them. She cannot be married to the older man, later, unless she holds him responsible, and takes him at his word. She cannot be married to the younger one, now, because he has already abandoned her. And further than that: to the extent that it is important to this woman's sense of her own identity, morally and personally, that she is his wife, he leaves her without anything clear to be, and so without anything clear to do. You cannot act in concert with one who does not act in concert with himself. Where our relations are constitutive of our ongoing identities, those with whom we have them must have ongoing identities too.[33]

So if you only apply the concepts of freedom and responsibility to yourself at the moments of deliberative choice, you do not have any sort of recognizable moral life at all. No Kingdom of Ends on earth can be sought or realized if responsibility is restricted to its original home in the first person deliberator's perspective.

But notice that all of the reasons I have just given are moral and practical ones. I have been suggesting that holding people responsible is something that we do for moral reasons. The reason we must view another as a fellow rational person rather than as a psycho-social phenomenon is not that he is *in fact* one of these things rather than the other. In fact, he is both. That another is responsible is what Kant calls a postulate of practical reason: a belief or attitude that can be formulated theoretically, but is practical and moral in its basis (C2 132–34). We hold others responsible in the same way that, according to Kant, we "will that there be a God," because it is a condition of our obedience to the commands of the moral law (C2 143). Or, when a more personal relation is at stake, because it is the condition of our submission to the imperatives of love.

No doubt this way of putting it makes it all sound more deliberate and voluntary than it really is. We do not, of course, simply decide whether to hold other people responsible in general; reciprocal relations and the attitudes that characterize them are, as Strawson argues, too deeply imbedded in the framework of human life to "come up for review," and reactive attitudes, or at least the feelings that accompany them, cannot always be helped.[34] But as Strawson himself observes we do make these decisions in particular cases, and even more frequently we make decisions about whether to identify with our reactive feelings or not. If I have decided not to hold someone responsible, I may view my rage at him as mere inevitable emotion, like the rage provoked in everyone except saints by recalcitrant home appliances and fractious infants. Still, it might be better to put my point a different way. The idea is not that we deliberately decide to hold people responsible in general, but that our commitment to this view of others and our commitment to the moral life issue together from the standpoint of practical reason. Holding others responsible is an inevitable concomitant of holding ourselves so, both in particular personal relations and in more general moral ones. To share our ends and reasons is to share the standpoint from which those ends and reasons are generated. The citizens of the Kingdom of Ends make their decisions in congress; the noumenal world is, above all, a place that we occupy *together*.

V   MITIGATING MORAL JUDGMENT

Now while this explains why we hold others responsible, and why our doing so has and must have a practical basis, it does not solve the problem of what now appears to be Kant's intransigence. The moral command that we hold others responsible seems as absolute as it would be if we had theoretical knowledge that they were indeed transcendentally free. Kant does not separate the grounds for holding people responsible in general, from the grounds for holding them responsible for particular actions. And so it seems as if holding someone responsible in general amounts to holding her responsible for everything she does. The flexibility with which I credited the practical account of attributions of responsibility does not seem to follow readily from Kant's view.

Some of the things Kant says, however, suggest that there is room for such flexibility. I will discuss two kinds of considerations, mentioned by Kant, which may be used to guide our decisions whether to hold people responsible for particular actions and reactions, and in particular, to mitigate the intransigence that seems required by the commitment to treating others as persons.

The first consideration springs from what I call Kant's practical compatibilism. Although Kant endorses both free will and determinism, he is not a theoretical compatibilist. Kant does not believe that these two things can be reconciled from a single point of view, as his contempt for Leibniz's *automaton spirituale*, which he says has "the freedom of a turnspit," shows (C2 97). And yet this does not stop him from adjuring politicians that "a good constitution is not to be expected from morality, but conversely, a good moral condition of a people is to be expected only under a good constitution" (PP 366).

Nor does it stop him from detailing a theory of moral education designed to awaken our sense of our own autonomy.[36] To the extent, or in the sense, that Kant believes that virtue can be taught, or made to flower by a good constitution, he must believe that it can be caused.[36]

Readers of Kant may want to deny this, for in the *Groundwork*, Kant says that insofar as we are members of the world of sense, our actions "must be regarded as determined by other appearances, namely, desires and inclinations" (G 453). But this remark is actually somewhat misleading. Insofar as we view our actions as phenomena we must view them as causally determined, but not necessarily as determined by mere desires and inclinations. We can still view them as determined by moral thoughts and moral aspirations; only from this point of view, those must themselves be viewed as determined in us. For instance, I might explain someone's doing the right thing by saying that she did it because she values humanity as an end in itself, and I might in turn explain that fact by showing how she received a moral education. And, for that matter, I might explain how that kind of education is possible by appealing to a psychological or even psychoanalytic theory, such as Freud's, of how human beings develop a conscience or superego. A deterministic account can be a deterministic account of moral motivation itself – it does not have to bypass morality and pretend we do everything for the sake of happiness. The element of truth in what Kant says is that a deterministic account necessarily leaves out what is distinctively good about moral motivation. From a merely theoretical and explanatory point of view moral interest is on a footing with inclination. We may imagine the cynic saying: "it doesn't really matter how she came to treat humanity as an end in itself. It is what she likes to do, so she is still pursuing her own happiness." When moral motivation is viewed theoretically, it can be distinguished from inclination only by its content. Its special *source*, in the agent's autonomy, does not show up.

Kant's practical compatibilism suggests that it may be reasonable, when we are deciding whether and when to hold people responsible, to take into account such things as upbringing and education. Depending on the particular circumstances, the fact that someone has had a good moral education may provide a special reason either for forgiveness or for blame, and our decisions about whether to hold him responsible may be governed accordingly. Or it may by itself, quite apart from prediction, provide a special reason for holding someone responsible. When the community has done all it can to make someone good, then there may be no further outlet for respect for humanity, than to blame him if he goes wrong.[37]

Another kind of consideration comes from Kant's iterated demand, in the *Metaphysical Principles of Virtue*, for generosity of interpretation. As I mentioned at the beginning of my discussion, Kant believes that we cannot know people's most fundamental or intelligible characters. But he censures contempt, calumny, and mockery as much for their disrespectful and ungenerous nature as for their lack of a theoretical basis (MPV 462–68). He says, for instance, "One should cast the veil of philanthropy over the faults of others, not merely by softening but also by silencing our judgments" (MPV 466). Our theoretical estimate of another person's character may be set aside in favor of our respect for the humanity within him. The reproach of vice, according to Kant,

... must never burst out in complete contempt or deny the wrongdoer all moral worth, because on that hypothesis he could never be improved either – and this latter is incompatible with the idea of man, who as such (as a moral being) can never lose all predisposition to good. (MPV 463–64)

Kant compares this to the duty, when someone makes an error, not just to deem him stupid but to try to determine how the mistaken view could have seemed reasonable to him. We are to do this in part in order to "preserve the mistaken individual's respect for his own understanding" (MPV 463). But regarding a person as stupid or making her errors seem reasonable are not our only options in these cases. Sometimes we can best preserve someone's self-respect, as well as our own respect for her, not by making her errors seem reasonable, but by laughing them off as the result of transitory emotion or exhaustion. The same is surely true in the moral realm. Respect for someone's humanity is not always best expressed by holding him responsible for each and every action. It may be better to admit that even the best of us can just slip. Indeed Kant's own doctrine of moral progress, in *Religion Within the Limits of Reason Alone*, has this implication. The phenomenal expression of a noumenally good will is not perfect action in all cases, but progress towards the better (R 47–48). If an anomalous action intrudes into a course of steady progress in virtue, we might find it in our hearts simply to dismiss it as atavistic or

transient, or sometimes without any explanation at all. We simply
say, "He isn't himself."

VI   CONCLUSION

On the whole, Kant's view is that we must always hold ourselves
responsible, and that we should as far as possible always hold other
people responsible. But this is not because people's noumenal freedom is known to us as a theoretical fact. It is because of the respect
which the moral law commands us to accord to the humanity in
every person. We hold one another responsible because this is essential to our interactions with each other as *persons*; because in this
way we together populate a moral world. We may disagree with Kant
about some of the details of how respect for humanity is best expressed, but his theory captures the essential idea that attributions
of responsibility have a practical basis. To view people theoretically,
as objects of knowledge, is to view them as part of the world that is
imposed upon us through the senses, and, to that extent, as alien.
But insofar as we are noumenal, or active beings, we join with others
in those intersubjective standpoints which we can occupy together,
either as thinkers or as agents. When we enter into relations of
reciprocity, and hold one another responsible, we enter together into
the standpoint of practical reason, and create a Kingdom of Ends on
earth.

NOTES

I have many people to thank for help with this paper. Ken Simons provided extensive and helpful comments which prompted me to make a
number of revisions. Sidney Axinn, Charlotte Brown, Dan Brudney, and
Jay Schleusener read and commented on various versions. I presented
the paper to several philosophy departments and found all of the discussions helpful; special thanks are owed to audiences at UCLA, the University of Vermont, and the University of Michigan. A short version of the
paper, entitled "Holding People Responsible," was presented at the VIIth
International Kant Congress and appears in *Akten des Siebeuten Internationalen Kant-Kongresses*, edited by G. Funke. Bonn: Bouvier, 1991.

1   *Nicomachean Ethics* IX.9 1170b 6–7, with parentheses removed. Hence-
forth cited parenthetically in the text as NE followed by the Bekker
page, column, and line references.

2 My reasons for these doubts will become apparent in the course of the paper, although I will not discuss them in the text. If the argument of this paper is correct, the decision whether to hold someone responsible is governed by a variety of considerations, rather than determined wholly by facts about the person. One might think that the legal use of the concept of responsibility requires that the issue of whether a person is responsible be determinable by such facts. Did he understand what he was doing? Does he know right from wrong? If so my view might cause difficulties for it, unless the legal use is not as continuous with the moral use as some believe. However, it is important to notice that my doubts concern the *particular* uses to which the concept of responsibility is sometimes put in our legal system. In a general and philosophical way, the justification of the penal system may rest on our will, as social contractors, to hold one another responsible. But *this* legal use of the concept of responsibility admits of the moral and practical foundation I describe in this paper, and indeed probably requires it. We have no general reason to believe that our fellow citizens are for the most part rational and moral people, who only occasionally go haywire or fall into sin. If I am right, we do have a general reason to hold them responsible: it is *because* they are our partners in the social contract.

3 This is clear from the structure of their theories. But for some more specific statements, see for example the opening paragraph of Francis Hutcheson's *Inquiry Concerning Moral Good and Evil* (in D.D. Raphael, *British Moralists*, p. 261); Hume's statement of the central question of his moral philosophy on p. 456 of *The Treatise of Human Nature*. The complaint applies less straightforwardly to Smith, whose theory in general is more sensitive to the perspective of the agent than those of his predecessors. But see, for instance, the opening lines of I.i.5 of *The Theory of Moral Sentiments*, p. 23.

4 Matthew 7:1.

5 We have two somewhat different uses of the term "responsible." When we say someone is responsible for an action or attitude, we imply that she is a candidate for praise or blame. But when we say someone is a responsible person, we imply that she is reliable, resourceful, trustworthy, and self-controlled. The notion I want is a combination of these but more like the second: we think of the person as someone who should be regarded as reliable and trustworthy and so forth, and *therefore* as a candidate for praise and blame.

6 See David Hume, *An Enquiry Concerning the Principles of Morals*, pp. 183–92. I borrow the term "circumstances of justice" from John Rawls in *A Theory of Justice*, pp. 126ff.

7 These remarks obviously assume a particular reading of Kant's Formula

of Humanity, according to which what is involved in treating someone
as an end-in-itself is respecting her as a rational being, whose choices
confer value on their objects, and whose actions must be left to her own
autonomous decision. I defend this reading in two articles, "Kant's Formula of Humanity," Chapter 4 in this volume, especially pp. 124–28;
and "The Right to Lie: Kant on Dealing with Evil," Chapter 5 in this
volume, especially pp. 137–43.

8 See note 14 for some remarks on this point.

9 Here, as several readers have pointed out to me, I am obviously discussing very close and intimate friendships, and saying things that do not
hold of less personal but still particular relationships. In these cases
perhaps the right thing to say is that reciprocity is heightened, but only
in a certain sphere of activity. The members of a committee or a department, for example, must take action and make decisions together, and
this involves a commitment to treating each other's contributions to
these decisions as responsible ones and each other's wishes about them
as having weight. This is a heightened form of reciprocity, although only
within a delimited sphere. But within this sphere what is involved is
like friendship. The comparison of factionalized departments to unhappy marriages is a good one. When reciprocity breaks down, and the
entity is held together only by formal institutional mechanisms, not
only its pleasantness but also its moral character deteriorates.

10 Sometimes Kant unfortunately changes his ground and says the problem
is precisely that we don't want the other person *qua* that person, but
only *qua* member of a particular gender (LE 164). This is nonsense, and
spoils what I take to be of interest in his point.

11 In the *Groundwork*, Kant suggests that in the Kingdom of Ends everything either has a market price, an affective price, or a dignity. Ordinarily commodities have market prices, art objects have affective prices,
and human beings have dignity (G 434–435). Thus my suggestion in the
text is that Kant is not worried that sexual desire reduces its object to
something with a market price, but to something with an affective price.
This suggests two further reflections. The first is interpretive. Whatever
has a price, Kant claims, can be replaced by something else as its equivalent. This is already an odd thing to say about art objects, but it may
explain why he was driven to make the bizarre claim mentioned in note
10 above: that we do not desire another as a person but as a member of a
gender. The second is more general. Many people seem to be more skeptical about the respectability of offering yourself as a direct object of
enjoyment than about the respectability of offering your services; especially, of course, if you are a woman. Actresses, entertainers, and models
have often been regarded as disreputable characters; while cleaning la-

dies, nurses, and sales clerks are not thought thereby to degrade themselves. People may even have the obscure feeling that the character actor
is more respectable than the movie star, and in this case Kant's analysis
fits; for what the movie star offers for our delight is not her talents but
simply herself. The view, perhaps surprising but not completely at odds
with our intuitions, is then this: being useful is no threat to your dignity,
but being delectable is. I do not say this to criticize movie stars, of
course, but rather to urge that they are unusually dependent upon the
good will and delicacy of their audiences.

12 Again Kant spoils his point, by making an oddly metaphysical-sounding
argument that the lover only wants your sexuality but that "It is not
possible to have the disposal of a part only of a person without having at
the same time a right of disposal over the whole person, for each part of a
person is integrally bound up with the whole" (LE 166). But perhaps the
argument that sexual love wants its object to be entirely at its disposal
can still be made, and made on more interesting grounds than the ones
Kant appeals to here. Pursuing this line of thought might have forced
Kant to admit that the problem he is concerned with here is more of a
problem about sexual love than about casual sexual encounters.

13 It is clear from the way Kant sets the problem up in the Lectures on
Ethics that he sees the problem as arising, so to speak, from the point of
view of the sexual object (LE 164). This point should be detachable from
the familiar view, which he also sometimes seems to have in mind, that
this fact makes the morality of sexuality more of a problem for a woman.

14 In public discussions of this paper, several people pointed out that more
needs to be said about the sense in which one is restored to oneself in
these relationships. Lawful freedom is not the same as lawless freedom;
the condition to which one is restored is not the same. Kant makes this
clear in a rather forceful way when he says that marriage produces a unity
of will. The kind of reciprocity I am discussing here is not mere exchange,
from which one can walk away. What is exchanged is a part of one's
practical identity, and what results is a transformation of that identity.
Kant's account of marriage is clearly based on Rousseau's account of the
social contract, in which "each person gives himself whole and entire"
and "in giving himself to all, each person gives himself to no one. And
since there is no associate over whom he does not acquire the same right
that he would grant others over himself, he gains the equivalent of everything he loses . . . " Rousseau certainly thinks that this produces a change
of identity, since he says it is what transforms a human being from "a
stupid, limited animal into an intelligent being and a man" (Rousseau,
On the Social Contract, p. 151). This aspect of Kant's view of personal
relations has a number of striking implications, among them some that

address contemporary criticisms of Kant. From a feminist perspective, Kant has sometimes been accused of denying that personal relationships can be constitutive of identity. See for instance Sally Sedgwick, "Can Kant's Ethics Survive the Feminist Critique?" (p. 74). And it has also been argued that his ethics requires that the moral agent be completely impartial among persons in some undesirable way. See for instance, Bernard Williams, "Persons, Character and Morality" in his *Moral Luck*, chapter 1, especially pp. 16–18. In my view Kant's theory of personal relations provides grounds for challenging both of these views. I hope to pursue these points sometime.

15 Not translated in Ladd. Kant does not draw *this* conclusion, of course. But he comes close. For he goes on to raise the obvious question whether the marriages of his time, which declare the husband to be master, are real marriages, and to assert absurdly that so long as the inequality is really only based on the natural superiority of the man's faculties it is no inequality at all. Both the feebleness and the moral irrelevance of this excuse for inequality suggest the conclusion in the text.

16 In *The Possibility of Altruism*, p. 83, Thomas Nagel argues that resentment, for instance, involves the thought that the person resented had a *reason* to act differently than he did. If this is right, and personal relations essentially involve the sharing of reasons, it is clear why personal relations especially involve such reactive attitudes.

17 See Strawson, *Freedom and Resentment and Other Essays*, p. 4.

18 In his discussion of Gauguin in "Moral Luck," Bernard Williams suggests that, even if we accept Gauguin's success in painting as a justification for his desertion of his family, his family need not do so. Williams thinks that this is because you can do something justified and yet leave some people with a justified complaint. Leaving aside that question, on my view we may at least say this: given Gauguin's belief in his vocation, *we* may find his desertion of his family understandable and forgivable – just another instance of the strains which the institution of marriage places on the moral life – while *his wife* certainly need not find in this a reason for forgiveness at all. See Williams, "Moral Luck" in his *Moral Luck*, chapter 2, especially pp. 36–37.

19 There are others, of course. For instance, one who knows you well may use his knowledge to manipulate you psychologically. And there is also the simple risk that while you are opening your heart, the other is holding back. Few things are as disconcerting as the discovery that someone in whom you have confided a certain kind of secret or thought or feeling has secrets or thoughts or feelings of a similar kind, which she has not in turn shared with you. This may make you feel exposed, watched, or objectified. You do not need to think that she was spying on

or judging you in order for this to hurt; the bare failure of reciprocity is enough.

20 We must suppose this, more specifically, to avoid falling into the third antinomy (C1 A444/B472; A452/B480).

21 In this sketch of Kant's view I skate over the differences between Kant's accounts of how we arrive at the idea of our own freedom in the Third Section of the *Groundwork of the Metaphysics of Morals* and in the *Critique of Practical Reason*. In the *Groundwork*, Kant's emphasis is on our consciousness of the spontaneity of reason in the production of ideas in general; in the *Critique of Practical Reason*, it is on our awareness of the moral law and of our ability to act from it (the Fact of Reason), which he says reveals our freedom to us (see the references in the text and C2 30–31). I believe that Kant revised his argument because the spontaneous production of ideas only places us among the noumena as thinkers. To be among the noumena as *agents*, we must be able to *act from* pure ideas, and for this, the positive conception of freedom which is found only in the categorical imperative, as well as our ability to act from that conception, are necessary.

22 This account, which of course is not Kant's, resembles the more traditional rationalist account: incentives incline but do not determine the will. Kant does think that this is how we must regard our own incentives from the practical point of view.

23 It is important to say that the claim is only that it is crazy to regard *Marilyn's* noumenal will, taken by itself, as standing behind the laws of nature. Whether Kant thinks that all rational wills taken together should be regarded as standing behind the laws of nature is a different question altogether.

24 Kant's language in *Groundwork III* could certainly lead one to believe that he holds this view; and it is this same language which gives rise to the paradoxes mentioned. If we always choose morally in the noumenal world, and if our noumenal choices govern our phenomenal ones, how do bad actions ever occur? And if they do occur, since they cannot be attributed to our noumenal will, how can we be held responsible for them? It is possible that at the time of writing the *Groundwork* Kant had not sufficiently distinguished (what I take to be) his own view from the one under discussion here. I discuss this further in note 29. I discuss the paradoxes about the possibility of evil and responsibility for evil in "Morality as Freedom," Chapter 6 in this volume, especially pages 171–76.

25 The knowability of pure activity or power is an important theme in modern philosophy, taken up by thinkers as diverse as Descartes and Hume. In the *Second Meditation*, Descartes argues that although we cannot "imagine" ourselves as pure thinkers, that is the role in which

we *know* ourselves best (i.e., most free from skeptical doubt). (*Medita-tions on First Philosophy* in *The Philosophical Works of Descartes*, Vol-ume I, p. 153.) Hume, who thinks we get all of our ideas from the senses and therefore cannot have ideas of what we cannot imagine or envision, supposes that we do *not* know ourselves as active thinkers. He tells us that "The uniting principle among our internal perceptions is as unintel-ligible as that among external objects, and is not known to us any other way than by experience" (A *Treatise of Human Nature*, p. 169). But the view comes out most clearly in the *Dialogues Concerning Natural Reli-gion*, in remarks like "But the ideas in a human mind, we see, by an unknown, inexplicable economy, arrange themselves as to form the plan of a watch or a house . . . " (p. 146) and "We have indeed, experience of ideas, which fall into order, of themselves, and without any known cause . . . " (p. 162). Kant's move here as everywhere is to find a path between empiricism and rationalism, using what is right in both posi-tions. Hume is correct in tying what we can know to what can be represented. The world must show itself to us before we can apply the concepts that give us understanding. But he is wrong in thinking we can only *have ideas* of the sorts of things we can know. What we can think is not exhausted by what we can know: our concepts do not all come from sensible intuition. Descartes is right in insisting that we can *think* about our activity. But he is wrong to suppose that we *know* ourselves as thinkers and agents. Our agency, although not knowable, is *intelligible*, and we must think of it (C1 A538/B566).

26 These remarks apply to the moral law, on the practical side, and to the regulative principles of reason, on the theoretical or speculative side. Something more complex must be said about the constitutive principles of the understanding, an issue which I here leave aside.

27 Including, in the theoretical or speculative realm, deciding how to pro-ceed with our investigation or theory construction. In fact, when describ-ing and explaining our behavior we must view ourselves both ways, since we appear in the role of thinker as well as that of object thought about.

28 The reader may wonder whether I am suggesting that Kant was simply wrong in the *Groundwork* when he said that insofar as we are members of the intelligible world we necessarily will according to the moral law, and that if we were only members of that world we would will always according to that law (G 453). The answer is no, but here I think it is significant that in the *Groundwork* Kant uses the language of "intelligi-ble" and "sensible" rather than that of "noumenal" and "phenomenal"; and also that he changes his language in the *Critique of Practical Rea-son*. As I understand these terms, the noumenal world is the intelligible

world insofar as it is thinkable. If we think of noumena at all, we must think of them as acting in the only way that is intelligible to us, which is according to the laws of freedom. But at the same time we must always admit the possibility that the noumenal world is unintelligible to us. The trouble with the way Kant phrases the argument in *Groundwork III* is that it can make it sound as if the normative force of the moral law followed from its descriptive application in the noumenal world: "Consequently if I were a member of only that world [the intelligible world], all my actions *would* always be in accordance with the autonomy of the will. But since I intuit myself at the same time as a member of the world of sense, my actions *ought* to conform to it" (G 454). If we suppose, naturally but incorrectly, that the normativity of morality enters the scene with the "ought," Kant seems to be deriving a normative sensible "ought" from a descriptive intelligible "is." But he is not, for the laws of the intelligible world are normative through and through. The moral law characterizes noumena insofar as they are intelligences (insofar as we can think of them) because acting according to it is the only thing it makes sense for them to *do*; and this is already a normative point.

29 This is slightly overstated, since Kant does think that insofar as we are free we think of ourselves as the causes of our action; and this idea plays an important role in his ethics at various crucial moments. But since he insists that free causality is an idea without a theoretical employment, the point still holds (C2 49; 56; 133–36).

30 Perhaps I should make it clear that the question I am asking here concerns the way we make this decision in a case where it is *already* clear that we *can* view the creature and its actions in either of these two ways. Kant thinks we can do this whenever the actions are performed by a human being. I am not concerned here with what justifies that view – that is, I am not discussing the question why we think that human beings are candidates for being held responsible while the other intelligent animals, who make some use of reason and with whom we may enter into some forms of relationship, are not. This is an important question, but it requires a separate treatment.

31 This remark again straddles the accounts in the *Groundwork* and in the *Critique of Practical Reason*, since I think that both elements are involved in Kant's best explanation of how we come to think of our own freedom. See my "Morality as Freedom," Chapter 6 in this volume, pp. 175–76.

32 See Derek Parfit, "Later Selves and Moral Principles," pp. 145ff.; and *Reasons and Persons*, pp. 327–28.

33 I discuss the practical construction of our own identities in "Personal Identity and the Unity of Agency: A Kantian Reply to Parfit," Chapter

13 in this volume. The issue of whether relationships can be constitutive of identity is touched on in note 14 above.

34 "This commitment ['the natural human commitment to ordinary inter-personal attitudes'] is part of the general framework of human life, not something that can come up for review as particular cases come up for review within this particular framework." Strawson, "Freedom and Resentment," p. 13.

35 Kant's theory is spelled out in the "Methodologies" of the *Metaphysical Principles of Virtue* (477–84) and of the *Critique of Practical Reason* (151–63), as well as in his book *Education.*

36 Kant denies that we can have a duty to promote the moral perfection of others, on these grounds: "For the perfection of another man as a person consists precisely in his being able to set his end for himself according to his own concepts of duty. And it is a contradiction to require (to make it a duty for me) that I ought to do something which no one except another himself can do" (MPV 387). But this, again, is overstated. Granted, that it would be both disrespectful to you, and unfair to me, to hold me responsible in a general way for your moral character. Yet it is clear that we have a duty to provide for the moral education of our children, and, Kant himself insists, our intimate friends (MPV 470). Choosing ends on another's behalf is as impossible as it would be disrespectful, but putting others in a good position to choose ends for themselves, and to choose them well, is the proper work of parents, teachers, friends, and politicians; providing for someone's moral education as well as nurturing her self-respect is an important part of the way we do this.

37 Nor is Kant unaware of the more direct educational benefits of holding others responsible, for he reminds us that "Examples of respect shown to others may also incite in them an endeavor to deserve it" (MPV 466). In *Ethics and the Limits of Philosophy*, Bernard Williams writes, "The institution of blame is best understood as involving a fiction, by which we treat the agent as one for whom the relevant ethical considerations are reasons. . . . This fiction has various functions. One is that if we treat the agent as someone who gives weight to ethical reasons, this may help to make him into such a person" (p. 193). It is presumably this form of "recruitment into the deliberative community," to use Williams's phrase, that he has in mind when he writes "The purity of morality conceals not only the means by which it deals with deviant members of its community, but also the virtues of those means" (p. 195). Williams thinks that "the fiction of the deliberative community is one of the positive achievements of the morality system" but adds "As with other fictions it is a real question whether its working could survive a clear understanding of how it works" (193–94). I want to make two com-

ments about these remarks. First, the view of persons we adopt from the practical point of view will seem "fictional" (if that is supposed to suggest some form of inferiority) only to those who privilege the theoretical standpoint and its concepts, or at least believe that all our concepts should be congruent with those. This suggests a certain view of what concepts in general are for. No doubt theoretical concepts are more firmly aimed at tracking the truth, but tracking the truth is not the primary business of ethical concepts, as Williams would certainly agree. In any case the term "fiction" is one adopted from the theoretical standpoint, and relativized in an obvious way to the purposes of theoretical reason. My second point concerns recruitment into the deliberative community. Kant himself apparently thought that we *can* understand how holding people responsible works – and even, as the quotation above suggests, that we can take notice of its more strategic benefits – and yet go on doing it. Of course it is a delicate business to manipulate someone into morality while maintaining the essentially non-manipulative attitude that morality demands. But, as Kant's remarks about error at MPV 463 (quoted in Section V) show, he rightly perceives this to be a quite general problem about education.

PART TWO

Comparative essays

8 Aristotle and Kant on the source of value

THREE KINDS OF VALUE THEORY

In this paper I discuss what I will call a "rationalist" account of the goodness of ends. I begin by contrasting the rationalist account to two others, "subjectivism" and "objectivism." Subjectivism identifies good ends with or by reference to some psychological state. It includes the various forms of hedonism as well as theories according to which what is good is any object of interest or desire. Objectivism may be represented by the theory of G. E. Moore. According to Moore, to say that something is good as an end is to attribute a property, intrinsic goodness, to it. Intrinsic goodness is an objective, nonrelational property of the object, a value a thing has independently of anyone's desires, interests, or pleasures.

The attraction of subjectivist views is that they acknowledge the connection of the good to human interests and desires. Most things that are good are good because of the interest human beings have in them, an interest that can be explained in terms of the physiological and psychological constitutions of human beings and the other conditions of human life. In Kantian language, we may say that just as means are "conditioned" goods because their value depends on the ends to which they are means, most of our ends are conditioned goods because their value depends on the conditions of human existence, and the needs and desires to which those conditions give rise. Objectivism reverses this relation between goodness and human interest. Instead of saying that what we are interested in is therefore good, the objectivist says that the goodness is in the object, and we ought therefore to be interested in it. This divorce of goodness from natural interest can make it seem too accidental that we are able to care about the things that are intrinsically good.

The advantage of objectivism is that it explains certain of our beliefs about the good that a subjectivist account cannot readily accommodate. We believe that people sometimes fail to care about what is good and sometimes have interests in or desires for things that are not good. Yet in subjectivist theories it seems as if anything one enjoys or desires is good at least ceteris paribus, and anything one does not enjoy or desire is not. A theory of intrinsic values allows us to make sense of beliefs such as that something may be good as an end even though a person gets no pleasure from it, or that a malicious pleasure may be intrinsically bad.

The rationalist theory may be seen as an attempt to combine these advantages. According to this view, an object or state of affairs is good if there is a sufficient practical reason for realizing it or bringing it about. The prima facie reason for it will be, as in subjectivist accounts, a reason springing from our nature, conditions, needs, and desires. The account must then provide a test for the sufficiency of this reason. Since not every such reason will turn out to be a sufficient one, not every interest or pleasure will establish the goodness of its object. The beliefs that motivate objectivism can be explained, but in a different way. The objectivist accounts for our failures of appropriate attachment to the good by cutting the tie between natural interest and the good in the first place. The rationalist accounts for these failures by appeal to the imperfect rationality of human beings. We sometimes fail to be motivated by reasons that are available to us and so do not want what is good. We sometimes are motivated by insufficient reasons and so want what is not good.

For the rationalist view what is required is some sort of test of the sufficiency of the reasons for the adoption of an end. It is important to emphasize that the three theories are being compared with respect to their assessments of single goods, or it will be hard to see what distinguishes the rationalist view. The subjectivist may of course say that a given pleasure – say, a malicious one – should not be brought about because of the pain that it causes to others. And an objectivist may say of some intrinsic good that it should not be realized because there are better things we can do. In these cases both the subjectivist and the objectivist may say that there is not a sufficient reason for the existence of some prima facie good. One may think of this as a *negative* test of sufficiency: the fact that something is pleasant or desired or intrinsically good is a sufficient reason for it as long as there is no extrinsic reason why not. By contrast, the rationalist account seeks a *positive* test of sufficiency and seeks this even for conditional goods taken singly. The rationalist thinks that if an object of pleasure or desire is only conditionally good in the first instance, then the fact that it does not interfere with other conditional goods is not sufficient to make it absolutely good.

This thought commits the rationalist to an extensive view of what practical reasoning consists in. Both the objectivist theory of intrinsic value and the subjectivist theories are characteristically associated with an empiricist view about the scope of practical reasoning: that it is primarily concerned with the means to preestablished ends.[1] Ends are marked out for us by something other than reasoning – our interests or their intrinsic value. If these ends are regarded as commensurable and the goal is to maximize the good, practical reasoning is all instrumental in form. If they are not commensurable, there will be another use for practical reasoning in combining and harmonizing various ends into the best compossible set. The rationalist is committed to a more extensive view of the scope of practical reasons since the test of the sufficiency of reasons will be a way of rationally assessing ends. An end provides the justification of the means; the means are good if the end is good. If the end is only conditionally good, it in turn must be justified. Justification, like explanation, seems to give rise to an indefinite regress; for any reason offered, we can always ask why. If complete justification of an end is to be possible, something must bring this regress to a stop; there must be something about which it is impossible or unnecessary to ask why. This will be something unconditionally good. Since what is unconditionally good will serve as the condition of the value of other good things, it will be the source of value. Practical reason, then, has the noninstrumental tasks of establishing what is unconditionally good and, in light of that, establishing whether particular conditional goods stand in the right relation to it and so really are fully justified.

What is unconditionally good is like what is intrinsically good in that it is objectively valuable, but there is an important difference.

Moore and other proponents of intrinsic values have thought that one cannot argue for them; they must be known through intuition. But you can argue about what is unconditionally valuable. The reason that there must be something that is unconditionally valuable is that there must be a source of value. Arguments about what is unconditionally valuable can proceed in terms of questions about what is suitable to be a source of value; only certain sorts of values are able to play this role.

In the rest of this paper I examine, or rather construct, such an argument. So far, the terms in which I have sketched the rationalist account are borrowed from Kant. In the next section, I argue that Aristotle's position on the superiority of the contemplative over the political life is also motivated by the rationalist conception of the good. Contemplation is the best activity because it can play the role of a source of value: it justifies other things. The effect of this way of looking at Aristotle's argument is to assign to contemplation the same role that Kant assigns to the good will. In the third section, I sketch the arguments Kant uses to establish that this role must be played by a good will. Finally, in the last section, I take up the question of why these two philosophers picked such different candidates for the source of value. What makes this interesting is not only the fact that they identify different things as unconditionally good, but that each philosopher comes close to denying that the other's candidate could be the source of value. Aristotle's argument implies that moral virtue could not be unconditionally good and so cannot be the source of value. Kant says explicitly that contemplation cannot.

ARISTOTLE: CONTEMPLATIVE ACTIVITY AS THE SOURCE OF VALUE

In 1.5 of the *Nicomachean Ethics*, Aristotle observes that there are three types of life thought to be happy: the life of enjoyment, the political life, and the life of contemplation. The life of enjoyment is a hedonistic life focused on conventional pleasures. The political life is the life of a statesperson. It may aim at despotic power, or be lived for the sake of winning public honors, but in its most proper form its aim is the exercise of moral virtue and political and practical wisdom in the governing of the state. The contemplative life, speaking generally, is the life of the philosopher or student of nature. But it is an important part of Aristotle's argument that the aim of this life is a quite particular activity. Contemplation, as Aristotle understands it, is not research or inquiry, but an activity that ensues on these: an activity that consists in understanding. We have understanding of something when we have grasped its essence – its nature, function, characteristic activity, and final purpose – and see how its other universal properties arise from its essence. The best objects of contemplation are God (the final purpose of the world) and the heavens. Aristotle also believes that what God does is to contemplate and that since God is the best thing, God must contemplate God. God is the activity of thinking on thinking and the aim of the contemplative life is to engage in this divine activity.[2]

Aristotle's own definition of happiness is that it is an activity of soul which follows or implies a rational principle, in accordance with excellence (1.7). In book 1, Aristotle tests this definition against some criteria which he believes any account of happiness or the good must meet. The good must be self-sufficient and final (1.7), it must consist in activity (1.5), and it must be pleasant (1.8). In book 10, Aristotle turns once more to the three kinds of life, to see which of them are happy. He does this by testing them against the criteria he used before – self-sufficiency, finality, pleasantness, and activity – as well as against his own definition from book 1. The result of this investigation is that the contemplative life is judged happiest, mainly on the grounds that contemplation is the only activity that is loved for itself alone (10.7). The political life is judged to be happy "in a secondary degree" (10.8) and the life of enjoyment is dismissed on the grounds that relaxation is "not an end" (10.6). These claims are surprising, for Aristotle has already argued that morally virtuous actions *are* done for their own sake by a virtuous person, and that pleasant amusements are engaged in for their own sake and are ends seems obvious.

In the next two sections, I examine the way two of Aristotle's criteria – finality and activity – can be used to establish the unconditional value of contemplation. Aristotle is not denying that either morally virtuous actions or amusements are ends. What he is arguing is rather that contemplation is an end in a special sense. It is unconditionally good and serves as a source of value for these other ends.

Finality

One of Aristotle's central arguments for the contemplative life rests on the claim that happiness must be a good that is final without qualification and that this is true only of contemplation, not of political activity. The argument depends on a proper understanding of the notion of finality. In book 1, Aristotle explains the notion this way:

Since there are evidently more than one end, and we choose some of these (e.g. wealth, flutes, and in general instruments) for the sake of something else, clearly not all ends are final ends; but the chief good is evidently something final. . . . Now we call that which is in itself worthy of pursuit more final than that which is worthy of pursuit for the sake of something else, and that which is never desirable for the sake of something else more final than the things that are desirable both in themselves and for the sake of that other thing, and therefore we call final without qualification that which is always desirable in itself and never for the sake of something else. (1.7.1097a)

The most natural way to read this passage is this: (1) by ends which are chosen for the sake of something else Aristotle intends what we would call means; (2) by ends which are desirable both in themselves and for the sake of something else Aristotle intends things that are both means and ends; and (3) by what is final without qualification Aristotle intends something that is an end but never a means.

The difficulty with this reading, however, is that it makes what Aristotle says absurd. Why should something be more valuable (and more final clearly does mean more valuable to Aristotle) just because it is useless? It is instructive to compare the passage in the *Republic* where a similar threefold classification is made. "In which of these classes do you place justice?" asks Glaucon. And Socrates replies, "It belongs in the fairest class, that which a man who is to be happy must love both for its own sake and for the results."[3] This seems more like what we should expect once the threefold classification is made – that the middle class is "fairest."

Aristotle points out that happiness is valuable in the way of things final without qualification, since "for this we choose always for itself and never for the sake of something else, but honour, pleasure, reason, and every virtue we choose indeed for themselves (for if nothing resulted from them we should still choose each of them), but we choose them also for the sake of happiness, judging that through them we shall be happy" (1.7.1097a–b). Soon after, Aristotle asserts that happiness must be self-sufficient in the sense that it cannot be increased by other goods. These remarks together have motivated some to take an "inclusive-end"[4] view of what Aristotle means by final without qualification. If happiness is a higher-order end, a coherent and efficient plan for realizing one's other ends, both remarks are explained. It cannot be increased by other goods because it by definition includes all that can be compossibly realized. And the threefold classification is now understood to be means, ends, and the higher-order inclusive end. Items in the middle category are both ends and means in the sense that they are valued both for their own sake and as constituents of the higher-order end. On this reading, Aristotle thinks that ends are justified by membership in a best compossible set.

The difficulty with this way of reading the threefold classification is that in book 10 Aristotle puts the classification to work on the three kinds of life in a way that seems to fit the simple reading (means, ends plus means, ends only) better than the inclusive-end reading. For contemplative activity, which is clearly not an inclusive end, is ranked above "practical activities" because they are also useful: "This activity alone would seem to be loved for its own sake; for nothing arises from it apart from the contemplating, while from practical activities we gain more or less apart from the action" (10.7.1177b). Thus we seem caught between a reading of the threefold classification which makes Aristotle wrong – the uselessness of contemplation is not a good reason for identifying it with happiness – and a reading which makes sense of the idea that what is final without qualification is best but which does not fit the use that Aristotle makes of the threefold classification in book 10.

If we suppose that Aristotle is giving a rationalist account of the good, his three categories are means, conditional ends, and unconditional ends. Conditional ends, for Aristotle, are ends valued for their own sake, given that we are human beings living in human conditions – among friends, in the city, with a nature both animal and rational to cope with. They "befit our human estate" (10.8.1178a, p. 266). The unconditional end plays a different role: it is what makes it worth it to be a human being and to live in human conditions. Although I will argue that the passages about ends in the *Nicomachean Ethics* are consistent with this reading, nothing in that work so decisively favors it as these remarks from *Eudemian Ethics* 1.5:

After all, many things that happen are such as to induce people to abandon life – disease, extremes of pain, storms, for example; *so that it is evident that on account of those things at any rate, it would, given the choice, have been worth choosing not to be born in the first place.* . . . In general, if we put together all the things that everyone does or undergoes, but not voluntarily (because they are not done or undergone for their own sake), . . . *no one would choose in order to have them to be alive, rather than not.* Nor again would anyone who was not a complete slave prefer to live solely for the pleasure associated with nutrition and sex. . . .

They say that Anaxagoras, when someone raised just these puzzles and asked him *what it was for which a person would choose to be born rather than not,* answered that it would be in order to apprehend the heavens and the order in the whole universe.[5]

In this passage it is quite clear that whatever is to play the role of happiness must be something that makes human life worthy of choice.

If we suppose that Aristotle distinguishes between the unconditional ends for which we would choose life and conditional ends which we choose given that we are alive but for which we would not choose life, I believe we can arrive at a more natural reading of the puzzling things Aristotle says about ends whenever he discusses the three lives. It will be the mark of a conditional end that it is also a means. But this "also" is not merely conjunctive; rather, its being a "means" or constituent of a worthwhile life will be what makes it possible to choose it as an end. The fact that something plays a certain instrumental or constitutive role in human life makes it worthy of choice. Its instrumentality may be regarded as essential to what it is; this is true of artifacts which are made for certain purposes and for activities understood as instances of, say, "recreation" or "exercise." When something which is essentially an instrumental or a constitutive activity is also interesting or beautiful or pleasant it may be chosen as an end under the condition of its utility.

I believe that this is how Aristotle regards amusements and conventional pleasures. When he is dismissing the life of amusements in 10.6, Aristotle says:

Happiness, therefore, does not lie in amusement; it would, indeed, be strange if the end were amusement, and one were to take trouble and suffer hardship all one's life in order to amuse oneself. For, in a word, everything that we choose we choose for the sake of something else – except happiness, which is an end. Now to exert oneself and work for the sake of amusement seems silly and utterly childish. But to amuse oneself in order that one may exert oneself, as Anacharsis puts it, seems right; for amusement is a sort of relaxation, and we need relaxation because we cannot work continuously. Relaxation, then, is not an end; for it is taken for the sake of activity. (10.6.1176b)

We cannot plausibly think that Aristotle is declaring amusement to be a mere means. It is absurd to suppose that if you read detective stories in the evening in order to relax, you do it in the same instrumental spirit in which you go to the dentist for repairs on your teeth. Given that you are a human being, and so cannot work continuously, and are capable of taking pleasure in reading detective stories, you do it for its own sake – that is, for the pleasure of it. But you would not choose to be a human being or "to take trouble and suffer hardship all your life" in order to read detective stories. Amusements have a place in human life because human beings need relaxation. But that place is not the center; the happy person does not live for them.[6]

Now something like this point can also be made about the political life, but this requires some care. For the political life is not, like the life of amusements, a mistake. Virtuous actions are done by the virtuous person for their own sake. The political life fits Aristotle's definition and meets the criteria for a happy life. But while the political life can be final for the individual, in a sense it cannot be final for the city. What Aristotle says about pleasant amusements for the individual can be said about virtuous actions for the city: that they play a necessary role, but that role cannot be the center.

And happiness is thought to depend on leisure; for we are busy that we may have leisure, and make war that we may live in peace. Now the activity of the practical virtues is exhibited in political or military affairs, but the actions concerned with these seems to be unleisurely. Warlike actions are completely so (for no one chooses to be at war, or provokes war, for the sake of being at war; anyone would seem absolutely murderous if he were to make enemies of his friends in order to bring about battle and slaughter); but the action of the statesman also is unleisurely, and aims – beyond the political action itself – at despotic power and honours, or at all events happiness, for him and his fellow citizens – a happiness different from political action, and evidently sought as being different. (10.7.1177b)

Political activity aims at setting up a context in which people can be happy. The statesperson makes laws and establishes conditions in which the citizens can have a good life; a life that will not consist of making laws and establishing conditions but, rather, of something else. And this something else will therefore be a more final good, for it will be what gives political activity its point. If we take a broader interpretation of the political life and include in it other forms of community service, the point still holds. The doctor cures people so that they may have the health that makes a good life possible. Imagine that the *only* good life is the life of a doctor. Then if the doctor were successful and everyone were healthy, there would be no point to life. In general, morally virtuous activity of the sort characteristic of a political life aims at the establishment of conditions for a good life and therefore cannot itself be the only good life or the most final.

It is clear that Aristotle thinks that the exercise of the moral virtues in a morally motivated project can be the final good of an individual's life. One can center one's life around, say, justice in fighting for oppressed people or courage in a military life or political and practical wisdom in making laws for the city. For an individual such an activity is a final good, for the virtuous person does these things for their own sake. But this sort of life of the moral virtues is conditional in a particular way, namely, on something's being wrong or imperfect. Engaging in politics is choiceworthy because there are injustices to put right, and being a soldier is choiceworthy because there are wars to be fought, and being a doctor is choiceworthy because illness is a recurrent flaw in human life and so on. But it would be better if life did not have these limitations and defects. Imagine that it doesn't: some Solon has made laws that deliver us from poverty, injustice, and inequality; medical science has taught us all to be healthy through simple daily dietary and exercise routines, and so forth. What in these idyllic conditions will make life worth choosing? A certain amount of business must be done in order to provide goods and services for the citizens, but these must be *for* something. And we may imagine that the people have a lot of leisure. What will they do with it? Will they now devote themselves to conventional amusements? These have already been dismissed as insufficient to make life worth living. Will morally virtuous actions give their life meaning? They will still need the moral virtues in an everyday way. They will need everyday justice to keep their promises and contracts and to return services. They will need the social graces of wit and friendliness in their dealings with one another. They will need temperance. But being just, friendly, and temperate in these ways cannot be the final goods or central activities of human life. Certainly, one would not choose a human life or choose to be a human being in order to keep one's promises and to exercise temperance. Even if one does do these things for their own sake, they are not final goods.

The value of the political life is conditioned by the limitations and defects of human life, just as the value of amusements is conditioned by the need for relaxation. Just as you would not choose to be a human being in order to do something that only makes sense because human beings need relaxation, so you could not choose to be a human being merely in order to overcome the defects and limitations of human life. Aristotle therefore looks for an activity that would make life worth living even if life had no defects and limitations to overcome – and so which makes them worth overcoming. This activity will be one whose value is unconditional. The mark of this will be that we do not gain anything apart from doing it.

It is to secure this unconditional character for happiness that Aristotle raises the question of how the gods spend their time. For the gods live a life that has no limitations and defects to overcome, and so the value of their activity cannot be in that way conditioned.

We assume the gods to be above all other beings blessed and happy; but what sort of actions must we assign to them? Acts of justice? Will not the gods seem absurd if they make contracts and return deposits, and so on? Acts of a brave man, then, confronting dangers and running risks because it is noble to do so? Or liberal acts? To whom will they give? It will be strange if they are really to have money or anything of the kind. And what would their temperate acts be? Is not such praise tasteless, since they have no bad appetites? If we were to run through them all, the circumstances of action would be found trivial and unworthy of gods. Still everyone supposes that they *live* and therefore that they are active; we cannot suppose them to sleep like Endymion. Now if you take away from a living being action, and still more production, what is left but contemplation? (10.8.1178b)

Without needs, fears, or bad appetites, a god could not make a life of overcoming limitations. What a god does must be something that is valuable just for the doing of it. If being human makes it possible to engage in such an activity, then there is a reason for being human: something that makes life worthy of choice. It is such an activity that Aristotle identifies as happiness and as the source of the value of the other ends of human life.

Activity

The distinction between conditional and unconditional ends as it functions in Aristotle can be illuminated by a distinction borrowed from Aristotle's metaphysics: that of process (*kinesis*) versus activity (*energeia*).[7] A process gets something done or effects a change, and it has a natural termination point: when the thing is done or the change effected. An action (as opposed to an activity) is a kind of process. An activity is a doing for its own sake. It is not (qua activity) an attempt to get anything done because it is its own end. Aristotle gives us various criteria for distinguishing activities and processes. An activity, Aristotle says, is complete at every moment, so that we can apply to it the following criterion: at every moment one Xs and has Xd. A process can be done quickly or slowly; in a sense an activity cannot. A process is done for the sake of its termination, for the sake of what one gets done; and an activity is done for its own sake. An example of a process is building a house. This is an attempt to get something done – to get a house built. It has a natural termination point – when the house is built. It is not complete at every moment: one cannot say that at every moment of building that one is building a house and one has built a house, because one cannot say one has built the house until it is over. One can build a house quickly or slowly. One does not build a house for its own sake; one does it in order to get the house. One of Aristotle's examples of an activity is seeing: at every moment one sees and has seen; one cannot see quickly or slowly; it is not an attempt to get something done, occupying a certain space of time and having a definite termination. Hence, seeing is the sort of thing that might be done for its own sake.

Confusion will be avoided if we keep in mind the following facts. First, the same physical movements will often be both process and activity, so that the difference is a matter of description. But this by no means trivializes the distinction, for the difference in description will be motivationally and rationally pertinent. Take walking. "Walking" is the name of a physical business, and one that can be involved in either processes or activities. Walking-to-the-bank is a process. It has a definite termination – arriving at the bank. It has a purpose outside of itself: being at the bank, so that I can make a transaction. It can be done quickly or slowly. I cannot say at every moment that I am walking-to-the-bank and that I have walked-to-the-bank: I can only say that I *have* walked-to-the-bank when I have arrived. Compare this to "taking-a-walk." Taking-a-walk is an activity. It does not have, in itself, a definite termination. I can, of course, facilitate my walk-taking by setting myself a termination, but this is a device. If when I get there I decide to go further, I am still taking-a-walk. On the other hand, if I am walking-to-the-bank and when I get there, decide to go farther, I am no longer walking-to-the-bank but now am just taking-a-walk. It is true at every moment that I am taking-a-walk and I have been taking-a-walk and almost whenever I stop I will have taken-a-walk. Furthermore, I can walk quickly or slowly while taking-a-walk, but I cannot take-a-walk quickly or slowly. (If I schedule a walk daily and usually spend an hour at it, and today being pressed for time I only spend half an hour, I might say that I took my walk quickly today. But this is a rather special circumstance and requires an explanation such as I have given: you would only say that you took your walk quickly today to someone who knew of your usual schedule.) Taking-a-walk is not done merely for the sake of the end result, but for its own sake; it is a pleasure.[8]

The second thing to keep in mind is that performing a certain process can be an activity. The notion of activity, *energeia*, is closely associated with the notion of *ergon*, function. In one of its uses, a function is one's work. Thus, although building a house is itself a *kinesis* or process, performing this process is the *ergon*, and so the *energeia*, of an architect. House building is what she does. Let us suppose that she does not do it in a bored and grudging manner and just for the money, but that she loves it, exercises artistic taste and engineering skill, and derives satisfaction from constructing a dwelling perfectly suited to her clients' needs. She does not do it just for the sake of the house (although the house gives the activity its point), for as soon as she finishes one she starts another, and – this is an important mark of an activity – she seeks the occasions (within decent limitations) of house building.

There are several important points to make about this. First, an activity is, ontologically speaking, the only thing that is appropriate to play the role of a final good.⁹ An action or process is not because an action or process is by its nature the sort of thing that is for the sake of something else, for the sake of the change effected or the product produced. If it aims at a product, the pertinent question is what it is good for. If it aims at producing a state or condition, the same question can be raised; life is activity, and being healthy or virtuous is pointless if one is going to sleep forever. Thus an activity, done for its own sake, is the appropriate sort of thing to be a final good, and to play the role of what ultimately justifies other things.¹⁰

As the case of the architect shows, however, this does not mean that something which is in itself a process cannot be an *individual's* final good. One can make a certain process one's activity. And this is in a sense what Aristotle envisions for the political life. For moral actions are in a sense processes: they have an aim outside themselves, and their occasions should not be created, though the political person seeks them. As long as there is occasion for them, however, they can be the activity of someone's life, just as architecture can, as long as there is a need for houses. But just as the architect's life and activity are only possible as long as someone – not necessarily the architect herself – needs and will enjoy the house, so the statesperson's life and activity are only possible as long as someone – the citizens – enjoy the benefits in the form of a different sort of happiness. And in general, for any activity that is also a process there will be this dependence: the possibility of its being an activity will depend upon someone's benefiting from the results of the process.

A process that is also an activity is a conditional end. Its being a process is what makes it conditional: it depends for its value on the value of its result or product. Its being an activity is what makes it an end. If it calls upon the resources of one's talents and virtues, exercises one's faculties, is pleasurable and impeded only by a (usually inoperative) factor of limited occasion or opportunity, then it can be the final good of someone's life. Of course most of the things that human beings do with themselves are of this nature. There are not very many "pure" activities – activities that are not also processes. But Aristotle thinks that there must be at least one. For the

results of any process (including the ones people make activities of)
must in turn be justified by the role that they play in some other
activity. Every justification must refer eventually to an activity. This
means that ultimately, if justification is to be complete, there must
be a pure activity, one that is not also a process. Now this is what
Aristotle thinks contemplation is: it is the purest of all activities.
For contemplation is not research but the exercise of the understanding; it does not involve change[11] or the overcoming of any limitation;
its occasions are inherently unlimited. It is because contemplation
is an activity that is not also a process that Aristotle identifies it as
the most final good. The structure of justification requires that ultimately all value must be traced to a pure activity. Only a pure
activity can be unconditionally good. Since Aristotle thinks that
contemplation is the only such activity, he thinks that it is the
source of value.

KANT: THE GOOD WILL AS THE SOURCE OF VALUE

The *Groundwork* opens with the claim that the only thing that can
be found anywhere of unconditional value is a good will. As Kant
envisions the structure of justification, the goodness of means is
conditioned by the goodness of the ends which they serve; the goodness of those ends which are not morally obligatory is conditioned
by their contribution to happiness, and the goodness of happiness is
conditioned by the possession of a good will, which "seems to constitute the indispensable condition even of worthiness to be happy" (G
393). Since a good will is the only unconditionally good thing, everything else must ultimately trace its justification to this: virtues such
as intelligence or calmness must be directed by it, happiness must
be deserved by it, particular ends must be chosen in accordance with
it. The good will is the source of value, and without it, nothing
would have any real worth.

As we saw, Aristotle's arguments that contemplation is the most
final good can be construed as being based on the claim that only
contemplation can serve as a source of value. To confer value on
other things, and so to justify them completely, the final good must
be something that makes human life worthy of choice and it must
be a pure activity. Contemplation is the final good and source of
value because it meets these conditions. In a similar fashion, Kant

will argue that the good will is unconditionally good because it is the only thing able to be a source of value. In order to follow this argument, it is necessary to keep in mind that on Kant's view a good will is a perfectly rational will. The argument is essentially that only human reason is in a position to confer value on the objects of human choice.

The point is made in both the *Groundwork* in the argument leading to the Formula of Humanity and in chapter 2 of the *Critique of Practical Reason*. In the *Groundwork*, Kant begins from the fact that, if there is a categorical imperative, then there must be something of unconditional value. For, if there is a categorical imperative, then there are actions dictated by pure reason, and the ends of these actions will be completely justified. It must be possible to formulate the moral law in terms of whatever the source of this justification is. Kant argues that only our humanity, or rational nature, can play this role. The objects of inclination have only a conditioned value, he says, for their worth depends on the inclinations themselves (the things we desire are good because we desire them, not the reverse). The inclinations, however, cannot confer value on their objects, for they are not themselves unconditionally valuable. Kant says that since they are sources of needs it would be better to be rid of them altogether, but it is sufficient for his point that they are not a sufficient condition for the goodness of their objects. The existence of an inclination is not enough to make its object good, for the inclination itself may be bad. Other things in nature are only means. But rational nature is an end in itself, for "man necessarily thinks of his own existence in this way; thus far it is a subjective principle of human actions. Also every other rational being thinks of his existence by means of the same rational ground which holds also for myself; [note] thus it is at the same time an object principle from which, as a supreme practical ground, it must be possible to derive all laws of the will" (G 429). The note refers us to the third section: the argument is that we necessarily think of our own existence as able to confer value on our ends because we necessarily think of ourselves as autonomous and so of our ends as freely and rationally chosen. Nothing else justifies our ends and actions; it is our rational autonomy itself that does so. The argument is in a simple sense transcendental: we regard some of our ends as good, even though they are obviously conditional; there must be a condition of their goodness, a source of their value; we regard them as good whenever they are chosen with full rational autonomy; so full rational autonomy itself is the source of their value. Since this holds for other rational beings as well as myself, I cannot act against their rational autonomy without violating my own; and so it turns out to be a good will that is the source of all value.

In the *Critique of Practical Reason*, Kant claims that good is a rational concept. This means that if ends are to be good, they must be determined by reason, not merely inclination or pleasantness; if ends were determined by pleasantness, only means could be called "good" since only they would be determined by reason (C2 62). It also means that "what we call good must be, in the judgment of every reasonable man, an object of the faculty of desire" (C2 60). Thus the reasons for "calling" a thing good must be universalizable. The sufficiency of a reason is tested by its universalizability. Behind the assumption that if every rational being could acknowledge something to be good (the reason for it is universalizable) then it is indeed good (the reason for it is sufficient) is the idea that it is rational beings who determine what is good; rational nature confers value on the objects of its choices and is itself the source of all value.[12]

In Aristotle, the question of what the final good is has a metaphysical as well as an ethical significance: contemplation is the final purpose not only of human life but also of the world. Kant makes an argument that is similar but in a way reverses the order in which these points are established. The final purpose for human beings must also be regarded as the final purpose of the world. Since whatever is chosen with a good will is good, we can construct the ideal of a totality of all good things. In the *Groundwork* this is the Kingdom of Ends: "A whole of rational beings as ends in themselves as well as of the particular ends which each may set for himself" (G 433). In the *Critique of Practical Reason* it is the Highest Good, "the unconditioned totality of the object of pure practical reason" (C2 108), virtue and the happiness merited by it for every rational being. This turns out to be the final purpose of the world as well as the good for humanity.

Theoretical reason, like practical reason, seeks the unconditioned: it keeps asking why until explanation is complete. Such complete explanation cannot be given in terms of mechanical laws, for even if we could explain everything in nature in terms of some set of mechanical laws, there would be no answer to the question why the world is organized according to these laws rather than some other set. For unconditional explanation we would need a teleological system of the world, in which every event and thing could be explained, justified, and fully comprehended in terms of some final purpose, to the realization of which everything else would be organized. This final purpose would have to be something unconditionally good: something for the sake of which nature might have been created. Of course, according to Kant we cannot have a metaphysical or teleological system of the world with the status of knowledge. We can and should think of the world in this way, using teleological concepts as tools of reflection, but we can have no knowledge that there is a God who created the world for the sake of some end. The rational ideal of the full and unconditional explanation of things cannot be realized; it is beyond the limits of our finitude and sensible nature. Yet we can say what would realize the speculative ideal of reason. It would be knowledge of the world as a Kingdom of Ends: "Teleology considers nature as a kingdom of ends; morals regards a possible kingdom of ends as a kingdom of nature. In the first case the kingdom of ends is a theoretical idea for explaining what exists. In the latter it is a practical idea for bringing about what does not exist but can be made actual by our conduct, i.e., what can be actualized in accordance with this very idea" (G 436n.).

The same ideal governs reason in theory and practice, that of a system of purposes. Such a system requires a final purpose. For practical reason, this is the good will. In the *Critique of Teleological Judgment* Kant argues that this is also the only possible candidate for the final purpose of a teleological system of nature. The only possible end of creation – if the world were known to be a purposive creation – would be humanity under moral laws. Kant begins by identifying human life as the purpose of the teleological organization of nature. If nature exists to set the stage for human life, then we must seek the justification of nature in some value realized by human life:

Without men the whole creation would be mere waste, in vain, and without final purpose. But it is not in reference to man's cognitive faculty (theoretical reason) that the being of everything else in the world gets its worth; he is not there merely that there may be someone to *contemplate* the world. For if the contemplation of the world only afforded a representation of things without any final purpose, no worth could accrue to its being from the mere

fact that it is known; we must presuppose for it a final purpose, in reference
to which its contemplation itself has worth. Again it is not in reference to
the feeling of pleasure or to the sum of pleasures that we think a final
purpose of creation is given. . . . It is that worth which [man] alone can give
to himself and which consists in what he does, how and according to what
principles he acts. . . . That is, a good will is that whereby alone his being
can have an absolute worth and in reference to which the being of the world
can have a *final purpose*. (C3 442–43)

Speculative and practical reason are linked in that their ultimate
ideal, their conception of a rationally intelligible world, is of a system of purposes organized around free rational beings taken as the
final purpose of the system, a Kingdom of Ends. But while speculative reason hopes vainly to discover or prove that this ideal of reason
is already realized in the world, practical reason – or morality – is
the attempt to impose this ideal on action and on the world insofar
as action shapes the world. We cannot prove that the standards of
reason are met by the world as it is in itself and independently of our
own impositions. But there is no bar to our organizing our own lives,
our actions, and our characters so that they will accord with the
standards of reason. Morality replaces metaphysics as the highest
expression of our rational nature. For Kant, this makes the good will,
rather than contemplative activity, the source of value.

ARISTOTLE AND KANT ON THE SOURCE OF VALUE

Aristotle and Kant agree that there are many things that are worthy
of choice as ends given that one is a human being with a certain
physical and psychological constitution, and with certain needs
and capacities for enjoyment as a result. They also agree that these
are conditional goods and that rationality demands more. These
values of a human life are only really worth pursuing if something
makes a human life worth living. Both look for something that
human beings can do that gives a point to being human. Both
believe that practical reason at once demands a deeper justification
for human existence and teaches us what will satisfy that demand.
Furthermore, both are led to seek what is unconditionally good in
the thought of what might be a final purpose for God, whose
choices and activities are not determined by any limiting condition. Aristotle thinks that God contemplates, while Kant thinks

that if God exists he must be conceived as bringing into being the Highest Good or Kingdom of Ends.

The similarities make the differences more striking. Why exactly do the two philosophers disagree? We have already seen why Aristotle puts the political life in second place: moral actions are processes with results, and we gain apart from them; it is only because of this gain that it makes sense to devote your life to them. Indeed the life of the statesperson may in some respects be better than the life of the contemplator but only because "though it is worth while to attain the end merely for one man, it is finer and more godlike to attain it for a nation or for city-states" (1.2.1094b). Thus for Aristotle, morality is not the final good because it has an object beyond itself. We might be tempted to oppose to this Kant's remarks, in the opening of the *Groundwork*, that the good will's goodness is independent of what it effects or accomplishes, and his view that neither the actual success of our efforts, nor the purpose for which we act, but only the grounds on which we choose our actions and purposes, matter to moral worth. But Aristotle denies none of this. His virtuous person does virtuous actions for their own sake and for the sake of the noble, and because they are directed by right reason. It is also important that Kant does not dismiss considerations of what is to be achieved by morality as irrelevant. The doctrine of practical religious faith is motivated by the fact that the virtuous person needs to believe that the ends that morality sets before her may be achieved through her efforts. The moral law makes the highest good our end and is threatened if the highest good is impossible to attain. This is not because of our private interest in our own happiness, but because the motivating thought of morality is the thought that autonomy means that one can make a difference – one is not just part of the causal chain but may help to bring about the highest good. Both philosophers believe that a good person does moral actions for their own sake – neither thinks this means it is unimportant whether they achieve the ends they aim at.

Kant has two kinds of argument against the unconditional value of contemplation. One is presented in the quotation from the *Critique of Judgment* given above. The world must have a final purpose in order to be worth contemplating, so contemplation cannot be that final purpose. The reply that Aristotle could give might seem convoluted. We contemplate God; yet God is also a contemplator – and what God contemplates is God, for God is thinking on thinking. Thus to the charge that contemplation cannot be the final purpose because the world needs a final purpose in order to be worth contemplating, the answer would be both that the world has a final purpose and is worth contemplating, and that contemplation is that final purpose. The conception may be alien to us, but the main idea is still clear: Aristotle thinks that we can participate in the final purpose of the world through contemplative activity.

And contemplation in this sense is not strictly speaking possible on Kant's view. For it involves a grasp of the teleological order of things and a participation in it through knowledge, through the theoretical faculty. But for Kant, scientific knowledge associated with this kind of understanding does not exist; teleological thinking is not knowledge, and such grounding as it has lies in practical religious faith and so in ethics. We cannot, through theoretical thinking, participate in the final purpose of the world. We can only do this in practice.

Kant's other argument against contemplation is found in the *Critique of Practical Reason*. There, Kant explicitly says that the pleasures of understanding are on a footing with the physical pleasures: "For the possibility of these pleasures, too, presupposes, as the first condition of our delight, the existence in us of a corresponding feeling" (C2 24). The capacity to enjoy the activities of understanding is as much the result of our constitution as the capacity to enjoy physical pleasures; and it is this capacity that makes both possible ends. Neither one, as Kant conceives it, could be assigned to God. Part of the problem here comes from an issue not taken up in this paper: Kant associates pleasure with passivity, with being affected, and this divorces it firmly both from autonomy and from divinity: pleasure goes with being susceptible to causes. Aristotle, by contrast, associates pleasure with activity and even supposes God to be in a state of pleasure.[13] Plato and Aristotle distinguish between pure or true pleasures, the activities of healthy faculties engaged in for their own sake and not provoked by the "pain" of needs and appetites; while Kant says explicitly that every inclination gives rise to a need, and this is his ground for saying that "the value of any object obtainable by our action is always conditioned." Yet Kant and Aristotle agree in placing unconditional value on activities that are unprovoked by needs and therefore done for their own sake unconditionally. This important characteristic is shared by autonomously chosen actions as conceived by Kant as well as contemplation and the pleasures of perception as conceived by Aristotle.

By combining these two objections we can see why Kant cannot agree with Aristotle about the unconditional value of contemplation. For Kant, reason's standards are our standards and we do not know whether the world as it is in itself meets them. What we know is that it is only intelligible *to us* if it does. One of the things that this means is that we cannot say that even contemplation is in Aristotle's sense a perfect activity. Like a physical pleasure, it satisfies a need of ours; this makes it a conditional end, and it may be nothing more. To reach the unconditioned in a world where reason itself may be a purely human thing we must regard humanity as unconditionally valuable. Even if Kant fully accepted the Aristotelian metaphysical vision of a world striving for a kind of divine activity as its final purpose, it would retain for him the status of a human creation, its value arising from the way in which it meets human demands and standards. Even the activities that seem most perfect to us, because we gain nothing apart from them and are able to take them as giving point and meaning to our lives, must actually get their value from our valuing them.

The difference between Kant and Aristotle on this point has its roots not directly in ethics – anyway, not in a different view of practical reasoning – but in their stance toward metaphysics. Aristotle and Kant disagree not so much on what it would take to bring value into the world as on what is available for the purpose. The impossibility of a teleological metaphysics and the limitation of theoretical knowledge to a mechanical account places the good squarely in the human realm. The good cannot be contemplated but only created by our efforts. What initially looks like a sort of moralism on Kant's part is really the consequence of his humanism. The only value there is is that which human beings give to their own lives. We must be the source of value.

NOTES

In writing this paper I have benefited from the comments of Richard Kraut and Holly Smith.
1 Some intuitionists may view the intuitions used to ascertain the good as

"rational." But no procedures are envisioned, and there is nothing distinctively practical about these intuitions – they do not even motivate.
So I am not counting this as a more extensive use of practical reason.

2 Readers of the *Nicomachean Ethics* often find a difficulty in understanding how contemplation as Aristotle describes it can be an activity on
which to spend time and so just what activity he has in mind. Space
constraints prevent my taking up this issue here. The brief description I
have given is gleaned from the *Posterior Analytics; Metaphysics Lambda*
7 and 9; and *Nicomachean Ethics* 6.7 and 10.7. Another issue I do not
address directly here is the notorious one of how single-mindedly the
contemplative life is lived. However, since I argue that Aristotle nowhere
implies that contemplation is the only end, my account should remove
some of the reasons for supposing that Aristotle envisions the contemplative person as devoting all of his time and resources to contemplation and
regarding everything else as a means to it.

3 Plato, *The Republic*, trans. Paul Shorey in *The Collected Dialogues of
Plato*, p. 605.

4 The term is borrowed from W. F. R. Hardie's "The Final Good in Aristotle's *Ethics*." Hardie argues that Aristotle confuses a "dominant end"
conception of the good which treats contemplation as the only end with
an "inclusive end" conception. This view of Aristotle is the one I am
opposing.

5 *Aristotle's Eudemian ethics*, 1215b–1216a, trans. Michael Woods, pp.
5–6. Emphases mine.

6 Anything pleasant can be an end, and the person who chooses the life of
amusements, although she is making a mistake, is not making the same
sort of mistake that the person who chooses the life of money-making is.
Money is a mere means, so the person who makes an end of it has really
inverted the values of things. (It is a mark of our agreement with Aristotle that we do not imagine the money-making life as really lived for
the sake of money. We imagine money as playing the same role in this
life that honor does in a common version of the political life: it is a sort
of external sign of one's entrepreneurial virtue.) The person who chooses
amusements is not mistaking a means for an end: he is mistaking a
conditional end for an unconditional one. Aristotle suggests that he does
not know anything better (10.6.1177b). Or, perhaps, if he is reflective, he
has denied the existence of unconditional goods and therefore placed all
goods and all pleasures on a level. This is why it is conventional to
defend the life of amusements by reflections on the shortness and absurdity of human life.

7 Aristotle's major discussions of this distinction are in *Metaphysics
Theta* 6 and *Nicomachean Ethics* 10.3. I have learned from J. L. Ackrill's

"Aristotle's Distinction between *Energeia* and *Kinesis*." Ackrill's discussion of the case of walking led to my reflections on that example. My account of the relations between *energeia* and *kinesis* is constructive, however. My remarks about things that are both processes and activities and about processes that are taken up as activities are not based directly on what Aristotle says.

8 Of course you may be walking for the sake of exercise (of which walking is an instance) and exercising for the sake of health (to which walking is a means). Taking a walk is a conditional end: it is both useful and pleasant. And this is not a mere conjunction: the human need for exercise is what *makes* it pleasant.

9 Here it matters that for Aristotle pleasure is activity (or so close to activity that the two are indistinguishable), and unimpeded activity is pleasure (7.12–13; 10.4). Though pleasure taken generally is not the final good, the final good will necessarily be a pleasure.

10 I have learned this from Warner Wick's "The Rat and the Squirrel, or the Rewards of Virtue."

11 Aristotle points out that contemplation is an activity that does not involve process at the end of *Nicomachean Ethics* 7.14. (The phrase is translated "activity of immobility.") Divine contemplation is also the purest activity for ontological reasons: it is immaterial and involves no potentiality.

12 These arguments are treated more thoroughly in my "Two Distinctions in Goodness," Chapter 9 in this volume, and "Kant's Formula of Humanity," Chapter 4 in this volume.

13 See *Metaphysics Lambda* 7.1072b and *Nicomachean Ethics* 7.14.1154b for the view that God is in a condition of pleasure.

9   Two distinctions in goodness

In this paper I describe two distinctions in goodness which are often conflated, and try to show the importance of keeping them separate. The two distinctions in question are: the distinction between intrinsic and extrinsic goodness, and the distinction between ends or final goods, and means or instrumental goods.

It will help to begin by delineating the kind of value and the kind of judgment of value with which I am primarily concerned here. I take it that there are three primary categories of value with which the moral philosopher is concerned: namely, the rightness or justice of actions, policies, and institutions; the goodness of objects, purposes, lives, etc.; and the moral worth or moral goodness of characters, dispositions, or actions. My concern here is not with what constitutes moral worth or moral goodness but with the second category – with goodness as a feature of ordinary ends and purposes, states of affairs, objects, activities, and other things – that is, with the kind of goodness that marks a thing out as worthy of choice.

Within this category, we can distinguish, admittedly with some artificiality, three kinds of judgments of goodness that we make. We judge something to be good of its kind when we judge it to have the virtues appropriate to that kind. We may also judge something to be a good kind of thing, as when we say of friendship or books or health that they are good. And we also sometimes judge particular things to be good absolutely, meaning that here and now the world is a better place because of this thing. I am mostly concerned with this third sort of judgment in this paper, though part of what is in question is its relation to the other two.

II

It is rather standard fare in philosophy to distinguish two kinds of this value of goodness, often called "intrinsic" and "instrumental."[1] Objects, activities, or whatever, have an instrumental value if they are valued for the sake of something else – tools, money, and chores would be standard examples. A common explanation of the supposedly contrasting kind, intrinsic goodness, is to say that a thing is intrinsically good if it is valued for its own sake, that being the obvious alternative to a thing's being valued for the sake of something else. This is not, however, what the words "intrinsic value" mean. To say that something is intrinsically good is not by definition to say that it is valued for its own sake: it is to say that it has its goodness in itself. It refers, one might say, to the location or source of the goodness rather than the way we value the thing. The contrast between instrumental and intrinsic value is therefore misleading, a false contrast. The natural contrast to intrinsic goodness – the value a thing has "in itself" – is *extrinsic* goodness – the value a thing gets from some other source. The natural contrast to a thing that is valued instrumentally or as a means is a thing that is valued for its own sake or as an end. There are, therefore, two distinctions in goodness. One is the distinction between things valued for their own sakes and things valued for the sake of something else – between ends and means, or final and instrumental goods. The other is the distinction between things which have their value in themselves and things which derive their value from some other source: intrinsically good things versus extrinsically good things. Intrinsic and instrumental good should not be treated as correlatives, because they belong to two different distinctions.

If intrinsic is taken to be the opposite of instrumental, then it is under the influence of a theory: a theory according to which the two distinctions in goodness are the same, or amount to the same thing. According to such a theory, final goods or things valuable as ends will be the same as intrinsic goods, and instrumental goods or things valuable as means will be the same as extrinsic goods. It is worth considering what such a theory might be like.

The first part of the equivalence – that ends and intrinsic goods are the same – might be held in two very different ways: (1) The claim might be that anything we value for its own sake is thereby "intrinsically good"; that is that this is all that can be meant by "intrinsically good." This amounts to a *reduction* of the intrinsic/extrinsic distinction to the end/means distinction; the significance of the former distinction drops out. This option, which in effect replaces the intrinsic/extrinsic distinction with the end/means distinction, is sometimes taken to render the conception of good "subjective," both in the sense of "relative to the person" and of "varying among individuals." The thought goes this way: good things (on this account) are just those valued for their own sakes, but different people value different things for their own sakes. (2) The second way one might equate ends and intrinsically good things is by claiming that those things which have intrinsic value are or ought to be treated as ends. In this case we have a significant, and rather metaphysical, claim about ethics and moral psychology: namely, that choice is or ought to be a response to an attribute that we perceive in things – the attribute of intrinsic goodness. Equating the two distinctions in goodness thus leads naturally to the idea that there are two alternative theories about final goods – either that "good" is subjective or that good things are the possessors of some particular attribute. Objectivity, in other words, is thought to amount to the possession of an attribute. I think that many people do have a tendency to think that these alternatives are exhaustive, and one thing I want to show is that if the two distinctions in goodness are kept separate, this need not be so.

The other side of the theory that equates the two distinctions is the equation of extrinsic with instrumental goods, or means. The consequences of this equation are serious. Since intrinsically good things (at least when "intrinsic" retains its significance) are thought to have their value *in* themselves, they are thought to have their goodness in any and all circumstances – to carry it with them, so to speak. If you find that a certain kind of thing is not good in any and all circumstances, that it is good in some cases and not in others, its goodness is extrinsic – it is derived from or dependent upon the circumstances. If extrinsic value and instrumental value are equated, you are then forced to say of all such things that they are means or instruments. This way of thinking is part of what is behind the tendency to conclude that the final good must be pleasure or some sort of experience. The argument proceeds as follows: take an activity that we would naturally say is valuable for its own sake – say, looking at a beautiful sunset. Now the question is raised: would you think this activity was a good one even if the person engaged in it found it tedious or painful? If you say "no" then you have admitted that the goodness of this activity is not intrinsic; that it depends, in some way, on the pleasantness of it. But if all extrinsic value is instrumental value, then the only option is that the activity is a *means* to pleasure. Now if the two distinctions are not equated, there is room for some other sorts of accounts of extrinsic value, and one may not be forced to this conclusion.

Because of these consequences this side of the equation has been more widely attacked than the other. It has been argued that instrumentality is not the only sort of extrinsic value, on the grounds that there are other sorts of contributions things can make to intrinsically good ends. So, for instance, it is common to identify a "part" of an intrinsically valuable "whole" as having "contributive" value. Another sort of value, suggested by C. I. Lewis, is called "inherent" value.[2] This is supposed to be the value that characterizes the object of an intrinsically good experience. A painting, for example, might have inherent value. The identification of these different kinds of extrinsic value serves as a reminder that things can bear other relations to good ends besides being their causes or tools for their production. Contributive value and inherent value, however, both share with instrumental value the fact of deriving their goodness from the contribution they make to the existence of a supposedly intrinsically good end.

Separating the two distinctions in goodness, however, opens up another possibility: that of something which is extrinsically good yet valued as an end. An example of this would be something that was good as an end because of the interest that someone took in it, or the desire that someone had for it, for its own sake. This is the case that I am going to be discussing in the rest of this paper. In particular, I am going to compare the very opposite treatments of this issue that appear in, on the one hand, the work of Moore and Ross at the beginning of our century and, on the other hand, Kant. These philosophers all separated the two distinctions, but they applied them to this case in opposite ways. Moore and Ross came to the conclusion that the goodness of ends is intrinsic and must be independent of the interest that people take in them or the desires that people have for them. You might value something as an end

because of its intrinsic goodness or in response to its intrinsic goodness, but a thing's possession of intrinsic goodness is quite independent of whether anyone cares about it or not. Kant's theory, on the
other hand, both allows for and depends upon the idea of extrinsically valuable ends whose value comes from the interest that people
take in them.

The fact that philosophers nowadays often oppose intrinsic to
instrumental value and equate intrinsic value with the value of ends
may just be taken to be sloppiness, of course. But it may also mean
that these philosophers are working with some theory of the sort I
have described – a theory of the equivalence of the two distinctions.
As the Kantian option shows, such a theory is a substantive philosophical position and restricts the possibilities open to us in serious
ways. It should not, in any case, be taken for granted.

III

In the early years of this century there was much discussion of the
question whether or not a good thing has its value as a result of
something like the interest taken in it or the desire someone has for
it. Influential philosophers such as G. E. Moore, W. D. Ross, R. B.
Perry, and others discussed this question at length. Probably the
interest in the issue was aroused by a common utilitarian argument
that pleasure is the only thing that is good in itself because it is the
only thing that we can desire for its own sake. It quickly became,
and still is, a commonplace discussion of utilitarianism to argue that
pleasure is not, after all, the only thing that we desire for its own
sake. But that leaves open the further question whether the things
we desire for their own sakes, whatever they might be, are therefore
good in themselves, or intrinsically good. Moore, and following him,
Ross, argued vigorously that this could not be so. Goodness, they
said, had nothing to do with mental attitudes taken towards things
at all – even though it turned out that, as a matter of fact, goodness
is a property of mental attitudes or a property of states of affairs that
always include mental states or attitudes.

The idea of intrinsic value is central to Moore's theory. He believed that right actions are those that maximize intrinsic goods.
Emphatically opposed to hedonism, he took the class of intrinsic

goods to consist of such things as the appreciation of beauty, friendship, and love. In his attempt to account for the goodness of these things, he came back to the question of the nature of intrinsic value over and over again.[3]

In his paper "The Conception of Intrinsic Value," Moore argues that people who object to the idea that goodness is subjective are really worried about something quite different: the idea that goodness is nonintrinsic. This is shown, according to Moore, by the fact that there are theories which would render goodness objective to which the same people would still be opposed, and for the same reason. Moore gives as his example the theory that "better" means "better fitted to survive" (CIV 256): People who object to subjectivity, he says, would also object to this, although it renders "good" objective. So the problem with a subjectivist theory of the good is not merely the lack of objectivity, but something else. According to Moore, it is that it excludes the possibility that things are intrinsically valuable. Moore defines intrinsic value as follows:

To say that a kind of value is "intrinsic" means merely that the question whether a thing possesses it, and in what degree it possesses it, depends solely on the intrinsic nature of the thing in question. (CIV 260)

Moore's definition of the intrinsic nature of a thing is rather complicated: he says that two things have a different intrinsic nature if they are not exactly alike; that the difference need not be a difference in qualities, since it may be in the degree of a quality or in the quality of a constituent; and that two numerically different things have the same intrinsic nature if they are exactly alike (CIV 260–265). In general, the intrinsic nature of a thing seems to consist of its non-relational properties, for Moore insists that a thing would have the same intrinsic nature if transferred to another world or placed in a different set-up of causal laws (CIV 256). This is what Moore supposes we *want* from the conception of intrinsic goodness, as his analysis of the trouble with the evolutionary account of goodness shows. He says that the difficulty is that the types better fitted to survive under our laws of nature would not be the same as the types better fitted to survive under other circumstances and with different laws of nature. "Good" therefore would not be dependent only on a thing's intrinsic nature but would be a property that is relative to the circumstances, even though in this case it would be objective. But the problem with subjectivism is the same: it makes "good" relative to the circumstances.

Intrinsic goodness is not an element in the thing's intrinsic nature, for to say that would be to commit the naturalistic fallacy. The elements in its intrinsic nature are natural properties and cannot be identified with the good. But it is dependent only on the thing's intrinsic nature and is just as constant: so long as the thing remains what it is, it has the same value: and the value is the same, of course, for everyone and so also objective. Since it is no part of a thing's intrinsic nature whether anybody likes it or not, intrinsic value is quite independent of people's desires and interests. To put it another way: the attribute of "being desired by somebody" is relational, and as such it obviously varies with the circumstances in which the thing is found.

In *Ethics*, Moore's definition is a little different. We judge a state of things to have intrinsic value when we judge that it would be a good thing for that state of things to exist, even if nothing else were to exist besides. Here again, the emphasis is on the thing's goodness being nonrelational in a certain way. This view of intrinsic goodness is behind Moore's method of determining which things have intrinsic goodness in *Principia Ethica:* the "method of isolation." In order to arrive at a correct decision on the question which things have intrinsic value, Moore says that we must consider whether a thing is such that, if it existed by itself, in absolute isolation, we should judge its existence to be good (PRIN 187). In *Ethics*, Moore says:

> We *can* consider with regard to any particular state of things whether it would be worth while that it should exist, even if there were absolutely nothing else in the Universe besides . . . we *can* consider whether the existence of such a Universe would have been better than nothing, or whether it would have been just as good that nothing at all should ever have existed. (E 68)

These definitions, along with the method of isolation they suggest, seem to Moore to exclude easily any connection between intrinsic value and what people desire for its own sake, for, he tells us, it is obviously possible to desire something for its own sake, or believe that someone else does, and yet not regard the thing as the sort of thing that would be good if it existed in isolation. Indeed you might regard it as a bad thing, worse than nothing, for it to exist quite alone. Moore concludes:

And if this is so, then it shows conclusively that to judge that a thing is intrinsically good is not the same thing as to judge that some man is pleased with it or desires it for its own sake. (E 69)

Moore, it should be noted, does not usually use the terminology of "relational" vs. "nonrelational" attributes in his discussions of intrinsic value, but these are the terms in which Ross and Perry, following Moore, take up the discussion. Ross, who is on Moore's side,[4] says that there are two kinds of theories of value. One kind treats value as an attribute, and the other treats it as a relation, usually to a state of mind such as interest or desire. If it is a relation, Ross complains, then nothing can be intrinsically good, since intrinsically good *means* "good even if nothing else exists." But, he says,

. . . in that case value would seem always to be borrowed, and never owned; value would shine by a reflected glory having no original source.[5]

Ross, like Moore, finds it virtually self-evident that "intrinsically valuable" is not the same as "desired as an end." He insists that:

It is surely clear that when we call something good we are thinking of it as possessing in itself a certain attribute and are not thinking of it as necessarily having an interest taken in it.[6]

The terms in which this discussion proceeded suggested that the question was whether final goods, whatever we ought to pursue, are intrinsically good and objective, the possessors of a property; or good because they are desired and therefore subjective, or at any rate "relational" and therefore unfixed. These are terms that those who followed Moore and Ross inherited.

IV

Kant, I am going to claim, was aware of and made use of the two distinctions in goodness, with results that were quite different from those arrived at by Moore and Ross.[7] In order to see this, we must begin by looking at Kant's own distinction between unconditioned and conditioned value. The *Groundwork of the Metaphysics of Morals* opens with the famous claim:

Nothing in the world – indeed nothing even beyond the world – can possibly be conceived which could be called good without qualification except a *good will*. (G 392–93)

As Kant presents the argument that follows, it becomes clear that what he means is that the good will is the only unconditionally good thing and "the supreme condition to which the private purposes of men must for the most part defer" (G 396). He says:

This will must indeed not be the sole and complete good but the highest good and the condition of all others, even of the desire for happiness. (G 396)

Happiness, by contrast to the good will, is referred to as a "conditional purpose" (G 396).

The fact that happiness is identified as a conditional purpose shows that the unconditioned/conditioned distinction is not the same as the end/means distinction, since happiness is certainly desired as an end. For Kant, the end/means distinction can be said to be a distinction in the *way* we value things. By contrast, the unconditioned/conditioned distinction is a distinction not in the way we value things but in the circumstances (conditions) in which they are objectively good. A thing is unconditionally good if it is good under any and all conditions, if it is good no matter what the context. In order to be unconditionally good, a thing must obviously carry its own value with it – have its goodness in itself (be an end in itself). Kant's notion of unconditional value therefore corresponds to the notion of intrinsic goodness as nonrelational that I have been discussing. The early passages of the *Groundwork* emphasize the independence of the value of the good will from all surrounding circumstances as well as from its results. It is good in the world or even beyond it (G 393); it is not good because of what it effects or accomplishes; it sparkles like a jewel in its own right, as something that has its full worth in itself. Later in the *Groundwork*, Kant uses the phrase "*inneren Wert,*" inner worth, to describe the special dignity of a morally good rational being as compared to the "*relativen Wert,*" relative worth, of anything else (G 435). But whereas Moore assigned intrinsic goodness to a range of things – to aesthetic appreciation, to friendship, and in general to the things that he thought we ought to pursue as ends – Kant assigns it only to the one thing, the good will.

If unconditional value is intrinsic value, conditional value is extrinsic value. Now a thing is conditionally valuable if it is good only when certain conditions are met; if it is good sometimes and not others. Thus, to elaborate on Kant's own examples, "the coolness of a villain makes him not only far more dangerous but also more directly abominable in our eyes than he would have seemed without it" (G 344), while coolness in a fireman or a surgeon is usually an excellent thing. Power, riches, and health are good or not depending upon what use is made of them. To say that a thing is conditionally valuable is to say that it is good when and only when the conditions of its goodness are met. We can say that a thing is good objectively (this is my terminology) either if it is unconditionally good or if it is a thing of conditional value and the conditions of its goodness are met. Here it is important to notice that "good objectively" is a judgment applying to real particulars: this woman's knowledge, this man's happiness, and so on. To say of a thing that it is good objectively is not to say that it is the type of thing that is usually good (a good kind of thing like knowledge or happiness) but that it contributes to the actual goodness of the world: here and now the world is a better place for *this*. We would not say that about the coolness of the villain or the happiness of the evil person: hence coolness and happiness are objectively good only when certain further conditions are met. Further, we might, under unusual conditions, attribute objective goodness to something that under more usual conditions is nearly always bad, as when a kind of occurrence normally unfortunate coincidentally contributes to someone's happiness.[8] When Kant says that the only thing good without qualification is a good will, he means that the good will is the one thing or kind of thing for which the whole world is always a better place, no matter "what it effects or accomplishes" (G 394).

The two distinctions interact in the following ways. When a thing is valued as a means or instrumentally (or is the sort of thing valued as a means) it will always be a conditionally or extrinsically valuable thing, and the goodness of the end to which it is a means will be a condition of its goodness. Instruments therefore can only be conditionally valuable. If the conditions of their goodness are met, however, they can be good objectively. The more important point is about things valued as ends. These are also conditionally or extrinsically good. In particular, happiness, under which Kant thinks all our other private purposes are subsumed, is only conditionally good, for:

It need hardly be mentioned that the sight of a being adorned with no feature of a pure and good will, yet enjoying uninterrupted prosperity, can never give

pleasure to a rational impartial observer. Thus the good will seems to constitute the indispensable condition even of worthiness to be happy. (G 393)

But although happiness is conditionally valuable, it is, when the
condition is met, objectively good.

In order to see this, it will help to keep in mind Kant's other uses
of the unconditioned/conditioned distinction. If anything is conditioned in any way, reason seeks its condition, continually seeking
the conditions of each condition until it reaches something unconditional. It is this characteristic activity of reason that generates the
antinomies of theoretical speculative reason described in the *Critique of Pure Reason*. The usual example is causal explanation – if
we explain a thing in terms of its cause, we then go on to explain the
cause itself in terms of its cause, and this process continues. Reason
does not want to rest until it reaches something that needs no explanation (although this turns out not to be available): say, something
that is a first cause or its own cause. A causal explanation truly
satisfying to reason would go all the way back to this evident first
cause, thus *fully* explaining why the thing to be explained must be
so. These are familiar sort of moves in philosophy, so there is no
need to belabor the point. To apply it here, it is only necessary to
point out that just as to explain a thing fully we would have to find
its unconditioned first cause, so to *justify* a thing fully (where justify
is "show that it is objectively good") we would have to show that all
the conditions of its goodness were met, regressing on the conditions until we came to what is unconditioned. Since the good will is
the only unconditionally good thing, this means that it must be the
source and condition of all the goodness in the world; goodness, as it
were, flows into the world from the good will, and there would be
none without it. If a person has a good will, then that person's
happiness (to the extent of his or her virtue) is good. This is why the
highest good, the whole object of practical reason, is virtue and
happiness in proportion to virtue: together these comprise all ends
that are objectively good – the unconditional good and the private
ends that are rendered good by its presence (C2 110). So also the
Kingdom of Ends, defined as "a whole of rational beings as ends in
themselves as well as of the particular ends which each may set for
himself" (G 433), is a kingdom in which the objectively good is fully
realized.

On the Kantian conception of goodness, then, an end is objectively good either if it is unconditionally (intrinsically) good *or* if it is conditionally good and the relevant conditions, whatever they are, are met. This conception of the good is used in his argument for one of the formulas of the categorical imperative, the Formula of Humanity as an End in itself. 9 It is this argument that establishes the role of the good will in conferring value upon the ends of the person who has it.

The argument shows how Kant's idea of justification works. It can be read as a kind of regress upon the conditions, starting from an important assumption. The assumption is that when a rational being makes a choice or undertakes an action, he or she supposes the object to be good, and its pursuit to be justified. At least, if there is a categorical imperative there must be objectively good ends, for then there are necessary actions and so necessary ends (G 427–28; MPV 384–85). In order for there to be any objectively good ends, however, there must be something that is unconditionally good and so can serve as a sufficient condition of their goodness. Kant considers what this might be: it cannot be an object of inclination, for those have only a conditional worth, "for if the inclinations and the needs founded on them did not exist, their object would be without worth" (G 428). It cannot be the inclinations themselves because a rational being would rather be free from them. Nor can it be external things, which serve only as means. So, Kant asserts, the unconditionally valuable thing must be "humanity" or "rational nature," which he defines as the capacity to set an end (G 437; MPV 387; MPV 392). Kant explains that regarding your existence as a rational being as an end in itself is a "subjective principle of human action." By this I understand him to mean that we must regard ourselves as capable of conferring value upon the objects of our choice, the ends that we set, because we must regard our ends as good. But since "every other rational being thinks of his existence by the same rational ground which holds also for myself" (G 429), we must regard others as capable of conferring value by reason of their rational choices and so also as ends in themselves. Treating another as an end in itself thus involves making that person's ends as far as possible your own (G 430). The ends that are chosen by any rational being, possessed of the humanity or rational nature that is fully realized in a good will, take on the status of objective goods. They are not intrinsically valuable, but they are objectively valuable in the sense that every rational being has a reason to promote or realize them. For this reason it is our duty to promote the happiness of others – the ends that they choose – and, in general, to make the highest good our end.

It is worth emphasizing that the relation of intrinsic to extrinsic value in this case – the case of extrinsically valuable ends – is entirely different from that in the cases of extrinsic value mentioned earlier. Instrumental value, contributive value, and Lewis's inherent value were all forms of extrinsic value that derived from the production of a supposedly intrinsically good end. The extrinsic value of an objectively good end – of something that forms part of the happiness of a good person – comes not from some further thing that that end promotes but from its status as the object of a rational and fully justified choice. Value in this case does not travel from an end to a means but from a fully rational choice to its object. Value is, as I have put it, "conferred" by choice. This formulation may seem paradoxical. A natural objection will be that the goodness of the chosen object is precisely what makes the choice rational, so that the choice cannot itself be what makes the object good. I will have more to say about this objection in the next section. The point I want to emphasize here is that the Kantian approach frees us from assessing the rationality of a choice by means of the apparently ontological task of assessing the thing chosen: we do not need to identify especially rational ends. Instead, it is the reasoning that goes into the choice itself – the procedures of full justification – that determines the rationality of the choice and so certifies the goodness of the object. Thus the goodness of rationally chosen ends is a matter of the demands of practical reason rather than a matter of ontology.[10] It is notable that on Kant's theory the goodness of means is handled the same way: it is not because of the ontological property of being productive of an intrinsically good end that means are good but rather because of the law of practical reason that "whoever wills the end, so far as reason has decisive influence on his action, wills also the indispensably necessary means to it that lie in his power" (G 417). Similarly, the argument for the objective goodness of the object of a rational choice is not an ontological one; rather, it is based on Kant's theory of rational action. If we regard our actions as rational, we must regard our ends as good; if so, we accord to ourselves a power of conferring goodness on the objects of our choice, and we must accord the same power – and so the same intrinsic worth – to others.

It will be helpful to pause for a moment to match up Kant's view and the Kantian terms to what has gone before. On Kant's view there is only one thing that has what he calls unconditional value and what Moore calls intrinsic value, and that is the power of rational choice (when the choices are made in a fully rational way, which is what characterizes the good will). The value of everything else whatever is extrinsic or conditional. Yet when a thing is conditionally valuable and the relevant conditions are met, the thing has objective value. Things that are valued for their own sakes or as ends have this status. Their value is conditional but can be objective, given the real circumstances of the case. Thus, although Kant, like Moore, firmly separates intrinsic value from a thing's being desired for its own sake, he has resources for saying that a thing is objectively good as an end *because* it is desired for its own sake. And most things that are good will in fact be good in this way: they will be good because they are part of the happiness of a deserving human being.

On Kant's theory, the goodness of most things is, in the way described by Ross, relational – relative to the desires and interests of people. But since it must also be appropriately related to one thing that has intrinsic value, it is not merely "subjective." Value does, in Ross's extravagant terms, "shine with a reflected glory," and it is "borrowed rather than owned" by most of the things that have it. But it does have an original source that brings it into the world – the value-conferring power of the good will.

v

In this section I want to focus on some advantages of the Kantian way of describing values. In the next section I will show how some of these advantages are shared by Moore. In the last section I will discuss what I take to be the most important advantage that Kant's theory of goodness has over Moore's.

Kant's treatment of the two distinctions and the relations between them allows us to describe certain kinds of everyday matters of value in a way that is more flexible and that I think is more natural than is available to us if the two distinctions are conflated or equated. This is especially so for certain cases of what we might call "mixed" values. I have in mind a variety of different mixtures. Take some examples: a luxurious instrument; a malicious pleasure; an unenjoyed exercise of one's higher faculties; or an undisplayed art object. Now the idea that a thing can have value under a condition, when combined with the reminder that instrumentality or usefulness is not the only possible condition (that is, some extrinsically good things are valued as ends), will help us to describe such cases.

Consider, for instance, a common symbol of aspiration – a mink coat. Is it valuable as a means or as an end? One hardly wants to say that it is valuable only as a means, to keep the cold out. The people who want mink coats are not willing to exchange them for plastic parkas, if those are better protection against the elements. A mink coat can be valued the way we value things for their own sakes: a person might put it on a list of the things he always wanted, or aspires to have some day, right alongside adventure, travel, or peace of mind. Yet it is also odd to say it is valued simply for its own sake. A coat is essentially instrumental: were it not for the ways in which human beings respond to cold, we would not care about them or ever think about them. To say that the coat is intrinsically or unconditionally valuable is absurd: its value is dependent upon an enormously complicated set of conditions, physiological, economic, and symbolic. Certainly, it does not pass Moore's isolation test, so far as I can see. A universe consisting of a mink coat or of someone's having one, without the associations that can only be provided by the particular relations and causal connections under which we live, is not really imaginable, much less valuable. What would a coat *be*? It seems hard even to apply the isolation test here, for one is tempted to say that its instrumentality *is* one of the elements in the "intrinsic nature" of a coat, even though it can hardly be said to be a property the coat would have under any set of laws of nature. If its instrumentality is not one of its intrinsic properties, then one is regarding the coat as something else – an animal skin sewed into a peculiar shape, perhaps. But then it seems as if one must strip away the practically relevant properties of the coat in order to ask about its intrinsic value – and that cannot be right. It is equally absurd to say of such a thing that it is a mere instrument, just because its value is conditioned. The Kantian distinctions allow us to say that the coat is valued in part for its own sake, although only under certain conditions. It even allows us to say of certain kinds of things, such as luxurious instruments, that they are valued for their own sakes under the condition of their usefulness. Mink coats and handsome china and gorgeously enameled frying pans are all things that human beings might choose partly for their own sakes under the condition of their instrumentality: that is, given the role such things play in our lives.

Another possible advantage is that the independent use of the two distinctions will provide us with a way of talking about the relation of pleasure, enjoyment, and appreciation to other kinds of value that does not turn these mental states into ends to which everything else is a means. Activities of various kinds might be thought to be good under the condition that we enjoy them and not good at all for those who, for one reason or another, cannot enjoy them, without forcing the conclusion that it is only for the sake of the enjoyment that they are valued. Certain difficulties concerning the "higher pleasures" described by Mill or those activities that Aristotle says are "pleasant in their own nature" although not necessarily "to a particular person" might be dealt with in this way. But this is a suggestion I cannot pursue here.

Consider also the example of an extraordinarily beautiful painting unsuspectedly locked up, perhaps permanently, in a closet. Now a beautiful painting, I am supposing, is valued for its own sake. If the two distinctions are equated, we must say it has intrinsic value. Yet it is locked in a closet, utterly unseen, and no one is the better for its existence. Consider Moore's isolation test: is a universe with such a painting locked up somewhere intuitively better than one without it? Is a universe consisting of such a painting better than a universe consisting of something quite plain, with no viewers in either? These are curious puzzles: and Moore's isolation test seems to force us to ask the metaphysical-sounding question whether the painting has this property, intrinsic value, or not. Yet we *know* what the practically relevant property of the painting is: it is its beauty. Now on the Kantian type of account we can say that the painting is valuable for its own sake, yet so long as it remains locked up and unseen, it is no good at all. The condition of its goodness – the condition of the goodness of its beauty – is not met. That condition is that the painting be viewed. Yet although its value is not intrinsic, the painting may be objectively good for its own sake. If it were viewed, and the viewer were enraptured, or satisfied, or instructed by its loveliness, then the painting would be an objectively good thing: for the world would be, really, a better place for it: it would be a substantive contribution to the actual sum of goodness of the world. Notice, too, that this does not in the least mean that we have to say that the painting is only valued as a means to the experiences of appreciation. Those experiences are not an end to which the painting is a means, but the condition under which its value as an end is realized.

I am not suggesting that the Kantian treatment solves all the difficulties in our thinking about these things, but only that it does not drive us immediately to the conclusion that all of these things, valued only under conditions and only in a network of relations, must be mere instruments or contributors to some further thing – pleasure or some "mental" state, which supposedly has the real value. The conflation of the two distinctions does tend to have this effect. In particular, when conflation leads us to the conclusion that a thing can only be valued as an end when it is intrinsically valuable, or valuable independently of all conditions and relations, we find ourselves led inevitably to the curious conclusion to which modern moral philosophers are indeed frequently led – that everything good as an end must be something mental, some kind of experience. I have already mentioned one line of argument that leads to this conclusion: some sort of experience, such as pleasure, seems to be a condition of goodness of so many good things. Another line of thought that leads this way is this: no matter how much the philosopher wants to insist that the value of a good thing must be intrinsic and so nonrelational, the sense remains that the goodness of a good thing must have something to do with its goodness *for us*. It cannot merely be a property, metaphysical and simple, which we perceive in things and respond to in an extraordinary way. So the fact that goodness must lie in some relation to human beings, evidently at odds with the theory that goodness must be entirely nonrelational, is dealt with by making goodness a property of something belonging directly to the human being – our experiences or states of mind. By making goodness lie in the experiences themselves, the philosopher rids us of the worry: but what if no one is around to care about this good thing? What good is it then? Kant's way of looking at it, on the other hand, enables us to explain why ordinary good things are good only in virtue of the fact that people are around to care about them without tempting us to the conclusion that the only good things are mental states and experiences.

To some, it may seem paradoxical to claim that things are good because we desire or choose them, rather than to say that we desire or choose them because they are good. Ross, for example, finds it clear that when we call something good we are thinking of it as having some attribute, not as an object of interest; he thinks of our interest as inspired by the perception of the thing's goodness. We choose the thing because it is good. This picture is part of what gives power to the theory that goodness is not relative to interest, and of course there is a way in which it is true. For instance, when we want a certain kind of thing, we usually want one with the virtues of that kind of thing. And it is also true that what makes a thing a good kind of thing is its virtues. In this sense our choice may be called forth by a thing's goodness, rather than the thing's being good because of our choice. But when we inquire into the basis for calling certain properties of a thing its "virtues," we always come back to something that is relative to certain conditions of human life. It is our interests and the bases of our interests that make certain qualities *virtues*; so these facts cannot make goodness a nonrelational attribute.

This shows up most clearly in the everyday kind of case of "mixed" value, in which the distinction between what we value for its own sake and what we value for the sake of something else is itself overstrained. Take this case: there are instrumental reasons, good ones, for eating. It keeps you alive. But most people could not really be said to eat in order to stay alive. Certainly, only someone who didn't enjoy eating, perhaps because of illness or some damage to the taste buds, would say that he ate "in order to stay alive." Are we then to say that eating is an activity that also has an *intrinsic* value? (Perhaps then we should be glad that we are so constituted that it is necessary for us?) Or shall we say that people eat for the sake of enjoyment – that pleasure is an end to which eating is a means? Of course, you cannot exchange another pleasure for it; hunger pains will prevent that. Perhaps then we should say we eat as a means, not to obtain life and health, but just to avoid pain. Now the philosopher wants to say: the real end is painlessness. But again, only someone in a particular situation would say that. Is this then a complicated case, to which the ends of life and health, enjoyment,

and painlessness contribute in various ways? And if this is a complicated case, where are we going to find a simple one? It is easier to say
that food is a good thing under the condition that you are hungry –
or rather, under the set of physiological and psychological conditions
that make it both necessary and pleasant for human beings to eat.
Those conditions determine what the virtues of a good meal are, and
not all of these virtues are instrumental properties. But this does not
mean that you choose the meal in response to a perception of its
intrinsic value, or of the intrinsic value of eating it. The conditions
of our lives make various things valuable to us in various ways, and
it is sometimes artificial to worry about whether we value those
things as means or as ends. It is the conditions themselves that
make the things good, that provide the various reasons for their
goodness. The question is not whether the thing possesses a special
attribute, but whether these reasons are sufficient to establish the
goodness of the thing.

  This point can be sharpened if we distinguish between the initial
condition that makes an object a candidate for choice and the full
complement of conditions that, when met, renders the thing good. In
the cases under discussion in this paper, the initial condition is the
thing's desirability as an end (or at least not merely as a means). I have
tried to show that the sense in which we can be said to desire things
because they are good – i.e., for their virtues – does not show that a
desirable thing need have a nonrelational property of goodness. What
we call virtues just are the features of the thing that, given our
constitution and situation, we find appealing or interesting or satisfying to our needs. It remains just as true, as far as this goes, to say that
the thing is good because we desire it as to say that we desire it
because it is good. For its virtues are still relative to our desires, or,
more accurately, to the conditions that give rise to those desires. The
reason that one cannot, on a Kantian account, rest with the perhaps
less paradoxical formulation that value is conferred by desire is that
desire is not by itself a *sufficient* condition of the goodness of its
object. This is shown initially by the sort of case in which one has a
desire which one would be better off without. Short of endorsing
Kant's view that "the inclinations themselves, as sources of needs,
however, are so lacking in absolute worth that the universal wish of
every rational being must be to free himself completely from them"
(G 428), we can agree that there are desires that conflict with one's

health or happiness or that are self-destructive or pathological or simply burdensome out of all proportion to any gratification their fulfillment can provide. This already shows that the existence of a desire is not by itself a sufficient reason for the realization of its object; further conditions exist. The criterion that reasons be universalizable will also, on Kant's account, limit the capacity of desires to serve as reasons and so to confer value. But although desirability is not a sufficient condition of goodness, it is still the initial condition of the goodness of many good things, and so a main source of the goodness of those things.[11] On the Kantian view, not everything valued as an end need be intrinsically valuable or self-justifying for there to be a sufficient reason for it. A conditionally valuable thing can still be fully justified, if the unconditioned condition of its goodness is met. Things that are not self-justifying can be justified by something else. In particular, ends whose condition is their desirability can be justified by the rational choices of human beings.

VI

But I have not meant to suggest that Moore himself is prey to all of the difficulties that arise when the two distinctions are conflated. Moore has his own way of dealing with these issues of "mixed" value, a problem in which he was keenly interested. In order to handle cases of mixed value, Moore introduced a device which he regarded as one of his best discoveries: the theory of organic unities. The theory of organic unities involves two important points. First, it turns out that intrinsic value, on Moore's account, usually belongs to "organic" wholes or complexes of certain kinds, not to simple things. Second, it is true of such a complex whole that its value "bears no regular proportion to the sum of the values of its parts":

It is certain that a good thing may exist in such a relation to another good thing that the value of the whole thus formed is immensely greater than the sum of the values of the two good things. It is certain that a whole formed of a good thing and an indifferent thing may have immensely greater value than that good thing itself possesses. It is certain that two bad things or a bad thing and an indifferent thing may form a whole much worse than the sum of badness of its parts. And it seems as if indifferent things may also be the sole constituents of a whole which has great value, either positive or negative (PRIN 27–28).

In his last chapter, "The Ideal," Moore provides various examples. For instance: the mere existence of what is beautiful has *some* intrinsic value, but so little as to be negligible, compared to the consciousness of beauty. If the consciousness of beauty is taken to be the cognition of beauty, then it in turn is made much more valuable if accompanied by an appropriate emotional response, which Moore identifies with the appreciation. Yet appreciation of beauty is not an end to which the beautiful object is a mere means. If this were so it would not matter whether the appreciation were produced in us by something genuinely beautiful or not, and it does: appreciating something that is ugly may be bad. Instead of saying that the value of the appreciation is conditional upon its appropriateness, as one might expect, Moore says that the great intrinsic value of appreciating beauty does not belong either to the object or the appreciative state but only to the complex whole formed of both. But the goodness of the whole is not the sum of the value of the parts. For we have seen that the value of the appreciation, in another context, can be absolutely negative. Moore has similar things to say about his other cases: for instance love itself is a good thing, but if your beloved is a good person, the whole is better by *more* than the addition of your beloved's goodness. These conclusions are arrived at by the method of isolation: we compare the value of various isolated wholes, with and without the relevant element. The important thing is to avoid the mistake of thinking that the element itself possesses all of the value of the difference its presence makes. It was because of this mistake that the Greeks attributed intrinsic value to knowledge. Moore explains that, really, knowledge by itself has little or no value, but that it "is an absolutely essential constituent in the highest goods, and contributes immensely to their value" (PRIN 199). Similarly, the great value that has been placed upon pleasure, and the delusion that pleasure is the sole good, is attributed to the fact that:

Pleasure does seem to be a necessary constituent of most valuable wholes; and since the other constituents, into which we may analyse them, may easily seem not to have any value, it is natural to suppose that all the value belongs to pleasure. (PRIN 93)

Indeed, getting the right account of the relation of pleasure to other sorts of value seems to have been one of Moore's major motives in introducing the idea of organic unities. Things like pleasure and knowledge have what the tradition has called "contributive value."

I hope it is evident from these examples that the principle of organic unities is meant to do the same job that the notion of a conditioned good in Kant's theory does: it allows us to say of certain things that they are valuable only under certain circumstances, or valuable only when certain other things are true or present, without forcing us to say that these kinds of things must be valuable merely as instruments. Contributive value takes on the role that conditional value plays in Kant's view. The remaining difference is that Moore makes no distinction between what would be in Kant's terms really unconditionally (or intrinsically) good and what would be objectively good as an end.

VII

The principle of organic unities is crucial to Moore, for it enables him to make some of the same distinctions and judgments that the Kantian divisions make possible. Like the Kantian distinctions, it gives us a more flexible way of talking about the value of everyday things; and like the Kantian distinctions, it makes it possible for us to explain the conditional character of a good thing without rendering that good thing a mere means. Moore, who separates pleasure from the consciousness of pleasure, even complains in one passage that if pleasure were the sole intrinsic good, consciousness would have to be regarded as a means to it (PRIN 89). But the principle of organic unities is also in a certain way perverse. The seeming difficulties that it solves in fact arise from the relational or conditional character of the value of most of the things that human beings regard as good. Yet it is precisely this relational character that Moore, with his insistence on intrinsic value, wants to deny.

Suppose someone said: on Kant's view happiness is a conditioned or extrinsic value and the good will its condition. But the happiness of a good person is, on Kant's view, always good, good under any and all circumstances, for its condition is met. So couldn't we say of this, as well as of the good will, that it is intrinsically valuable? What this would amount to would be constructing an organic unity out of happiness and the good will, and showing that on Moore's account it has intrinsic value. Then the Kantian notion of "objective value" and Moore's "intrinsic value" are not so different after all.[12]

And the answer to that is that there is still a difference. For Moore's view, and the intuitionistic method of isolation, veil or obscure the internal relations within the organic unity in virtue of which the organic unity has its value. Whereas the Kantian account, which focuses on rather than ignoring the internal relations of the valuable whole, allows us to see why happiness is valuable in just this case and not in another case. Moore can only say that the combination of happiness and good will works (is a good recipe, so to speak) while happiness plus the bad will does not. Kant can say that happiness in the one case is good because the condition under which it is fully justified has been met (roughly, because its having been decently pursued makes it deserved). Those internal relations reveal the *reasons* for our views about what is valuable, while Moore's view tends to cover up these reasons. And this might be true in other cases as well: if we think that aesthetic response is only valuable when the object responded to is genuinely beautiful, or that friendship is only valuable when your friend is good, or even if we think that aesthetic response and friendship are just *more* valuable in these cases, then this has something to do with the reasons we think these kinds of things are valuable at all. On Moore's account the only relation in which the elements of an organic whole stand to each other is the relation of being elements in a single organic whole. They are all on a footing with one another. But if Kant is right there is an order within "valuable wholes," a conditioning of some elements by others, that is hidden by treating these elements as just so many *ingredients.* This order reflects the reason why the wholes are good.

Another way to put the point is this: Moore's theory drives a wedge between the reason why we care about something and the reason why it is good. Or rather, since on Moore's theory it is a mistake to talk about why something is good, we should say that it drives a wedge between our natural interest in something and our moral interest in it. On Moore's theory if you say that the reason something is good is because someone cares about it, that could only mean that the person's interest was an element in an organic whole which had intrinsic value. But according to Moore the question why such a whole has intrinsic value must not be raised: it just has the property of intrinsic value; there is no reason why it has that property (PRIN 142–144). Yet it is because it has intrinsic value that we ought to make it an end in our actions. A thing's goodness becomes a property that we intuit and respond to in a way that seems curiously divorced from our natural interests.

The interesting thing about that is that Moore took up the idea of intrinsic value because he saw that objectivity was not all that we wanted from a theory of value. He was certainly right to think that the same people who are discouraged by subjectivism are discouraged by an evolutionary theory or others of that kind. But to me it seems that this discouragement has to do with the way in which such theories undermine the nature of our concern for the good. For instance, if goodness is mere fitness to survive, then the only way goodness matters is the way the biological survival of the species matters – and that doesn't cover everything we feel about the importance of living a good life. But what is the nature of our concern for intrinsic values as Moore describes them? Moore seems to find it obvious that when we have determined what is intrinsically good we shall have an interest in bringing that into the world. His antinaturalistic arguments prevent him from giving any account of why this nonnatural property should be so appealing to us. Of course, the isolation test by which intrinsic values are discerned guarantees that we will only attribute them to something that appeals to us. But that does not provide a justification of our interest in the intrinsically valuable or even a motivational explanation of it. On the Kantian account, by contrast, the good end is the object of a rational choice. The things that we want, need, care for, are good so long as certain conditions of rational choice are met. Thus, the reasons that things are good bear a definite relation to the reasons we have for caring about them.

The primary advantage of the Kantian theory of goodness is that it gives an account of the "objectivity" of goodness that does not involve assigning some sort of property to all good things. Good things are good in the way that Ross describes as relational, because of attitudes taken up towards them or because of other physical or psychological conditions that make them important to us. Only one thing – the good will itself – is assigned an intrinsic value or inner worth, and even the argument for that is not ontological. If we regard ourselves as having the power to justify our ends, the argument says, we must regard ourselves as having an inner worth – and we must treat others who can also place value on their ends in virtue of their humanity as having the same inner worth.

If human beings have an intrinsic value by virtue of the capacity for valuing things, then human beings bring goodness into the world. The distinction between a thing that is intrinsically good and a thing that is extrinsically good yet valuable as an end allows for the possibility that the things that are important to us have an objective value, yet have that value because they are important to us. Objective goodness is not a mysterious ontological attribute. The things that are important to us can be good: good because of our desires and interests and loves and because of the physiological, psychological, economic, historical, symbolic and other conditions under which human beings live.

NOTES

1 Intrinsic is often directly opposed to instrumental: equally commonly, "extrinsic" is opposed to intrinsic but then "consequential" or "instrumental" is offered as a definition or explanation of that term. Or, in some of the literature, "intrinsic" is taken to be a particular theory about how ends are valued, and accepted or dismissed as such. All of these usages more or less imply the equivalence of the two distinctions; none leaves room for the Kantian theory described in this paper.·

2 C. I. Lewis, *An Analysis of Knowledge and Valuation.*

3 Moore's views on intrinsic value are mostly presupposed in *Principia Ethica* (hereinafter cited as "PRIN") but they are addressed explicitly in *Ethics* (hereinafter cited as "E."); "The Conception of Intrinsic Value" in his *Philosophical Studies* (hereinafter cited as "CIV"); and a symposium reply entitled "Is Goodness a Quality?" published in the Aristotelian Society Supplement in 1932 and reprinted in *Philosophical Papers* (1959). In the last, Moore tends to give way to a view that his earlier accounts avoid – namely, that only experiences can be intrinsically good. For that reason and because of its polemical nature I have not used it in this paper.

4 In *The Right and the Good*, Chapter IV, Ross argues explicitly in favor of Moore and against Ralph Barton Perry, who, in his *General Theory of Value*, argues that value is relative to interest. The Kantian view defended in this paper is classified by Perry as one in which value is "the

object of a qualified interest" and opposed by him in favor of the view
that value is "the object of any interest."

5 *The Right and the Good*, p. 75.
6 *The Right and the Good*, p. 81.
7 I am not the first to set up Kant's view in opposition to Moore's. The
   same is done by H. J. Paton in "The Alleged Independence of Goodness."
   Paton, however, is not concerned with the two distinctions, and he
   focuses on the goodness of actions, which he claims is relative to the
   circumstances in which they are performed. Moore's rather impatient
   response is to incorporate the choice into the action and consideration of
   the circumstances into the choice: thus under different circumstances
   you have different actions. Moore's reply may be fair in the case discussed, but it is an instance of a general strategy which I discuss in the
   paper: when someone brings forward an example of a good thing whose
   goodness seems relative to the circumstances, Moore and Ross incorporate the circumstances into the thing to maintain the nonrelational
   character of the goodness.
8 I am indebted to the Editors of the *Philosophical Review* for this point.
9 A much fuller treatment of the ideas of this section is in my paper
   "Kant's Formula of Humanity," Chapter 4 in this volume.
10 Insofar as Moore's point in identifying the naturalistic fallacy is to deny
   the identity of goodness with any particular natural property and so to
   insist on the autonomy of ethical discourse, Kant could agree. But
   whereas Moore concludes that goodness must therefore be a nonnatural
   property, Kant understands it to be a practical, rather than a theoretical,
   characterization.
11 I would like to thank the Editors of *The Philosophical Review* for
   prompting me to clarify the roles of desire and choice in conferring
   value.
12 Ross does something very like this in his discussion of the relation of
   virtue and pleasure in *The Right and the Good*, pp. 135 ff.

10 The reasons we can share: An attack on the distinction between agent-relative and agent-neutral values

To later generations, much of the moral philosophy of the twentieth century will look like a struggle to *escape* from utilitarianism. We seem to succeed in disproving one utilitarian doctrine, only to find ourselves caught in the grip of another. I believe that this is because a basic feature of the consequentialist outlook still pervades and distorts our thinking: the view that the business of morality is to *bring something about.* Too often, the rest of us have pitched our protests as if we were merely objecting to the utilitarian account of *what* the moral agent ought to bring about or *how* he ought to do it. Deontological considerations have been characterized as "side constraints," as if they were essentially restrictions on ways to realize ends.[1] More importantly, moral philosophers have persistently assumed that the primal scene of morality is a scene in which someone does something *to* or *for* someone else. This is the same mistake that children make about another primal scene. The primal scene of morality, I will argue, is not one in which I do something to you or you do something to me, but one in which we do something· together. The subject matter of morality is not what we should bring about, but how we should relate to one another. If only Rawls has succeeded in escaping utilitarianism, it is because only Rawls has fully grasped this point. His primal scene, the original position, is one in which a group of people must make a decision together. Their task is to find the reasons they can share.[2]

In this essay, I bring these thoughts to bear on a question which has received attention in recent moral philosophy. In contemporary jargon, the question is whether reasons and values should be understood to be agent-relative or agent-neutral, or whether reasons and values of both kinds exist. In slightly older terms, the question is whether reasons and values are subjective, existing only in relation to individuals, or objective, there for everyone. I begin by explaining the distinction in more detail, and then examine two kinds of examples which have been used to support the claim that values of both kinds must exist. By explicating the structure of the values in these examples, I hope to show that employing the distinction between agent-relative and agent-neutral is not the best way to account for their normative force. Values are neither subjective nor objective, but rather are *intersubjective*. They supervene on the structure of personal relations.[3]

I   AGENT-RELATIVE AND AGENT-NEUTRAL VALUES

In what I have said so far, I have assumed an equivalence or at least a direct correspondence between values and practical reasons: to say that there is a practical reason for something is to say that the thing is good, and vice versa. In this I follow Thomas Nagel, whose work will be the focus of what I have to say (VFN 139).[4] Although assuming this equivalence gives us a variety of ways to characterize the distinction in question, it still turns out to be a delicate matter to do so.

According to Nagel, a subjective or agent-relative reason is a reason only for a particular agent to promote something; an objective reason is a reason for anyone to promote the thing.[5] "Subjective" in this context is not meant to suggest "unreal" or "illusory." Subjective reasons are real and in one sense universal – they are alike for everyone – but they are personal property. Objective reasons, by contrast, are common property. Formally speaking, a subjective reason exists when the formulation of the reason predicate contains a "free-agent variable" and an objective reason exists when it does not (PA 90ff.).[6] Thus, suppose we say, "There is a reason for any agent to promote *her own* happiness." This gives me a reason to promote my happiness and you a reason to promote yours, but it does not give you a reason to promote mine or me a reason to promote yours. On the other hand, suppose we say, "There is a reason for any agent to promote *any person's* happiness." This gives each of us a reason to promote not only her own happiness but the other's as well.

Formulated in terms of values, it is tempting to say that subjective reasons capture the notion of "good-for," while objective reasons capture the notion of "good-absolutely." If there is a reason for any agent to promote *her own* happiness, then my happiness is good-for me and yours is good-for you. But if there is a reason for any agent to do what will promote any person's happiness, then any person's happiness is good-absolutely. Human happiness is an objective value which as such makes a claim on all of us. This way of putting the point, however, obscures an important distinction, which I will discuss in the next section.

In *The Possibility of Altruism*, Nagel argued that all subjective reasons and values must be taken to have objective correlates. If it is good-for me to have something, then we must regard it as good-absolutely that I should have it. I cannot do justice to Nagel's complex argument here, but its central idea can easily be conveyed. Nagel associates a commitment to the objectivity of value with a conception of oneself as one person among others who are equally real. I act on certain considerations which have normative force *for me:* they are subjective reasons. I am capable, however, of viewing myself from an impersonal point of view – as simply a person, one among others who are equally real. When I view myself this way, I still regard these considerations as having normative force.[7] This is especially clear, Nagel argues, when I consider a situation in which someone else fails to respond to my reasons. This is why we ask, "How would you like it if someone did that to you?" when we are trying to get someone to see the normative force of another's reasons. If I am tormenting someone, say a stranger, the question invites me to consider the case where a stranger is tormenting me. According to Nagel, I should see that I would not merely dislike this, I would also resent it, and my resentment carries with it the thought that my tormentor would have a reason to stop. That reason is the same as my reason for wanting it to stop: that I don't like it. I would expect my tormentor to respond to *my* reason (PA 82–85). And yet, to a stranger, I am just a person, some person or other. This shows that I view my reasons as having normative force simply insofar as they are a person's reasons, and expect others to do so as well. And that commits me to the view that other people's reasons have normative force for me.[8] Where there is a subjective reason, then, there is also an objective one, to which everyone should respond.

Later Nagel changed his mind about this conclusion. But before considering that, we must ask more exactly what this argument, if it works, establishes.

II   TWO INTERPRETATIONS OF AGENT-NEUTRAL VALUE

Earlier I mentioned that there is a problem with understanding the distinction between relative and neutral values in terms of the distinction between good-for and good-absolutely. The problem is that the claim that something is a reason for everyone may be understood in two different ways, one of which the phrase "good-absolutely" tends to conceal.

An agent-neutral value might be a value that is not relative to what agents actually value. According to this interpretation, the goodness of, say, my happiness, has what G. E. Moore called an intrinsic value, a property that is independent either of my interest in promoting it or yours.[9] It provides a reason for both of us the way the sun provides light for both of us: because it's out there, shining down. And just as the sun would exist in a world devoid of creatures who see and respond to light, so values would exist in a world devoid of creatures who see and respond to reasons. I call this interpretation of agent-neutral values *Objective Realism*.[10] On a less metaphysical view, agent-neutrality does not mean independence of agents as such, but neutrality with respect to the individual identities of agents. On this reading, values are intersubjective: they exist for all rational agents, but would not exist in a world without them. I call this view of agent-neutral values *Intersubjectivism*.[11]

The difference between these two interpretations of neutral value is naturally associated with two other differences. First, the two views will normally involve a different priority-ordering between subjective or relative and objective or neutral values. According to Objective Realism, subjective values are *derived from* objective ones: an individual comes to value something by perceiving that it has (objective) value. Our relation to values, on this account, is epistemological, a relation of discovery or perception. According to Intersubjectivism, objective values are derived or, better, constructed from subjective ones. Our individual, subjective interests become intersubjective values when, because of the attitude we take towards one another, we come to share each other's ends.[12] On this view, our relation to values is one of creation or construction. The second and related difference concerns the possibility of adding and subtracting value across the boundaries between persons. On an Intersubjectivist interpretation, neutral reasons are shared, but they are always initially subjective or agent-relative reasons. So on this view, everything that is good or bad is so because it is good or bad *for* someone. This makes it natural for an Intersubjectivist to deny that values can be added across the boundaries between people. My happiness is good for me and yours is good for you, but the sum of these two values is not good *for* anyone, and so the Intersubjectivist will deny that the sum, as such, is a value.[13] But an Objective Realist, who thinks that the value is in the object rather than in its relation to the subject, may think that we can add values. Two people's happinesses, both good in themselves, will be better than one. Since consequentialism depends upon the possibility that values may be added, an Objective Realist about value may be a consequentialist, while an Intersubjectivist will not.[14]

This leaves us with some important questions. We shall want to know how Intersubjectivism could be true, and what there is to choose between it and Objective Realism. These are questions to which I will return in due course. More immediately, I want to raise a question about Nagel. Which kind of agent-neutral values did he intend to defend? This turns out to be a little difficult to establish. In a postscript he later attached to *The Possibility of Altruism*, Nagel says:

This book defends the claim that only objective reasons are acceptable, and that subjective reasons are legitimate only if they can be *derived from* objective ones. I now think that the argument actually establishes a different conclusion: That there are objective reasons corresponding to all subjective ones. It remains possible that the *original subjective reasons from which the others are generated* retain some independent force and are not completely subsumed under them. (PA vii; my emphases)

The first part of this is misleading, since nothing in *The Possibility of Altruism* really requires that subjective reasons be "derived from" objective ones. What the argument establishes (if it works) is that if you are to act in harmony with a conception of yourself as one person among others who are equally real, then you must regard your own and others' subjective reasons and values as being objective as well. This is consistent with the view that the objective values are constructed from – or as Nagel himself says here "generated from" – the subjective ones, and so consistent with an Intersubjectivist interpretation.

In *The View from Nowhere*, Nagel says his project is to bring the method of objectivity to bear on the will (VFN 4, 138). You are to see, first, to what extent your motives are really reasons, with normative force for you, by seeing to what extent they may be confirmed or corrected when you view yourself more objectively, as simply a person, one person among others. You are then to see whether these agent-relative reasons can support a still more objective normative force, by considering whether from this point of view they could be taken to have normative force for everyone. This could describe a practical project: the project would be to bring our subjective motives into the impersonal point of view, conferring objective normative force or value upon them as far as that can consistently be done. The result would be Intersubjectivism, and sometimes Nagel sounds as if this is what he has in mind. But at other times he seems to think of it as an epistemological project, one of *discovering* whether what seem to us, subjectively, to be reasons are objectively real. He suggests that we should take reasons to be objectively real if (or to the extent that) the best account of why it seems to us that there are reasons and values is that they are really there (VFN 141). This sounds like a form of Objective Realism, not about Platonic entities of some sort, but about reasons themselves. But it is not perfectly clear what Nagel thinks is involved in the existence of a reason.[15] He says that the existence of reasons is dependent on the existence of creatures who can see and respond to reasons:

The reasons are real, they are not just appearances. To be sure, they will be attributed only to a being that has, in addition to desires, a general capacity to develop an objective view of what it should do. Thus, if cockroaches cannot think about what they should do, there is nothing they should do. (VFN 150)

This, however, is in tension with the claims that Nagel makes when he is arguing for the existence of neutral values. For instance:

The pain can be detached in thought from the fact that it is mine without losing any of its dreadfulness. It has, so to speak, a life of its own. That is why it is natural to ascribe to it a value of its own. (VFN 160)

... suffering is a bad thing, period, and not just for the sufferer. (VFN 161)

An Intersubjectivist account of neutral values does not require that suffering be a bad thing in itself and not just for the sufferer. It requires only that suffering be a bad thing for everyone *because* it is bad for the sufferer. So here Nagel again seems to be an Objective Realist. But on a realist conception of the badness of pain, surely the pains of animals who cannot think objectively about what they should do must be bad in the same way as the pain of animals who can. If so, there would be reasons and values, even in a world without creatures who can see and respond to them.[16]

Finally, when discussing the temptation to think that a maximally objective account of values must be the best one, Nagel remarks:

This idea underlies the fairly common moral assumption that the only real values are impersonal values, and that someone can really have a reason to do something only if there is an agent-neutral reason for it to happen. That is the essence of traditional forms of consequentialism: the only reason for anyone to do anything is that it would be better in itself, considering the world as a whole, if he did it. (VFN 162–63)

Evidently, Nagel thinks that the position that there are only agent-neutral values commits one to consequentialism. Relatedly, he thinks that agent-neutral values are correctly described as reasons for things to happen, reasons that are concerned with what is "better in itself." This again suggests Objective Realism. Nagel's position, I think, is not fully consistent. On the whole, it seems as if he takes himself to be defending the existence of agent-neutral reasons in an Objective Realist sense, although his project can be understood as an Intersubjectivist one.

It is not necessary to settle the question of how to categorize Nagel's position here. But two points are important to the rest of my argument. First, if we distinguish between agent-relative or subjective values on the one hand, and agent-neutral values *understood on the Objective Realist model* on the other, we leave out an important option. Values may be intersubjective: not part of the fabric of the universe or external truth, but nevertheless shared or at least shareable by agents.[17] Second, if the status of values is essentially intersubjective, then the question arises why we should suppose that a value must be shared by everyone – why Intersubjectivism must be universal. If values arise from human relations, then there are surely more possibilities. The claims springing from an acknowledgement of our common humanity are one source of value, but the claims springing from friendships, marriages, local communities, and common interests may be others.

III   WHY NOT ALL VALUES ARE AGENT-NEUTRAL

By the time he wrote *The View from Nowhere*, Nagel had decided that not all subjective values have objective correlates.[18] He argues that an individual may have agent-relative or subjective reasons which have a legitimate normative force for her, but which have no normative force for others.

Nagel was moved to modify his earlier position, I believe, by a general consideration and by reflection on certain familiar categories of value which seem to illustrate that consideration. The general consideration is familiar to us from criticisms of utilitarianism, especially those of Bernard Williams.[19] According to Williams, utilitarianism deprives the moral agent of her integrity or individual character, because it does not allow her actions to be guided by commitments to a set of people and projects that are distinctively her own. But these are the very commitments which make us who we are as individuals and give us reasons for caring about our own lives. A person may surely find that some project or person is the most important thing in the world *to her* without having to suppose that it is the most important thing in the world *absolutely*. A theory that requires impartial allegiance to a system of agent-neutral values gives individuals insufficient space in which to lead their own lives. In Samuel Scheffler's words, it ignores "the independence and distinctness of the personal point of view."[20]

In *The View from Nowhere*, Nagel discusses three categories of values which, he thinks, must be understood as agent-relative for these reasons (VFN 164ff.). The first category springs from the agent's special relationship to his own projects. Nagel calls these "reasons of autonomy." He gives the example of someone with a desire to climb to the top of Kilimanjaro. This desire, he supposes, could give the person a good reason to make the climb, without giving others a reason to help him make it (VFN 167). Because he has the desire, his climbing Kilimanjaro is good-for him, but this does not make it good-absolutely, nor need he suppose that it does. The second category, and the most difficult to understand, is the category of "deontological reasons." These are traditional moral restrictions, which forbid performing certain types of actions even when the consequences of doing so are good. According to Nagel, they spring from an agent's special relationship to his own actions. Although it may be best absolutely that someone should lie, or break faith, or kill another, because of the good consequences that will in this way be produced, it may be better *for him* not to do so (VFN 180). The last category is "reasons of obligation" which, Nagel says, "stem from the special obligations we have toward those to whom we are closely related: parents, children, spouses, siblings, fellow members of a community or even a nation" (VFN 165). Because of my special obligation to my own child, for instance, it might be the most important thing in the world *to me* that my child be successful or happy. I can have this attitude without supposing that my child is objectively any more important than any other child.

In each of these three cases, it appears as if an agent has excellent subjective reasons for doing things which from an objective point of view are either completely worthless or obviously inferior to other things which she might do. Of course, there are familiar strategies for dealing with these appearances, many of which have been generated by the utilitarian tradition. The most revisionist strategy is to dismiss them, and to castigate people who spend their time on worthless activities as irrational, and people who pursue the happiness of their loved ones at the expense of the greater good as selfish. A more moderate strategy is to produce extraneous justifications for giving one's personal concerns extra weight. The good is maximized, say, by everyone looking after her own special friends. But there are also well-known objections to these strategies.[21] Rather than supposing that a special concern for your own projects, loved ones, and actions is either irrational or in need of an extraneous justification, Nagel thinks we should allow that there are some values which are purely agent-relative. Accordingly, in *The View from Nowhere*, he offers us explanations of why reasons of the first two kinds, reasons of autonomy and deontological reasons, might be thought to exist. In what follows I examine these accounts.

IV   AMBITION

In *The View from Nowhere*, Nagel suggests that some of an agent's interests and desires give rise to agent-neutral values and some only to agent-relative values. The obvious question is how we are to draw the line. Nagel expects the two categories to sort along these lines: Our interests in avoiding pains and having pleasures, in the satisfaction of what we would intuitively call basic needs, and in the possession of freedom, self-respect, and access to opportunities and resources, give rise to neutral values (VFN 171). But more idiosyncratic personal projects, such as the desire to climb to the top of Kilimanjaro or to learn to play the piano, have only relative value. Rather than using Nagel's label "reasons of autonomy," I am going to call these idiosyncratic projects "ambitions."²² The claim is that ambitions give those who have them reasons to do things, but do not give others reasons to help or to care whether these things get done. The question then is why the normative force of ambitions is limited in this way.

According to Nagel, it is a matter of how far an individual's authority to confer value may appropriately be thought to extend (VFN 168). In order to explain this it is helpful to introduce another distinction. Nagel believes that values may differ in what he calls their degree of externality, their independence from the concerns of sentient beings (VFN 152–53). Some valuable things clearly get their value from their relation to people. Consider for instance chocolate. We could account for the value of chocolate in either of two ways. One is to say that its value is intrinsic, and that the reason why we like it so much is because we recognize that fact. If we failed to like chocolate, we would have failed to appreciate something of value. The other is to say that eating chocolate is valuable to human beings *because* we like it so much. In the case of chocolate, that seems like a much more sensible thing to say. Chocolate is not an independent value which our taste buds recognize (as if they were an epistemological faculty, a way of knowing about values). Instead, chocolate gets its value *from* the way it affects us. We *confer* value on it by liking it.

In other cases it is less obvious whether this sort of analysis applies. Consider the value of a beautiful sunset or a work of art. Here, people are much more tempted to say that the value, the beauty, is in the object itself, and that what we do is recognize it. If we didn't like it, we would be failing to see a value that is really there. This is the kind of value that Nagel calls external.[23] Obviously, this kind of value is only possible if we accept an Objective Realist interpretation of agent-neutral or objective values. An Intersubjectivist must say that the value of beauty arises in the same way as the value of chocolate, only by a more complex process. In this case, aesthetic value would also be a value that we confer.[24]

Leave aside the question whether there are any external values. Suppose that we are talking about those values which we confer. Some of these values are conferred collectively – as aesthetic values are, if they are conferred – while others are conferred individually. This is the phenomenon which Nagel refers to as the individual's authority. The individual's authority is his right to confer objective value on something by desiring, or enjoying, or being interested in it. Whenever we say that an agent-neutral value arises from someone's desire, we in effect allow the agent to confer agent-neutral or objective value on some state of affairs. If all desires gave rise to agent-neutral reasons, every desire would be an act of legislation – it would create a value for the whole human race. The question therefore is how far the individual's right to legislate runs: what range of things an individual has the authority to confer neutral or objective value on.

Nagel believes that it is appropriate to give the individual the authority to confer objective value on her own inner states and the conditions that determine what living her life is like, but that it is not appropriate to give an agent the authority to confer objective value on things that are completely outside of herself (VFN 169–71). Suppose, for example, that it is my ambition that my statue should stand on campus. It seems very odd to say that everyone has a reason to work to bring this about merely because I desire it. Why should I be the right person to determine what state of the campus is objectively good?[25] On the other hand, I seem to be exactly the right person to determine what state of *me* is objectively good. If I'm not the person to determine this, who could possibly be? This is why everyone has a reason to help me to achieve things like pleasure and freedom, but no one has a reason to help me get my statue put up on campus.

Two facts complicate what I have just said – facts which we must notice in order to avoid confusion. The first is that the satisfaction of a desire often brings pleasure, and Nagel supposes that pleasure has neutral value. In one sense, then, you do have a reason to help me arrange to get my statue on campus, but the reason is not, directly, that I want it. It is that, given that I want it, it will give me pleasure. To see that these two reasons are different, we need only remind ourselves that desire and pleasure can be prized apart. We can have desires for the realization of states of affairs in which we will not personally take part, and desires whose satisfactions we will never even know about.

The other complication comes from one of Nagel's other categories of agent-relative reasons. It seems natural to believe that people have a special obligation to try to promote the projects of those with whom they have personal relationships (VFN 168). If I am your friend, I should be concerned with whether or not you achieve your ambitions, regardless of whether your doing so serves some objective or neutral value.[26] To correct for these complications, we should imagine a case where all that is relevant is that some randomly selected person has an ambition, and ask whether that ambition, *in itself*, provides others with normative reasons, as is does the person who has it. Suppose I want my statue to stand on campus after I am dead (VFN 169). I will not be one of those who uses or even sees the campus, nor will I even be around to enjoy the thought that my ambition has been achieved. Someone who takes this desire to be in itself the source of an objectively normative reason must be prepared to let me control campus aesthetics from beyond the grave. According to Nagel, my authority should not extend so far.

This way of putting the question makes Nagel's answer seem reasonable. But it ignores the fact that most people do not regard the value of pursuing their ambitions as grounded merely in their own desires.[27] Here it helps to appeal to a distinction Nagel himself used in *The Possibility of Altruism* – the distinction between unmotivated and motivated desires (PA 29ff.). An unmotivated desire is one which is simply caused in us; a motivated desire is one for which we can give reasons. In *The View from Nowhere*, Nagel says nothing about why his exemplar wants to play the piano or climb to the top of Kilimanjaro (VFN 167). But most people *do* have reasons for their personal ambitions, and in this sense, their ambitions are motivated.[28] Attention to this fact reveals that the structure of a reason of ambition is rather complex.

Suppose it is my ambition to write a book about Kant's ethics that will be required reading in all ethics classes. I do not care whether or not I live to see my book required. Following Nagel's analysis, we will say that this ambition is agent-relative, since it gives me a reason to try to bring it about that my book is required reading, but it does not give anyone else a reason to require my book. This seems to fit, for surely no reason for anyone to require my book could spring from the bare fact that I *want* it that way. The only conceivable reason for anyone to require my book would be that it was a good book.

But this way of describing the situation implies a strange description of my own attitude. It suggests that my desire to have my book required is a product of raw vanity, and that if I want to write a good book, this is merely as a means to getting it required. This does not correctly reflect the structure of my ambition. Part of the reason that I want to write a good book on Kant's ethics is that I think such a book would be a good thing, and my ambition is not conceivable without that thought. It is an ambition to do something good, and it would not be served by people's requiring my book regardless of whether it were good. For now, let us describe this by saying that I think *someone* should write a book on Kant's ethics good enough that it will be required reading. I think that this would have neutral value.   ·

This does not, however, mean that my ambition is just a disinterested response to that neutral value. It is essential not to sanitize the phenomena here, or we shall go wrong. I may be interested in personal adulation, I may really like the idea of my book's being required reading, and I may even harbor competitive feelings towards others engaged in similar projects. I do not just want it to be the case that someone writes the book. I want to *be the someone* who writes that book. That element in my ambition is ineliminably agent-relative; no one else, except possibly my friends, has a reason to care whether I write the book or someone else does.

So the structure of this ambition is not:

(1) I want my book to be required reading (where that is an agent-relative end);
(2) therefore: I shall write a good book (as a means to that end);

but rather:

(1) Someone should write a book on Kant good enough that it will be required reading (where that is an agent-neutral end);
(2) I want to be that someone (agent-relative motive).

In other words, to have a personal project or ambition is not to desire a special object which you think is good for you subjectively, but rather to want to stand in a special relationship to something you think is good objectively.

Ambition so characterized clearly does have an agent-relative component: you want to stand in a special relationship to what is good. Is this component the source of subjective reasons for action? On the one hand, the agent-relative component does seem to *motivate* me to do a lot of work I would not otherwise do. It is often true that without the personal element in ambition, people would not be able to bring themselves to carry out arduous tasks. There are, therefore, neutral reasons for encouraging the personal desires associated with ambitions. But should the agent herself treat these personal desires as the sources of reasons? If I took it seriously that my desire that *I* should be the one to write the book was a reason for action, then I would have a reason to prevent one of the other Kant scholars from writing *her* book. But in fact, neither I nor anybody else thinks I have a reason to do this, even if in competitive moments I am tempted to feel it. This is not an expression of ambition, but rather a very familiar perversion of it.

It is important to see that reasons of personal obligation characteristically have this form. Although I may not suppose that the happiness of my loved ones is objectively more important than that of anyone else, I certainly do suppose that their happiness is objectively good. The structure of reasons arising from love is similar to that of reasons of ambition. I think that someone should make my darling happy, and I want very much to *be that someone*. And others may have good reason to encourage me in this. But if I try to prevent someone else from making my darling happy or if I suppose that my darling's happiness has no value unless it is produced by me, that is no longer an expression of love. Again, it is a very familiar perversion of it.[29]

Where there is no agent-neutral value anywhere in the structure of the ambition – where the ambition is not an ambition to do something good – we might feel inclined to deny that it provides any kind of a reason, even an agent-relative reason for its agent. This is a plausible way of dealing with my ambition to have my statue on campus. That is just a stupid piece of vanity, and one might well think that such a desire does not provide even *me* with a reason for trying to arrange its satisfaction.

But there is an important objection to the way I have handled these cases. I have been trading on the claim that a good book on Kant's ethics would be an objectively good thing. You may of course, deny that. But even if you accept it, you might point out that not every ambition is *in that way* an ambition to do or produce something good. Is someone who wants to climb a mountain "because it is there" committed to the view that someone ought to climb this mountain (as if it needed climbing), or perhaps that climbing a mountain is an intrinsically valuable action, whose occurrence everyone has a reason to promote? Does someone who wishes to collect stamps or coins or barbed wire, or to excel at bowling or billiards, have to believe that these are activities with an intrinsic value of their own?

Perhaps that does not seem quite right. But neither does it seem right to say that those who pursue such projects are in the grip of unmotivated desires, or view themselves as being so. There are reasons for caring about these things, reasons which are communicable and therefore at least potentially shareable. Ask a mountain climber why she climbs and she need not be mute: she may tell you things about the enlarged vistas, the struggle with the elements, the challenge of overcoming fears or surpassing physical limitations. She takes her desire to climb mountains to be a motivated desire, motivated by recognizably good features of the experience of climbing. She does not take the value of the climb to be conferred on it simply by her desire to do it. Someone who says "I *just* want to" is not offering you his reason; he is setting up a bulwark against incomprehension. You may be the problem, or he may feel himself inarticulate: many people do. But listen to the articulate talk about their projects and you hear the familiar voice of humanity, not the voice of alien idiosyncrasies.

Or if you don't, perhaps you should. For it is at this point that the difference between Objective Realism and Intersubjectivism becomes important. An Objective Realist interpretation of the value of climbing mountains, or of collecting stamps or coins or barbed wire, or of excelling at bowling or billiards, is not very tempting.[30] Neither, I think, is an Objective Realist interpretation of the value of a good book on Kant's ethics. These are not intrinsic values, already there in the universe, which we have discovered, but rather are expressions of our own distinctively human capacity to take an interest, and to find something interesting, in whatever we find around us. To share another's ends, or at least to grant that they could be shared, is to see them as expressions of that capacity, and so as expressions of our common humanity. The Intersubjectivist sees the other as human, and *therefore* shares or tries to share the other's ends. That is why she helps others to pursue their ambitions. But the Objective Realist sees no reason to help unless he *first* sees the other's ends as ones that he can share. His relationship to others is mediated by his relationship to their ends. According to the Intersubjectivist this is not only a mistake in moral theory but a moral wrong. We should promote the ends of others not because we recognize the value of those *ends*, but rather out of respect for the humanity of those who have them.

I am not here concerned to argue, as Nagel is in *The Possibility of Altruism*, that we are always obliged to promote everyone's ambitions, and that therefore we must find some "combinatorial principles" for weighing up the many reasons they provide (PA 133ff.). I do not myself believe that reasons *can* be added across the boundaries of persons. And since we cannot always act for everyone's reasons, that cannot be our duty. But according to this argument we are obliged to see the ends of others as providing reasons for action, and this means that the claims of proximity may bring them into play. Someone in your neighborhood, in immediate need of help in order to carry out his ambition, does present you with a reason to act. In that sense, reasons springing from ambitions are agent-neutral. But they spring from our respect for one another, rather than from our respect for one another's ends.

But one form of proximity is especially important. For of course it is also true that you might come to share the ambition of another in a deeper way. For if what I have said is right, you ought to be committed to the view that another *could* explain to you what is good about the world as she sees it through the eyes of her ambition.[31] You may come to see the value of mountain climbing, or philosophical ethics, or stamp collecting, and to take it as your own. And then, between the two of you, the value functions *as if* it were a value in the Objective Realist sense. It is a fact about your relationship that you both see this as a good thing, which you share a reason to promote. This is why those who share particular ambitions form communities which acknowledge special and reciprocal obligations to one another. In this way, Intersubjective values can come to function like Objective Realist values with respect to the very communities which they themselves create.

V DEONTOLOGY

Deontological reasons are reasons for an agent to do or avoid certain actions. They do not spring from the consequences of those actions, but rather from the claims of those with whom we interact to be treated by us in certain ways. One who believes in deontological values believes that no matter how good our ends are, we are not supposed to hurt people, or tell lies, or break promises in their pursuit. Deontological reasons are the source of the traditional moral thou-shalt-nots.

It is important to see why Nagel thinks these reasons must be agent-relative. Three other accounts of them, which construe them as objective or agent-neutral, may seem more plausible at first glance.

First, we might think that they derive directly from the agent-neutral or objectively valuable interests of the other people involved, the potential victims of wrongdoing. We might think that the reason not to hurt people is that it is objectively bad for them to be hurt, or that the reason not to lie to people is that it is objectively good for them to know the truth, or that the reason not to break promises springs from the objective badness of disappointed expectations. In short, we might think that wrongdoing is bad because of the *specific* harm that it does to the victim.

The second account of deontological values is modeled on one utilitarian account of them. John Stuart Mill argued that deontological principles are a kind of inductive generalization from particular utility calculations.[32] We apply the principle of utility directly in a large number of individual cases, and discover that, almost always, telling lies or breaking promises does more harm than good. Usually, this will be for the kind of reason mentioned in the first account – say, that pain, ignorance, or disappointment is bad – together with certain more long-range considerations, such as the bad effects of setting an example or making a habit of performing such actions.[33] The actions are bad because of the *general* harm which they do.

Third, we might think that the actions forbidden by deontological reasons are simply bad in themselves, objectively so – not (just) because of the harm that they do, but because of a specific form of badness, namely *wrongness*.

But there are problems with all of these attempts to construe deontological values as agent-neutral. To see this, consider Bernard Williams's by now famous example:

> Jim finds himself in the central square of a small South American town. Tied up against the wall are a row of twenty Indians, most terrified, a few defiant, in front of them several armed men in uniform. . . . The captain in charge explains that the Indians are a random group of the inhabitants who, after recent acts of protest against the government, are just about to be killed to remind other possible protestors of the advantages of not protesting. However, since Jim is an honored visitor from another land, the captain is happy to offer him a guest's privilege of killing one of the Indians himself. If Jim accepts, then as a special mark of the occasion, the other Indians will be let off. . . . [I]f Jim refuses . . . Pedro here will do what he was about to do when Jim arrived, and kill them all.[34]

Utilitarians are committed to the view that it is *obvious* that Jim should kill an Indian, but few people can imagine themselves in Jim's position without some sense of a dilemma. Many think that in Jim's shoes they would kill an Indian, but they do not see it as a happy opportunity for doing some good. Some think that Jim should not let the captain co-opt him into participating in a murder and should refuse. Still others think that it is essential to find out, if possible, what the Indians want Jim to do.[35] Nagel thinks that if all values are objective or agent-neutral we should have *no* sense of dilemma in cases like this, since that we do the *most* good by killing the Indian is obvious.

This problem can be dealt with in various ways. A consequentialist may claim that it is salutary for us to be subject to some hesitation to kill, even when the hesitation is irrational. Someone who favors the second account of deontological reasons, in terms of general harm, is especially likely to make this argument: killing is certainly something that usually does more harm than good, so a natural reluctance to do it has a consequentialist value of its own.[36] Another possible solution is suggested by the fact that the problem seems to depend on the assumption that values can be added across the boundaries between persons. If we deny this assumption, we may deny that killing twenty Indians is a worse thing than killing one. This move is not open to those who hold that the badness of a wrong act rests in the *general* harm that it does. But those who think that the badness rests in the specific harm to the victim, or in the wrongness of the act itself, may simply refuse to add. According to this view, not only hesitating but refusing to kill the Indian is perfectly intelligible.

But this does not entirely solve the problem. Suppose we do think that the badness of killing this Indian rests either in his own resulting death or in the badness of the act of killing him. We refuse to add values. Now it looks as if the badness is the same whether the Indian is shot by Jim or by Pedro: there will be a death, and a killing, either way. So perhaps Jim should flip a coin? This does not seem right either: most of us think that if Jim does not suppose he is going to do any good by killing the Indian then he *certainly* should not kill him. But if the same amount of evil is done either way, then Jim's reason for declining to kill the Indian must be agent-relative.

To make the problem clearer, imagine a peculiar theory of value. According to this theory, value is always objective or agent-neutral, and the only thing that has value is the keeping of promises. This theory will not tell us always to keep our promises, surprising as this may seem. First, assume that we can add values. Then there could be a case like this: by breaking your promise, you could cause five other people to keep theirs; while, if you keep yours, they will break theirs. You produce more promise-keeping by breaking your promise than by keeping it, and so that is what the theory tells you to do. Second, suppose we say that the promise-breakings must be bad for someone, and that their badness cannot be added across the boundaries between persons. For whom are they bad? It does not matter which view we take. If the badness is for the victim, I have no reason to care whether I inflict it on him or you do. I should flip a coin. If the badness is for me, the agent, I may have a reason to care, but it could be an agent-relative one.

Nagel concludes that deontological reasons, if they exist, are agent-relative. The special relation in which you stand to an action when you are the one who performs it carries a special weight, like the special relations in which you stand to your own ambitions or loved ones. In taking this position, Nagel joins Samuel Scheffler, who had earlier argued that deontological values are agent-relative. In *The Rejection of Consequentialism*, Scheffler argues for what he calls an "agent-centered prerogative," a right, under certain conditions, to neglect what will conduce to the overall good in favor of one's personal commitments.[37] Such a prerogative does the work of Nagel's "reasons of autonomy." But Scheffler finds the idea of an "agent-centered restriction" – that is, a deontological requirement – paradoxical. He claims that the idea that there could be a reason not to do certain actions which is not equally a reason to prevent them from being done has "an apparent air of irrationality," which any account of them must dispel.[38] Although Nagel undertakes to explain how deontological reasons arise, it is clear that he shares Scheffler's attitude. He characterizes deontological constraints as "obscure" and "peculiar"; he wonders how what we *do* can be so much more important than what *happens* (VFN 175, 180–81). At one point he says:

One reason for the resistance to deontological constraints is that they are formally puzzling, in a way that the other reasons we have discussed are not. We can understand how autonomous agent-relative reasons might derive from the specific projects and concerns of the agent, and we can understand how neutral reasons might derive from the interests of others, giving each of us reason to take them into account. But how can there be relative reasons to respect the claims of others? How can there be a reason not to twist someone's arm which is not equally a reason to prevent his arm from being twisted by someone else? (VFN 178)

Despite his doubts, Nagel gives an account of why such reasons exist.

In cases where a deontological restriction is at issue, performing the *action* puts you into a direct relationship with another human being – your "victim" as Nagel puts it. In performing the action, you

will have to aim directly at evil for your victim, even if your larger
purpose is good. Robert Nozick, in his remarks on the apparent
paradox of deontology, puts the point in more Kantian language. In
violating a deontological requirement, you will have to treat your
victim as a mere means.[39] I will come back to the question of what
there is to choose between these two formulations. In any case, the
force of deontological restrictions, according to Nagel, rests in the
immediate badness of victimizing someone.

Nagel illustrates his point with an example (VFN 176). You need
the cooperation of a reluctant elderly woman in order to save someone's life, and you find that you can only secure it by twisting the
arm of her grandchild so that his screams will induce her to act. You
are faced with using the child as a means to saving a life, and in this
case, that involves hurting the child. If the grandmother does not
give in, you have to try to hurt the child more. You have to *will* to
hurt the child more, and so, in a sense, to want to (VFN 182). The
louder the child screams, the better for you. But there he is, a child, a
vulnerable human being to whom everyone owes protection. From
your point of view, this is a terrible thing to *do*.

You might think that this analysis does not apply in some of the
other cases I have mentioned. Consider Williams's Indians. The one
you kill is going to die anyway, whether he is shot by you all alone or
along with his compatriots by Pedro. So you are not bringing about
an evil for him which he would not have endured otherwise. But
there is still a sense in which *you* are aiming directly at his evil. You
must pick up a rifle, aim it at his heart, and fire. You must be
gratified if the bullet kills him, just as you must be gratified if the
child screams louder. And, despite appearances, there is also a sense
in which you are treating him as a mere means. You are killing him
in order to save the others. The fact that he is going to die anyway
does not really change the fact that this is what *you* are doing.

According to Kant, you treat someone as a mere means whenever
you treat him in a way to which he could not possibly consent (G
430).[40] Kant's criterion most obviously rules out actions which depend upon force, coercion, or deception for their nature, for it is of
the essence of such actions that they make it impossible for their
victims to consent. If I am forced, I have no chance to consent. If I
am deceived, I don't know what I am consenting to. If I am coerced,
my consent itself is forced by means I would reject.[41] So if an action

depends upon force or deception or coercion, it is impossible for me to consent to *it*. To treat someone as an end, by contrast, is to respect his right to use his own reason to determine whether and how he will contribute to what happens.

This is why it is important to establish, if you can, what the Indians themselves think should happen. Suppose the oldest Indian steps forward and says, "Please go ahead, shoot *me*, and I forgive you in advance." This does not make things wonderful but it does help. *Very* roughly speaking, you are not treating him as a mere means if he consents to what you are doing.[42] Of course, the Indian does not in general consent to be shot, and his gesture does not mean that after all he has not been wronged. In the larger moral world he has. But if you and the Indians are forced to regard Pedro and the captain as mere forces of nature, as you are in this case, then there is a smaller moral world within which the issue is between you and them, and in that world this Indian consents. On the other hand, suppose the Indians are pacifists and they say, "We would rather die than ask you, an innocent man, to commit an act of violence. Don't do what the captain asks, but go back up north, and tell our story; make sure people know what is happening down here." Now the decision *not* to shoot looks much more tempting, doesn't it? Now you can at least imagine refusing. But you may still take the rifle from Pedro's hands and say, "You cannot ask me to kill to save you, and yet I will," and pick an Indian to shoot. This is a different kind of decision to kill than the earlier one, for it involves a refusal to share the Indians' moral universe; from the perspective of the Indians who live, it has a slight taint of paternalism.

Surprisingly, the fact that you are treating someone as a mere means operates even in the peculiar cases of breaking a promise so that other people will keep theirs, or telling a lie so that others will tell the truth. You can see this by imagining the kind of case in which you could be faced with such a decision. If I tell the truth, I predict, three of you will tell lies that you should not tell. On what basis could I make this prediction? Perhaps I think that if I tell the truth I will reveal information which will show you that it is in your interest to lie, and I also think that you are unscrupulous people who will lie if it is in your interest. Or perhaps I believe that the truth will confuse you, and that you will tell the lies as a result of the muddle. Or perhaps I think you have a wrongheaded moral system, and knowing this particular truth will make you wrongly conclude that you ought to lie. However it goes, if I tell a lie in order to *get you* to tell the truth, I am treating you as somehow inferior creatures whose tendency to go wrong must be controlled by my superior wisdom. Since this is a way of being treated to which you could not possibly consent, I am treating you as a mere means. Here I am not necessarily aiming at anything evil for you: I may be paternalistic, protecting you from going wrong. This shows, I think, that Nagel is mistaken when he emphasizes that you are aiming at your victim's *evil*. The problem is that you are treating your victim as a mere means. But suppose that with this revision we accept Nagel's account. It is the particular badness of treating someone as a means that explains deontological reasons. It is the horribleness of looking right into a pair of human eyes, while treating their owner like a piece of furniture or a tool. And yet by violating the restriction you may be doing what is best. So the badness of violating it is a badness that is for you. The reason is agent-relative.

Now this does not seem right at all. Surely when you violate a deontological restriction, it is bad for your victim as well as for you. Your victim may surely object to being treated as a mere means, even when he understands the larger good which is thereby produced. And his objection is not only to being harmed; it is to being *used*. Nagel believes that his theory can accommodate the victim's right to complain. He says:

The deontological constraint permits a victim always to object to those who aim at his harm, and this relation has the same special character of normative magnification when seen from the personal perspective of the victim that it has when seen from the personal perspective of the agent. Such a constraint expresses the direct view of the person on whom he is acting. *It operates through that relation.* The victim feels outrage when he is deliberately harmed even for the greater good of others, not simply because of the quantity of the harm but because of the assault on *his value* of having my actions guided by his evil. (VFN 184; my emphases)

This is absolutely right. But the theory that deontological reasons are agent-relative or only subjectively normative *cannot* accommodate it. If the deontological reason were agent-relative, merely *my* property, my victim would not have the right to demand that I act on it. Consider a comparison. If you have an agent-relative reason to climb Kilimanjaro, and don't do it, I may entertain the thought that you are being irrational. I can see what your reasons are. But if I have no reason to bring it about that you climb Kilimanjaro, as Nagel supposes, then I have no reason to talk you into doing it. I have no reason to do anything about your relative reasons, even to think about them, although I may happen to. I certainly don't have a reason to complain of your conduct when you don't act on them, and if I do, you may justifiably tell me that it is none of my business. If deontological reasons were *agent*-relative, the same thing would hold for victims. My victim could entertain the thought that I have a reason not to treat him this way, but that thought would give him no grounds for complaint. Astonishingly enough, it turns out to be none of his business.

Earlier, I mentioned two reasons why you might be moved to do something by someone else's subjective or relative reasons. One is to give her the agent-neutral good of pleasure. The other springs from the third category of agent-relative reasons, the reasons of personal obligation. If you stand in a personal relation to someone, you may therefore interest yourself in her subjective reasons. This seems like a natural thing to say, and it has weight against the points I have just been making. Although we may resent it when strangers point out to us that we are not doing what we have reason to do, we do not resent such reminders from friends, and we do not tell them that it is none of their business.

Nagel suggests, in the passage quoted above, that the deontological constraint "operates through the relation" between agent and victim. So it is tempting to suppose that what he has in mind is something like this: the relationship of agents and victims, like that of love or friendship, is a *personal* relationship. Perhaps *that* is what gives the victim a stake in the agent's relative reasons, and so entitles him to complain.[43]

But the violation of a deontological constraint *always* involves an agent and a victim, and thus if this account is correct, deontological reasons are always shared reasons. They cannot be the personal property of individual agents. Instead, they supervene on the relationships of people who interact with one another. They are intersubjective reasons.

In fact, Nagel's primal scene, the confrontation of agent and victim, shows us how agent-neutral reasons are *created* in personal interaction. My victim complains; he says: "How would you like it if someone did that to you?" I see not merely that I wouldn't like it, but that I would resent it. I am treating my victim as a means, and it is the essence of treating another as a means that his consent is dispensed with. It would be impossible for me to consent to be so treated and so I would have to rebel. That is why I would feel resentment. "How would you like it if someone did that to you?" In asking me this question my victim demands that I either cease using him as a means, or give up my own claim not to be so used by others. But the latter is impossible: one cannot consent to be used as a means. And so *he obligates me* to desist, and to treat him instead as an end in himself.[44] This of course is a variant of Nagel's own argument in *The Possibility of Altruism* (PA 82ff.). And as his arguments there show, my recognition that others must be treated as ends in themselves explains altruistic reasons as well. We resent those who regard our plight with indifference, in much the same way that we resent those who use us as means.

But now we have arrived at a picture of neutral or objective value that is different from the one Nagel had intended to give us. According to this account, *all* neutral reasons for action arise from a category which Nagel had thought of as a source of relative reasons – the category of personal relationships. But this is no special category: for *all* human interaction is personal. It is because or to the extent that we regard one another as *persons* that we acknowledge the force of deontological reasons. As persons, others demand that we treat them in ways to which they can consent; as persons, we find we must respond to that demand. But we also express our respect for one another's humanity by sharing in each other's ends. As persons, we have a claim on one another's help when it can readily be given or is desperately needed. It is the status of humanity, as the source of normative claims, that is the source of all value. The argument, in other words, has brought us back to Kant.

VI   POSTSCRIPT

Let me conclude by going back to the thoughts with which I began. In both *The Possibility of Altruism* and *The View from Nowhere*, Nagel's arguments take an unexpected turn. In both he starts from recognizably Kantian ideas, working in *The Possibility of Altruism* with motivation derived from a metaphysical conception of the person, and in *The View from Nowhere* with a two-standpoints account. And yet in both he ends up having to construct elaborate arguments to fend off the conclusion that his ideas will lead to utilitarianism. Why does this happen? It happens because Nagel presupposes that the business of morality is to bring something about.[45] This presupposition infects Nagel's arguments in many ways. In *The Possibility of Altruism*, Nagel treats all reasons as reasons to *promote* something (PA 47ff.). In *The View from Nowhere*, he substitutes the idea of aiming at someone's evil for that of treating him as a means. Nagel is puzzled by deontology because he finds it odd that we could have reasons not to do things which are not equally reasons to *prevent* those things from being done (VFN 177). He does not mention the difference between preventing an action by asking its agent not to do it or talking him out of it, and preventing an action by the use of force or tricks. If you suppose that all that matters is what you are bringing about, this is merely a difference in *method*. If morality is concerned with the character of human relationships, this difference is *everything*.[46] It is no accident that in order to explain deontology, Nagel must finally imagine his agents and victims *talking* to each other.[47] Nagel is in danger of ending up with consequentialism because that is where he started.

For the view that the business of ethics is to bring something about is the legacy of utilitarianism and, in turn, of the scientific aspirations of the utilitarian tradition. According to consequentialist conceptions of ethics, ethics if the most sublime form of technical engineering, the one that tells us how to bring about The Good. The questions that it answers are questions about what we should do with the world. These *are* the questions we must face when we confront issues of population control or the preservation of the environment, issues with which utilitarians have been nonaccidentally obsessed. But deontological restrictions predate these global issues, and were already recognized at a time when all we had to do with the world was to live in it together.

One way in which you might be tempted to describe the position I have defended in this essay leaves the distinction between neutral and relative values in place. It might be thought that I am defending this position: that persons have agent-neutral value, while all other values are agent-relative. And then I add that you express your sense of the neutral value of others by sharing in their agent-relative ends. This *is* close to the Kantian position I want to defend, but it is a misleading way to put it. It makes the value of persons a metaphysical reality, perhaps in need of a metaphysical defense; and to some minds, it will suggest that people are a good thing, and therefore that many people are better than a few. I do not believe these things.

Ask yourself, what is a reason? It is not just a consideration on which you in fact act, but one on which you are supposed to act; it is not just a motive, but rather a normative claim, exerting authority over other people and yourself at other times. To say that you have a reason is to say something *relational*, something which implies the existence of another, at least another self. It announces that you have a claim on that other, or acknowledges her claim on you. For normative claims are not the claims of a metaphysical world of values upon us: they are claims we make on ourselves and each other. It is both the essence of consequentialism and the trouble with it that it treats The Good, rather than people, as the source of normative claims.

The acknowledgment that another is a person is not exactly a reason to treat him in a certain way, but rather something that stands behind the very possibility of reasons. I cannot treat my own impulses to act as *reasons*, rather than mere occurrent impulses, without acknowledging that I at least exist at other times. I cannot treat them as *values*, exerting at least a possible claim on others, without acknowledging that other persons do indeed exist. That is the lesson of Nagel's own argument in *The Possibility of Altruism*. The title of this essay is a tautology: the only reasons that are possible are the reasons we can share.

NOTES

This essay leaves me with many debts. It is the result of a number of years teaching Thomas Nagel's books, and I owe a great deal to my students for many helpful comments and pressing challenges. In the fall of 1990, when I was developing my own responses to Nagel in class, I benefited especially from comments by Andrew Livernois and David Sussman; over the course of the last few years, my ideas on these topics have been shaped by conversations with Scott Kim. Arthur Kuflik read drafts of the material at two different stages and commented usefully and extensively both times. I received helpful written comments on an earlier draft from many people, among them James Dreier, Barbara Herman, Andrews Reath, and Amélie Rorty; and benefited from conversations with Catherine Elgin, Patricia Greenspan, Michael Hardimon, and Samuel Scheffler. A discussion with Thomas Scanlon and the members of his seminar on value theory in the spring of 1992 provided me with many useful suggestions and clarifications. And I am sure I have been influenced by Stephen Darwall, who makes many of the same points I do in this essay in part III of his book *Impartial Reason*. But my greatest debt here is of course to Thomas Nagel, whose ideas I have found endlessly fertile even when I have disagreed. I thank all of these people.

1 The term is used by Robert Nozick in *Anarchy, State, and Utopia*. I should emphasize that it is the *term* that I am criticizing here. Nozick's account of side constraints anticipates some of what I will say in this essay about deontological reasons: in particular, that they are based on the Kantian notion that people must not be treated as means (p. 30), and that they will seem puzzling only to someone who assumes that "a moral concern can function only as a moral goal" (p. 28).

2 John Rawls, *A Theory of Justice*. See especially pp. 139–42.

3 This formulation may give rise to the misapprehension that I do not think that there can be duties to the self, or that questions of value cannot arise for the self. What I actually think is that the relations between stages of a self have many of the same features as the relations between separate persons; if stages of the self are to lay each other under normative demands, they too owe each other reasons they can share. But, for reasons indicated in Section IV of this essay, it follows that the self cannot have a reason it *could* not, in principle, share with others. This gives the question of the reasons we can share with others a certain priority, and that is the focus of this essay. Duties to the self do not get an adequate treatment here.

4 In this chapter, references to Nagel's works will be inserted into the text. The abbreviations used are: "PA" for *The Possibility of Altruism* and "VFN" for *The View from Nowhere*.

5 In *The Possibility of Altruism*, Nagel uses the terms "subjective" and "objective." But these terms are awkward because they are used in so many different ways. "Subjective" may be used in a metaphysical sense, to refer to *how things are for someone*, assuming that things might be different for others. Or it may be used in an epistemological sense, to refer to *how things seem to someone*, assuming that things might in fact be different from the way they seem. To avoid confusion, notice that in *this* sense the subjective need not be personal or individual. Something could seem the same way to every human being and yet not be that way

from some more objective point of view. A mirage, although seen by everybody, is in this sense a subjective illusion; more controversially, one might say that colors are a feature of the subjective experience of creatures with color vision. In *The Possibility of Altruism*, Nagel uses "subjective" in a metaphysical sense: a subjective value is one that is good-for some individual. In *The View from Nowhere*, however, Nagel uses that term to refer to what *seems* to be a reason. Here his project is first to assert that it *seems* to us as if we had reasons and values (from a subjective or personal standpoint), and then to raise the question whether or not, from a more objective or impersonal standpoint, that appearance reveals itself as an illusion of the subjective standpoint (VFN ch. 8). For this reason, Nagel borrows Derek Parfit's terms to cover his earlier distinction. What he had called a subjective value becomes an agent-relative value, which is a source of reasons for a particular agent, but not necessarily for others. What he had called an objective value becomes an agent-neutral value, which is a source of reasons for any agent (VFN 152). Parfit introduces these terms in *Reasons and Persons*, p. 143.

6 James Dreier has pointed out to me that in styling my project an attack on the distinction between relative/subjective and neutral/objective, I might give the impression that I think this logical distinction is not exhaustive, which it obviously is. My quarrel, as will emerge, is really with Nagel's account of the source of these reasons, which suggests that values and reasons originate either from personal, idiosyncratic desires or from metaphysical realities of some kind. I thank Dreier for the point.

7 More accurately, Nagel's view is that if I do not, I will suffer from dissociation between the personal and impersonal views I can take of myself (PA ch. 11).

8 Or, as one might put it, that every person, being equally real, is a source of value. But Nagel does not put it that way: he moves, as we shall see, from a focus on the (equal) reality of people to a focus on the reality of their reasons. In one sense, I believe his mistake lies here, and that he would have arrived at a more Kantian and, as I think, more correct position if he had not made this move.

9 See especially G. E. Moore, "The Conception of Intrinsic Value," in his *Philosophical Studies*. Values could be independent of agents in this sense and still always involve agents in another sense: agents and their experiences might always be parts of the complex "organic unities" which G. E. Moore thought were the loci of value. See note 24. I thank Arthur Kuflik for prompting me to be clearer about this.

10 Another view makes good-for-ness objective in this sense. It is a fact about the universe that a certain thing is good for me or for you. I *think*

that this is the view that G. E. Moore, from whom I borrow the idea of formulating these notions in terms of good-for and good-absolutely, found incoherent. See Moore, *Principia Ethica*, pp. 97ff. I do not know whether it is incoherent, but it is not tempting.

11 For another account of Intersubjectivism, see Stephen Darwall, *Impartial Reason*, part III.

12 It may help to give examples of the sort of position I have in mind here. I am thinking, as will become clear, of Kant's claim that respect for the humanity in the person of another requires you to share his ends; or of Hume's view that the virtues get their value from a shared evaluative standpoint. According to Kant's argument, a person's subjective ends become objective ends in the eyes of those who respect his humanity; according to Hume's, the character traits subjectively valued by the members of a person's own "narrow circle" become objectively valued when viewed from a general point of view which we share. As I suggest below in the text, one may read Nagel's projects as forms of Intersubjectivist constructivism as well. I do not know whether an Intersubjectivist position *must* be one in which objective values are constructed from subjective ones, but the Intersubjectivist positions with which I am familiar do take this form.

13 This is not to say that there cannot be values that are best understood as "good for *us*." But these will not be the results of addition. They will exist when the two of us stand in a relationship to which the value in question is relevant. In this way the birth of a child might be good for a couple, or the conclusion of a treaty might be good for a nation. These are collective, not aggregative, goods.

14 Obviously, the array of logically possible positions goes far beyond the two that are schematically described in the text. One could be an Intersubjectivist and yet think that values can be added across the boundaries of persons. One could be an Objective Realist and yet deny that values can be added – not only across the boundaries of people, but at all. In *Reasons and Persons*, for example, Derek Parfit explores the possibility that weighing and compensation cannot take place even within the boundaries of a life (pp. 342–45). I am not concerned to discuss all possible theories of neutral value, but only the two I find most natural. I shall assume throughout this essay that if there is any objection to adding values, it comes from the consideration that everything that is good or bad is good or bad for somebody, and that values can be added within individual lives. I shall also assume that the view that everything that is good or bad is good or bad for someone is most naturally associated with some form of Intersubjectivism.

15 Sometimes, Nagel seems to imply that all it amounts to for a reason to

be "really there" *is* that it can be assimilated to the objective standpoint without contradiction or incoherence. This unites the practical and the epistemological projects described in the text, and the result would be an Intersubjectivist form of realism. Nagel's values would be part of reality because we put them there, rather than the way that, according to Kant, causes are part of empirical reality. This view would have the merit of giving us realism without metaphysics. But it would require a transcendental argument for the category of objective value, and I do not myself see how, in the absence of Kant's own firm division between theoretical and practical reason, this is to be achieved.

16 Nagel might reply that all that follows is that, if we exist, we have reason to stop the animal's pain. But if pain has a value of its own it seems more natural to say that there just is a reason to stop the animal's pain, although the animal cannot see and respond to it.

17 One reason I take this option to be important is this: I think that its lack of ontological or metaphysical commitments is a clear advantage of Intersubjectivism; we should not be Objective Realists unless, so to speak, there is no other way. This is not just because of Ockham's razor. A conviction that there are metaphysical truths backing up our claims of value must rest on, and therefore cannot explain, our confidence in our claims of value. Metaphysical moral realism takes us the long way around to end up where we started – at our own deep conviction that our values are not groundless – without giving us what we wanted – some account of the source of that conviction.

18 Nagel backed off from his earlier position by degrees. At the time he added the postscript to *The Possibility of Altruism* (quoted above), he had decided that it was possible that an individual's subjective reasons may sometimes have a legitimate normative force for her that goes beyond that of their objective correlates. If my happiness is good-absolutely, we both have a reason to pursue it, but perhaps I find an additional or a stronger reason in the fact that it is good-for-me. This seems to be an intermediate position between the views of *The Possibility of Altruism* and *The View from Nowhere*.

19 *Utilitarianism: For and Against*, pp. 100ff.; and "Persons, Character, and Morality," in his *Moral Luck*, chapter 1.

20 See Samuel Scheffler, *The Rejection of Consequentialism*, p. 41. I discuss Scheffler's views briefly in Section V below.

21 Many of which can be found in the two pieces by Williams cited in note 19.

22 Several readers have pointed out to me that this label, together with the example I go on to discuss, might suggest that all personal projects are in some way competitive. I do not mean to imply that, and in fact I discuss

some noncompetitive ones below. But the choice of an example of a personal project which is competitive seems to me to be useful, since such projects are especially resistant to objectification of either an Objective Realist or an Intersubjectivist kind.

23 Barbara Herman has pointed out to me that the external account works better for natural beauty than for art, since works of art are socially embedded and therefore their value seems more relative to our interests.

24 One may wonder whether an Objective Realist can accommodate the cases of clearly relational value, like the case of chocolate. The answer is yes. The Objective Realist does not have to place the intrinsic value in the chocolate. He can place it in the experience of a human being enjoying eating the chocolate. That is to say, he can construct what G. E. Moore called an organic unity and place the value-creating relationship inside of it. (See Moore, *Principia Ethica*, ch. 6.) The trouble with this strategy is that it conceals the fact that the value is really relational. For further discussion, see my "Two Distinctions in Goodness," Chapter 9 in this volume, especially pp. 268–70.

25 Of course, this way of putting it assumes that no one else has any desires about the campus that could weigh against mine. In that sense, it assumes that I am the only person in the world who cares about the campus. Some people, when they realize that, are tempted to think that under those improbable circumstances I *would* be the right person to determine what counts as a good state of the campus.

26. This includes your happiness or pleasure, which perhaps makes what I say here controversial. I am claiming that if I care about you I want your ambitions to be fulfilled, and not only in order to make you happy. I want them to be satisfied simply because you do. This is why deathbed wishes are entrusted to loved ones. Of course, this does not mean that I will never oppose your pursuit of an ambition if I foresee that it will make you miserable. But that is a matter of weighing, not a matter of refusing to give the ambition any weight of its own. Something here depends on one's views about rationality. There are people who hold that it is only rational to fulfill those ambitions that will make us happy. If you hold this view about rationality, you are likely to encourage and help your friends only to do what will make them happy, just as you are likely to give up your own more dangerous ambitions. But if you hold that it is sometimes rational just to do what you think is important without regard for your happiness, you are likely to respect a friend's desire to do what he thinks is important without regard to his happiness as well. Of course, if you hold the view that happiness just consists in doing what you think is most important, these issues cannot even arise.

27 On this point, see also Stephen Darwall, *Impartial Reason*, p. 139.

28 When introducing the idea (PA 29), Nagel writes as if a motivated desire
were one arrived at through deliberation. But on his own view prudence
is a motivated desire, and most of us can hardly be said to have arrived at
it through deliberation. You arrive at it through the simple recognition
of a reason – that it is your own future – without deliberation. I am
using the term in this looser sense; I do not think that most people arrive
at their ambitions through deliberation.

29 I am not suggesting that there is something perverted about *sexual* jeal-
ousy. The desire to make love to someone is not primarily the desire to
be the one who provides him with a certain kind of experience. The
desire to make someone happy can be an expression of either morality or
of love, but in neither case is it their essence. For further discussion, see
my "Creating the Kingdom of Ends: Reciprocity and Responsibility in
Personal Relations," Chapter 7 in this volume.

30 One may say that human talents and powers are developed and refined
by these activities, and that this is an objective human good. Indeed,
when people talk about what they like about these activities, these are
the things they talk about. But this does not mean that what they care
about are these supposedly objectively valuable features of their chosen
activities rather than the particular activities themselves. Other activities, which people are not always prepared to substitute for the ones they
actually choose, may refine and develop similar human powers. And one
may even accept these other activities as substitutes *if it is necessary* (as
when one turns to a less strenuous sport in old age). But we should not
take that to mean that the "objective" goods embodied in the activities
were all that the actors cared about. The problem here is like the problem associated with the fact that we love particular people even though
what we can say we love about them is general. You love a particular
person, not just his warmth, intelligence, and sense of humor. It is not
true that any other person with these attributes would do just as well,
even though it is true that if he leaves you, you may seek another person
with these attributes to replace him. No adequate theory of value can
ignore these complex facts.

31 There are several ways to motivate this thought. Daniel Warren has
pointed out to me, in conversation, that without this thought the requirement to share ends could be met by someone who took a sort of
patronizing attitude towards the ambitions of others: "Oh, well, *you*
like it, so I suppose we shall have to count it as good." Scott Kim
points out that a parallel problem exists on the recipient's side: If you
accept help from someone who does not in any way enter into your
ambitions, you may be regarding him somewhat instrumentally. The
point of these remarks is not to show that there is something *wrong*

with either helping or accepting help among those who do not really enter into each other's interests, but that the moral attitude required of us is less than perfectly realized in such cases. This in turn shows that there is a kind of continuum between the sense of "shared ends" defined in the previous paragraph and the sense defined in this paragraph. One may share the ends of others in the sense of (i) agreeing to promote them because they are another's ends; (ii) trusting that there must really be something interesting about them because they are another's ends; (iii) seeing what is interesting about them; amd (iv) coming to have them as your own ends. I thank Thomas Scanlon for prompting me to be clearer about this point, and Amélie Rorty for reminding me of the importance of the possibility that one may stop at step (iii); e.g., one may come to have a much better appreciation of what a certain school of art was trying to do without actually coming to enjoy the works or find them beautiful.

32 See John Stuart Mill, *Utilitarianism*, pp. 23–24.

33 Mill, *Utilitarianism*, p. 22.

34 Williams, *Utilitarianism: For and Against*, p. 98.

35 I think this point is sometimes overlooked in discussions of this example. Williams, to be fair, specifies that the Indians are begging Jim to accept the offer (p. 99). But he obscures the importance of this point when he says that this is "obviously" what they would be doing.

36 This is a familiar move: when reminded that a person is likely to experience a negative moral emotion such as guilt, regret, hesitation, or squeamishness about doing something which according to our theory is right, the philosopher points out that the action in question is *usually* wrong and that it is therefore healthy to be equipped with some reactions which will make it hard for us to do it or will make us think twice before doing it. The assumption seems to be that our emotions are clunkier, more mechanical, less sensitive to the details of a situation, and altogether less refined than our thoughts. This view seems to be a byproduct of the modern conception of the emotions; the emotions are conceived as feelings or reactions, not as perceptions. Aristotle, for instance, would not have said this about the trained emotions of the virtuous person.

37 Scheffler, *The Rejection of Consequentialism*, pp. 14ff.

38 Scheffler, *The Rejection of Consequentialism*, p. 82.

39 See note 1.

40 See my "The Right to Lie: Kant on Dealing with Evil," Chapter 5 in this volume; and Onora O'Neill, "Between Consenting Adults," in her *Constructions of Reason: Explorations of Kant's Practical Philosophy*, chapter 6.

41 There are familiar philosophical puzzles about all of these notions. This

is perhaps especially true of coercion, notoriously hard to distinguish in any formal way from bribery or the mere offer of an incentive. This is not the place to take these puzzles up, but this should pose a problem only for readers who are actually skeptical about whether there is such a thing as coercion.

42 That is a remark that needs *many* qualifications. Actual consent – in the sense of saying yes – can easily be spurious. As Onora O'Neill argues, a better test of whether someone was able to consent is whether the person had an authentic opportunity to say no. See Onora O'Neill, "Justice, Gender, and International Boundaries."

43 Thomas Scanlon has drawn my attention to a footnote in Nagel's paper "War and Massacre" in which Nagel mentions that Marshall Cohen says that according to Nagel's view, shooting at someone establishes an I-thou relationship. See *Mortal Questions*, p. 69. I agree with Cohen, and think that so interpreted Nagel is *right*.

44 Strictly speaking, this is only an account of what Kant would call the "incentive" of morality; we are not obligated until we acknowledge the necessity of adopting this incentive as law. A related point is this: several readers, among them Barbara Herman and Arthur Kuflik, have pointed out to me that this account says nothing about why I must recognize the other as a person, only about what follows from the fact that I do. For now, I can only acknowledge that the argument is incomplete in these ways. I hope to say more on these points elsewhere.

45 A similar point, I think, can be made about Scheffler. He says that it is "natural" to interpret Nozick's defense of side constraints as an appeal to the disvalue, the badness, of violating those constraints (Scheffler, *The Rejection of Consequentialism*, p. 88). But it is only "natural" if you ignore Nozick's reminder that a moral constraint does not have to function as a moral goal – that is, only if you presuppose that the business of morality is the realization of goals.

46 Several readers have suggested to me that I am not really rejecting consequentialism but only proposing an alternative account of what we should aim at: decent human relationships. This suggestion is similar to the familiar consequentialist reply to standard counterexamples: "If justice matters, we can include it among the results." That kind of inclusion results in the curious view discussed above: that we should commit injustice if it will bring about more justice. Scheffler imagines his consequentialist saying: "And if you are worried that a violation of R [the deontological requirement] corrupts the relationship between the agent and the victim, and that the corruption of a human relationship is a bad thing, then why isn't it at least as permissible to corrupt one valuable relationship if that is the only way to prevent the corruption of five

equally valuable human relationships?" (Scheffler, *The Rejection of Consequentialism*, pp. 89–90.) A commitment to mutual respect in human relationships is not merely a commitment to bringing respectful relations about, any move than a commitment to justice is merely a commitment to bringing justice about. For example: In the early stages of our friendship, I might be tempted to conceal things from you in order to help bring about a condition of mutual trust; I might be afraid that you will reject me too quickly if you find certain things out before you know me better. But if mutual trust is ever to be *achieved*, the day must come when my calculations about the effects of my telling you things stops; that is what it *means* for *me* to trust *you*. The point here is that having decent relationships with people is not the same as bringing them about and to some extent is inconsistent with regarding them as things to be brought about. And my suggestion in this essay is that *having* decent human relationships, not bringing them about, is the primary concern of morality.

47 Nor is it an accident that many of my own examples in this essay, especially the ones concerning Jim and the Indians, focus on what the protagonists might *say* to each other. Many of Rawls's arguments invite us to imagine people talking to each other, to consider what it would be like to say certain things to another person. His argument against the utilitarian account of what is wrong with slavery, in "Justice as Reciprocity" (pp. 242–68), in effect invites us to consider the absurdity of a slaveholder who says to a protesting slave: "But my gains *outweigh* your losses!" His consideration of the effects of publicizing principles of justice on people's self-respect are also related to this theme (see *Theory of Justice*, pp. 177ff.). Part of the appeal of the difference principle is that it is the source of justifications which you can offer *to anyone* without embarrassment.

11 Skepticism about practical reason

The Kantian approach to moral philosophy is to try to show that ethics is based on practical reason: that is, that our ethical judgments can be explained in terms of rational standards that apply directly to conduct or to deliberation. Part of the appeal of this approach lies in the way that it avoids certain sources of skepticism that some other approaches meet with inevitably. If ethically good action is simply rational action, we do not need to postulate special ethical properties in the world or faculties in the mind, in order to provide ethics with a foundation. But the Kantian approach gives rise to its own specific form of skepticism, skepticism about practical reason.

By *skepticism about practical reason*, I mean doubts about the extent to which human action is or could possibly be directed by reason. One form that such skepticism takes is doubt about the bearing of rational considerations on the activities of deliberation and choice; doubts, that is to say, about whether "formal" principles have any content and can give substantive guidance to choice and action. An example of this would be the common doubt about whether the contradiction tests associated with the first formulation of the categorical imperative succeed in ruling out anything. I will refer to this as *content skepticism*. A second form taken by skepticism about practical reason is doubt about the scope of reason as a motive. I will call this *motivational skepticism*. In this paper my main concern is with motivational skepticism and with the question whether it is justified. Some people think that motivational considerations alone provide grounds for skepticism about the project of founding ethics on practical reason. I will argue, against this view, that motivational skepticism must always be based on content skepticism. I will not address the question of whether or not content skepticism is justified. I want only to establish the fact that motivational skepticism has no independent force.

I

Skepticism about practical reason gets its classical formulation in the well-known passages in the *Treatise of Human Nature* that lead Hume to the conclusion that

Reason is, and ought only to be the slave of the passions, and can never pretend to any other office than to serve and obey them.[1]

According to these passages, as they are usually understood, the role of reason in action is limited to the discernment of the means to our ends. Reason can teach us how to satisfy our desires or passions, but it cannot tell us whether those desires or passions are themselves "rational"; that is, there is no sense in which desires or passions are rational or irrational. Our ends are picked out, so to speak, by our desires, and these ultimately determine what we do. Normative standards applying to conduct may come from other sources (such as a moral sense), but the only standard that comes from reason is that of effectiveness in the choice of means.

The limitation of practical reason to an instrumental role does not only prevent reason from determining ends; it even prevents reason from ranking them, except with respect to their conduciveness to some other end. Even the view that those choices and actions which are conducive to our overall self-interest are rationally to be preferred to self-destructive ones is undermined by the instrumental limitation. Self-interest itself has no rational *authority* over even the most whimsical desires. As Hume says:

'Tis not contrary to reason to prefer the destruction of the whole world to the scratching of my finger. 'Tis not contrary to reason for me to chuse my total ruin, to prevent the least uneasiness of an *Indian* or person wholly unknown to me. 'Tis as little contrary to reason to prefer even my own acknowledg'd lesser good to my greater, and have a more ardent affection for the former than the latter. (T 416)

x

Under the influence of self-interest [or of "a general appetite to good, and aversion to evil, consider'd merely as such" (T 417)] we may rank our ends, according to the amount of good that each represents for us, and determine which are, as Hume puts it, our "greatest and most valuable enjoyments" (T 416). But the self-interest that would make us favor the greater good need not itself be a stronger desire, or a stronger reason, than the desire for the lesser good, or than any of our more particular desires. Reason by itself neither selects nor ranks our ends.

Hume poses his argument as an argument against "the greatest part of moral philosophy, ancient and modern" (T 413). Moral philosophers, Hume says, have claimed that we ought to regulate our conduct by reason, and either suppress our passions or bring them into conformity with it; but he is going to show the fallacy of all this by showing, first, that reason alone can never provide a motive to any action, and, second, that reason can never oppose passion in the direction of the will. His argument for the first point goes this way: all reasoning is concerned either with abstract relations of ideas or with relations of objects, especially causal relations, which we learn about from experience. Abstract relations of ideas are the subject of logic and mathematics, and no one supposes that those by themselves give rise to any motives. They yield no conclusions about action. We are sometimes moved by the perception of causal relations, but only when there is a pre-existing motive in the case. As Hume puts it, if there is "the prospect of pleasure or pain from some object," we are concerned with its causes and effects. The argument that reason cannot oppose a passion in the direction of the will depends on, and in fact springs directly from, the argument that reason by itself cannot give rise to a motive. It is simply that reason *could* oppose a passion only if it could give rise to an *opposing motive*.

What is important to notice in this discussion is the relation between Hume's views about the possible content of principles of reason bearing on action and the scope of its motivational efficacy. The answer to the question what sorts of operation, procedure, or judgment of reason exist is presupposed in these passages. In the first part of the argument Hume goes through what by this point in the *Treatise* is a *settled* list of the types of rational judgment. The

argument is a sort of process of elimination: there are rational
judgments concerning logical and mathematical relations; there are
empirical connections such as cause and effect: Hume looks at
each of these in turn in order to see under what circumstances it
might be thought to have a bearing on decision and action. In other
words, Hume's arguments against a more extensive practical employment of reason depend upon Hume's own views about what
reason is – that is, about what sorts of operation and judgment
are "rational." His motivational skepticism (skepticism about the
scope of reason as a motive) is entirely dependent upon his content
skepticism (skepticism about what reason has to *say* about choice
and action).

Yet Hume's arguments may give the impression of doing something much stronger: of placing independent constraints, based
solely on motivational considerations, on what might count as a
principle of practical reason. Hume seems to say simply that all
reasoning that has a motivational influence must start from a passion, that being the only possible source of motivation, and must
proceed to the means to satisfy that passion, that being the only
operation of reason that transmits motivational force. Yet these are
separate points: they can be doubted, and challenged, separately.
One could disagree with Hume about his list of the types of rational judgment, operation, or possible deliberation, and yet still
agree with the basic point about the source of motivation: that all
rational motivation must ultimately spring from some nonrational
source, such as passion. At least one contemporary philosopher,
Bernard Williams, has taken something like Hume's argument to
have this kind of independent force, and has so argued in his essay
"Internal and External Reasons,"[2] which I will take up later in this
paper.

The Kantian must go further, and disagree with Hume on both
counts, since the Kantian supposes that there are operations of
practical reason which yield conclusions about actions and which
do not involve discerning relations between passions (or any pre-
existing sources of motivation) and those actions. What gives
rise to the difficulty about this further possibility is the question
of how such operations could yield conclusions that can motivate us.

II

The problem can best be stated in some terms provided by certain recent discussions in moral philosophy. W. D. Falk, William Frankena, and Thomas Nagel, among others, have distinguished between two kinds of moral theories, which are called "internalist" and "externalist."[3] An *internalist* theory is a theory according to which the knowledge (or the truth of the acceptance) of a moral judgment implies the existence of a motive (not necessarily overriding) for acting on that judgment. If I judge that some action is right, it is implied that I have, and acknowledge, some motive or reason for performing that action. It is part of the sense of the judgment that a motive is present: if someone agrees that an action is right, but cannot see any motive or reason for doing it, we must suppose, according to these views, that she does not quite know what she means when she agrees that the action is right. On an *externalist* theory, by contrast, such a conjunction of moral comprehension and total unmotivatedness is perfectly possible: knowledge is one thing and motivation another.

Examples of unquestionably external theories are not easy to find. As Falk points out (125–26), the simplest example would be a view according to which the motives for moral action come from something wholly separate from a grasp of the correctness of the judgments – say, an interest in obeying divine commands. In philosophical ethics the best example is John Stuart Mill (see Nagel 8–9), who firmly separates the question of the proof of the principle of utility from the question of its "sanctions." The reason why the principle of utility is true and the motive we might have for acting on it are not the same: the theoretical proof of its truth is contained in chapter IV of *Utilitarianism*, but the motives must be acquired in a utilitarian upbringing. It is Mill's view that *any* moral principle would have to be motivated by education and training and that "there is hardly anything so absurd or so mischievous" that it cannot be so motivated.[4] The "ultimate sanction" of the principle of utility is *not* that it can be proved, but that it is in accordance with our natural social feelings. Even to some who, like Mill himself, realize that the motives are acquired, "it does not present itself . . . as a superstition of education, or a law despotically imposed by the power of society, but as an attribute which it would not be well for them to be without."[5] The modern intuitionists, such as W. D. Ross and H. A. Prichard, seem also to have been externalists, but of a rather minimal kind. They believed that there was a distinctively moral motive, a sense of right or desire to do one's duty. This motive is triggered by the news that something is your duty, and only by that news, but it is still separate from the rational intuition that constitutes the understanding of your duty. It would be possible to have that intuition and not be motivated by it.[6] The reason why the act is right and the motive you have for doing it are separate items, although it is nevertheless the case that the motive for doing it is "because it is right." This falls just short of the internalist position, which is that the reason why the act is right is the reason, and the motive, for doing it: it is a practical reason. Intuitionism is a form of rationalist ethics, but intuitionists do not believe in practical reason, properly speaking. They believe there is a branch of theoretical reason that is specifically concerned with morals, by which human beings can be motivated because of a special psychological mechanism: a desire to do one's duty. One can see the oddity of this if one considers what the analogue would be in the case of theoretical reasoning. It is as if human beings could not be convinced by arguments acknowledged to be sound without the intervention of a special psychological mechanism: a belief that the conclusions of sound arguments are true.

By contrast, an internalist believes that the reasons why an action is right and the reasons why you do it are the same. The reason that the action is right is both the reason and the motive for doing it. Nagel gives as one example of this the theory of Hobbes: the reason for the action's rightness and your motive for doing it are both that it is in your interest. The literature on this subject splits, however, on the question of whether the Kantian position is internalist or not. Falk, for instance, characterizes the difference between internalism and externalism as one of whether the moral command arises from a source outside the agent (like God or society) or from within. If the difference is described this way, Kant's attempt to derive morality from autonomy makes him a paradigmatic internalist (see Falk 125, 129). On the other hand, some have believed that Kant's view that the moral command is indifferent to our desires, needs, and interests –

that it is categorical – makes him a paradigmatic externalist.[7] Since Kant himself took the categorical character of the imperative and autonomy of the moral motive to be necessarily connected, this is a surprising difference of opinion. I will come back to Kant in section VII.

This kind of reflection about the motivational force of ethical judgments has been brought to bear by Bernard Williams on the motivational force of reason claims generally. In "Internal and External Reasons" Williams argues that there are two kinds of reason claims, or two ways of making reason claims. Suppose I say that some person P has a reason to do action A. If I intend this to imply that the person P has a motive to do action A, the claim is of an internal reason; if not, the claim is of an external reason. Williams is concerned to argue that only internal reasons really exist. He points out (106–7) that, since an external-reason claim does not imply the existence of a motive, it cannot be used to explain anyone's action: that is, we cannot say that the person P did the action A because of reason R; for R does not provide P with a motive for doing A, and *that* is what we need to explain P's doing A: a motive. Nagel points out that if acknowledgment of a reason claim did not include acknowledgment of a motive, someone presented with a reason for action could ask: Why do what I have a reason to do? (9; see also Falk 121–22). Nagel's argument makes from the agent's perspective the same point that Williams makes from the explainer's perspective, namely, that unless reasons are motives, they cannot prompt or explain actions. And, unless reasons are motives, we cannot be said to be practically rational.

Thus, it seems to be a requirement on practical reasons, that they be capable of motivating us. This is where the difficulty arises about reasons that do not, like means/end reasons, draw on an obvious motivational source. So long as there is doubt about whether a given consideration is able to motivate a rational person, there is doubt about whether that consideration has the force of a practical *reason*. The consideration that such and such action is a means to getting what you want has a clear motivational source; so no one doubts that this is a reason. Practical-reason claims, if they are really to present us with reasons for action, must be capable of motivating rational persons. I will call this the *internalism requirement*.

In this section I want to talk about how the internalism requirement functions – or, more precisely, malfunctions – in skeptical arguments. Hume winds up his argument by putting the whole thing
in a quite general form. Reason is the faculty that judges of truth
and falsehood, and it can judge our ideas to be true or false because
they represent other things. But a passion is an original existence or
modification of existence, not a copy of anything: it cannot be true
or false, and therefore it cannot in itself be reasonable or unreasonable. Passions can be unreasonable, then, only if they are accompanied by judgments, and there are two cases of this kind. One is
when the passion is founded on the supposition of the existence of
objects that do not exist. You are outraged at the mocking things
you heard me say about you, but I was talking about somebody
else. You are terrified by the burglars you hear whispering in the
living room, but in fact you left the radio on. It is of course only in
an extended sense that Hume can think of these as cases where a
passion is irrational. Judgments of irrationality, whether of belief or
action, are, strictly speaking, relative to the subject's beliefs. Conclusions drawn from mistaken premises are not *irrational*.[8] The
case of passions based on false beliefs seems to be of this sort.

The second kind of case in which Hume says that the passion
might be called unreasonable is

... when, in exerting any passion in action, we chuse means insufficient for
the design'd end, and deceive ourselves in our judgment of causes and effects. (T 416)

This is in itself an ambiguous remark. Hume might, and in fact does,
mean simply that we base our action on a false belief about causal
relations. So this is no more genuinely a case of irrationality than
the other. Relative to the (false) causal belief, the action is not irrational. But it is important that there is something else one might mean
in this case, which is that, knowing the truth about the relevant
causal relations in the case, we might nevertheless choose means
insufficient to our end or fail to choose obviously sufficient and
readily available means to the end. This would be what I will call
true irrationality, by which I mean a failure to respond appropriately
to an available reason.

If the only possibility Hume means to be putting forward here is the possibility of action based on false belief about causes and effects, we get a curious result. Neither of the cases that Hume considers is a case of true irrationality: relative to their beliefs, people *never* act irrationally. Hume indeed says this:

... the moment we perceive the falsehood of any supposition, or the insufficiency of any means, our passions yield to our reason without any opposition. (T 416)

But it looks as if a theory of means/end rationality ought to allow for at least one form of true irrationality, namely, failure to be motivated by the consideration that the action is the means to your end. Even the skeptic about practical reason admits that human beings can be motivated by the consideration that a given action is a means to a desired end. But it is not enough, to explain this fact, that human beings can engage in causal reasoning. It is perfectly possible to imagine a sort of being who could engage in causal reasoning and who could, therefore, engage in reasoning that would point out the means to her ends, but who was not motivated by it.

Kant, in a passage early in the *Groundwork*, imagines a human being in just such a condition of being able to reason, so to speak, theoretically but not practically. He is talking about what the world would have been like if nature had had our happiness as her end. Our actions would have been controlled entirely by instincts designed to secure our happiness, and:

... if, over and above this, reason should have been granted to the favored creature, it would have served only to let it contemplate the happy constitution of its nature. (G 395)

The favored creature is portrayed as able to see that his actions are rational in the sense that they promote the means to his end (happiness); but he is not motivated by their reasonableness; he acts from instinct. Reason allows him to admire the rational appropriateness of what he does, but this is not what gets him to do it – he has the sort of attitude toward all his behavior that we in fact might have toward the involuntary well-functioning of our bodies.

Being motivated by the consideration that an action is a means to a desirable end is something beyond merely reflecting on that fact. The motive force attached to the end must be transmitted to the means in order for this to be a consideration that sets the human body in motion – and only if this is a consideration that sets the human body in motion can we say that reason has an influence on action. A practically rational person is not merely capable of performing certain rational mental operations, but capable also of transmitting motive force, so to speak, along the paths laid out by those operations. Otherwise even means/end reasoning will not meet the internalism requirement.

But the internalism requirement does not imply that nothing can interfere with this motivational transmission. And generally, this is something there seems to be no reason to believe: there seem to be plenty of things that could interfere with the motivational influence of a given rational consideration. Rage, passion, depression, distraction, grief, physical or mental illness: all these things could cause us to act irrationally, that is, to fail to be motivationally responsive to the rational considerations available to us.[9] The necessity, or the compellingness, of rational considerations lies in those considerations themselves, not in us: that is, we will not necessarily be motivated by them. Or rather, to put the point more properly and not to foreclose any metaphysical possibilities, their necessity may lie in the fact that, when they do move us – either in the realm of conviction or in that of motivation – they move us with the force of necessity. But it will still not be the case that they necessarily move us. So a person may be irrational, not merely by failing to observe rational connections – say, failing to see that the sufficient means are at hand – but also by being "willfully" blind to them, or even by being indifferent to them when they are pointed out.[10]

In this respect practical reason is no different from theoretical reason. Many things might cause me to fail to be convinced by a good argument. For me to be a theoretically rational person is not merely for me to be capable of performing logical and inductive operations, but for me to be appropriately *convinced* by them: my conviction in the premises must carry through, so to speak, to a conviction in the conclusion. Thus, the internalism requirement for theoretical reasons is that they be capable of convincing us – insofar as we are rational. It is quite possible for me to be able to perform these operations without generating any conviction, as a sort of game, say, and then I would not be a rational person.

Aristotle describes the novice in scientific studies as being able to repeat the argument, but without the sort of conviction that it will have for him later, when he fully understands it. In order for a theoretical argument or a practical deliberation to have the status of reason, it must of course be capable of motivating or convincing a rational person, but it does not follow that it must at all times be capable of motivating or convincing any given individual. It may follow from the supposition that we are rational persons and the supposition that a given argument or deliberation is rational that, if we are not convinced or motivated, there must be some explanation of that failure. But there is no reason at all to believe that such an explanation will always show that we had mistaken reasons, which, if true, would have been good reasons. Many things can interfere with the functioning of the rational operations in a human body. Thus there is no reason to deny that human beings might be practically irrational in the sense that Hume considers impossible: that, even with the truth at our disposal, we might from one cause or another fail to be interested in the means to our ends.

IV

My speculation is that skepticism about practical reason is sometimes based on a false impression of what the internalism requirement requires. It does not require that rational considerations always succeed in motivating us. All it requires is that rational considerations succeed in motivating us insofar as we are rational. One can admit the possibility of true irrationality and yet still believe that all practical reasoning is instrumental. But once this kind of irrationality is allowed in the means/end case, some of the grounds for skepticism about more ambitious forms of practical reasoning will seem less compelling. The case of prudence or self-interest will show what I have in mind. I have already mentioned Hume's account of this matter: he thinks that there is "a general appetite to good, and aversion to evil" and that a person will act prudently insofar as this calm and general passion remains dominant over particular passions. It is under the influence of this end that we weigh one possible satisfaction against another, trying to determine which conduces to our greater good. But if this general desire for the good does not remain predominant, not only the motive, but the reason, for doing what will conduce to one's greater good, disappears. For Hume says it is not contrary to reason to prefer an acknowledged lesser good to a greater.

Suppose, then, that you are confronted with a choice and, though informed that one option will lead to your greater good, you take the other. If true irrationality is excluded, and you fail to take the means to some end, this is evidence either that you don't really have this end or that it is not the most important thing to you. Thus, in this imagined case, where you do not choose your greater good, this is evidence either that you do not care about your greater good or that you do not care about it as much as you do about this particular lesser good. On the other hand, if you do respond to the news that one option leads to your greater good, then we have evidence that you do care about your greater good. This makes it seem as if your greater good is an end you might care about or not, and rationality is relative to what you care about. But, once we admit that one might from some other cause fail to be responsive to a rational consideration, there is no special reason to accept this analysis of the case. I do not mean that there is a reason to reject it, either, of course; my point is that whether you accept it depends on whether you *already* accept the limitation to means/end rationality. If you do, you will say that the case where the lesser good was chosen was a case where there was a stronger desire for it, and so a stronger reason; if you do not, and you think it *is* reasonable to choose the greater good (because prudence has rational authority), you will say that this is a case of true irrationality. The point is that the motivational analysis of the case *depends* upon your views of the content of rational principles of action, not the reverse. The fact that one might or might not be motivated to choose a certain course of action by the consideration that it leads to the greater good does not by itself show that the greater good is just one end among others, without special rational authority, something that some people care about and some people do not. Take the parallel case. The fact that one might or might not be motivated to choose a certain course of action by the consideration that it is the best available means to one's end does not show that taking the means to one's ends is just one end among others, an end some people care about and some people do not. In both cases, what we have is the fact that people are sometimes motivated by considerations of this sort, and that we all think in the latter case and some think in the former case that it is rational to be so motivated.

The argument about whether prudence or the greater good has

any special rational authority – about whether it is a rational consideration – will have to be carried out on another plane: it will have to be made in terms of a more metaphysical argument about just what reason does, what its scope is, and what sorts of operation, procedure, and judgment are rational. This argument will usually consist in an attempt to arrive at a general notion of reason by discovering features or characteristics that theoretical and practical reason share; such characteristic features as universality, sufficiency, timelessness, impersonality, or authority will be appealed to.[11] What the argument in favor of prudence would be will vary from theory to theory; here, the point is this: the fact that someone might fail to be motivated by the consideration that something will serve her greater good cannot by itself throw any doubt on the argument, whatever it is, that preferring the greater good is rational. If someone were not convinced by the logical operation of conjunction, and so could not reason with conviction from "A" and from "B" to "A and B", we would not be eager to conclude that conjunction was just a theory that some people believe and some people do not. Conjunction is not a theory to believe or disbelieve, but a principle of reasoning. Not everything that drives us to conclusions is a theory. Not everything that drives us to action need be a desired end (see Nagel 20–22).

v

An interesting result of admitting the possibility of true irrationality is that it follows that it will not always be possible to argue someone into rational behavior. If people are acting irrationally only because they do not know about the relevant means/end connection, they may respond properly to argument: point the connection out to them, and their behavior will be modified accordingly. In such a person the motivational path, so to speak, from end to means is open. A person in whom this path is, from some cause, blocked or nonfunctioning may not respond to argument, even if this person understands the argument in a theoretical way. Aristotle thinks of the incontinent person as being in a condition of this sort: this happens to people in fits of passion or rage, and the condition is actually physiological.[12] Now this is important; for it is sometimes thought, on the basis of the internalism requirement, that if there is a reason to do something it must be possible to argue someone into doing it: anyone who understands the argument will straightaway act. (The conclusion of a practical syllogism is an action.) Frankena, for example, argues against an internalist construal of the moral "ought" on the grounds that even after full reflection we do not always do what is right (71). But if there is a gap between understanding a reason and being motivated by it, then internalism does not imply that people can always be argued into reasonable conduct. The reason motivates someone who is capable of being motivated by the perception of a rational connection. Rationality is a condition that human beings are capable of, but it is not a condition that we are always in.

It is for this reason that some ethical theories centered on the idea of practical reason are best thought of as establishing ideals of character. A person with a good character will be, on such a view, one who responds to the available reasons in an appropriate way, one whose motivational structure is organized for rational receptivity, so that reasons motivate in accord with their proper force and necessity. It is not an accident that the two major philosophers in our tradition who thought of ethics in terms of practical reason – Aristotle and Kant – were also the two most concerned with the methods of moral education. Human beings must be taught, or habituated, to listen to reason: we are, as Kant says, imperfectly rational.

In fact, the argument of the last section can be recast in terms of virtues. Suppose that it *is* irrational not to prefer the greater good: this need have nothing at all to do with having the greater good *among* your desired ends. It is of course true that some people are more steadily motivated by considerations of what conduces to their greater good than others: call such a person *the prudent person*. The fact that the prudent person is more strongly motivated by reasons of greater good need not be taken to show that he has stronger reasons for attending to his greater good. (People have varying theoretical virtues too.[13]) We may indeed say that the prudent person "cares more" about his greater good, but that is just another way of saying that he responds more strongly to these kinds of consideration, that he has the virtue of prudence. It need not be taken to imply that his greater good is a more heavily weighted end with him and that, therefore, it really does matter more to him that he achieve his greater good than it does to another person, an imprudent person, that he achieve his. It makes more sense to say that this other person ignores reasons that he has. Again, take the parallel: some people respond much more readily and definitely to the consideration that something is an effective means to their end. We might call such a person a *determined* or *resolute* person. Presumably no one feels like saying that the determined or resolute person has a stronger reason for taking the means to her ends than anyone else does. We all have just the same reason for taking the means to our ends. The fact that people are motivated differently by the reasons they have does not show that they have different reasons. It may show that some have virtues that others lack. On a practical-reason theory, the possibility of rationality sets a standard for character; but that standard will not always be met. But this is not by itself a reason for skepticism about the scope of the deliberative guidance that reason *can* provide. This is a reason for skepticism only about the extent to which that guidance will ever be taken advantage of.

VI

Nevertheless, the fact that a practical reason must be capable of motivating us might still seem to put a limitation on the scope of practical reason: it might be thought that it is a subjective matter which considerations can motivate a given individual and that, therefore, all judgments of practical reason must be conditional in form. In Hume's argument, this kind of limitation is captured in the claim that motivation must originate in a passion. In the means/end case, we are able to be motivated by the consideration that action *A* will promote purpose *P* because, and only if, we have a pre-existing motivational impulse (a passion) attached to purpose *P*. As Hume says, a relation between two things will not have any motivational impact on us unless one of the two things has such impact. This does not limit practical reason to the means/end variety, but it might seem to impose a limitation of this sort: practical-reason claims must be reached by something that is recognizably a rational deliberative process from interests and motives one already has. This position is advocated by Bernard Williams in "Internal and External Reasons." Williams, as I have mentioned, argues that only internal reasons exist; but he takes this to have a strong Humean implication. Williams takes it that internal reasons are by definition relative to something that he calls the agent's "subjective motivational set": this follows from the fact that they can motivate. The contents of this set are left open, but one kind of thing it will obviously contain is the agent's desires and passions. Internal reasons are reasons reached by deliberation from the subjective motivational set: they can motivate us because of their connection to that set. Means/end deliberation, where the end is in the set and the means are what we arrive at by the motivating deliberation, is the most characteristic, but not the only, source of reasons for action. Williams calls the means/end view the "sub-Humean model", and he says this:

The sub-Humean model supposes that ϕ-ing [where ϕ-ing is some action we have a reason for doing] has to be related to some element in [the subjective motivational set] as causal means to end (unless perhaps it is straightforwardly the carrying out of a desire which is itself that element in [the subjective motivational set].) But this is only one case. . . . there are much wider possibilities for deliberation, such as: thinking how the satisfaction of elements in [the subjective motivational set] can be combined, e.g. by the time ordering; where there is some irresoluble conflict among the elements of [the subjective motivational set] considering which one attaches most weight to . . . or again, finding constitutive solutions, such as deciding what would make for an entertaining evening, granted that one wants entertainment. (104–5)[14]

Anything reached by a process of deliberation from the subjective motivational set may be something for which there is an internal reason, one that can motivate. External reasons, by contrast, exist regardless of what is in one's subjective motivational set. In this case, Williams points out, there must be some rational process, not springing from the subjective motivational set and therefore not relative to it, which could bring you to acknowledge something to be a reason and at the same time to be motivated by it. Reason must be able to produce an entirely new motive, the thing that Hume said could not be done.

Thus, Williams takes up one part of the skeptic's argument: that a piece of practical reasoning must start from something that is capable of motivating you; and drops the other, that the only kind of reasoning is means/end. One might suppose that this limits the operations of judgments of practical reason to those functions which are natural extensions or expansions of the means/end variety, and the things Williams mentions in this passage, such as making a plan to satisfy the various elements in the set, or constitutive reasoning, are generally thought to be of that sort. But in fact this is not Williams' view, nor is it necessitated by his argument, as he points out.

The processes of deliberation can have all sorts of effect on [the subjective motivational set], and this is a fact which a theory of internal reasons should be very happy to accommodate. So also it should be more liberal than some theorists have been about the possible elements in the [subjective motivational set]. I have discussed [the subjective motivational set] primarily in terms of desires, and this term can be used, formally, for all elements in [the subjective motivational set]. But this terminology may make one forget that [the subjective motivational set] can contain such things as dispositions of evaluation, patterns of emotional reaction, personal loyalties, and various projects, as they may abstractly be called, embodying commitments of the agent. (105)

Williams can accommodate the case of someone's acting for reasons of principle, and in this case the form the deliberation will take is that of applying the principle or of seeing that the principle applies to the case at hand. The advocate of the view that all deliberation is strictly of the means/end variety may claim to assimilate this case by the formal device of saying that the agent must have a desire to act on this principle, but this will not change the important fact, which is that the reasoning in this case will involve the application of the principle, which is not the same as means/end reasoning.[15]

In this kind of case, Williams' point will be that in order for the principle to provide reasons for a given agent, acceptance of the principle must constitute part of the agent's subjective motivational set. If the principle is not accepted by the agent, its dictates are not reasons for her. Reasons are relativized to the set. If this is true, it looks at first as if all practical reasons will be relative to the individual, because they are conditioned by what is in the subjective motivational set. Reasons that apply to you regardless of what is in your subjective motivational set will not exist.

This argument, however, having been cut loose from Hume's very definite ideas about what sort of rational operations and processes exist, has a very unclear bearing on claims about pure practical reason. If one accepts the internalism requirement, it follows that pure practical reason will exist if and only if we are capable of being motivated by the conclusions of the operations of pure practical reason as such. Something in us must make us capable of being motivated by them, and this something will be part of the subjective motivational set. Williams seems to think that this is a reason for doubting that pure practical reasons exist, whereas what seems to follow from the internalism requirement is this: if we can be motivated by considerations stemming from pure practical reason, then that capacity belongs to the subjective motivational set of every rational being. One cannot argue that the subjective motivational set contains only ends or desires; for that would be true only if all reasoning were of the means/end variety or its natural extensions. What sorts of items can be found in the set does not limit, but rather depends on, what kinds of reasoning are possible. Nor can one assume that the subjective motivational set consists only of individual or idiosyncratic elements; for that is to close off without argument the possibility that reason could yield conclusions that every rational being must acknowledge and be capable of being motivated by. As long as it is left open what kinds of rational operations yield conclusions about what to do and what to pursue, it must be left open whether we are capable of being motivated by them.

Consider the question of how an agent comes to accept a principle: to have it in her subjective motivational set. If we say that the agent comes to accept the principle through reasoning – through having been convinced that the principle admits of some ultimate justification – then there are grounds for saying that this principle is in the subjective motivational set of every rational person: for all rational persons could be brought to see that they have reason to act in the way required by the principle, and this is all that the internalism requirement requires. Now this is of course not Williams' view: he believes that the principles are acquired by education, training, and so forth, and that they do not admit of any ultimate justification.[16] There are two important points to make about this.

First, consider the case of the reflective agent who, after being raised to live by a certain principle, comes to question it. Some doubt, temptation, or argument has made her consider eliminating the principle from her subjective motivational set. Now what will she think? The principle does not, we are supposing, admit of an ultimate justification, so she will not find that. But this does not necessarily mean that she will reject the principle. She may, on reflection, find that she thinks it better (where this will be relative

to what other things are in her motivational set) that people should
have and act on such a principle, that it is in some rough way a good
idea – perhaps not the only but an excellent basis for community
living, etc. – and so she may retain it and even proceed to educate
those under her influence to adopt it. The odd thing to notice is that
this is almost exactly the sort of description Mill gives of the reflective utilitarian who, on realizing that his capacity to be motivated
by the principle of utility is an acquirement of education, is not
sorry. But Mill's position, as I mentioned earlier, is often taken to be
the best example of an *externalist* ethical position.

More immediately to the point, what this kind of case shows is
that for Williams, as for Hume, the motivational skepticism depends on what I have called the "content skepticism." Williams'
argument does not show that if there were unconditional principles
of reason applying to action we could not be motivated by them. He
only thinks that there are none. But Williams' argument, like
Hume's, gives the appearance of going the other way around: it looks
as if the motivational point – the internalism requirement – is supposed to have some force in limiting what might count as a principle
of practical reason. Whereas in fact, the real source of the skepticism
is a doubt about the existence of principles of action whose content
shows them to be ultimately justified.

VII

The internalism requirement is correct, but there is probably no
moral theory that it excludes. I do not think that it even excludes
utilitarianism or intuitionism, although it calls for a reformulation
of the associated views about the influence of ethical reasoning or
motivation. The force of the internalism requirement is psychological: what it does is not to refute ethical theories, but to make a
psychological demand on them.

This is in fact how philosophers advocating a connection between
morality and practical reason have thought of the matter. From considerations concerning the necessity that reasons be internal and
capable of motivating us which are almost identical to Williams',
Nagel, in the opening sections of *The Possibility of Altruism*, argues
that investigations into practical reason will yield discoveries about
our motivational capacities. Granting that reasons must be capable

of motivating us, he thinks that if we then are able to show the existence of reasons, we will have shown something capable of motivating us. In Nagel's eyes, the internalism requirement leads not to a limitation on practical reason, but to a rather surprising increase in the power of moral philosophy: it can teach us about human motivational capacities; it can teach us psychology.[17]

As Nagel points out, this approach also characterizes the moral philosophy of Kant. By the end of the Second Section of the *Groundwork*, there is in *one* sense no doubt that Kant has done what he set out to do: he has shown us what sort of demand pure reason would make on action. Working from the ideas that reasons in general (either theoretical or practical) must be universal, that reason seeks the unconditioned, and that its binding force must derive from autonomy, he has shown us what a law of pure reason applying to action would look like. But until it has been shown that we can be motivated to act according to the categorical imperative, it has not been completely shown that the categorical imperative really exists – that there really is a law of pure practical reason. And this is because of the internalism requirement. The question how the imperative is possible is equated to that of "how the constraint of the will, which the imperative expresses in the problem, can be conceived" (G 417). Thus, what remains for proof by a "deduction" is that we are capable of being motivated by this law of reason: that we have an autonomous will. In the *Groundwork III*, Kant does try to argue that we can be motivated by the categorical imperative, appealing to the pure spontaneity of reason as evidence for our intelligible nature and so for an autonomous will (G 452). In the *Critique of Practical Reason*,[18] however, Kant turns his strategy around. He argues that we know that we are capable of being motivated by the categorical imperative and therefore that we know (in a practical sense) that we have an autonomous will. Again, explorations into practical reason reveal our nature. It is important, however, that although in the *Critique of Practical Reason* Kant does not try to argue *that* pure reason can be a motive, he has detailed things to say about *how* it can be a motive – about how it functions as an incentive in combatting other incentives.[19] Something is still owed to the internalism requirement: namely, to show what psychological conclusions the moral theory implies.

It may be that we are immune to motivation by pure practical reason. But, for that matter, it may be that we are immune to motivation by means/ends connections. Perhaps our awareness of these in cases where we seem to act on them is epiphenomenal. In fact we are quite sure that we are not immune to the reasons springing from means/ends connections; and Kant maintained that, if we thought about it, we would see that we are not immune to the laws of pure practical reason: that we know we can do what we ought. But there is no guarantee of this; for our knowledge of our motives is limited. The conclusion is that, if we are rational, we will act as the categorical imperative directs. But we are not necessarily rational.

VIII

I have not attempted to show in this paper that there is such a thing as pure practical reason, or that reason has in any way a more extensive bearing on conduct than empiricism has standardly credited it with. What I have attempted to show is that this question is open in a particular way: that motivational considerations do not provide any reason, in advance of specific proposals, for skepticism about practical reason. If a philosopher can show us that something that is recognizably a law of reason has bearing on conduct, there is no special reason to doubt that human beings might be motivated by that consideration. The fact that the law might not govern conduct, even when someone understood it, is no reason for skepticism: the necessity is in the law, and not in us.

To the extent that skepticism about pure practical reason is based on the strange idea that an acknowledged reason can never fail to motivate, there is no reason to accept it. It is based on some sort of a misunderstanding, and I have suggested a misunderstanding of the internalism requirement as a possible account. To the extent that skepticism about pure practical reason is based on the idea that no process or operation of reason yielding unconditional conclusions about action can be found, it depends on – and is not a reason for believing – the thesis that no process or operation of reason yielding unconditional conclusions about action can be found. To the extent that skepticism about pure practical reason is based on the requirement that reasons be capable of motivating us, the correct response is that if someone discovers what are recognizably reasons bearing on conduct and those reasons fail to motivate us, that only shows the limits of our rationality. Motivational skepticism about practical reason depends on, and cannot be the basis for, skepticism about the possible content of rational requirements. The extent to which people are actually moved by rational considerations, either in their conduct or in their credence, is beyond the purview of philosophy. Philosophy can at most tell us what it would be like to be rational.

NOTES

I would like to thank Timothy Gould, Charlotte Brown, and audiences of an earlier version of this paper at Columbia and the University of Chicago, for comments on and discussions of the issues of this paper, from which I have learned a great deal.

1 David Hume, *Treatise of Human Nature* p. 415. Hereinafter cited as "T" followed by page reference.
2 This paper was originally published in Ross Harrison, ed., *Rational Action* (New York: Cambridge, 1980), and is reprinted in Williams, *Moral Luck* pp. 101–113. Page references to Williams are to this article, as it appears in *Moral Luck*.
3 Actually, Falk and Frankena speak of internalist and externalist senses of 'ought'. See Falk, " 'Ought' and Motivation," in his, *Ought, Reasons and Moralism: The Collected Papers of W. D. Falk*, chapter 1 and Frankena's discussion, "Obligation and Motivation in Recent Moral Philosophy," *Perspectives on Morality: Essays of William K. Frankena*, chapter 6. Nagel's discussion is in *The Possibility of Altruism*, part I.
4 *Utilitarianism*, p. 30.
5 Mill, *Utilitarianism*, p. 33.
6 See Prichard, "Duty and Interest," in his *Moral Obligation and Duty and Interest*. Falk's original use of the distinction between internal and external senses of 'ought' in " 'Ought' and Motivation" is in an argument responding to Prichard's paper.
7 See Frankena, "Obligation and Motivation," p. 63, for a discussion of this surprising view.
8 I am ignoring here the more complicated case in which the passion in question is parent to the false beliefs. In my examples, for instance, there might be cases such as these: irritation at me predisposes you to think my insults are aimed at you; terror of being alone in the house makes you more likely to mistake the radio for a burglar. Hume does discuss this phenomenon (T 120). Here, we might say that the judgment is irrational, not merely false, and that its irrationality infects the passions and actions based on the judgment. If Hume's theory allows him to say that the judgment is irrational, he will be able to say that some

passions and actions are truly irrational, and not merely mistaken, although he does not do this.

9 "Available to us" is vague, for there is a range of cases in which one might be uncertain whether or not to say that a reason was available to us. For instance there are (1) cases in which we don't know about the reason, (2) cases in which we couldn't possibly know about the reason, (3) cases in which we deceive ourselves about the reason, (4) cases in which some physical or psychological condition makes us unable to see the reason, and (5) cases in which some physical or psychological condition makes us fail to respond to the reason, even though in some sense we look it right in the eye. Now no one will want to say that reason claims involving reasons people do not know about are therefore external, but as we move down the list there will be a progressive uneasiness about whether the claim is becoming external. For toward the end of the list we will come to claim that someone is psychologically incapable of responding to the reason, and yet that it is internal: capable of motivating a rational person. I do not think there is a problem about any of these cases; for all that is necessary for the reason claim to be internal is that we can say that, if a person did know and *if nothing were interfering with her rationality*, she would respond accordingly. This does not trivialize the limitation to internal reasons as long as the notion of a psychological condition that interferes with rationality is not trivially defined.

10 I have in mind such phenomena as self-deception, rationalization, and the various forms of weakness of will. Some of these apply to theoretical as well as practical reason, and for the former we can add the various forms of intellectual resistance or ideology (though "willful" is not a good way to characterize these). For some reason, people find the second thing that I mention – being indifferent to a reason that is pointed out to you – harder to imagine in a theoretical than in a practical case. To simply shrug in the face of the acknowledged reason seems to some to be possible in practice in a way that it is not in theory. I think part of the problem is that we can push what the practically paralyzed person accepts over into the realm of theory: he *believes* "that he ought to do such-and-such," although he is not moved to; whereas there seems to be nowhere further back (except maybe to a suspense of judgment) to push what the theoretically paralyzed person accepts. It may also be that the problem arises because we do not give enough weight to the difference between being convinced by an argument and being left without anything to say by it, or it may be just that what paralysis *is* is less visible in the case of belief than in the case of action.

11 Universality and sufficiency are appealed to by Kant; timelessness and impersonality by Nagel, and authority by Joseph Butler.

12 *Nicomachean Ethics*, VII.3, 1147b 5–10.

13 The comparisons I have been drawing between theoretical and practical reason now suggest that there should also be something like an ideal of good theoretical character: a receptivity to theoretical reasons. The vision of someone free of all ideology and intellectual resistance might be such an ideal.

14 Williams uses the designation 'S' for 'subjective motivational set', but I have put back the original phrase wherever it occurs; hence the brackets.

15 It is true that the application of a principle may be so simple or immediate that it will be a matter of judgment or perception rather than deliberation. In such a case there will be some who want to deny that practical reason has been used. On the other hand, the reasoning involved in applying a principle may be quite complicated (as in the case of the contradiction tests under the categorical imperative), and so be such that anyone should be willing to call it reasoning. If the fact that you hold the principle gives motivational force to either the insight or the deliberative argument to the effect that this case falls under the principle, then the result is a practical reason.

16 Williams himself remarks that the "onus of proof about what is to count as a 'purely rational process' . . . properly belongs with the critic who wants to oppose Hume's general conclusion and to make a lot out of external reason statements" (108). Although I think he is quite right in saying that the burden of proof about what is to count as a purely rational process – about *content* – belongs to Hume's opponents, I am arguing that there is no reason to suppose that if this burden is successfully picked up the reasons will be external.

17 *The Possibility of Altruism*, p. 13. Nagel calls this a "rebellion against the priority of psychology" (11) and accordingly distinguishes two kinds of internalism: one that takes the psychological facts as given and supposes that we must somehow derive ethics from them in order to achieve an internalist theory, and one that supposes that metaphysical investigations – investigations into what it is to be a rational person – will have psychological conclusions. Hobbes would be an example of the first kind and Kant of the second.

18 See especially C2 30, 41–50.

19 In Chapter III of the Analytic of the *Critique of Practical Reason*, where Kant's project is "not . . . to show a priori why the moral law supplies an incentive but rather what it effects (or better, must effect) in the mind, in so far as it is an incentive" (C2 72).

12 Two arguments against lying

I

In recent years philosophers have welcomed the development of a widespread interest in philosophical ethics. In their concern about the bewildering ethical questions generated by medical technology, legal practice, and the power and responsibility of the modern corporation, members of the professions and of the public have turned to philosophy, traditional repository of rigorous moral thought. This concern has provided philosophers with an opportunity to show that our subject is important and useful, and that we have knowledge on which others might draw. And so the profession has responded with the development of courses, textbooks, and a vast literature on the questions of "applied ethics."

Yet a gap between traditional ethical philosophy and the solution of ethical problems remains. Writers on applied ethics do not seem to draw very heavily on traditional theories, and certainly do not draw on their details. Often the "application" consists simply in borrowing a principle which the theory defends. And often that principle gives an answer which seems too facile and too extreme. Theorists, in turn, know that you can have a real mastery of the concepts and arguments of a complex ethical theory and yet, when confronted by an ethical problem, find that you have no idea what resolution the theory provides. To some extent this gap is sociologically produced, for often different people are drawn to the different kinds of work. But it may also be that we have not thought enough yet about what sort of an activity "applying" an ethical theory is.

This paper is an attempt to begin to think about that question. The moral problem I will consider is whether and to what extent we may tell benevolent or paternalistic lies. I take this to be an important problem about which we need theoretical help, because while most of us agree that there is a general presumption against paternalistic lies, we also agree that some of them are legitimate. The question is which ones and why. I will look at what happens when two of the most important moral theories in our tradition – those of Sidgwick and Kant – are applied to this problem. In each case, I will approach the question of when paternalistic lies are permissible by asking why they are in general wrong, so that we can identify the cases in which the consideration that disallows them does not hold. Sidgwick and Kant were both deeply concerned about the practical side of ethics and wrote more than most traditional moral philosophers about casuistical questions. Yet their views exemplify the tendency of theory to go to extremes, for Sidgwick's theory mandates benevolent deception on a massive scale, while Kant's apparently allows none.[1] I will show how the difference in their conclusions can be traced to the different requirements they impose on ethical concepts. One of the tasks of theoretical ethics is to provide an account of the status of ethical concepts – where they come from and why we are justified in using them. I will argue that differences in the status of ethical concepts can make a difference in how we decide which objects to apply them to. If this is right, theoretical and applied ethics are inseparable, not only because the principles are borrowed from the theories, but because each theory must teach us how its own principles and concepts apply to the objects and events we encounter in our lives.

II

A consequentialist is committed to the view that the rightness or wrongness of an action depends entirely on its consequences. The right action is the one with the best possible consequences realizable under the circumstances. The consequences considered may be either the direct consequences of the particular action, or the consequences of a general rule the action instantiates, a disposition it expresses, or an institution or practice it serves. In any case, the value of the consequences must be determinable before the rightness of the action can be ascertained. Consequentialist reasoning

about what is right must start from a knowledge of which consequences are good.

On a consequentialist view, lies will be wrong only if they do
more harm than good. Whether they do so is a question of empirical fact. But most consequentialists have found it so obvious that
lies tend to be harmful that they do not bother to argue the point.
Sidgwick says simply that "... it is generally a man's interest to
know the truth ..."[2] But it is clear how the argument should go,
for knowledge of the truth is necessary for success at the instrumental reasoning by which the consequentialist believes the good is
pursued. So we achieve the best results when we can rely upon one
another to be sources of true information.

But benevolent lies are aimed at achieving good results, so if there
is even a *general* presumption against them, it must be because they
are normally misguided. This in turn would have to be because of
some general empirical tendency. I think that the argument many
consequentialists would use to explain the presumption against benevolent lies is that an individual is normally in the best position to
judge what is good or bad for herself. If you lie to someone for her
own good, it is because you think that you know better than she
does what it will be good for her to know. Perhaps you think that she
should be spared painful information, or diverted from making a
poor decision. Usually, according to this argument, you will be
wrong as a matter of fact, because she is in the best position to judge
what is good in her own case.

A tension in this argument emerges when one reflects on two of
the assumptions on which it depends. One of the assumptions of the
consequentialist approach generally is that we can have determinate
knowledge about what consequences are good or bad. This account
of the presumption against benevolent lies assumes that persons are,
as a matter of fact, the best judges of what is good or bad for themselves. These assumptions do not harmonize well together. We
might ask, with Socrates, why the science of the good is the only
science in which everyone is supposed to be equally expert.[3]

The most important school of philosophical consequentialists,
the utilitarians, of course have an answer to this question. They
believe that what is good or bad for a person depends on some sort of
psychological state to which the person has special access: what is

good is either pleasure, or the satisfaction of desire, and what is bad is pain or frustration. Sidgwick defines pleasure as "feeling which the sentient individual at the time of feeling it implicitly or explicitly apprehends to be desirable," making it by definition something to which the individual has special access (ME 131). If a person has a special ability to identify what is good in her own case, then there is some reason to believe she is in the best position to make choices for herself. Since she needs the truth in order to make her choices well, we can argue on utilitarian grounds that she has a right to the truth.[4]

But this kind of consideration does not show that the individual is best at predicting what will *bring about* good results in her own case. She may lack the appropriate technical knowledge. And among the many problems involved in the assessment of pleasure and pain which Sidgwick describes, there are some that put the individual in an especially poor position to judge what she will find pleasant at a later stage.[5] For example, in certain emotional states you cannot properly imagine the pleasures and pains attendant upon emotional states of an opposite kind (ME 144–45). And persons are unable to properly anticipate how much they will enjoy certain things later in life (ME 147). So the general rule that persons can make the best choices for themselves will often fail, and will not support a strong presumption against benevolent lies. Accordingly, the utilitarian will see many benevolent lies not merely as excusable, but as straightforwardly right.

Sidgwick explicitly acknowledges this. He thinks that the morality of Common Sense is "unconsciously utilitarian", and that its long-term logical and historical tendency is towards a more thoroughgoing utilitarianism (ME 423–57). And one of the cases he adduces to show this is the case of the Common Sense attitude to benevolent lies:

. . . where deception is designed to benefit the person deceived, Common Sense seems to concede that it may sometimes be right: for example, most persons would not hesitate to speak falsely to an invalid, if this seemed the only way of concealing facts that might produce a dangerous shock: nor do I perceive that any one shrinks from telling fictions to children, on matters upon which it is thought well that they should not know the truth. But if the lawfulness of benevolent deception in any case be admitted, I do not see how we can decide when and how far it is admissible, except by consider-

ations of expediency; that is, by weighing the gain of any particular deception against the imperilment of mutual confidence involved in all violation
of truth. (ME 316)

Sidgwick here employs a slippery slope argument common in de-
fenses of utilitarianism. We may lie to children and invalids because
it is for their own good. So why shouldn't we lie to other persons
when it is for their own good? That Sidgwick himself is prepared to
endorse large-scale benevolent deception becomes clear later in *The
Methods of Ethics*, when he discusses the question whether utilitarianism should be publicly promulgated. Sidgwick believes he has
established that according to utilitarianism, an action done in secret
may sometimes be right which, if found out, would be wrong, because of the bad effects of publicity. But he thinks that ordinary
persons will be misguided by this truth, and that they are better off
believing they may only do what may be done openly. Because of
this, utilitarianism, if true, should be kept "esoteric" for utilitarian
reasons. With an evident relish for his paradox he concludes:

Thus the Utilitarian conclusion, carefully stated, would seem to be this;
that the opinion that secrecy may render an action right which would not
otherwise be so should itself be kept comparatively secret; and similarly it
seems expedient that the doctrine that esoteric morality is expedient should
itself be kept esoteric. Or if this concealment be difficult to maintain, it may
be desirable that Common Sense should repudiate the doctrine which it is
expedient to confine to an enlightened few. (ME 490)

Of course, this is a recommendation for concealment rather than
directly for deception, but it seems clear enough that deception will
be involved; the "enlightened few" will almost certainly have to
voice moral opinions they do not hold. Sidgwick thus favors whole
sale deception of the public concerning important moral truths by
an intellectual elite.[6]

Suppose that Common Sense, confronted by this unattractive result, digs in its heels and insists that the difference between a child
and an adult is morally significant. While we may deceive a child for
its own good, we may not do that to an adult. Sidgwick will reply
that the distinction between a child and an adult is morally arbitrary
because it is a difference of degree, a matter of placement on a continuum. There seems to be no non-arbitrary place on the continuum to

draw the line. If we do draw the line at some selected place, we will get irrational results: I may lie to you for your own good the day before your eighteenth birthday, say, but not the day after. Yet all that has happened is that you are two days older, and that doesn't seem to be a good reason for the difference. This violates one of the fundamental axioms of ethics, which is that we must not treat different cases differently without a good reason (ME 209, 379). Moral issues cannot be settled by appeal to arbitrary distinctions like this, but must be settled by the principle of utility, because that principle will give us a clear justification for lying in some cases and not in others. Sidgwick's commitment to this kind of argument is explicit in a discussion of the principle that everyone should be equally free. He argues:

> ... it seems obviously needful to limit the extent of its application. For it involves the negative principle that no one should be coerced for his own good alone; but no one would gravely argue that this ought to be applied to the case of children, or of idiots, or insane persons. But if so, can we know *a priori* that it ought to be applied to all sane adults? since the above-mentioned exceptions are commonly justified on the ground that children, etc., will manifestly be better off if they are forced to do and abstain as others think best for them; and it is, at least, not intuitively certain that the same argument does not apply to the majority of mankind in the present state of their intellectual progress. Indeed, it is often conceded by the advocates of this principle that it does not hold even in respect of adults in a low state of civilisation. But if so, what criterion can be given for its application, except that it must be applied wherever human beings are sufficiently intelligent to provide for themselves better than others would provide for them? and thus the principle would present itself not as absolute, but merely a subordinate application of the wider principle of aiming at the general happiness or well-being of mankind. (ME 275)

This passage exemplifies a kind of slippery slope argument that Sidgwick employs frequently in his debunking of Common Sense morality. This kind of slope is especially slippery because it has two sources. One is the usual utilitarian source: Sidgwick claims that we coerce children because they will be better off, and if this is a reason in one case, it will be a reason in another. But the other source of slipperiness is that the moral principle is operating with what I will call a pragmatic, as opposed to a metaphysically precise, concept. If a concept is metaphysically precise, its application is determined wholly by features of the thing we apply it to. If it is pragmatic, its application is indeterminate – there are borderline cases – and it can only be made determinate artificially. A concept which divides a continuum is often pragmatic, and must for practical purposes be to some extent arbitrarily set. This need not mean that we have no good reason for drawing the line at the point that we do (although it might), but it will mean our reasons are considerations other than features of the objects to which the concept is applied. The distinctions between the child and the adult, the deeply troubled and the mentally ill, the "idiotic" and the slow, are in this way pragmatic. These are divisions of continuums, and where exactly we should draw the line is unclear. To some extent the way that these distinctions are made does depend on features external to the persons in question – such as the kinds of work and the kinds of care that are available in the societies and cultures in which the distinctions are employed.

We all recognize that the concepts with which our positive laws operate are in this way pragmatic. For instance, we are content to define a legal adult as anyone over eighteen or twenty-one. This is not because although some people are "really" adults by that age and some are not, we must have the same law for everyone. Perhaps there is a temptation to think that there must be a certain degree of something – rationality, intelligence, self-control – that qualifies you as a metaphysically real adult, and that the ideal legal system would identify that and assign legal majority only when it is present. But rationality, intelligence, and self-control are themselves matters of degree, and the degree of them required for adulthood will in turn have to be determined pragmatically. This sort of consideration teaches us to resist the temptation to look for metaphysical precision in the concepts employed in the positive laws, and to accept the artificiality and cultural mutability of the concepts they employ.

But many people are resistant to the idea that moral laws might operate with concepts of this kind as well. There is a temptation to think that a moral principle can only operate with a metaphysically precise concept, one whose application is at least in principle perfectly clear. This gives rise to a slippery slope argument that is a commonplace in moral debate. For example, some people believe that we cannot settle the question of the morality of abortion until we find a metaphysically precise distinction between mere fetuses and persons. As in the case of adult and child, there is no reason to believe that there is a precise distinction, or that one adopted would not itself be in part determined by pragmatic considerations, for the difference is one of degree. Now there are people who will use the fact that the mere-fetus/person distinction is one of degree as an argument against abortion. They create a slippery slope from killing fetuses to killing infants to killing still older persons, and say where will it all end. The only real difference here is a difference in the degree of dependence, and any setting of a certain amount of independence as a criterion of personhood will be arbitrary. This kind of argument is also sometimes used against vegetarianism. The ultimate indeterminateness of the plant/animal distinction can be used to create a slippery slope. These arguments are similar to the argument that we may be paternalistic towards adults because we are paternalistic towards children and the only real difference is one of degree. The philosophical instinct behind these arguments is that moral principles can only operate with metaphysically precise concepts or natural kinds and not with pragmatic concepts.

These slippery slope arguments are notoriously weak. The trouble is that which way the slope runs depends on which end of it your intuitions are most securely fastened to. Imagine someone who argues that the benefit to a child is not a sufficient reason for coercing him, for at that rate we might sometimes coerce adults. Or imagine someone arguing that there is no reason we should not euthanize a seriously disabled and disfigured infant, just as we would not hesitate to abort a seriously disabled and disfigured fetus. (You just raise up the lower end of the slope and the ball slides back into the other fellow's lap.) These arguments are not as commonly made as their conservative counterparts, but they are no worse – and no better. That is the trouble – the slippery slope produced by the pragmatic concept can prove nothing, but at best is a heuristic device that shows us where we must look for some principles that will help.

Now Sidgwick is deeply concerned with this sort of problem. He believes that ethics should proceed from self-evident principles, and that one of the criteria of a self-evident principle is that "the terms of the proposition must be clear and precise" (ME 338). Because pragmatic distinctions either are not clear and precise, or are only arbitrarily so, they destroy the self-evidence of the principles that employ them (ME 293n). In a discussion of whether government is justified by consent of the governed as expressed in voting, Sidgwick remarks that if it is voting that legitimates government then even children must be allowed to vote. And, he complains:

... if to avoid this absurdity we exclude children, an arbitrary line has to be drawn ... (ME 298)

This destroys the self-evidence of the principle. Sidgwick believes that an arbitrary and pragmatic character infects many of the concepts used in Common Sense moral principles, and he directs his account of Common Sense morality to freeing "the common terms of Ethics, as far as possible, from objection on this score" (ME 339). Because he thinks that his efforts to do this are unsuccessful, he thinks that only the principle of utility can resolve moral problems. This comes out clearly in Sidgwick's recurring reflections about the concept of "veracity" itself. Discussing the "Intuitional" view that veracity is right regardless of consequences, Sidgwick says:

... we find that in the common notion of different kinds of actions, a line is actually drawn between the results included in the notion and regarded as forming part of the act, and those considered as its consequences. For example, in speaking truth to a jury, I may possibly foresee that my words, operating along with other statements and indications, will unavoidably lead them to a wrong conclusion as to the guilt or innocence of the accused, as certainly as I foresee that they will produce a right impression as to the particular matter of fact to which I am testifying: still, we should commonly consider the latter foresight or intention to determine the nature of the act as an act of veracity, while the former merely relates to a consequence. We must understand then that the disregard to consequences which the Intuitional view is here taken to imply, only relates to certain determinate classes of action (such as Truth-speaking) where common usage of terms adequately defines what events are to be included in the general notions of the acts, and what regarded as their consequences. (ME 97)

But later Sidgwick *denies* that common usage adequately defines which consequences are to count as rendering a communication veracious:

... we found no clear agreement as to the fundamental nature of the obligation; or as to its exact scope, i.e. whether it is our actual affirmation as understood by the recipient which we are bound to make correspondent to fact (as far as we can), or whatever inferences we foresee that he is likely to draw from this, or both. (ME 355)

This sort of problem becomes especially acute when a gradual change in our linguistic practices renders it uncertain what inferences the recipient of our words will draw from them.

In the case of formulae imposed by law – such (e.g.) as declarations of religious belief . . . a difficulty is created by the gradual degradation or perversion of their meaning, which results from the strong inducements offered for their general acceptance; for thus they are continually strained and stretched until a new general understanding seems gradually to grow up as to the meaning of certain phrases; and it is continually disputed whether we may veraciously use the phrases in this new signification. A similar process continually alters the meaning of conventional expressions current in polite society. When a man declares that he 'has great pleasure in accepting' a vexatious invitation, or is 'the obedient servant' of someone whom he regards as an inferior, he uses phrases which were probably once deceptive. If they are so no longer, Common Sense condemns as over-scrupulous the refusal to use them where it is customary to do so. But Common Sense seems doubtful and perplexed where the process of degradation is incomplete and there are still persons who may be deceived. . . . (ME 314–15)[7]

Sidgwick also emphasizes our doubts about whether the use of such devices as *suppressio veri* and *suggestio falsi* is within the scope of veracity (ME 316–17, 448–49). The implication of these remarks is that the very concept of veracity is a pragmatic one, which therefore cannot play a role in a self-evident principle.

For Sidgwick, a large part of the appeal of the principle of utility is that it enables us to settle questions in a definite way. It enables us to apply the concepts of right and wrong firmly to cases by linking them, at least in principle, to solid empirical facts, facts about pleasure and pain. It bypasses the use of pragmatic distinctions like those between veracity and falsehood, adults and children. *The Methods of Ethics* is littered with questions like: "We seem to condemn either extreme: yet what clear and accepted principle can be stated for determining the true mean?" (ME 249) "Where then is the limit to be fixed?" (ME 334) "But if the rule does not hold for an extreme case, where can we draw the line?" (ME 308) and the answer is always "We do not seem able to obtain any clear and generally accepted principle for deciding this point, unless the Utilitarian for-

mula be admitted as such" (ME 348). Utility is the central concept of
ethics because it is the only one with the precision requisite to
render its principle self-evident.[8]

III

The Kantian begins from an altogether different theory of value. Kant
distinguishes those things which are unconditionally good – things
which are good in themselves and so in any and all conditions – from
things which are only conditionally good – that is, things whose goodness depends upon external conditions. According to Kant, the only
unconditionally good thing is a good will (G 393). Everything else
which is good has only a conditional value. In the argument that
culminates in the second formula of the categorical imperative, the
Formula of Humanity, Kant tells us that "All objects of inclinations
have only a conditional worth, for if the inclinations and the needs
founded on them did not exist, their object would be without worth"
(G 428). In other words, the things we desire have value, because we
want and need them, not the reverse. Our desire is a condition of their
value. Our wanting them is not enough to make them good, however,
for obviously many of the things we want are not good. Even if we
want them we will not judge them good unless they are conducive to
our happiness. And:

It need hardly be mentioned that the sight of a being adorned with no feature
of a pure and good will, yet enjoying uninterrupted prosperity, can never give
pleasure to a rational impartial observer. Thus the good will seems to constitute the indispensable condition even of worthiness to be happy. (G 393)

When an object is conditionally good, we must determine whether
the condition of its goodness is met. Say the initial condition is that
someone desires that a certain state of affairs be realized. Then we
can raise the further question why it should be good that this person's desire should be satisfied. If we say it makes him happy, we can
ask why it is good that he should be happy. In this way we give rise
to a regressive argument, a search for the unconditioned condition of
the goodness of the thing. In Kant's view, this condition will always
be the presence of a good will. A good will confers value on the
objects of choice of the person who has it, for

... rational nature exists as an end in itself. Man necessarily thinks of his own existence in this way; thus far it is a subjective principle of human actions. Also every other rational being thinks of his existence by means of the same rational ground which holds also for myself; thus it is at the same time an objective principle from which, as supreme practical ground, it must be possible to derive all laws of the will. The practical imperative, therefore, is the following: Act so that you treat humanity, whether in your own person or in that of another, always as an end and never as a means only. (G 429)

By "humanity" Kant means the power of free rational choice, for "the capacity to propose an end to oneself is the characteristic of humanity" (MPV 392) and in fact "rational nature is distinguished from others in that it proposes an end to itself" (G 437). According to Kant the choice of an end is always an act of freedom (MPV 386). We regard the objects of our own free rational choices as good (this is a "subjective principle of our actions") and so we must regard the objects of the free rational choices of others as good as well. This makes humanity, or the power of free rational choice, the limiting condition of the rationality of choice itself. That is to say: for a choice to be rational, it must be consistent with the supreme and unconditional value of the power of free rational choice.[9]
    One of the examples that follow the Formula of Humanity is the case of a lying promise. A man is in need of money and "borrows" some, falsely promising to pay it back although he knows he will not be able to. Kant explains what is wrong with the action this way:

For he whom I want to use for my own purposes by means of such a promise cannot possibly assent to my mode of acting against him and cannot contain the end of this action in himself . . . he who transgresses the rights of men intends to make use of the persons of others merely as a means, without considering that, as rational beings, they must always be esteemed at the same time as ends, i.e., only as beings who must be able to contain in themselves the end of the very same action. (G 430–31)

When Kant says that the other "cannot assent to my mode of acting against him," he does not mean merely that if the other knew I was lying he would find my conduct objectionable. This is probable, of course, but he might not. The case might be trivial and he might not care how I act; it must still turn out to be true that he "cannot assent to my mode of acting" if this is a correct analysis of what is wrong.

Similarly, when Kant says that the other is "unable to contain the end of this action in himself," he does not merely mean that the other cannot happen to have the same purpose. Obviously he can. In the example, for instance, the deceived lender may be a generous person who was longing for a way to give me the money outright without wounding my pride. Surely this fact would not mitigate the wrongness of my deception. What Kant means, I believe, is that the other person cannot assent to my action because he is not in a position to. This is because he is deceived. By the nature of the case, he doesn't know how I am acting, and you cannot assent to a transaction you do not know is occurring.[10] In the same way, he cannot "contain in himself" the end of the same action because he is not in a position to. He doesn't know what the real end of the action is, and is therefore not in a position to make it his own – to choose, freely, to contribute to its realization. In the example, the other person believes the end of the action is my temporary possession of his money, when in fact it is my indefinite possession of it. What makes my action wrong is not that he *would* not have chosen to cooperate in promoting that outcome, but simply that he *did* not.[11]

If our way of acting is to be consistent with the unconditional value of free rational choice, others must be able to assent to the transactions in which we engage them, and be in a position to voluntarily choose to further the ends at which those transactions are aimed. There are two things that interfere with these requirements: coercion and deception. The person who is forced to engage in a transaction or further an end, and the person who is fooled into it, cannot be said to assent to the transaction or choose the end. These persons are therefore being treated as mere means to the ends of others. As free rational beings, persons must be allowed to choose for themselves what transactions they will engage in and what ends they will promote. This is what it means to treat persons as ends in themselves.

This argument not only shows why lying is wrong, but that it is one of the two most fundamentally wrong things you can do to others. Coercion and deception are the two ways of using others as mere means. Lies are therefore wrong in themselves, regardless of whether they are told with good intentions or bad. Kant condemns benevolent lies for exactly the same reason as mischievous or malicious ones. But Kant's theory of value implies something even stronger than this. A coercive or deceptive character not only renders an action wrong, but robs the end of the action of its value. For the goodness of the end depends upon the rationality of the choice of the end, but an end pursued by way of a bad action has not been rationally chosen. The condition of its goodness – consistency with the value of free rational choice – is not met, and so it is not a good end. In this way, Kant's value theory leads to a sort of unanimity criterion of value.[12] "Good" is a concept of practical reason, and so "what we call good must be, in the judgment of every reasonable man, an object of the faculty of desire, and the evil must be, in everyone's eyes, an object of aversion" (C2 60–61). For an end to be good, it must be possible for everyone to agree to it.

... reason has no dictatorial authority; its verdict is always simply the agreement of free citizens, of whom each one must be permitted to express, without let or hindrance, his objections or even his veto. (C1 A738–39/ B766–67)

An end achieved through a lie violates this condition, for the deceived person has not had a chance to agree or to cast his veto. Thus, a lie for a *good* end is not only wrong. It appears to be, strictly speaking, *impossible*.

Now this result seems much too strong. For most of us think that there are some cases in which benevolent lies are permissible. The ends in these cases will be ones which, whatever Kant's theory says, we would certainly regard as good if they could be achieved by honorable means. For example, there is Sidgwick's case of the lie told to an invalid to spare him a dangerous shock. Sidgwick points out that we allow the use of coercion on children, idiots, and the insane; as we have seen Kant ranks deception and coercion together. Kant would have to agree that we may sometimes use coercion on such persons, for their own safety and that of others. And if we may use coercion, then we may lie. Presumably there will be cases in which lying is the preferable strategy, since coercion may well involve violence. If there are cases where benevolent deception is allowable, how can Kant's theory account for those cases?

One thing that we cannot do is handle such cases by saying *simply* that the person to whom we lie *would* agree to the end for which the lie is told. This would be to adopt the reading of Kant's "possibility of containing the end" criterion which I have rejected. For one thing, this would justify manipulative conduct towards those who happen to share our ends (as in the case of the false promise made to one who would be glad to give you the money outright). Furthermore, for me to make the *judgment* that you would agree to this end is already for me to take the decision out of your hands in the way that the theory forbids. Although Kant agrees that we have a duty to promote the happiness of others, "What they count as belonging to their happiness is left up to them to decide" (MPV 388). So benevolence cannot override the essential duty to let others determine their own ends. If I lie with the excuse that you would agree to my end, I am attempting to justify preempting your free use of your reason by appealing to an idea that I have arrived at because I have already preempted it. This clearly will not do.

We could get a more promising argument for permissible lies if we could establish in the pertinent cases that the deceived one would, to use Kant's phrase, "assent to my mode of acting against him." This has some of the same difficulties about preemptive judgment as the rejected suggestion, but at least it will only excuse lies to those who would specifically agree to be lied to, not to everyone who shares the purpose for which the lie was told. But in order to keep these two excuses distinct, we must not allow the inference that someone would agree to be lied to, simply *because* they would agree to the purpose for which the lie was told. Otherwise we will be back where we started. In any case, that inference seems incorrect. The requirement that each person be allowed the free use of her own reason in determining her actions and ends is a procedural one. It is important not only that the choice be the one that a person would have made, but that she actually gets to make it.

So our argument that the person would agree to be lied to must not appeal to, or appeal only to, the end for which the lie is told. We must justify the lie more directly. It seems clear that in order to annul the procedural requirement that each person decide for herself we must show that the procedure could not in any case be carried out. We must argue that the agent is not in a position to make a free rational decision – that she is not (at present, perhaps) autonomous, and that were she rational she would agree that someone in her (actual) condition may be lied to or coerced. Of course, we do not want to justify telling *any* lies whatever to non-autonomous persons. The hypothetical acceptance of *both* the mode of action *and* the end must be defended. And this is the usual way of justifying our manipulative transactions with children, the mentally handicapped, and the insane. We argue both that they are not autonomous because of their conditions, and that they would if rational agree that *such* persons may be manipulated for *these* ends to be realized.

The ends must be ones that we can fairly presume that non-autonomous persons would hold if they were rational. How can we tell what ends they would choose without being guilty of preemptive judgment? One end that we can attribute to them without pre-emptive judgment is their humanity itself, their power of free rational choice. Since this is unconditionally valuable, this is an end they would hold if they were rational. Presumably we may lie to someone who lacks autonomy if our end is to restore or preserve her autonomy, or to restore or preserve things which are necessary conditions of it, such as physical well-being. Since all human beings want to be happy, we can also safely attribute this end to them (G 415), but we will be on less firm ground here because we cannot without preemptive judgment determine what they would count as part of their happiness. And this must be treated as secondary to the restoration of autonomy, if that is possible.

Because we cannot justify the lie by appeal to its purpose alone, but must also appeal to the lack of autonomy of the person lied to, we will not be able to determine which paternalistic lies are permissible unless we have some criteria for determining who is autonomous. But here we run into a difficulty. Autonomy in the ordinary sense appears to be a matter of degree. Children are thought to acquire it little by little, for instance. So again we get Sidgwick's question about where to draw the line – how we are to decide what counts as autonomous enough to ground a claim against paternalism. Sidgwick thinks that we should refrain from using coercion on those who are "sufficiently intelligent to provide for themselves." Presumably Sidgwick thinks that "intelligence" is a matter of degree, and a certain degree of it is sufficient for expedient self-government. Whether you have this degree of intelligence will show up in various ways, among them the choices you actually make when left to your own devices. The one deciding whether to resort to paternalism judges whether the other is making her choices well. Now the Kantian cannot solve the problem about ascertaining and measuring autonomy this way, for several reasons. First, because

Kant does not have an empirical theory of value, we are not in a position to judge the quality of the choices of others. Of course we can see in the ordinary way if someone is poor at the choice of means, and we can ascertain whether his choices are immoral. But because each person determines for himself what he will count as part of his happiness, a person's choice of the ends he will pursue is not otherwise open to assessment. We cannot decide someone is insufficiently autonomous merely because he makes some choices we would not have made in his place. But further: we cannot decide someone is not autonomous because he is regularly making decisions we know are bad in the sense of immoral. It is the capacity for autonomy, not its actual exercise, which gives a person the right to self-government. Kant's theory may allow us to use manipulative tactics on children and the insane, on grounds of insufficient autonomy. It does not allow us to use them on persons who are immoral. We must have a way to distinguish persons who should be regarded as capable of autonomous conduct, however they may actually behave, who therefore are held responsible when they go wrong, and to whom we have no excuse for lying, from persons who should be regarded as incompletely developed or ill, who therefore are not held responsible when they go wrong, and to whom we may lie under the conditions described above.[13]

What makes this especially difficult is that the capacity for free rational choice, as Kant understands it, is not really a natural attribute at all. Freedom of the will is an idea of pure practical reason, and, according to Kant, a property that we ascribe to ourselves when we act. We ascribe it to ourselves because the moral law commands categorically, and we recognize that we can do what we ought (C2 30; 42). We do not ascribe it to ourselves because we have theoretical evidence of its presence – that would be impossible, for in Kant's philosophy freedom is beyond the limits of theoretical knowledge. Similarly, we ascribe it to other persons not because we have theoretical evidence that they have it but because it is a duty to do so. Respect for humanity in the persons of others demands that we attribute to them the capacity for free choice and action, regardless of how they are acting:

Thus it is also with the reproach of vice, which must never burst out in complete contempt or deny the wrongdoer all moral worth, because on that hypothesis he could never be improved either – and this latter is incompatible with the idea of man, who as such (as a moral being) can never lose all predisposition to good. (MPV 463–64)

Actual conduct, then, does not provide evidence for or against freedom. Furthermore, since every human being is imperfectly rational, we all fall short of acting completely autonomously. But then how are we to distinguish the psychotic, whose conduct should not be attributed to freedom, from the evil person, whose conduct should? We cannot appeal directly to the kind of explanation their conduct admits of. Kant's view is that *all* conduct, viewed theoretically, admits of a deterministic causal explanation. An evil person's conduct is attributed to but not *explained* by free choice. The idea of freedom has no explanatory role at all. Freedom is something we attribute to ourselves and others for moral purposes only (C2 51–58; 134–37).

In Kant's view, moral concepts generally are concepts of pure practical reason. They do not describe or explain anything about the world. They get their hook into the world via the practical reason of each one of us, as individuals who make choices and decisions, who are therefore bound by the moral law, and who in light of that must attribute freedom to ourselves and others. Practical concepts are ideal concepts, and the things in the world to which we apply them, under the direction of the moral law, fall short of them. No one exhibits perfect rationality, and so no one exhibits the perfect freedom which the moral law teaches us that we have. But this means that facts about the world will not decisively settle the question which natural objects these concepts are to be applied to and which not. What we find in the world is a continuum of more or less imperfectly rational beings. As a rule we are obliged to treat them as capable of perfect rationality. If we decide that somewhere along that continuum we will draw a line, beyond which we are excused from that obligation, the decision will be to some extent arbitrary. Or in any case, it will not be made by seeing how close various persons come to actual freedom. We cannot say: "children are not yet *in fact* fully free." Theoretical statements about freedom have no standing. The most we could say is that children should not be treated as fully free. But the grounds for this practical statement are unclear. The pressure of the moral law is towards treating every human being as a free rational being, regardless of actual facts.

IV

Both Sidgwick and Kant uncover problems about applying moral concepts to the world. Sidgwick thinks they are usually imprecise, and that ultimately we should be guided instead by the precise concept, utility. Kant thinks that they are precise in themselves but don't exactly fit the things we find in the world, because they are ideals. He thinks we should apply them anyway, without regard for the world's imperfections. In this section I discuss another example of a moral concept about which it is particularly clear that the lines between Sidgwick and Kant are drawn in the way I have suggested.

The concept in question is that of "legitimate government." Both Kant and Sidgwick consider the question when a government established by revolutionary overthrow of a previous government becomes legitimate. Sidgwick says:

All are agreed that usurpation ought to be resisted; but as to the right behavior towards an established government which has sprung from a successful usurpation, there is a great difference of opinion. Some think that it should be regarded as legitimate as soon as it is firmly established: others that it ought to be obeyed at once, but under protest, with the purpose of renewing the conflict on a favourable opportunity: others think that this latter is the right attitude at first, but that a usurping government, when firmly established, loses its illegitimacy gradually, and that it becomes, after a while, as criminal to rebel against it as it was originally to establish it. And this last seems, on the whole, the view of Common Sense; but the point at which the metamorphosis is thought to take place can hardly be determined otherwise than by considerations of expediency. (ME 300)[14]

Kant, on the other hand, places himself firmly in the first camp Sidgwick mentions. As is well known, Kant believes that any revolution is wrong, since the existing government must be taken to represent the general will of the people. For a revolt to be legitimate, it would have to be in *accordance* with the general will of the people, since coercion that does not meet this condition is mere illegitimate violence. But since the existing government represents the general will of the people, the revolutionary party of course does not (MPJ 318–21). However, Kant also holds that if a revolution succeeds, the new government is immediately legitimate and owed the same allegiance as the old was (MPJ 323). Taxed by a reviewer[15] with the oddity of this position, Kant replies:

Every matter of fact is an object that is an appearance (of sense); on the other hand, that which can be represented only through pure reason and which must be included among the Ideas – that is the thing in itself. No object in experience can be given that adequately corresponds to an Idea. A perfect juridical [just] constitution among men would be an example of such an Idea.

When a people are united through laws under a suzerain, then the people are given as an object of experience conforming to the Idea in general of the unity of the people under a supreme powerful Will. Admittedly, this is only an appearance; that is, a juridical constitution in the most general sense of the term is present. Although the [actual] constitution may contain grave defects and gross errors and may need to be gradually improved in important respects, still, as such, it is absolutely unpermitted and culpable to oppose it. If the people were to hold that they were justified in using violence against a constitution, however defective it might be, and against the supreme authority, they would be supposing that they had a right to put violence as the supreme prescriptive act of legislation in the place of every right and Law. (MPJ 371–72)

The legitimate state, like the autonomous moral person, is an idea of pure practical reason. Kant is clear that the form of government that corresponds to this idea is a republic: a constitutional government in which legislation is carried on by representatives of the citizens (MPJ 340–41; PP 349–53) and in which every adult is or can become a free, equal, and independent citizen (MPJ 313–15). But it is also clear that no actual government is adequate to this idea. Still, we don't feel like saying that no government has ever really been legitimate. Once again we get the problem of saying what comes close enough. Perhaps it seems as if in this case we can easily say what comes close enough: the existence of a constitution and a legislative body of elected representatives. But even this would mean that there had been no legitimate governments until very recent history. And if we suppose a legitimate government must meet another criterion which seems minimal and obvious – universal adult suffrage – then there have been no legitimate governments until this past century (our own, not Kant's). Thus, rather than deciding how close a government has to be to the ideal before we will call it legitimate, Kant thinks we should simply treat *any* existing government as legitimate. Like Sidgwick, although for a different reason, he does not see where to draw the line.

v

The two theories that I have been examining take extreme positions on paternalistic lies. Sidgwick allows too many, Kant apparently allows none. I have traced the extremism of both views to a common source: a problem about applying ethical concepts to the world. Both reject a popular model of applied ethics, according to which we work like this: we find out which objects in the world fit the ontological categories with which our principles operate (for instance, which things are in fact mere fetuses and which are persons), and then marshall in the principles to see what they say about those kinds of objects. On this popular model the real work – the hard work – of applied ethics is not ethical thought at all, but ontology or metaphysics. Once the ontological issues are settled, the ethical principles are easy to apply. Sidgwick and Kant both reject this model, because of a mismatch each perceives between the world and the concepts we employ in ethical thought. The ontological issues cannot be settled in the way proposed.

For Sidgwick, the problem arises because the concepts of Common Sense morality are imprecise. A clear and precise concept would be one that picks out its objects in a way that is non-arbitrary and decisive.[16] Only a precise concept can function in a real self-evident moral principle. Since the concepts of "adult," "sane" and "veracious" are all imprecise, "never lie to a sane adult" could not possibly be a self-evident moral principle. The concept of utility is precise. Pleasure and pain seem to have clear moral weight, yet they are also matters of theoretical fact. So utility allows us to map practical concepts onto theoretical ones perfectly. It makes the concepts of "right" and "wrong" fit the contours that the world provides – or more precisely, that the set of concepts we use in theoretically explaining the world provides.

For Kant the problem arises not because moral concepts are imprecise, but because they are ideals of pure practical reason. Nothing we find in the world is fully adequate to them, yet we must apply them to things that we find there anyway, for moral reasons. Thus, each person ought to be treated like a free rational being, despite our imperfect rationality, just as each government ought to be treated as the embodiment of the general will of the people, though most real governments are corrupt despotisms born of illegitimate violence.

One must not lie to a free rational being, or revolt against the general will of the people. If lying for a good end, or revolting for a better government, were *justified* simply because actual persons and states fall short of the ideal, a slippery slope argument would quickly lead to extreme conclusions, since all persons fall short of perfect autonomy and all governments fail to embody the general will of the people.

So perhaps we should say that what we are looking for is not good *reasons* for paternalism or revolution, since there are not good reasons for what the moral law disallows, but *excuses* for these kinds of action. We think we may be excused from treating certain persons as autonomous and certain governments as legitimate. But in order to decide that there are some human beings to which we will not apply the concepts of full autonomy, or some governments too despotic to count as legitimate, we apparently will have to draw some lines that are not firmly grounded either in theoretical facts about those persons and governments or in the moral law. We must *decide* who to count as a free rational being, and what makes a state legitimate. These decisions cannot be based on finding out which objects in fact are free rational beings or really embody the general will, because there are no such facts. If applied ethics is done this way, its work is not metaphysical, but ethical and practical all the way down. Kant's own solution is to treat every government as legitimate and (almost) every human being as free and rational. This is already a pragmatic decision, and it may seem to us to be – not the incorrect one, because this is not a matter of correct or incorrect – but a poor one. But now we must ask what the criteria for making these decisions should be. If we don't pick those who must be treated as free rational beings by determining who is in fact a free rational being, how do we do it? We need some alternative method, or our decisions will be arbitrary.

The answer is that of course such decisions don't have to be *completely* arbitrary. In deciding what objects to apply our ethical concepts to, we use available theoretical concepts that approximate them.[17] Although we cannot find a perfect match between ethical concepts and natural facts, theoretical considerations do provide guidance. After all, it is theoretical facts which teach us which things are even potentially rational beings. The ethical concept of a moral person is mapped on to the naturalistic concept of a human being. And theoretical facts do teach us that there is a sense in which children and the insane are not as "autonomous" – that is, not as much in control of themselves – as ordinary adult persons are. The sense of "in control of oneself" here will not be very determinate. It will be a matter of degree, and hardly adequate to Kant's notion of transcendental freedom. But we must use it for casuistical purposes, because it is all we have.[18]

Although Sidgwick wants to use the principle of utility directly for decision-making rather than for concept-formation, one can imagine a Sidwickean proposal that we make the notion of an autonomous rational agent precise by tying it to considerations of utility.[19] If what is at issue is not that the concept be applied correctly, but that it be applied well, the utilitarian will read "well" as "expediently." So the Sidgwickean might urge us to count persons as autonomous when it is expedient – in utilitarian terms – to do so. This would give us a clear way of deciding – in terms of theoretical facts – who was to be counted as autonomous and who was not. Applied ethics would then recover the intellectual cleanliness of the popular model – the real work would be theoretical. But the trouble with the proposed way of achieving precision is that it would make the notion of autonomy *subordinate* to that of utility. Freedom would not function as an independent value at all. To only be truthful when it is useful is to care only for utility, not for freedom. If we adopt the Sidgwickean strategy, we can seek empirical goals, but we cannot live up to rational ideals. Besides, if we are going to use values in deciding how to apply our ethical concepts, why should we only use utility? To say that our concepts can be applied well or badly needn't mean well or badly in the utilitarian sense. Why shouldn't we apply them in a way that maximizes fairness or personal freedom?

A natural objection is that if we work this way there is a danger that we will simply adjust our ethical categories and principles reciprocally until we get whatever result we want. We could just decide, for example, that all of the categories of persons to whom we are tempted to tell benevolent lies should count as incompletely autonomous. Or that benevolent lies in certain cases aren't really lies at all. Of course there are dangers of this kind, but it is not clear that we have any option but to face them, and to try to be intellectually honest. If the concepts we use in ethics cannot be tied down to the world by firm theoretical criteria, the precision of the popular model of applied ethics is just not available.

It is true that the principle of utility gives us a way of recovering that precision. But as we have seen, the price of defining autonomy in terms of utility is to give it no real weight at all. So now we must ask whether Sidgwick's demand for precision in ethical concepts is worth the cost of giving up rational ideals. It is clear enough why in scientific discourse we should want concepts that fit as neatly as possible onto the world. It is not at all clear why that should be appropriate for normative discourse. If there are ideals of practical reason, which outstrip the things we find in the world, we cannot give them up merely because they make applying ethical principles a difficult and uncertain enterprise. If we value the Kantian ideal of free and non-manipulative relations among rational beings, for instance, and we want to approximate that ideal in the empirical human community, we must learn to be truthful and straightforward with one another, regardless of our imperfect autonomy, and the bad results to which it may sometimes lead. In ethics, we cannot always trim our concepts so that they will fit neatly onto the world. Sometimes what we must do instead is try to reshape the world so that it will be more adequate to our concepts.

NOTES

1 For a discussion of the way various moral theories handle this issue, and of the tendency of utilitarian and Kantian approaches to go to extremes, see Igor Primoratz, "Lying and the Methods of Ethics."

2 Henry Sidgwick, *The Methods of Ethics*, p. 448. Hereinafter cited as "ME" followed by page reference.

3 See, for example, *Apology* 19e–20c and 24d–25c; *Laches* 186c; *Protagoras* 319bff.; and *Meno* 89eff.

4 In the sense of "right" developed in chapter V of Mill's *Utilitarianism:* we have whatever rights it is useful that we should have.

5 Sidgwick rejects Mill's view that some pleasures are better qualitatively than others which are similar or greater in quantity (ME 94–95, 127–28). If one does accept Mill's view, the problems about paternalism might seem to be worse, for the better pleasures can only be identified by those who have training in and experience of them. It will be better for the rest of us to have this training foisted upon us, but we will only be able to see

this after the training. In Chapter III of *On Liberty*, however, Mill argues that these pleasures are best cultivated in the course of choosing a life for oneself.

6 Interestingly, one of the reasons for concealing the utilitarian news from the general public is that "... the concealment [of those actions which are only right when concealed] would in most cases have importantly injurious effects on the agent's habits of veracity" (ME 490). The enlightened few will also have to take into account the danger to their habits of veracity, as Sidgwick has made clear earlier (ME 482).

7 Kant also worries about polite salutations. He asks, "Can an untruth from mere politeness (e.g. "your obedient servant" at the end of a letter) be taken as lying? Nobody is deceived by it" (MPV 431). Probably both Kant and Sidgwick would have appreciated the irony of the fact that the formula that occupies this place in modern official letters is "sincerely."

8 Actually, Sidgwick is not even sure of this. The concept of utility is only precise if pleasures and pains are in fact commensurable among themselves and with each other, and this could only be proved if we could have two different sensations at the same time, which is impossible. So "the belief that every pleasure or pain has a definite intensive quantity or degree must remain an *a priori* assumption, incapable of positive empirical verification." The only reason he gives for its acceptance is that "the belief in its general validity is irresistibly suggested in reflection on experience, and remains at any rate uncontradicted by experience" (ME 146).

9 This reading of the argument for the Formula of Humanity is explained and defended in more detail in my "Kant's Formula of Humanity," Chapter 4 in this volume.

10 Even if you happen to know that the person is lying to you, there is a sense in which you cannot assent to the transaction. If you say to her: "I know you don't mean to pay me back, but here's the money," the nature of the transaction is changed. You are not assenting to a false promise, but giving a handout.

11 This argument is explained more fully in my "The Right to Lie: Kant on Dealing with Evil," Chapter 5 in this volume.

12 It follows from this theory of value that some states of affairs cannot be assessed as good or bad directly. The cases I have in mind are those involving competition. If two persons both want the same particular, irreplaceable object (a job, say, or a house), practical reason does not say which outcome is good. It can only say that whatever outcome results from procedures which (according to the categorical imperative) are fair is good.

13 I should say that it is not clear to me whether Kant always saw that this theory has the troublesome consequences about making these distinctions that I am about to describe. In the *Anthropology*, for instance, he says confidently: "Simple, misguided, stupid, foppish, foolish or offensively silly people differ from the mentally deranged not merely in the degree but also in the kind of their mental disorder. . ." (ANTH 202). One wonders what makes him so sure. When discussing the question when someone may be exempt from punishment on grounds of insanity, he claims that philosophers and not the medical faculty must settle the question because it is "purely psychological." But then he says that this is only because of lack of scientific knowledge; there could be a physical cause of the action, but "physicians and physiologists in general have not yet reached a deep enough understanding of the mechanical element in man" (ANTH 213–14). So I cannot claim that the aspect of Kantianism which I am expounding was explicitly acknowledged by Kant, at least as far as judgments about the autonomy of actual persons is concerned. In the next section, however, I will show that he acknowledged it explicitly about another moral concept, that of legitimate government.

14 In general, Sidgwick cannot see how the consideration of how much time has passed can possibly make a difference *by itself*. Time is a continuum, and so as in the other cases we have been looking at, dividing points seem to be arbitrary if we cannot determine them by expediency. Another case where this worries Sidgwick is that of sexual purity. He says:

... where divorce by mutual consent, with subsequent marriage, is legalised, we do not call this an offence against Purity: and yet if the principle of free change be once admitted, it seems paradoxical to distinguish purity from impurity merely by less rapidity of transition. . . . (ME 358)

If I have a new lover every ten years surely I am not promiscuous. If I have a new lover every ten days perhaps I am. But where, in between shall we draw the line? Every five years? Every two years? Every month? In his footnote Sidgwick says:

It should be observed that I am not asking for an exact quantitative decision, but whether we can really think that the decision depends upon considerations of this kind. (ME 358n)

It is clear that he thinks that the temporal considerations must work in connection with "expediency" (utility) before they can make a difference.

15 Professor Friedrich Bouterwek of Göttingen, in the *Göttingen Journal* (Number 28, February 18, 1797). Kant appended his replies to Bouterwek to the second edition of *The Metaphysical Principles of Justice*.

16 In a slightly different way, Derek Parfit is concerned about the same problem. He is not concerned about precision as a criterion for self-evidence. But after showing us (stunningly) that our concept of a person is not as metaphysically precise as we might have thought, he concludes that personal identity is "not what matters." See Derek Parfit, *Reasons and Persons*.

17 But we do not have to be slavishly attached to the use of theoretical concepts. For example: In Kant's theory one of the ideas of practical reason is property. To say something is my property is to say that I am injured, or wronged, if someone uses it without my permission (MPJ 245). It is clear why I am injured if someone wrests something from my hand, so we have an empirical notion of possession as physical detention. But his does not exhaust our idea of property, since if something is my property I am injured if another uses or removes it even if I am not present. This shows that the notion of property is rational and not empirical (MPJ 250). Kant traces the notion to practical reason by an argument that shows that if we could not own things we could not successfully use them, and if we could not use them our freedom of action would be restricted for no reason (MPJ 246). But the important thing for my purposes here is the flexibility of the way this concept is imposed on the world. In many cases, the objects we own are ordinary physical objects, and there are good reasons of simple convenience for this. But we don't always own ordinary physical objects. Your right to a library book you have checked out would be a piece of property in Kant's theory (all "acquired rights" are property); but in that case what you own is not the physical object (you may not use it for kindling or tear out the pages for scratch paper), but only the privilege of reading from it for a certain length of time. Or think of the way you own the furniture in your office, or shares in a corporation's stock. The point is that we may divide the world into owned objects quite differently than we divide it into physical objects. And as the case of library books shows, our reasons for dividing it differently may be moral and evaluative. The library loan system makes the "intelligible" book available to more people, and so may be defended either in terms of utility or fairness.

18 I do not mean to imply that we should just use the *intuitive* notion of, say, "being in control of oneself." We should map our practical concepts onto theoretical ones that are as philosophically well-defined and respectable as we can make them. Here the philosopher will have much to learn from the scientist. Those working on applied ethics must learn as much as possible about the conditions of the persons about whom these decisions must be made from, say, psychiatrists, child psychologists, and doctors. The notion of self-control must be analyzed carefully. But it will

still never turn out to be adequate to the ideal of transcendental freedom, and so decisions about cutoff points will still just have to be made.
19 Although Sidgwick does not make this proposal about deliberate concept-
formation, there is some suggestion in the *Methods* that he thinks that
historically, considerations of utility have influenced the formation of
our ethical concepts (ME 423–59). If this were true it would give one sense
in which Common Sense morality would be "unconsciously utilitarian."

13 Personal identity and the unity of agency: A Kantian response to Parfit

A person is both active and passive, both an agent and a subject of experiences. Utilitarian and Kantian moral philosophers, however, characteristically place a different emphasis on these two aspects of our nature. The utilitarian emphasizes the passive side of our nature, our capacity to be pleased or satisfied, and is concerned with what happens to us. The Kantian emphasizes our agency, and is concerned with what we do. Alternatively, we may say that the utilitarian focuses first on persons as objects of moral concern, and asks, "what should be done for them?" whereas the Kantian addresses the moral agent, who is asking, "what should I do?"

One might think that this can only be a difference of emphasis. Any acceptable moral philosophy must take both sides of our nature into account, and tell us both how people ought to be treated and what we ought to do. Yet the difference of emphasis can lead to substantive moral disagreement. Kantians believe in what are sometimes called "agent-centered" restrictions, obligations which are independent of the value of the outcomes they produce.[1] Even when thinking of persons as objects of moral concern, the Kantian is more likely to focus on agency. The question "what should be done for them?" is answered, roughly, by "they should be given the freedom to make their own choices, and to do things for themselves." Rawls believes that asking the agentless "what should be done for them?" leads to distortion in the utilitarian view of moral and political decision. The idea that burdens for some people can be justified simply by benefits to others "arises from the conception of individuals as separate lines for the assignment of benefits, as isolated persons who stand as claimants on an administrative or benevolent largess. Occasionally persons do so stand to one another; but this is

363

not the general case."² When persons are viewed as agents who are making agreements with one another, this way of looking at their relations is not the natural one.

Of course the utilitarian claims to take agency into account. He acknowledges that persons do not just want things to be done for them but want to do things; he can argue, with Mill, that persons should be free to make their own choices because it makes them happy.³ The utilitarian regards agency as an important form of experience; he includes actions and activities among the things that *happen to us*. This is characteristic of the empiricist tradition in which utilitarianism has its roots, and is nowhere more evident than when Hume writes: "I desire it may be observ'd, that by the *will*, I mean nothing but *the internal impression we feel and are conscious of, when we knowingly give rise to any new motion of our body, or new perception of our mind.*"⁴ Hume here identifies the will not with our power to initiate action, but with the feeling we experience when we exercise that power.

And of course our actions and activities are among the things we experience. But in an equally undeniable sense, having experiences is among the things that we *do*. Activity and passivity are aspects of our nature, not parts, and each can be reduced to a form of the other. I will argue, however, that from a moral point of view it is important not to reduce agency to a mere form of experience. It is important because our conception of what a person is depends in a deep way on our conception of ourselves as agents. My argument is directed against the views about personal identity advanced by Derek Parfit in *Reasons and Persons*.⁵ I believe that Parfit's arguments depend on viewing the person primarily as a locus of experience, and agency as a form of experience. If we regard persons primarily as agents, we will reach different conclusions both about the nature of personal identity and about its moral implications.⁶

I   PARFIT'S THEORY OF PERSONAL IDENTITY

According to what Parfit calls "the standard view" of identity, the persistence of an object over time can be understood in terms of spatiotemporal continuity under a concept (RP 203). So long as we can draw a continuous line through space-time at every point on which there is an object falling under the concept X, we say that the object is the same X, persisting. It is generally acknowledged that this criterion is loose and admits of many exceptions. Some objects may be dismantled and reconstructed later on (RP 203). Or an object that does persist through space-time may change so radically that we do not call it the same one even though it falls under the same concept. Finally, the indeterminacy of our concepts often leaves us uncertain whether to say that an object falling under a given concept still exists or not.[7] In such cases, what we say about identity must be governed by pragmatic considerations. There is no metaphysical fact of the matter about whether the earlier object and the later one are the same. The question whether the thing is the same is, as Parfit says, an empty question (RP 213). It may have a best answer, if the pragmatic considerations are decisive, but it does not have a true answer (RP 260).

The standard view works best for physical objects. According to the physical criterion of personal identity, a person is, or coincides exactly with, a spatiotemporally continuous living human body. But some people think that physical continuity is neither necessary nor sufficient for personal identity. It is insufficient, because a human being could conceivably change so radically that he would not really be the same person. A great deal of what matters to us in ourselves and others is psychological – our memories, characters, tastes, interests, loves, hates, and so forth. To take an extreme case, a human being who lost all of his memories, and began to exhibit a very different character, would not be, in any important sense, the same person. For similar reasons, some think that physical continuity is not necessary for identity. They think it conceivable that the very same psychological person could occupy a different body, or, as in some religious conceptions, that a person could become independent of a body altogether. These people believe that a different kind of continuity characterizes personal identity, a continuity which Parfit calls psychological continuity.

Parfit defines psychological continuity in terms of another relation, psychological connection (RP 205–6). A psychological connection exists when a psychological state at one time is causally related in an appropriate way to a psychological state at an earlier time. For instance, if Marilyn remembers something because Norma Jean experienced it, if Marilyn does something because Norma Jean intended it, if Marilyn believes something because Norma Jean was taught it, then Marilyn and Norma Jean are psychologically connected.[8] If there are many such connections they are strongly connected, and if there are overlapping chains of strong connection then Marilyn is psychologically continuous with Norma Jean. In this case, what Parfit calls "Relation-R" – psychological connectedness and continuity – holds between Marilyn and Norma Jean. Under normal circumstances, this means that Marilyn is Norma Jean at a later date.

There are two views about what makes psychological connectedness possible. Some believe that psychological connections hold because of something psychological that persists in the person. The easiest way to conceive this is dualistically: the person has a soul or a "Cartesian Ego" that is the common subject of all her experiences and links them. Or, Parfit suggests, even without being a dualist one may believe that the persistence of a psychological subject is a "deep further fact" about a person. Parfit calls these views "Non-Reductionist," since the persisting subject of experiences is regarded as an irreducible entity. On a Non-Reductionist view, the person is the psychological subject of experiences; the holding of Relation-R results from identity, rather than being constitutive of it.[9] But a physicalist is more likely to believe that psychological connectedness can be explained simply by physical continuity. No persisting psychological *entity* is needed to explain connectedness. Parfit calls this view "Reductionist," since the existence of a person can be reduced to "the existence of a brain and body, and the occurrence of a series of interrelated physical and mental events" (RP 211). When this view is combined with the view that Relation-R is more important to personal identity than physical continuity, Relation-R becomes constitutive of personal identity.[10]

It is important to notice that for the Reductionist who favors a psychological criterion of the person, physical continuity is neither necessary nor sufficient for personal identity.[11] The importance of physical continuity is that it is the *normal* cause of psychological connectedness and so of psychological continuity. But Parfit argues convincingly that nothing important depends on the cause being normal. Even if physicalism is true, the physical basis of our psychological attributes will lie in what we may call, in a broadly Aristotelian sense, the "formal" rather than the "material" properties of the nervous system.[12] That is, it will rest in something about the way the matter is *organized*, not in the particular matter used. If this is cor-

rect, psychological connectedness can have other causes. Suppose
you are about to lose your memory because a portion of your brain is
dying, but a surgeon can make a copy of this portion of your brain,
including the configuration that carries memory but without the disease, and substitute it for the dying part. For you, this should be just as
good as remembering in the normal way. After all, this is what the rest
of your body is always doing – replacing old parts with fresh ones like
them. The continuity appropriate to a living being is this "formal"
continuity.[13] Indeed, Parfit argues, what we normally count as persisting identity is simply formal continuity plus uniqueness – that is,
being the only formal continuer of a past self.

But it is the continuity and not the uniqueness that really matters. For if the essential aspect of a person is formal or copiable,
then in principle it seems that we could make two equally good
copies of a whole person. Both of them would be formally continuous with the original person; each would have that person's memories, character, ambitions and loves; each would believe, or at least
feel, that he is the original person. In this case, the question which
of them is the same person as the original is an empty question.
And it may not matter, or it may depend on circumstance, what we
ought to say about it. And so personal identity is not important.
Rather, Relation-R is what matters.

But Relation-R, unlike identity, is a relation we can bear to more
than one person. If this is what is important, what matters to me in
my survival is not whether "I" survive, but whether someone who is
sufficiently R-related to me does. Whether or not that person is *me*
may not be important; it may even, in science-fictional cases, be an
empty question. But we do not need to appeal to science fiction to
make the point. We need only grant to Parfit that it does not matter
what the cause of connectedness is. I may do something because I
intended it; but so may my lawyer, secretary, executor, or slave. I
may believe something because I convinced myself of it; so, indirectly, may my students, children, or friends. Although others will
not directly remember events because they happened to me, they
may certainly know of events because they happened to me. To the
extent that such connectedness, and not identity, is what matters to
us in our survival, the second kind of connection may be nearly as
good as the first.[14] Yet the second kind of connection is consistent
with my death.

Parfit believes that his arguments show that the very existence of "persons" as a distinct kind of entity is less "deep" than we normally take it to be. Reductionists hold that a person just consists in "the existence of a brain and body, and the occurrence of a series of interrelated physical and mental events" (RP 211). They also hold that "these facts can be described without presupposing the identity of this person, or explicitly claiming that the experiences in this person's life are had by this person, or even explicitly claiming that this person exists. These facts can be described in an *impersonal* way" (RP 211). Parfit believes that the primary challenge to the possibility of an impersonal description is the claim that there must be a *subject* of experiences. To this, he replies:

In one sense this is clearly true. Even Reductionists do not deny that people exist. And, on our concept of a person, people are not thoughts and acts. They are thinkers and agents. I am not a series of experiences, but the person who *has* these experiences. A Reductionist can admit that, in this sense, a person is *what has* experiences, or the *subject of experiences*. This is true because of the way in which we talk. What a Reductionist denies is that the subject of experiences is a separately existing entity, distinct from a brain and body, and a series of physical and mental events. (RP 223)

Parfit believes that accepting Reductionism may change our minds about many issues concerning rationality and morality. Non-Reductionists think that personal identity constitutes a *special* relation I have to my past and future selves. I am responsible for my past self, and I bear the guilt for her crimes and the obligations created by her promises. I am responsible to my future self, for whose happiness, since it will one day be mine, it is rational for me to provide. Parfit thinks that such beliefs result from thinking of the self as a separately existing entity, a subject of experiences or Cartesian Ego, which moves through the course of a life, collecting memories and responsibilities as it goes. If there is no continuing subject of experiences, he argues, these claims about a special relation to oneself, and their rational and moral implications, are less plausible. Relation-R may bear the weight of some of these special relations, but it is a relation we may have to various persons and to varying degrees. Alternatively, Relation-R may not establish *any* special relation between myself and the subject of experiences who will occupy my body in the future. In either case, there should be changes in our views about morality and rationality wherever those views depend on claims about personal identity.

Suppose Parfit has established that there is no deep sense in which I am identical to the subject of experiences who will occupy my body in the future.[15] In this section I will argue that I nevertheless have reasons for regarding myself as the same rational agent as the one who will occupy my body in the future. These reasons are not metaphysical, but practical.

To see this, first set aside the problem of identity over time, and think about the problem of identity at any given time. Why do you think of yourself as one person now? This problem should seem especially pressing if Parfit has convinced you that you are not unified by a Cartesian Ego which provides a common subject for all your experiences. Just now you are reading this article. You may also be sitting in a chair, tapping your foot, and feeling hot or tired or thirsty. But what makes it one person who is doing and experiencing all this? We can add to this a set of characteristics which you attribute to yourself, but which have only an indirect bearing on your conscious experiences at any given time. You have loves, interests, ambitions, virtues, vices, and plans. You are a conglomerate of parts, dispositions, activities, and experiences. As Hume says, you are a bundle.[16] What makes you one person even at one time?

In *On the Soul*, Aristotle says that the practical faculty of the soul must be one thing.[17] We think of it as having parts, of course, because we sometimes have appetites that are contrary to practical reason, or experience conflict among our various desires. Still, the faculty that originates motion must be regarded as a single thing, because we do act. Somehow, the conflicts are resolved, and no matter how many different things you want to do, you in fact do one rather than another.

Your conception of yourself as a unified agent is not based on a metaphysical theory, nor on a unity of which you are conscious. Its grounds are practical, and it has two elements. First, there is the raw necessity of eliminating conflict among your various motives. In making his argument for Reductionism, Parfit appeals to a real-life example which has fascinated contemporary philosophers: persons with split brains (RP 245–46). When the corpus callosum, the network of nerves between the two hemispheres of the brain, is cut, the two hemispheres can function separately.[18] In certain experimental situations, they do not work together and appear to be wholly unconscious of each other's activities. These cases suggest that the two hemispheres of the brain are not related in any metaphysically deeper way than, say, two people who are married. They share the same quarters and, with luck, they communicate. Even their characteristic division of labor turns out to be largely conventional, and both can perform most functions. So imagine that the right and left halves of your brain disagree about what to do. Suppose that they do not try to resolve their differences, but each merely sends motor orders, by way of the nervous system, to your limbs. Since the orders are contradictory, the two halves of your body try to do different things.[19] Unless they can come to an agreement, both hemispheres of your brain are ineffectual. Like parties in Rawls's original position, they must come to a unanimous decision somehow. You are a unified person at any given time because you must act, and you have only one body with which to act.

The second element of this pragmatic unity is the unity implicit in the *standpoint* from which you deliberate and choose. It may be that what actually happens when you make a choice is that the strongest of your conflicting desires wins. But that is not the way you think of it when you deliberate. When you deliberate, it is as if there were something over and above all your desires, something that is *you*, and that *chooses* which one to act on. The idea that you choose among your conflicting desires, rather than just waiting to see which one wins, suggests that you have reasons for or against acting on them.[20] And it is these reasons, rather than the desires themselves, which are expressive of your will. The strength of a desire may be counted *by you* as a reason for acting on it; but this is different from *its* simply winning. This means that there is some principle or way of choosing that you regard as expressive of *yourself*, and that provides reasons that regulate your choices among your desires. To identify with such a principle or way of choosing is to be "a law to yourself," and to be unified as such. This does not require that your agency be located in a separately existing entity or involve a deep metaphysical fact. Instead, it is a practical necessity imposed upon you by the nature of the deliberative standpoint.[21]

It is of course important to notice that the particular way you choose which desires to act on *may* be guided by your beliefs about certain metaphysical facts. Parfit evidently thinks that it should. When he argues about the rationality of concern about the future, Parfit assumes that my attitude about the desires of the future inhabitant of my body should be based on the metaphysics of personal identity. That is, I should treat a future person's desires as *mine* and so as normative for me if I have some metaphysical reason for supposing that she is *me*.[22] But this argument from the metaphysical facts to normative reasons involves a move from "is" to "ought" which requires justification. I will argue shortly that there may be other, more distinctively normative grounds for determining which of my motives are "my own"; metaphysical facts are not the only possible ground for this decision. For now, the important points are these: First, the *need* for identification with some unifying principle or way of choosing is imposed on us by the necessity of making deliberative choices, not by the metaphysical facts. Second, the metaphysical facts do not obviously settle the question: I must still decide whether the consideration that some future person is "me" has some special normative force for me. It is practical reason that requires me to construct an identity for myself; whether metaphysics is to guide me in this or not is an open question.

The considerations I have adduced so far apply to unification at any given moment, or in the context of any given decision. Now let us see whether we can extend them to unity over time. We might start by pointing out that the body which makes you one agent now persists over time, but that is insufficient by itself. The body could still be a series of agents, each unified pragmatically at any given moment. More telling considerations come from the character of the things that human agents actually choose. First of all, as Parfit's critics often point out, most of the things we do that matter to us take up time. Some of the things we do are intelligible only in the context of projects that extend over long periods. This is especially true of the pursuit of our ultimate ends. In choosing our careers, and pursuing our friendships and family lives, we both presuppose and construct a continuity of identity and of agency.[23] On a more mundane level, the habitual actions we perform for the sake of our health presuppose ongoing identity. It is also true that we think of our activities and pursuits as interconnected in various ways; we think that we are carrying out plans of life. In order to carry out a rational plan of life, you need to be one continuing person. You normally think you lead one continuing life because you are one person, but according to this argument the truth is the reverse. You are one continuing person because you have one life to lead.

You may think of it this way: suppose that a succession of rational agents *do* occupy my body. I, the one who exists now, need the cooperation of the others, and they need mine, if together we are going to have any kind of a *life*. The unity of our life is forced upon us, although not deeply, by our shared embodiment, together with our desire to carry on long-term plans and relationships. But actually this is somewhat misleading. To ask why the present self should cooperate with the future ones is to assume that the present self has reasons with which it already identifies, and which are independent of those of later selves. Perhaps it is natural to think of the present self as necessarily concerned with present satisfaction. But it is mistaken. In order to make deliberative choices, your present self must identify with something from which you will derive your reasons, but not necessarily with something present. The sort of thing you identify yourself with may carry you automatically into the future; and I have been suggesting that this will very likely be the case. Indeed, the choice of any action, no matter how trivial, takes you some way into the future. And to the extent that you regulate your choices by identifying yourself as the one who is implementing something like a particular plan of life, you need to identify with your future in order to be *what you are even now.*[24] When the person is viewed as an agent, no clear content can be given to the idea of a merely present self.[25]

Still, Parfit might reply that all this concedes his point about the insignificance of personal identity. The idea that persons are unified as agents shares with Reductionism the implication that personal identity is not very deep. If personal identity is just a prerequisite for coordinating action and carrying out plans, individual human beings do not have to be its possessors. We could, for instance, always act in groups. The answer to this is surely that for many purposes we do; there *are* agents of different sizes in the world. Whenever some group wants or needs to act as a unit, it must form itself into a sort of person – a legal person, say, or a corporation. Parfit himself likes to compare the unity of persons to the unity of nations. A nation, like a person, exists, but it does not amount to anything more than "the existence of its citizens, living together in certain ways, on its territory" (RP 211–12). In a similar way, he suggests, a person just amounts to "the existence of a brain and body, and the occurrence of a series of interrelated physical and mental events" (RP 211). On the view I am advancing, a better comparison would be the state. I am using "nation" here, as Parfit does, for a historical or ethnic entity, naturalistically defined by shared history and traditions; a state, by contrast, is a moral or formal entity, defined by its constitution and deliberative procedures. A state is not merely a group of citizens living on a shared territory. We have a state only where these citizens have constituted themselves into a single agent. They have, that is, adopted a way of resolving conflicts, making decisions, interacting with other states, and planning together for an ongoing future. For a group of citizens to view themselves as a state, or for us to view them as one, we do not need to posit the state as a separately existing entity. All we need is to grant an authoritative status to certain choices and decisions made by certain citizens or bodies, as its legislative voice. Obviously, a state is not a deep metaphysical entity underlying a nation, but rather something a nation can make of itself. Yet the identity of states, for practical reasons, must be regarded and treated as more determinate than the identity of nations.

But the pragmatic character of the reasons for agent unification does not show that the resulting agencies are not *really* necessary. Pragmatic necessity can be overwhelming. When a group of human beings occupy the same territory, for instance, they have an imperative need to form a unified state. And when a group of psychological functions occupy the same human body, they have an even more imperative need to become a unified person. This is why the human body must be conceived as a unified agent. As things stand, it is the basic kind of agent.

Of course if our technology were different, individual human bodies might not be the basic kind of agent. My argument supports a physical criterion of identity, but only a conditional one. *Given the technology we have now*, the unit of action is a human body. But consider Thomas Nagel's concept of a "series-person." Nagel imagines a society in which persons are replicated in new matter once every year after they reach the age of thirty. This prevents them from aging, and barring accidents and incurable diseases, may even make them immortal (RP 289–90). On my concept, a series-person, who would be able to carry out unified plans and projects, and have ongoing relations with other persons, would be a person.[26] But the fact that the basic unit of action might be different if technology were different is neither here nor there. The relevant necessity is the necessity of acting and living, and it is untouched by mere technological possibilities. The main point of the argument is this: a focus on agency makes more sense of the notion of personal identity than a focus on experience. There is a necessary connection between agency and unity which requires no metaphysical support.

III   THE UNITY OF CONSCIOUSNESS

Many will feel that my defense of personal unity simply bypasses what is most unsettling in Parfit's arguments. Parfit's arguments depend on what we may broadly call an "Aristotelian" rather than a "Cartesian" metaphysics of the person. That is, matter is essentially particular; form is essentially copiable; and form is what makes the person what she is, and so is what is important about her. The "Cartesian" metaphysics, by contrast, holds that the important element of a person is something essentially particular and uncopiable, like a Cartesian Ego. What tempts people to believe this is an entrenched intuition that something like a Cartesian Ego serves as the locus of the particular consciousness that is mine and no one else's. And my argument about the unity of agency in no way responds to this intuition.

Parfit writes: "When I believed that my existence was a further fact, I seemed imprisoned in myself. My life seemed like a glass tunnel, through which I was moving faster every year, and at the end of which there was darkness. When I changed my view, the walls of my glass tunnel disappeared. I now live in the open air" (RP 281). Parfit's glass tunnel is a good image of the way people think of the unity of consciousness. The sphere of consciousness presents itself as something like a room, a place, a lit-up area, within which we do our thinking, imagining, remembering, and planning, and from out of which we observe the world, the passing scene. It is envisioned as a tunnel or a stream, because we think that one moment of consciousness is somehow directly continuous with others, even when interrupted by deep sleep or anesthesia. We are inclined to think that memory is a deeper thing than it is, that it is *direct* access to an earlier stage of a continuing self, and not merely one way of knowing what happened. And so we may think of amnesia, not merely as the loss of knowledge, but as a door that blocks an existing place.

The sense that consciousness is in these ways unified supports the idea that consciousness requires a persisting psychological subject. The unity of consciousness is supposed to be explained by attributing all one's experiences to a single psychological entity. Of course, we may argue that the hypothesis of a unified psychological subject does nothing to *explain* the unity of consciousness. It is simply a figure for or restatement of that unity. Yet the idea of such a subject seems to have explanatory force. It is to challenge this intuition that Parfit brings up the facts about persons with divided brains. People are often upset by these facts because they think that they cannot imagine what it is like to be such a person. When the hemispheres function separately, the person seems to have two streams of consciousness. If consciousness is envisioned as a sort of place, then this is a person who seems to be in two places at the same time. If consciousness requires a subject, then this person's body seems, mysteriously, to have become occupied by two subjects. Here, the hypothesis of a psychological subject brings confusion rather than clarity.

Parfit's own suggestion is that the unity of consciousness "does not need a deep explanation. It is simply a fact that several experiences can be co-conscious, or be the objects of a single state of awareness" (RP 250). Split-brain people simply have experiences which are not co-conscious, and nothing more needs to be said. This seems to me close to the truth but not quite right. Privileging the language of "having experiences" and "states of awareness" gives the misleading impression that we can count the experiences we are now having, or the number of objects of which we are aware, and then ask what unifies them. The language of activities and dispositions enables us to characterize both consciousness and its unity more accurately.[27]

Consciousness, then, is a feature of certain activities which percipient animals can perform. These activities include perceiving; various forms of attending such as looking, listening, and noticing; more intellectual activities like thinking, reflecting, recalling, remembering, and reading; and moving voluntarily. Consciousness is not a state that makes these activities possible, or a qualification of the subject who can perform them. It is a feature of *the activities themselves*. It is misleading to say that you must be conscious in order to perform them, because your being able to perform them is all that your being conscious amounts to.

Voluntary motion is an important example because of a distinction that is especially clear in its case. When we move voluntarily, we move consciously. But this is not to say we are conscious that we are moving. Much of the time when we move nothing is further from our minds than *the fact* that we are moving. But of course this does not mean that we move unconsciously, like sleepwalkers. It is crucial, in thinking about these matters, not to confuse *being engaged in a conscious activity* with *being conscious of an activity*. Perhaps such a confusion lies behind Descartes' bizarre idea that nonhuman animals are unconscious. In the direct, practical sense, an adult hunting animal which is, say, stalking her prey, knows exactly what she is doing. But it would be odd to say that she is aware *of* what she is doing or that she knows anything *about* it. What she is aware of is her environment, the smell of her prey, the grass bending quietly under her feet. The consciousness that is inherent in psychic activities should not be understood as an inner *observing* of those activities, a theoretic state. An animal's consciousness can be entirely practical.

The unity of consciousness consists in one's ability to coordinate and integrate conscious activities. People with split brains cannot integrate these activities in the same way they could before. This would be disconcerting, because the integration itself is not something we are ordinarily aware of. But it would not make you feel like two people. In fact, such persons learn new ways to integrate their psychic functions, and appear normal and normally unified in everyday life. It is only in experimental situations that the possibility of unintegrated functioning is even brought to light.[28]

What makes it possible to integrate psychic functions? If this is a causal question, it is a question for neurologists rather than philosophers. But perhaps some will still think there is a conceptual necessity here – that such integration requires a common psychological subject. But think again of persons with split brains. Presumably, in ordinary persons the corpus callosum provides means of communication between the two hemispheres; it transmits signals. When split-brain persons are not in experimental situations, and they function normally, the reason appears to be simply that the two hemispheres are able to communicate by other means than the corpus callosum. For example, if the left hemisphere turns the neck to look at something, the right hemisphere necessarily feels the tug and looks too.[29] Activities, then, may be coordinated when some form of communication takes place between the performers of those activities. But communication certainly does not require a common psychological subject. After all, when they can communicate, two different people can integrate their functions, and, for purposes of a given activity, become a single agent.

Communication and functional integration do not require a common subject of conscious experiences. What they do require, however, is the unity of agency. Again, there are two aspects of this unity. First, there is the raw practical necessity. Sharing a common body, the two hemispheres of my brain, or my various psychic functions, must work together. The "phenomenon" of the unity of consciousness is nothing more than the *lack* of any perceived difficulty in the coordination of psychic functions. To be sure, when I engage in psychic activities *deliberately*, I regard myself as the subject of these activities. *I* think, *I* look, *I* try to remember. But this is just the second element of the unity of agency, the unity inherent in the deliberative standpoint. I regard myself as the employer of my psychic capacities in much the same way that I regard myself as the arbiter among my conflicting desires.

If these reflections are correct, then the unity of consciousness is simply another instance of the unity of agency, which is forced upon us by our embodied nature.

IV AGENCY AND IDENTITY

At this point it will be useful to say something about why I take the view I am advancing to be a Kantian one. Kant believed that as rational beings we may view ourselves from two different standpoints.[30] We may regard ourselves as objects of theoretical understanding, natural phenomena whose behavior may be causally explained and predicted like any other. Or we may regard ourselves as agents, as the thinkers of our thoughts and the originators of our actions. These two standpoints cannot be completely assimilated to each other, and the way we view ourselves when we occupy one can appear incongruous with the way we view ourselves when we occupy the other. As objects of theoretical study, we see ourselves as wholly determined by natural forces, the mere undergoers of our experiences. Yet as agents, we view ourselves as free and responsible, as the authors of our actions and the *leaders* of our lives. The incongruity need not become contradiction, so long as we keep in mind that the two views of ourselves spring from two different relations in which we stand to our actions. When we look at our actions from the theoretical standpoint our concern is with their explanation and prediction. When we view them from the practical standpoint our concern is with their justification and choice. These two relations to our actions are equally legitimate, inescapable, and governed by reason, but they are separate. Kant does not assert that it is a matter of theoretical fact that we are agents, that we are free, and that we are responsible. Rather, we must view ourselves in these ways when we occupy the standpoint of practical reason – that is, when we are deciding what to do. This follows from the fact that we must regard ourselves as the causes – the first causes – of the things that we will. And this fundamental attitude is forced upon us by the necessity of making choices, regardless of the theoretical or metaphysical facts.[31]

From the theoretical standpoint, an action may be viewed as just another experience, and the assertion that it has a subject may be, as Parfit says, "because of the way we talk." But from the practical point of view, actions and choices must be viewed as having agents and choosers. This is what *makes* them, in our eyes, our own actions and choices rather than events that befall us. In fact, it is only from the practical point of view that actions and choices can be distinguished from mere "behavior" determined by biological and psychological laws. This does not mean that our existence as agents is asserted as a further fact, or requires a separately existing entity that should be discernible from the theoretical point of view.[32] It is rather that from the practical point of view our relationship to our actions and choices is essentially *authorial:* from it, we view them as *our own*. I believe that when we think about the way in which our own lives matter to us personally, we think of ourselves in this way. We think of living our lives, and even of having our experiences, as something that we *do*. And it is this important feature of our sense of our identity that Parfit's account leaves out.[33]

What sort of difference does this make? To put it in Parfit's terms, it privileges certain kinds of psychological connection – roughly speaking, authorial ones – over others. In discussing the events that according to Reductionism constitute a person's life, Parfit introduces the idea of a *boring* event – for instance, the continued existence of a belief or a desire (RP 211). His point in including these, of course, is to cover the fact that one of the things that makes you the same person at time$_2$ that you were at time$_1$ is that certain things about you have remained the same. But we can distinguish beliefs and desires that continue merely because, having been acquired in childhood, they remain unexamined, from beliefs and desires that continue because you have arrived at, been convinced of, decided on, or endorsed them. In an account of personal identity which emphasizes agency or authorship, the latter kind of connection will be regarded as much less boring than the former. This is because beliefs and desires you have actively arrived at are more truly your own than those which have simply arisen in you (or happen to inhere in a metaphysical entity that is you).[34] Recall Mill's complaint:

Not only in what concerns others, but in what only concerns themselves, the individual or the family do not ask themselves, what do I prefer? or, what would suit my character and disposition? or, what would allow the best and highest in me to have fair play and enable it to grow and thrive? . . . I do not mean that they choose what is customary in preference to what suits their own inclination. It does not occur to them to have any inclination except for what is customary. Thus the mind itself is bowed to the yoke: even in what people do for pleasure, conformity is the first thing thought of; they like in crowds . . . , and are generally without either opinions or feelings of home growth, or *properly their own*.[35]

It is, I think, significant that writers on personal identity often tell stories about mad surgeons who make changes in our memories or characters.[36] These writers usually emphasize the fact that after the surgical intervention we are altered, we have changed. But surely part of what creates the sense of lost identity is that the person is changed by *intervention*, from outside. The stories might affect us differently if we imagined the changes initiated by the person herself, as a result of her own choice. You are not a different person *just* because you are very different.[37] Authorial psychological connectedness is consistent with drastic changes, provided those changes are the result of actions by the person herself or reactions for which she is responsible.[38]

It is important to see how these claims do and do not violate Parfit's thesis that we should not care what the causal mechanism of connection is (RP 286). Given a suitable understanding of the idea of a causal mechanism, the Kantian can agree. If I can overcome my cowardice by surgery or medication rather than habituation I might prefer to take this less arduous route. So long as an authentic good will is behind my desire for greater courage, and authentic courage is the result, the mechanism should not matter. But for the Kantian it does matter who is initiating the use of the mechanism. Where I change myself, the sort of continuity needed for identity may be preserved, even if I become very different. Where I am changed by wholly external forces, it is not. This is because the sort of continuity needed for what matters to me in my own personal identity essentially involves my agency.

V   THE MORAL DIFFERENCES

Parfit believes that accepting Reductionism should modify many of our views about rationality and morality. In particular, he believes that Reductionism lends support to utilitarian attitudes about paternalism and distributive justice. In this section, I show how a more agent-centered conception of personal identity blocks the utilitarian implications which Parfit anticipates. Yet the agent-centered conception of the person shares with Reductionism the idea that persons are not deeply or metaphysically separated. And some modification of conventional philosophical views, therefore, does emerge.

Future concern and paternalism

Parfit's argument that Reductionism lends support to paternalism has two parts. First, he argues that Reductionism grounds a challenge to a standard view of rationality: that we have reason to be equally concerned about all parts of our own future. What matters is not identity but Relation-R, and part of that relation, connectedness, is a matter of degree. Two possible conclusions may be drawn about the rationality of special concern about one's own future. What Parfit calls the "Extreme Claim" is that I have *no* reason to be especially concerned about my own future. (More properly speaking, I have no reason of the form "she's me" to be especially concerned about any particular future person.) The "Moderate Claim" is that my personal concern about any future person who is R-related to me may (rationally) be a matter of degree (RP 307–8).

The disquieting result, according to Parfit, is that we cannot always criticize great imprudence as irrational. There may be no irrationality in my imposing a disproportionate burden on a person who will be R-related to me in the future for the sake of myself now. Even if we accept the "Moderate Claim," my future self may be too weakly connected to me to require great concern on my part. The result is disquieting because great imprudence "ought to be criticized" (RP 318). However we characterize it, most of us agree that there is something wrong about engaging in activities and relationships that pose a bad risk to one's future self-esteem, health, or welfare. Parfit proposes, therefore, that we should regard such conduct, even where not irrational, as immoral. Imposing the burdens of diminished self-respect, ill health, or misery on your later self should be regarded as wrong in exactly the same way that imposing these burdens on other persons is.

But this, in turn, may change our view about "paternalistic" intervention. Parfit writes:

The person we coerce might say: 'I may be acting irrationally. But even if I am, that is my affair. If I am only harming myself, I have the right to act irrationally and you have no right to stop me.' This reply has some force. We do not believe that we have a general right to prevent people from acting irrationally. But we do believe that we have a general right to prevent people from acting wrongly. This claim may not apply to minor wrong-doing. But we believe that it cannot be wrong, and would often be our duty, to prevent others from doing what is seriously wrong. Since we ought to believe that great imprudence is seriously wrong, we ought to believe that we should prevent such imprudence, even if this involves coercion. (RP 321)

There is more than one problem with this proposal. First, Parfit bases his analysis on an account of ordinary morality which I believe is mistaken. Most people *already* believe that great imprudence is morally wrong. The ruined or wasted life, with health, opportunity, and talent squandered, seems to us not merely stupid but reprehensible. And strictures against a lack of proper self-concern also follow from most ethical theories. The Greeks arguably made a form of self-concern the basis of their ethical theories, and unarguably included self-regarding virtues alongside others without hesitation. Of the eighteenth-century moralists perhaps only Hutcheson, who thought all virtue grounded in benevolence, was prepared to argue that self-regarding attributes could be virtues only indirectly.[39] For the utilitarian, lack of self-concern is the cause of needless pain and grief; for the Kantian, it evinces a lack of respect for the humanity in one's own person;[40] for the religious moralist, it is a failure of responsibility for what has been placed in one's special care.

The reason we do not feel entitled to interfere with imprudence is not, as Parfit claims, based on the difference between irrationality and immorality. He is also mistaken when he says that we believe that we may always interfere with immorality unless it is minor. The difference here is rather that between the realm of public right and the realm of private virtue. We enforce public right even when it is trivial; we cannot interfere with private vice even when it is as major as the concerns of human life can be. We may use coercion to prevent you from parking your car in your neighbor's unused private driveway or running a red light on a deserted road. We may not use coercion to prevent you from breaking your lover's heart or demolishing your spouse's self-esteem. A person has a right to the disposition of his driveway, but no one has a right not to have his heart broken.[41] This is certainly not because the latter is a minor wrong, but because of the moral territory we are in.

I have claimed that what matters personally is, or at least essentially involves, the view of myself as an agent, as one who chooses and lives a particular life. And, as things stand, it is qua the occupant of this particular body that I live a life, have ongoing relationships, realize ambitions, and carry out plans. So long as I occupy this body and live this life, I am this rational agent, the same one. As I argued earlier, it is misleading to ask whether my present self has a reason to be concerned with my future selves. This way of talking presupposes that the present self is necessarily interested in the quality of present experiences, and needs a further reason to care for more than that. But insofar as I constitute myself as an agent living a particular life, I will not in this way oppose my present self to future ones. And so I do have a personal reason, whether or not I also have a moral one, to care for my future.

But this kind of reason for future concern is going to weigh against extensive paternalistic intervention. This is not for the standard utilitarian reasons Parfit mentions – that people should learn from their own mistakes, and are in the best position to know whether their own actions are bad for them (RP 321). If it matters to me to live my own life, and that includes making my own choices and arriving at my own beliefs, then obviously I will not want others to intervene paternalistically unless it is necessary to prevent me from killing or crippling myself. I can live my own life only to the extent that I am free of such interference. We should be opposed to paternalism, then, not because self-concern lies outside morality, but because freedom is a condition of living one's own life, or even, as we say, of being one's own person.

But this is not to say that the considerations against deep personal separateness that Parfit and I both endorse have no consequences for the standard philosophical model of rationality. I have suggested that agents come in different sizes, and that the human body is merely the basic one. If we grant that the unity of agency is a reason for future concern, then we should grant that I also have reasons to care for the future of larger agencies of which I am a part. Just as I have a personal concern for my physical future, I may have a *personal* concern for the future of my family, the organization for which I work, a project in which I have been active, or the state of which I am a citizen. In fact our existing attitudes reflect this. We are glad if another country makes difficult changes to secure equality for an oppressed minority, but proud if our own does so; sorry if another country has recourse to needless military bluster, but ashamed when ours does. We care not just about the purposes involved here, but about our own involvement in them, even where it is distant. And this kind of personal concern often extends to the future of the agencies of which we are a part. The territory of practical reasons is not split into two domains – self-interested rationality concerned with the occupant of this particular body on the one hand, and reasons of impartial morality on the other. Instead, the personal concern which begins with one's life in a particular body finds its place in ever-widening spheres of agency and enterprise, developing finally into a *personal* concern for the impersonal – a concern, that is to say, for the fate of one's fellow creatures, considered merely as such.

Compensation and distributive justice

Parfit's treatment of distributive justice begins from consideration of an objection to utilitarianism advanced by Rawls (RP 329ff.). In burdening one person in order to benefit another, Rawls argues, utilitarianism improperly treats social choice as if it were just like individual choice.[42] The difficulty can be brought out in terms of *compensation*. If I am burdened today in order to get a benefit tomorrow, *I* am compensated. But if I am burdened so that *you* can get a benefit, no one is compensated. Therefore, while burdening myself for a future benefit is rational, burdening one person to benefit another is not. This is part of the reason for what Parfit calls "the objection to balancing," that is, balancing the gains of one person against the losses of another (RP 337).

Parfit agrees that one person cannot be compensated by a benefit to another. But he thinks that Reductionism makes this fact less important. One formulation of his argument is revealing:

Even those who object to balancing think that it can be justified to impose burdens on a child for his own greater benefit later in his life. Their claim is that a person's burden, while it can be morally outweighed by benefits to him, cannot ever be outweighed by mere benefits to others. This is held to be so even if the benefits are far greater than the burdens. The claim thus gives to the boundaries between lives – or to the fact of non-identity – overwhelming significance. It allows within the same life what, over different lives, it totally forbids. (RP 338–39)

Parfit thinks that Reductionism makes this position less rational. But notice his equation of "the boundaries between lives" with "the fact of non-identity." This is explicit in the next paragraph when he says: "The fact that we live different lives is the fact that we are not the same person. If the fact of personal identity is less deep, so is the fact of non-identity" (RP 339). But this conclusion does not follow even from Reductionism. Or, rather, it follows only if we also adopt a peculiarly agentless conception of what it is to live a life. Living a life as Parfit sees it is a matter of having a series of experiences. Since the idea of a continuing subject of experiences, as anything more than a grammatical convenience, has been discredited, Parfit supposes that the unity of a life has been discredited as well. He concludes that distributive policies should focus on the quality of experiences rather than on lives. But when living a life is conceived as something done by an agent we do not get this result. Lives conceived of as led by agents may be completely separate even if the unity of those agents is pragmatic rather than metaphysically deep. And if living a life in this sense is what matters, distribution should be over lives, and the agents who lead them. As things stand, the basic leader of a life is a human being, and this is what makes the human being the unit of distribution.[43] If technology changes this – for instance, if series-persons become possible – then the appropriate unit of distribution may change.

But still, one might envisage some change in our views as a result of our coming to believe that the fact that we lead separate lives *can be* less deep. Not just human beings, but marriages, friendships, institutions, and states all have lives. If we suppose that I participate in various lives, then there may be more scope for compensation than the objection to balancing allows. I *may* sometimes be compensated for a personal burden by a benefit to a larger life in which I participate. This is not an unfamiliar or revisionist idea, but is already realized in the attitudes most people have towards their friends and family. The efforts we make for the sake of those we love, and for the sake of keeping our relationships alive, are not regarded as uncompensated burdens, any more than the sacrifices we make today in order to benefit ourselves tomorrow are. I do things for my friend not because I calculate that she will do as much for me, but because she is my friend. This is just as comprehensible a reason, all by itself, as doing something for myself because I am myself. So perhaps it would be all right to impose a burden on me in order to benefit one of my close friends.[44]

But notice that *nothing* in this line of reasoning suggests that I can be compensated for a burden by a benefit to a person whose life is unconnected to, and not part of, my own. Even if personal identity is less deep, and our lives can be connected to those of others in much the same way they are connected within, it does not follow that our lives are equally connected to any lives whatever. And they are not. So a utilitarian criterion for distribution does not follow from this line of thought.

Still, one might think that even a limited expansion of the scope of possible compensation will change our views about distributive justice. But the argument against paternalism just given bears against this conclusion. And indeed to draw it would be to miss an important part of Rawls's point about the essential difference between private and political decision. Even in the most straightforward case of compensation, where a burden is imposed on a person from which she herself will later benefit, compensation by itself does not do the justificatory work. That I will be compensated may give me a reason to accept a burden; it does not give you a reason to impose one on me. The only reason you have to impose one on me is that *I do accept it.*[45] This fact may be obscured if we start, as Parfit does, from the example of a child, who is a legitimate object of paternalism, and on whose acceptance we cannot wait. In the case of an adult, it is the acceptance, not the compensation, that does the justificatory work.

VI   CONCLUSION

Some of the discussion of Parfit's work has revolved around the question whether we can, or even should, use a morally neutral, metaphysical conception of the person to support one moral theory over others.[46] I believe that the answer depends on what "morally neutral" is taken to mean. When we say a conception is morally neutral, we may mean that it is constructed without regard to the fact that we are going to employ it in moral thinking; or we may mean that it is constructed without prior dependence on any particular moral theory. I see no point in being neutral with respect to the purposes of moral thinking, nor do I see that metaphysics achieves that kind of neutrality any better than, say, psychoanalysis or biology.[47] On the other hand, if we are to find a basis for deciding among competing moral theories, an initial neutrality with respect to particular theories might be worth having. But Parfit's conception of the person does not have this kind of moral neutrality.

According to Parfit, utilitarians disagree with those who insist on compensation and other distributive values because utilitarians think that the question "to whom does it happen?" is like the question "when does it happen?" They regard both of these as "mere differences in position" (RP 340). Reductionism supports this parallel between the two questions because the Reductionist holds that an impersonal description of life is possible. Persons can be said to exist, but, according to Parfit, "this is true only because we describe our lives by ascribing thoughts and actions to people" (RP 341). It is a matter of grammatical convenience. Therefore "it becomes more plausible, when thinking morally, to focus less upon the person, the subject of experiences, and instead to focus more upon the experiences themselves" (RP 341).

So Parfit thinks that Reductionism supports the thesis that the quality of experiences is what matters, and so supports a utilitarian theory of value. But I believe instead that Parfit has assumed this theory of value from the start. The metaphysical argument about whether a person is a separately existing subject of experiences, or merely a stream of experiences with no separately existing subject, is preceded by an essentially *moral* assumption – the assumption that life is a series of experiences, and so that a person is first and foremost a locus of experiences. If you begin with the view that a person is a subject of experiences, and take away the subject, you are indeed left with nothing but experiences. But you will begin with that view only if you assume from the start that having experiences is what life is all about.

This assumption dictates the reduction of agency to a mere form of experience which I described at the beginning of this article. That is, it involves regarding our actions and activities as among the things that happen to us, and so, once the subject is removed, as simply among the things that happen. Because they regard doings as mere happenings, Parfit and other utilitarians suppose that the question "who does it?" is like the question "to whom does it happen?": according to them, it is merely a question about position.[48] But from the deliberative standpoint our relationship to our actions and our lives is not merely one of position. It is essential to us that our actions are our own, and we regard living our lives as something that we do.

Unless persons are separately existing entities, Parfit supposes, the ascription of actions to people is a matter of mere grammatical convenience. The Kantian reply is that neither metaphysics nor grammar is the basis for such ascriptions. Rather, the conception of ourselves as agents is fundamental to the standpoint of practical reason, the standpoint from which choices are made. And it is from this standpoint that we ask moral questions, and seek help from moral philosophy. This makes the conception of the agent, along with its unity, an appropriate one to employ in moral thinking. In fact, it is from the standpoint of practical reason that moral thought and moral concepts – including the concept of the person – are generated.

NOTES

I am pleased to acknowledge my debt to Thomas Hill, Jr. The original stimulus for this article came from an opportunity to comment on his paper "Pains and Projects: Justifying to Oneself," in his *Autonomy and Self-Respect*, chapter 12, at the Twenty-Seventh Annual Oberlin Philosophy Colloquium in April 1987, and his paper suggested some of the ideas in it. Section II contains a version of some of my comments on that occasion. I have also had the benefit of extensive comments on earlier versions of the chapter from Peter Hylton, Steven Wagner, John Broome, and the Editors of *Philosophy & Public Affairs*; colloquium discussions with the philosophy departments at Princeton University and Union College; and discussions on the material in Section III with Jay Schleusener. I would like to thank them all.

1 I borrow the term from Samuel Scheffler's *Rejection of Consequentialism*. Thomas Nagel, who also discusses such restrictions in *The View from Nowhere*, calls them "deontological." But that term may be misleading: the mark of such restrictions is not merely that they are not aimed at good consequences. Even utilitarians accept nonconsequentialist requirements as indirect ways to maximize utility. And other consequentialists may count the performance of a required action as itself a good consequence: when you tell the truth there is a good outcome, an act of honesty has occurred. What is distinctive of agent-centered restrictions is that you are not supposed to violate them even in order to prevent other similar violations. For instance, you are to tell the truth even if doing so will have the foreseeable result that several other people will tell lies, while your lying would prevent them from lying. This shows that neither the indirect utility of truth-telling nor the occurrence of acts of honesty exhausts the value of truth-telling for you; you must be in a special way concerned with what *you* do. This may seem paradoxical or self-indulgent to consequentialists. Scheffler, for instance, describes it as prima facie irrational (*The Rejection of Consequentialism*, p. 83). Kantians, however, reject the consequentialist description of the situation as morally misleading. It is inconsistent with respect for others to regard their actions as simply a *consequence* of what *you* do.

2 John Rawls, "Justice as Reciprocity," p. 267.

3 See especially John Stuart Mill, *On Liberty*, chap. III.

4 David Hume, *A Treatise of Human Nature*, p. 399.

5 Derek Parfit, *Reasons and Persons*. Hereinafter cited as "RP" followed by page reference.

6 Several commentators have noticed that Parfit's conclusions do not square well with the conception of persons as agents. See for instance Samuel Scheffler, "Ethics, Personal Identity, and Ideals of the Person," and Stephen Darwall's reply, "Scheffler on Morality and Ideals of the Person." See also Bart Gruzalski, "Parfit's Impact on Utilitarianism."

7 While I draw on Parfit's account of the standard view, mine is somewhat different. In particular, the idea that identity is continuity under a concept, and that some spurious identity problems arise from the indeterminacy of concepts, is not emphasized in his account. Yet it does come up when he discusses the possibility that his own views have implications for the morality of abortion and euthanasia (RP 321–23). In these cases, the empty question is not whether a fetus or a comatose body is or is not some particular person, but whether they are persons at all.

8 It may be urged that a concept like "remember" conceptually implies underlying identity; in a strict sense, I can "remember" only what happened to me. To cover this conceptual objection, Parfit introduces the idea of a "quasi-memory" (or quasi-intention, or whatever). If someone else's memory traces are copied into my brain, say, so that I seem to remember things that happened to her, we can say that I quasi-remember those things (RP 219–22). If Parfit is correct in his claim, discussed shortly, that any cause is appropriate for connection, the quasi-memory will count as a psychological connection of the right sort for psychological continuity.

9 Some further account must then be given, of course, of the continuing identity of the psychological subject of experiences. One of the standard complaints about dualism might be thought to apply, *mutatis mutandis*, here: to say that I remain the same because of a psychic entity within me that remains the same is like saying I am conscious because of a psychic entity within me that is conscious. This only pushes the problem back.

10 As Parfit himself is at pains to point out (e.g., RP 209, 241), it is not logically necessary that a dualist be a Non-Reductionist or that a physicalist be a Reductionist. The dualist may believe that the person still reduces to "a series of interrelated physical and mental events"; the physicalist may hold that the person's existence as a continuing subject of experiences is a "deep further fact," even though that subject is not a separate or special kind of substance. Still, physicalism makes Reductionism a more natural view to hold, and I think it is helpful to keep this in mind.

11 In the text I argue that the same person could occupy a different body. Could the same body come to have a new person in it? Suppose psycho-

logical changes are so extensive that we say that the person has become "someone else." The physical changes that necessarily accompany these drastic psychological changes need not themselves be so drastic that we feel like saying that even the body is a new one. This seems obvious, and it is partly on the basis of this intuition that the psychological criterion of identity is favored. But it is worth remembering that the obviousness of the intuition depends on whether we classify the *expressive* features of the body as physical or psychological. If we classify them as physical, then we should expect the physical changes accompanying drastic psychological changes to be drastic as well. Someone who has begun to walk, sit, stand, and hold her limbs and facial muscles differently might without too much strain be said "even to have a different body." In any event, the phenomenon of expressiveness should remind us that the physical/psychological dichotomy is not as hard and fast as we are inclined to suppose.

12 The Aristotelian terminology used here and throughout this section is mine, not Parfit's.

13 We do not need to appeal to the importance of psychological continuity to establish this conclusion, since it may be argued that it is only the formal aspect of even our physical attributes that matters to us. For more detailed arguments against the importance of material persistence, see Parfit, *Reasons and Persons*, chap. 13 and appendix D, "Nagel's Brain" (RP 468–77).

14 It is not clear to me whether Parfit would agree with this. He defines Relation-R in terms of *direct* connections, without specifying what he means by "direct." Intuitively, knowing something because you remember it does seem more "direct" than knowing something because you are told it. In the second case there is an "extra" step – another person must first remember and then tell you. But Parfit also argues that we should accept any sort of cause of psychological connectedness and continuity. His examples of other sorts of causes are things like having someone else's memory traces copied into your brain. It is not clear to me that this *is* a more direct way of knowing something than being told. No doubt it would have a more direct *feel* to it, since it would feel like a memory, but that should make no difference. There is still an extra step: the other person must first remember and then the memory is transplanted into your brain.

15 This formulation is not, I believe, quite right. Parfit's arguments show that there is not a one-to-one correspondence between persons and human animals, but of course there is no implication that a person ever exists apart from a human animal. So perhaps we should say that what his arguments show is that the subject of *present* experiences is not the

person, but the animal on whom the person supervenes. There are several difficulties with this way of talking, for there are pressures to attribute experiences to the person, not to the animal. It is the person to whom we attribute memory of the experience, and what the person remembers is "such and such happened to me," not "such and such happened to the animal who I was then." And, to the extent that the character of your experiences is conditioned by memories and character, we should say that the character of your experiences is more determined by which person you are than by which animal you are (see note 27 below). In fact, however, none of this blocks the conclusion that the animal is the subject of experiences in the sense that it is immediately conscious of them when they are present. And I will suggest that we attribute experiences to the person in a different sense: the person is the agent in whose activities these experiences figure, the one who is engaged in having them. It is only if we insist on saying that the person and not the animal is the conscious subject of present experiences that we can get the conclusion in the text.

16 Hume, *Treatise of Human Nature*, p. 252. Hume, however, would not accept the description of the problem I have just given, for two reasons. First, he thinks that we do not experience more than one thing at a time, but rather that our perceptions "succeed each other with an inconceivable rapidity" (*Treatise*, p. 252). Second, he is talking only about the persistence of a subject of "perceptions," or as he puts it, "personal identity, as it regards our thought or imagination," which he separates from personal identity "as it regards our passions or the concern we take in ourselves" (*Treatise*, p. 253). Taken together, these two points leave Hume with only the diachronic problem of what links a perception to those that succeed and follow it.

17 Aristotle, *On the Soul*, III.9–10.

18 In my account of these persons, I rely on Thomas Nagel's "Brain Bisection and the Unity of Consciousness," in his *Mortal Questions*, chapter 11.

19 This is not an entirely fantastic idea. In one case, a man with a split brain attempted to push his wife away with one hand while reaching out to embrace her with the other. See Parfit, *Reasons and Persons*, p. 246, and Nagel, "Brain Bisection and the Unity of Consciousness," in *Mortal Questions*, p. 154.

20 See Stephen Darwall, "Unified Agency," in *Impartial Reason*, pp. 101–13.

21 The problem of personal identity often gets compared to the problem of free will, as both are metaphysical issues that bear on ethics. I hope it is clear from the above discussion that there is another similarity between them. The conception of myself as one and the conception of myself as

free (at least free to choose among my desires) are both features of the deliberative standpoint. And from this standpoint both conceptions find expression in my identification with some principle or way of choosing.

22 This view is also found in Sidgwick. When Sidgwick attempts to adjudicate between egoistic and utilitarian conceptions of practical reason, the consideration that favors egoism is this: "It would be contrary to Common Sense to deny that the distinction between any one individual and any other is real and fundamental, and that consequently, 'I' am concerned with the quality of my existence as an individual in a sense, fundamentally important, in which I am not concerned with the quality of the existence of other individuals: and this being so, I do not see how it can be proved that this distinction is not to be taken as fundamental in determining the ultimate end of rational action" (*The Methods of Ethics*, p. 498). But the utilitarian, appealing to metaphysics rather than common sense, replies, "Grant that the Ego is merely a system of coherent phenomena, that the permanent identical 'I' is not a fact but a fiction, as Hume and his followers maintain; why, then, should one part of the series of feelings into which the Ego is resolved be concerned with another part of the same series, any more than with any other series?" (*Methods*, p. 419). Parfit endorses the basic form of Sidgwick's argument explicitly in *Reasons and Persons*, p. 139. Neither Sidgwick nor Parfit shows why these metaphysical views are supposed to have the normative force suggested.

23 As Susan Wolf points out, "Love and moral character require more than a few minutes. More to the point, love and moral character as they occur in the actual world occur in persons, or at any rate in psychophysical entities of some substantial duration" ("Self-Interest and Interest in Selves," 709).

24 This way of looking at things places a constraint on how we formulate the reasons we have for desiring to carry on long-term projects and relationships. We cannot say that we want them because we expect to survive for a long time; instead, these things give us reasons for surviving. So the reasons for them must be independent of expected survival. See Bernard Williams, "Persons, Character, and Morality," in his *Moral Luck*, chapter 1, especially the discussion of Parfit on pp. 8–12.

25 I would like to thank the Editors of *Philosophy & Public Affairs* for prompting me to be clearer on this point.

26 On the other hand, Williams's person-types, of whom a number of copies (tokens) exist simultaneously, are not persons, since the tokens would not necessarily lead a common life. See Parfit, RP 293–97, and Bernard Williams, "Are Persons Bodies?" in his *Problems of the Self*, chapter 5.

27 I have argued that the idea of a momentary agent is unintelligible; I would also like to suggest, perhaps more surprisingly, that even the idea of a momentary experience is suspect. Consider, for instance, what seems to be one of the clearest cases of a temporally localized experience: physical pain. There is a clear sense in which pain is worse if you have been in pain for a long while. If pain is a momentary experience, we must suppose that this particular form of badness can be explicated in terms of the quality of the experience you are having now – so that, I suppose, a clever brain surgeon by stimulating the right set of nerves could make you have exactly the experience of a person who has been in pain for a long while even if you have not. The idea that the intrinsic goodness or badness of an experience can always be explicated in terms of the felt quality of the experience at the time of having it is defended in Sidgwick's *Methods of Ethics*, bk. II, chaps. II–III, and bk. III, chap. XIV. I do not think Sidgwick's arguments are successful, but at least he sees that the point needs defending. A more complex challenge to Sidgwick's thesis comes from the fact that there is a sense in which a pain (I feel like saying: the *same* pain) can be worse if in the face of it you panic, or lose your sense of humor, or give way to it completely. And this will be determined not just by how bad the pain is, but by your character. There is a kind of courage that has to do with how one handles pain, and this suggests that even "experiencing pain" is something that can be *done* in various ways. Privileging the language of conscious states or experiences can cause us to overlook these complications.

28 Nagel, in "Brain Bisection and the Unity of Consciousness," also arrives at the conclusion that the unity of consciousness is a matter of functional integration, but he believes that there is something unintuitive or unsatisfactory about thinking of ourselves in this way.

29 Nagel, "Brain Bisection," in *Mortal Questions*, p. 154.

30 No single reference is adequate, for this conception unfolds throughout Kant's writings. But for the most explicit account of the "two standpoints" view see *Groundwork III*.

31 Some people suppose that this means that freedom and agency are an *illusion* produced by the practical standpoint. But this presupposes the primacy of the theoretical standpoint, which is in fact the point at issue. Free agency and, according to my argument, unified personal identity are what Kant calls "Postulates of Practical Reason" (see C2 132ff.).

32 Contrary to the view of Gruzalski in "Parfit's Impact on Utilitarianism." Gruzalski claims that a deep further fact is required to support any conception of agency more libertarian than Hume's (*Treatise*, p. 767).

33 That it is lives and not merely experiences that matter, and that lives cannot be understood merely as sequences of experiences, is a point that

several of Parfit's commentators have made. Thus Wolf urges that "the value of these experiences depends on their relation to the lives of the persons whose experiences these are" ("Self-Interest and Interest in Selves," p. 709). And Darwall, commenting on Scheffler's response to Parfit, emphasizes "a conception of the kind of life one would like oneself and others to lead as opposed to the kind of things that befall people" ("Scheffler on Morality and Ideals of the Person," pp. 249–50).

34 Other critics of Parfit have stressed the importance of what I am calling the authorial connection. Darwall, in "Scheffler on Morality and Ideals of the Person," reminds us that "the capacity to choose our ends, and rationally to criticize and assess even many of our desires, means that our future intentions and desires do not simply befall us; rather, they are to some degree in our own hands" (p. 254). And in "Self-Interest and Interest in Selves" Wolf writes, "Being a rational agent involves recognizing one's ability to make one's own decisions, form one's own intentions, and plan for one's own future" (p. 719). Alternatively, a desire or a belief that has simply arisen in you may be reflectively endorsed, and this makes it, in the present sense, more authentically your own. See Harry Frankfurt, "Freedom of the Will and the Concept of a Person," "Identification and Externality," and "Identification and Wholeheartedness," in his *The Importance of What We Care About*, chapters 2, 5, and 12. Parfit himself suggests that Reductionism "gives more importance to how we choose to live" (RP 446).

35 Mill, *On Liberty*, pp. 58–59 (emphasis added).

36 Some of Parfit's own stories involve surgical intervention, and in this he follows Bernard Williams in "The Self and the Future," in his *Problems of the Self*, chapter 4. It is also significant, in a related way, that these writers focus on the question of future physical pains. Although it is true that there is an important way in which my physical pains seem to happen to *me* and to no one else, it is also true that they seem to have less to do with who I am (which *person* I am) than almost any other psychic events. (But see note 27 above for an important qualification of this remark.) The *impersonal* character of pain is part of what makes it seem so intrusive. Williams uses pain examples to show how strongly we identify with our bodies. One might say, more properly, that they show how strongly we identify with the animals who we (also) are. It is important to remember that each of us has an animal identity as well as our more specifically human identity and that some of the most important problems of personal integration come from this fact (see note 15 above). One might say, a little extravagantly, that the growing human animal is disciplined, frustrated, beaten, and shaped until it becomes a person – and then the person is faced with the task of reintegrating the

animal and its needs back into a human life. That we are not much good at this is suggested by psychoanalytic theory and the long human history of ambivalence (to say the least) about our bodily nature. Pain examples serve to show us how vulnerable our animal identity can make our human identity.

37 One of the few things I take issue with in Wolf's "Self-Interest and Interest in Selves" is a suggestion that persons who regarded themselves as R-related to rather than identical with their future selves would be less likely to risk projects that might involve great psychological change. Wolf reasons that great changes would be viewed as akin to death (p. 712). It should be clear from the above that I think this depends on how one envisages the changes arising.

38 Parfit does notice the difference between deliberate changes and those brought about by "abnormal interference, such as direct tampering with the brain" (RP 207), but he seems to take it for granted that those who feel that identity is threatened by the latter kind of changes are concerned about the fact that they are *abnormal*, not the fact that they are *interference*. Of course the sorts of considerations that feed worries about free will and determinism make it hard to distinguish cases in which a person has been changed by external forces from cases in which she has changed herself. Surgical intervention seems like a clear case of external interference because the person's prior character plays no role in producing the result. But what of someone who changes drastically in response to tragedy or trauma? I do not take up these problems here, but only note that from our own perspective we do distinguish cases in which we change our minds, desires, or characters from those in which the changes are imposed from without.

39 See Francis Hutcheson, *An Inquiry concerning the Original of Our Ideas of Virtue or Moral Good* (1725), sec. II. The relevant passages may be found in *British Moralists 1650–1800*, ed. D. D. Raphael, 1:271.

40 Of course a Kantian does not believe in the split between rationality and morality that underlies Parfit's analysis in the first place. In a Kantian view, as I have been arguing, no aim is *my own* unless it is the object of my own choice. And if Kant is right in supposing that a choice I may regard as truly my own must also be a universalizable choice, no split between personal rationality and morality is possible. In other words, Kant supposes that the view of the person that I have been arguing for leads to the adoption of a particular unifying principle of action, the categorical imperative. I have not tried to argue for this more ambitious thesis here.

41 I am using "right" here in the strict sense usual in the contract theory tradition, where a right is something that may be coercively enforced;

396   COMPARATIVE ESSAYS

since Parfit is discussing the possible use of coercion, this seems appropriate. Of course, the difference between using coercion and trying to *persuade* the wrongdoer to desist is essential here. But even the latter is normally permitted only to close friends or relatives of the people involved. As Steven Wagner has pointed out to me, we do say things like "You had no right to treat her that way" in private contexts where coercion is not at issue. A Kantian would say that we use this language because of the way the private duties of respect model the public, and enforceable, duties of justice. (When we speak this way, we do not mean merely that it was not *benevolent* to treat her that way.) Although coercion obviously cannot be used to make me respect another, I should regard my respect as something to which she has a claim, just as she does to her rights; respect is not something we give to others out of generosity (MPV 449–50; 462–68).

42 John Rawls, *A Theory of Justice*, sec. 5, esp. pp. 26–27.

43 In fact, for economic purposes the unit is often the family, and this is because family members are presumed to share their lives, although of course in an economic rather than a metaphysical sense.

44 Friendship is not a form of altruism. In routine cases, the question of "making a sacrifice" – if that is supposed to be an uncompensated burden – does not even come up. Where a burden is large, one may speak of "making a sacrifice" for one's friend. But then, where a burden is large, one may also speak of "making a sacrifice" for one's career or health. Sometimes, the impossibility of compensation springs from the incommensurability of values, not from who gets what. My friend's happiness may be incommensurable with other things I care about, without being any the less a part of my own happiness for all that.

45 It will help to recall here that, according to the social contract theory accepted by Kantians, the burdens of social life are supposed to be ones that the citizens accept, through their representatives. Any coercive measure must have this kind of backing.

46 See, for instance, John Rawls, "The Independence of Moral Theory," pp. 15–20; Norman Daniels, "Moral Theory and the Plasticity of Persons," p. 269; Samuel Scheffler, "Ethics, Personal Identity, and Ideals of the Person," pp. 240ff.; and Bart Schultz, "Persons, Selves, and Utilitarianism," pp. 721–45, esp. 741ff.

47 Parfit might reply that the point of appealing to a metaphysical conception is not merely that it is neutral, but that it is deep. It is what we most truly are. But both the truth and the force of this consideration are questionable. Parfit's conception of the person is recognizably metaphysical in that it is concerned with the theoretical conditions of identity and counting, certainly traditional concerns of metaphysics. It is

also as minimal as possible. But our metaphysical concerns about countability and ontological economy are still just some concerns among others. And they are not obviously the important ones for ethics.

48 This is related to the utilitarian's perplexity about agent-centered restrictions, discussed in note 1 above. In his discussion of his now well-known example of Jim, who is invited by a South American soldier to kill one Indian in order to save the lives of nineteen others, Bernard Williams says that the utilitarian solution of the problem regards Jim as "the agent of the satisfaction system who happens to be at *a particular point at a particular time:* in Jim's case, our man in South America." See *Utilitarianism: For and Against,* p. 115 (emphasis added).

Bibliography

Ackrill, J. L. "Aristotle's Distinction between *Energeia* and *Kinesis*," in *New Essays on Plato and Aristotle*. Edited by Renford Bambrough. London: Routledge & Kegan Paul, 1965.

Acton, H. B. *Kant's Moral Philosophy*. London: Macmillan, St. Martin's Press, 1970.

Allison, Henry E. "Empirical and Intelligible Character in the *Critique of Pure Reason*," in *Kant's Practical Philosophy Reconsidered*. Edited by Yirmiyahu Yovel. Dordrecht: Kluwer Academic Publishers, 1989.

Ameriks, Karl. "Kant's Deduction of Freedom and Morality." *Journal of the History of Philosophy* 19 (January, 1981): 53–79.

Anscombe, G. E. M. *Ethics, Religion, and Politics: Collected Philosophical Papers of G. E. M. Anscombe*. Volume III. Minneapolis: University of Minnesota Press, 1981.

Aristotle. *Aristotle's Eudemian Ethics*. Translated by Michael Woods. Oxford: Clarendon Press, 1982.

Aristotle. *The Complete Works of Aristotle*. Edited by Jonathan Barnes. Princeton: Princeton University Press, 1984.

Aristotle. *The Nicomachean Ethics*. Translated by David Ross and revised by J. L. Ackrill and J. O. Urmson. Oxford: Oxford University Press, 1980.

Aune, Bruce. *Kant's Theory of Morals*. Princeton: Princeton University Press, 1979.

Balguy, John. *The Foundation of Moral Goodness*. London: John Pemberton, 1728–1729. Reprinted in New York: Garland Publishing Company, 1976. Selections from this work may also be found in D. D. Raphael, *British Moralists 1650–1800*.

Beck, Lewis White. *Essays on Kant and Hume*. New Haven: Yale University Press, 1978.

Beck, Lewis White. *A Commentary on Kant's Critique of Practical Reason*. Chicago: University of Chicago Press, 1960.

Beck, Lewis White, *Early German Philosophy: Kant and His Predecessors.* Cambridge, MA: Harvard University Press, 1969.

Beck, Lewis White. *Immanuel Kant: Critique of Practical Reason and Other Writings in Moral Philosophy.* Chicago: University of Chicago Press, 1949; reprinted in New York: Garland, 1976.

Blackall, Eric A. *The Emergence of German as a Literary Language, 1700–1775.* Cambridge: Cambridge University Press, 1959.

Bok, Sissela. *Lying.* New York: Vintage Books, 1979.

Bradley, F. H. *Ethical Studies.* (1876; 2nd Edition, 1927). Oxford: Clarendon Press, 1927.

Butler, Joseph. *Fifteen Sermons Preached at the Rolls Chapel* (1726). The most influential of these are collected in Butler, *Five Sermons Preached at the Rolls Chapel and a Dissertation upon the Nature of Virtue.* Edited by Stephen Darwall. Indianapolis: Hackett, 1983. This is the edition I have cited.

Cassirer, Ernst. *Kant's Life and Thought.* New Haven: Yale University Press, 1981.

Clarke, Samuel. *A Discourse Concerning the Unchangeable Obligations of Natural Religion, and the Truth and Certainty of the Christian Revelation: The Boyle Lectures 1705,* in *The Works of Samuel Clarke.* London: J. and P. Knapton, 1738; reprinted in New York: Garland Publishing Company, 1978. I have also cited the selections from D. D. Raphael, *British Moralists 1650–1800.*

Daniels, Norman. "Moral Theory and the Plasticity of Persons." *Monist* 62 (1979): 265–287.

Darwall, Stephen. "Scheffler on Morality and Ideals of the Person." *Canadian Journal of Philosophy* 12 (1982): 247–264.

Darwall, Stephen. *Impartial Reason.* Ithaca: Cornell University Press, 1983.

Descartes, René. *The Philosophical Works of Descartes.* Translated by Elizabeth S. Haldane and G. R. T. Ross. Cambridge: Cambridge University Press, 1911.

Dietrichson, Paul. "Kant's Criteria of Universalizability," in *Kant: Foundations of the Metaphysics of Morals: Text and Critical Essays.* Edited by Robert Paul Wolff. Indianapolis: Bobbs-Merrill, 1969.

Falk, W. D. *Ought, Reasons, and Morality: The Collected Papers of W. D. Falk.* Ithaca: Cornell University Press, 1986.

Frankena, William K. *Perspectives on Morality: Essays of William K. Frankena.* Edited Kenneth E. Goodpaster. Notre Dame: University of Notre Dame Press, 1976.

Frankfurt, Harry G. *The Importance of What We Care About.* Cambridge: Cambridge University Press, 1988.

Gooch, G. P. *Germany and the French Revolution*. New York: Russell & Russell, 1966.

Gorovitz, Samuel, editor. *Mill: Utilitarianism: Text and Critical Essays*. Indianapolis: Bobbs-Merrill, 1971.

Gregor, Mary J. *Laws of Freedom: A Study of Kant's Method of Applying the Categorical Imperative in the "Metaphysik der Sitten."* Oxford: Basil Blackwell, 1963.

Gruzalski, Bart. "Parfit's Impact on Utilitarianism." *Ethics* 96 (1986): 760–783.

Hardie, W. F. R. "The Final Good in Aristotle's Ethics." *Philosophy* 40 (1965): 277–295. Rpt. in *Aristotle: A Collection of Critical Essays*. Edited by J. M. E. Moravscik. Notre Dame: The University of Notre Dame Press, 1968.

Hart H. L. H. *The Concept of Law*. Oxford: Carendon Press, 1961.

Hegel, G. W. F. *Hegel's Philosophy of Right*. Translated by T. M. Knox. Oxford: The Clarendon Press, 1952.

Hegel, G. W. F. *Phenomenology of Spirit*. Translated by A. V. Miller. Oxford: Oxford University Press, 1977.

Henrich, Dieter. "Die Deduktion des Sittengesetzes: Über die Gründe der Dunkelheit des letzten Abschnittes von Kants *Grundlegung zur Metaphysik der Sitten*," in *Denken in Schatten des Nihilismus*. Edited by Alexander Schwan. Darmstadt: Wissenschaftliche Buchgesellschaft, 1975.

Herman, Barbara. *The Practice of Moral Judgment*. Cambridge, MA: Harvard University Press, 1993.

Hill, Thomas, Jr. *Autonomy and Self-Respect*. Cambridge: Cambridge University Press, 1991.

Hill, Thomas, Jr. *Dignity and Practical Reason in Kant's Moral Theory*. Ithaca: Cornell University Press, 1992.

Hobbes, Thomas. *Leviathan*. Edited by Richard Tuck, Cambridge: Cambridge University Press, 1991.

Hume, David. *A Treatise of Human Nature*. (2nd Edition). Edited by L. A. Selby-Bigge and P. H. Nidditch. Oxford: Clarendon Press, 1978.

Hume, David. *Dialogues Concerning Natural Religion*. Edited by Norman Kemp Smith. New York: Macmillan Library of Liberal Arts, 1947.

Hume, David. *Enquiry Concerning the Principles of Morals*, in *David Hume: Enquiries Concerning Human Understanding and Concerning the Principles of Morals*. (3rd Edition). Edited by L. A. Selby-Bigge and P. H. Nidditch. Oxford: Clarendon Press, 1975.

Hutcheson, Francis. *Illustrations on the Moral Sense*. (Part II of *An Essay of the Nature and Conduct of the Passions and Affections with Illustra-*

tions on the Moral Sense (1728)). Edited by Bernard Peach. Cambridge, MA: Harvard University Press, 1971. Selections from this work may also be found in D. D. Raphael, *British Moralists 1650–1800*.

Hutcheson, Francis. *Inquiry Concerning the Original of Our Ideas of Beauty and Virtue* (1725). I have quoted from Volume I of D. D. Raphael, *British Moralists 1650–1800*. Two Volumes. Indianapolis: Hackett Publishing Company, 1991. Reprint of an edition published in Oxford: Clarendon Press, 1969.

Kant, Immanuel. *Education*. Translated by Annette Churton. Ann Arbor: The University of Michigan Press, 1971.

Kemp, J. "Kant's Examples of the Categorical Imperative," in *Kant: Foundations of the Metaphysics of Morals: Text and Critical Essays*. Edited by Robert Paul Wolff. Indianapolis: Bobbs-Merrill, 1969.

Korsgaard, Christine M. "Aristotle on Function and Virtue." *History of Philosophy Quarterly* 3 (July 1986): 259–279.

Leibniz, G. W. *Discours de métaphysique* (1686) and *Monadologie* (1714). Translated by George R. Montgomery in *Leibniz: Discourse on Metaphysics/Correspondence with Arnauld/Monadology*. La Salle, IL: Open Court, 1973.

Lewis, C. I. *An Analysis of Knowledge and Valuation*. La Salle, IL: Open Court, 1946.

Mill, John Stuart. *On Liberty*. Edited by Elizabeth Rapaport. Indianapolis: Hackett Publishing Company, 1978.

Mill, John Stuart. *The Subjection of Women*. Edited by Susan Moller Okin. Indianapolis: Hackett, 1988.

Mill, John Stuart. *Utilitarianism*. Edited by George Sher. Indianapolis: Hackett, 1979.

Moore, G. E. *Ethics*. Oxford: Oxford University Press, 1912.

Moore, G. E. *Philosophical Papers*. New York: Collier Books, 1966.

Moore, G. E. *Philosophical Studies*. London: Kegan Paul, 1922.

Moore, G. E. *Principia Ethica*. Cambridge: Cambridge University Press, 1971.

Nagel, Thomas. *Mortal Questions*. Cambridge: Cambridge University Press, 1979.

Nagel, Thomas. *The Possibility of Altruism*. Oxford: Clarendon Press, 1970. Reprinted in Princeton: Princeton University Press, 1978.

Nagel, Thomas. *The View from Nowhere*. New York: Oxford University Press, 1986.

Nell (O'Neill), Onora. *Acting on Principle: An Essay on Kantian Ethics*. New York: Columbia University Press, 1975.

Newman, John Henry. *Apologia Pro Vita Sua: Being a History of His Religious Opinions*. London: Longmans, Green & Co, 1880.

Nozick, Robert. *Anarchy, State, and Utopia.* New York: Basic Books, 1974.
O'Neill, Onora. "Agency and Anthropology in Kant's *Groundwork,*" in *Kant's Practical Philosophy Reconsidered.* Edited by Yirmiyahu Yovel. Dordrecht: Kluwer Academic Publishers, 1989.
O'Neill, Onora. "Justice, Gender, and International Boundaries." *The Quality of Life.* Edited by Martha Nussbaum and Amartya Sen. Oxford: Clarendon Press, 1992.
O'Neill, Onora. *Constructions of Reason: Explorations of Kant's Practical Philosophy.* Cambridge: Cambridge University Press, 1989.
Parfit, Derek. "Later Selves and Moral Principles," in *Philosophy and Personal Relations.* Edited by A. Montefiore. London: Routledge & Kegan Paul, 1973.
Parfit, Derek. *Reasons and Persons.* Oxford: Clarendon Press, 1984.
Paton, H. J. "The Alleged Independence of Goodness." *The Philosophy of G. E. Moore.* Edited by Paul Schilpp. (Library of Living Philosophers, Volume 4.) Chicago: Northwestern University Press, 1942.
Paton, H. J. *The Categorical Imperative: A Study in Kant's Moral Philosophy.* London: Hutchinson's University Library, 1947. Reprinted in Philadelphia: University of Pennsylvania Press, 1971.
Perry, Ralph Barton. *A General Theory of Value.* Cambridge, MA: Harvard University Press, 1926.
Plato. *The Collected Dialogues.* Edited by Edith Hamilton and Huntington Cairns. Princeton: Princeton University Press, 1961.
Price, Richard. *A Review of the Principal Questions in Morals.* Edited by D. D. Raphael. Oxford: Clarendon Press, 1948. Selections may also be found in Raphael, *British Moralists 1650–1800.*
Prichard, H. A. *Moral Obligation and Duty and Interest. Essays and Lectures by H. A. Prichard.* Edited by W. D. Ross and J. O. Urmson. Oxford: Oxford University Press, 1968.
Primoratz, Igor. "Lying and the 'Method of Ethics.' " *International Studies in Philosophy* 16 (1984): 35–57.
Raphael, D. D., editor. *British Moralists 1650–1800.* Two Volumes, Indianapolis: Hackett Publishing Company, 1991. Reprint of an edition published in Oxford: Oxford University Press, 1969.
Rawls, John. "Justice as Reciprocity," in *Mill: Utilitarianism: Text and Critical Essays.* Edited by Samuel Gorovitz. Indianapolis: Bobbs-Merrill, 1971.
Rawls, John, "Kantian Constructivism in Moral Theory: The Dewey Lectures 1980." *The Journal of Philosophy* 77 (September 1980): 515–572.
Rawls, John. "The Independence of Moral Theory." *Proceedings and Addresses of the American Philosophical Association* 47 (1974–1975): 5–22.

Rawls, John. "Two Concepts of Rules." *Philosophical Review* 64 (January 1955): 3–32.

Rawls, John. *A Theory of Justice.* Cambridge, MA: Harvard University Press, 1971.

Reath, Andrews. "Hedonism and Heteronomy." *Pacific Philosophical Quarterly* 70 (March 1989): 42–72.

Reiss, Hans. "Kant and the Right of Rebellion," in *The Journal of the History of Ideas*, XVII, 2 (April 1956): 179–192.

Reiss, Hans. *Kant's Political Writings.* Cambridge: Cambridge University Press, 1970.

Ross, W. D. *Kant's Ethical Theory.* Oxford: Clarendon Press, 1954.

Ross, W. D. *The Right and the Good.* Oxford: Clarendon Press, 1930.

Rousseau, J. J. *On the Social Contract* in *The Basic Political Writings.* Translated by Donald Cress. Indianapolis: Hackett Publishing Company, 1987.

Scheffler, Samuel. "Ethics, Personal Identity, and Ideals of the Person." *Canadian Journal of Philosophy* 12 (1982): 229–246.

Scheffler, Samuel. *The Rejection of Consequentialism.* Oxford: Clarendon Press, 1982.

Schilpp, Paul. *Kant's Pre-Critical Ethics.* Chicago: Northwestern University Press, 1938. Reprinted in New York: Garland Publishing, 1971.

Schultz, Bart. "Persons, Selves, and Utilitarianism." *Ethics* 96 (1986): 721–745.

Sedgwick, Sally. "Can Kant's Ethics Survive the Feminist Critique?" *Pacific Philosophical Quarterly* 71 (1990): 60–79.

Sidgwick, Henry. *The Methods of Ethics.* Indianapolis: Hackett Publishing Company, 1981.

Singer, Marcus. *Generalization in Ethics.* New York: Atheneum, 1961.

Smith, Adam. *The Theory of Moral Sentiments.* Edited by D. D. Raphael and A. L. Macfie. Indianapolis: Liberty Classics, 1982.

Strawson, Peter. *Freedom and Resentment and Other Essays.* London: Methuen & Co., 1974.

Wick, Warner. "The Rat and the Squirrel, or the Rewards of Virtue." *Ethics* 82 (1971): 21–32.

Williams, Bernard, and Smart, J. J. C. *Utilitarianism For and Against.* Cambridge: Cambridge University Press, 1973.

Williams, Bernard. *Ethics and the Limits of Philosophy.* Cambridge, MA: Harvard University Press, 1985.

Williams, Bernard. *Moral Luck.* Cambridge: Cambridge University Press, 1981.

Williams, Bernard. *Morality: An Introduction to Ethics.* New York: Harper Torchbooks, 1972.

Williams, Bernard. *Problems of the Self.* Cambridge: Cambridge University Press, 1973.

Wittgenstein, Ludwig. *Philosophical Investigations.* Translated by G. E. M. Anscombe. New York: Macmillan, 1953.

Wolf, Susan. "Self-Interest and Interest in Selves." *Ethics* 96 (1986): 704–720.

Wolff, Christian. *Preliminary Discourse on Philosophy in General.* Translated by Richard J. Blackwell. Indianapolis: Bobbs-Merrill Library of Liberal Arts, 1963.

Wolff, Robert Paul, editor. *Kant: Foundations of the Metaphysics of Morals: Text and Critical Essays.* Indianapolis: Bobbs-Merrill, 1969.

Wood, Allen W. *Kant's Moral Religion.* Ithaca: Cornell University Press, 1970.

Wood, Allen. "Kant on False Promises." *Proceedings of the Third International Kant Congress.* Edited by Lewis White Beck. Dordrecht: D. Reidel, 1972.

Yovel, Yirmiyahu, editor. *Kant's Practical Philosophy Reconsidered.* Dordrecht: Kluwer Academic Publishers, 1989.

Sources

The thirteen essays in this volume have all been previously published. I hold the copyright for the first; the others are reprinted here with the generous permission of the original publishers. Inevitably my views have evolved over the more than ten years during which I wrote these essays; there are many things in them I would say somewhat differently if I were writing them today, and some tensions among them. In my own eyes the most noticeable of these concerns the value of humanity. Does Kant think, or should a Kantian think, that human beings simply have unconditional or intrinsic value, or is there a sense in which we must confer value even upon ourselves? In earlier essays (Chapters 4 and 9) I lean towards the former view, although even there not always consistently; in later ones (Chapters 7 and 10) I can see myself migrating towards the latter, the view I now hold. I have not modified the essays to eradicate that tension or to reflect my current views; it does not seem to me to matter that much to the work that those essays are primarily meant to do. The reader can find my current views explained in *The Sources of Normativity*, forthcoming from Cambridge University Press. I have changed the essays only to ensure that the translations used, titles, and system of references to Kant's works are, as far as possible, consistent throughout the collection; and to simplify and update the bibliographical references.

1. "An Introduction to the Ethical, Political, and Religious Thought of Kant" was first published as "Kant" in *Ethics in the History of Western Philosophy*, edited by Robert Cavalier, James Gouinlock, and James Sterba. New York: St. Martin's Press, 1989, pp. 201–243.

2. "Kant's Analysis of Obligation: The Argument of *Groundwork* I" was first published as "Kant's Analysis of Obligation: The Argument of *Foundations* I" in the *Monist*, Volume 72, Number 3 (July 1989): 311–340. It is reprinted here by the permission of the publisher.

3. "Kant's Formula of Universal Law" was first published in *Pacific Philosophical Quarterly*, Volume 66, Numbers 1&2 (January/April 1985): 24–47. It is reprinted here by the permission of the publisher.

4. "Kant's Formula of Humanity" was first published in *Kant-Studien*, 77. Jahrgang, Heft 2 (1986): 183–202. It is reprinted here by the permission of the publisher.

5. "The Right to Lie: Kant on Dealing with Evil" was first published in *Philosophy and Public Affairs*. Volume 15, Number 4 (Fall 1986): 325–349. It is reprinted here by the permission of Princeton University Press.

6. "Morality as Freedom" was first published in *Kant's Practical Philosophy Reconsidered*, edited by Yirmiyahu Yovel. Dordrecht: Kluwer Academic Publishers, 1989, pp. 23–48. It is reprinted here by the permission of Kluwer Academic Publishers. © 1989 Kluwer Academic Publishers.

7. "Creating the Kingdom of Ends: Reciprocity and Responsibility in Personal Relations," by Christine M. Korsgaard, appeared in *Philosophical Perspectives 6: Ethics, 1992*, edited by James Tomberlin (copyright by Ridgeview Publishing Co., Atascadero, CA). Reprinted by permission of Ridgeview Publishing Company.

8. "Aristotle and Kant on the Source of Value" was first published in *Ethics*, Volume 96, Number 3 (April 1986): 486–505. It is reprinted here by the permission of the University of Chicago Press. © 1986 by The University of Chicago. All rights reserved.

9. "Two Distinctions in Goodness" was first published in *The Philosophical Review*, Volume 92, Number 2 (April 1983): 169–195. It is reprinted here by the permission of Cornell University Press.

10. "The Reasons We Can Share: An Attack on the Distinction Between Agent-Relative and Agent-Neutral Values" was first published in *Social Philosophy & Policy*, Volume 10, Number 1 (January 1993): 24–51. It is reprinted here by permission of the publisher.

11. "Skepticism about Practical Reason" was first published in *The Journal of Philosophy*, Volume 83, Number 1 (January 1986): 5–25. It is reprinted here by the permission of the publisher.

12. "Two Arguments Against Lying" was first published in *Argumentation*, Volume 2, Number 1 (February 1988): 27–49. It is reprinted here by the permission of Kluwer Academic Publishers. © 1988 Kluwer Academic Publishers.

13. "Personal Identity and the Unity of Agency: A Kantian Response to Parfit" was first published in *Philosophy and Public Affairs*, Volume 18, Number 2 (Spring 1989): 101–132. It is reprinted here by the permission of Princeton University Press.

Other publications by the author

The Sources of Normativity. Lectures with commentary by G. A. Cohen, Raymond Geuss, Thomas Nagel, and Bernard Williams, edited by Onora O'Neill. Cambridge: Cambridge University Press, forthcoming. A shorter version of the lectures is available in *The Tanner Lectures on Human Values*, Volume 15, edited by Sterling M. McMurrin. Salt Lake City: University of Utah Press, 1994.

"The Normativity of Instrumental Reason," in *Ethics and Practical Reason*, edited by Garrett Cullity and Berys Gaut. Oxford: Clarendon Press, forthcoming.

"Taking the Law into Our Own Hands: Kant on the Right to Revolution," in *Reclaiming the History of Ethics: Essays for John Rawls*, edited by Andrews Reath, Barbara Herman, and Christine M. Korsgaard. New York: Cambridge University Press, forthcoming.

"From Duty and for the Sake of the Noble: Kant and Aristotle on Morally Good Action," in *Aristotle, Kant, and the Stoics: Rethinking Happiness and Duty*, edited by Stephen Engstrom and Jennifer Whiting. New York: Cambridge University Press, 1996.

"Aristotle on Function and Virtue," *The History of Philosophy Quarterly*, Volume 3, Number 3 (July 1986): 259–279.

"Rawls and Kant: On the Primacy of the Practical," in the *Proceedings of the Eighth International Kant Congress, Memphis 1995*, edited by Hoke Robinson. Milwaukee: Marquette University Press, 1995.

"A Note on the Value of Gender-Identification," in *Women, Culture, and Development: A Study of Human Capabilities*, edited by Martha Nussbaum and Johnathan Glover. Oxford: The Claredon Press, 1995.

"Commentary on Amartya Sen's 'Capability and Well-Being' and Gerald Cohen's 'Equality of What? On Welfare, Goods, and Capabilities'" in *The Quality of Life,* edited by Martha Nussbaum and Amartya Sen. Oxford: Clarendon Press, 1993.

"Holding People Responsible" (A shorter version of "Creating the Kingdom of Ends: Reciprocity and Responsibility in Personal Relations.") in *Akten des Siebenten Internationalen Kant-Kongresses,* edited by Gerhard Funke. Bonn: Bouvier, 1991; pp. 535–550.

Articles on "Theories of the Good" and "Teleological Ethics" in the *Routledge Encyclopedia of Philosophy,* edited by Edward Craig. London: Routledge, forthcoming.

Articles on "Conscience" and "Formalism" in *Philosophy of Education: An Encyclopedia,* edited by J. J. Chamblis. New York: Garland Publishing Company, 1996.

Articles on "Immanuel Kant," "John Rawls," and "Richard Price" in *The Garland Encyclopedia of Ethics,* edited by Lawrence C. Becker. New York: Garland Publishing, 1992.

The Standpoint of Practical Reason (Dissertation, 1981). Published in Garland's *Distinguished Harvard Dissertations* series, 1990.

Index

abortion, 341–42, 389 n.7

Ackrill, J. L., 247–48 n.7

acting from duty, 12–13, 55–60, 107–09

acting under the idea of freedom, 26, 57, 162–63, 206; *see also*: two standpoints; deduction of the moral law

action, *see* agency

activity, vs. passivity, 168–69, 177–78, 180, 203–05, 363–64, 379; vs. process, in Aristotle's theory, 236–39; as a final good, 238–39; and pleasure, 245

Acton, H. B., 86

adding values, across boundaries between persons, 279, 290, 293, 304 n.13, 304 n.14

affirmative action, 148

agency: conception of, belongs to the practical standpoint, 203–05, 205–09; emphasized by Kant, 363; vs. experience, 363, 364, 374, 384–85, 387–88; the unity of agency, 369–74; unity at a particular time, 369–71, and over time, 371–74; central to our conception of our identity, 208, 377–80, 382–83; individual human being the basic kind of agent, 373, but

group agency is possible, 372, 383, 385; *see also* activity

agent-relative vs. agent-neutral values and reasons: explanation of the distinction, 276–78, 302–03 n.5, 303 n.6; Objectivist vs. Intersubjectivist interpretations of agent-neutral value, 278–82, 285, 289–90, 298–99, 304 n.11, 304 n.12, 304 n.14, 305 n.17, 306 n.24; not all values agent-neutral, 282–83; whether reasons springing from "ambitions" or personal projects are agent-relative, 284–91, 305–06 n.22; whether deontological reasons are agent-relative, 363, 388 n.1, 397 n.48, but see more considered discussion at 291–99

Allison, Henry, 184 n.1

ambitions (personal projects): 284–91; Nagel thinks them agent-relative, 284–86; but they do not spring from unmotivated desires, 286, 289; and seem to involve agent-neutral values, 286–90; which are best understood as Intersubjective rather than Objective, 289–90; 305–06 n.22, 306 n.25, 306 n.26, 307 n.30

413

is what the gods do, 235–36, 243;
purest activity, 238–39, 248 n.11;
cannot be final purpose of the
world, according to Kant, 242–43,
244–46; nature of the contemplative life, 247 n.2
contradiction in conception test,
14–15, 38 n.19, 38 n.20, 77–78,
103 n.7; interpretations of, 78,
81–101; see also: contradiction in
the will test; Universal Law, Formula of
contradiction in the will test, 14,
15–16, 77–78, 79, 81, 82–83, 95–
97, 104 n.24; see also: contradiction in conception test; Universal
Law, Formula of
conventional actions, see natural
vs. conventional actions
Copp, David, 154n
Crusias, Christian August, 11
culture, 33, 110, 114, 129–30
Cummiskey, David, 75 n.57

Daniels, Norman, 396 n.46
Darwall, Stephen, 67 n.1, 154n,
302n, 304 n.11, 306 n.27, 389 n.6,
393–94 n.33, 394 n.34
Davis, Michael, 154n
deception: coercion and deception,
violate perfect duty to others, under the Formula of Humanity, 17,
138–40, 295–96, 346–48; teleological argument against, 88;
Kant's apparent rigorism about,
134–35; argument against, under
the Formula of Universal Law,
135–36; argument against, under
the Formula of Humanity, 137–
40; how coercion and deception
treat others as means, 137–43;

lying to deceivers, under the Formula of Universal Law, 136, 154–
55 n.2; lying to deceivers, as self-
defense, 144, 145–46, 155 n.3,
156–57 n.10; whether there is a
duty to lie to the murderer at the
door, 145–46; consenting to being
lied to, 155 n.5; paternalistic deception, problem of, 336; paternalistic deception, wrongness of, according to consequentialists, 336–
38, and according to Sidgwick,
337–45, 355, 359 n.6; unclarities
about what counts as deception,
according to Sidgwick, 343–44; paternalistic deception, in a Kantian
account, 348–52, 355; insincere
salutations, 359 n.7; see also lying
promise example
deduction of the moral law, 12, 24–
27, 46, 68–69 n.10, 106, 160–175,
330; Second Critique argument
for the moral law, 26–27, 170,
175, provides a credential for the
moral law, 11–12, 160, 161;
whether the Groundwork and Second Critique arguments are different, 40 n.29, 161, 170, 217 n.21,
330; the two arguments combined, 175; see also: analytic/
synthetic; spontaneity
deontological reasons: denial of
them based on the idea that the
business of morality is to produce
something, 27, 300; why Nagel
thinks them agent-relative, 282–
83, 291–94; attempts to construe
them as agent-neutral, 291–92;
paradoxical, according to Nagel
and Scheffler, 294, 388 n.1; spring
from requirement not to treat others as means, 295–97; Inter-

diction in the will test, 14, 135;
involve failures to value humanity, 17–18, 137; imperfect distinguished from broad, 20–21, 83–
84, 179, 186 n.25; whether they
should be understood as forms of
obligation, 70 n.23; secondary to
perfect duties, 145; see also: categories of duty; perfect duties
impurity of the will, 21, 58–59
incentives: defined, 165; sensible incentives do not make us evil, 40–
41 n.30; moral law needs no end
as an incentive, 109; fundamental
principles of volition rank incentives of inclination and of morality, 165, 202; incentives and the
problem of moral interest, 167–
71; idea of intelligible world or intelligible existence as the moral
incentive, 168–71, 175–76 (see
also 27); 309 n.44, 330; incentives
and the need for ends, 176–78; incentives take the form of ways of
perceiving the world, 180
incest, 195–96
inclination, see desires and inclinations
instrumental reasoning: instrumental reasoning not just causal reasoning, 35–36 n.1; and the idea of
a practical contradiction, 93–94,
101–02; Hume's argument supposedly limits reason to instrumental role, 312; but if so should
allow instrumental irrationality,
319; instrumental reason does
not give reasons for ranking ends,
312; arguments about instrumental reason and prudence
compared, 322–23, 324–25; internalism seems to imply a limita-

tion to instrumental reason and
things like it, 325–27; but does
not, 327–329; see also hypothetical imperative
intelligible and sensible worlds, 26,
27, 167–76; and moral motivation, 26–27, 28–29, 167–71, 175–
76, 185 n.16; and freedom, 27,
159–60, 172, 183, 201–05; relation between noumena and the intelligible world, 26, 218–19 n.28;
see also: noumena and phenomena; two standpoints
internalism (vs. externalism), 43–
76, 311–34; 20th century debate
about, compared to 18th century
debate about obligation, 43–45,
48–49; 18th century rationalists
were internalists, 53–54; but
Ross and Prichard were externalists, 54; 20th century debate
characterized, 315–17; confu-
sions about its implications gives
rise to skepticism about practical
reason, in Hume's argument,
318–21, in general, 321–23, and
in Williams's argument, 325–29;
does not rule out pure practical
reason, 329–32
Intersubjectivism, see agent-relative
vs. agent-neutral values and reasons
intrinsic value: 249–74; intrinsic/
extrinsic distinguished from
final/instrumental, 250–53;
Moore's account, 253–56, 278,
306 n.24; intrinsic value not possessed by right action, but by acting from the motive of duty, according to Ross, 54; how related
to unconditional goodness, 117,
227–28, 257–73 (esp. 262); as an

metaphysics (*cont.*)
Kant's critical views, 8–9; and rejection of dogmatic metaphysics
in ethics, 46; personal identity
practical rather than metaphysical, 371, 386–88, 391–92 *n.21*,
392 *n.22*, 396–97 *n.47*; *see also*:
construction of values; realism
(or objectivism) about values; teleology; two standpoints
Mill, John Stuart: criticism of
Kant's Formula of Universal Law,
80, 81; security, as the interest
protected by justice, 99; interpretation of hedonism, 131 *n.2*; on
higher pleasures, 264, 358–59
n.5; interpretation of
deontological principles, 291–92;
externalist account of the moral
sanction, 315–16, 329; rights, 358
n. 4; on value of agency, 364;
agency and personal identity,
379–80
mockery, 21, 141
Moore, G. E., naturalistic fallacy,
66, 274 *n.10*; irrationality of egoism, 132 *n.6*, 303–04 *n.10*; objectivist theory of goodness, 225,
278; cannot give reasons why
things are good, 227–28, 271–73;
theory of intrinsic value, 252,
253–56, 278; method of isolation
for determining value, 255, 263,
264, 271; theory of organic unities, 268–70, 274 *n.7*, 303 *n.9*; organic unities assessed, 270–73,
306 *n.24*; Moore's intrinsic values
compared to Kant's unconditional
value, 131 *n.4*, 257, 270–73; development of his views, 273 *n.3*
moral faith: 3, 27–31, 169–70, 183,
208, 244, 245; as Kant's response to

the problems of non-ideal theory,
149; *see also*: God; immortality;
postulates of practical reason
moral sense theory, *see* sentimentalism
motivation, moral: in Wolff, 5; in
Kant, 22–23, 25–27, 55–67, 107–
09, 162–71, 175–76, 210 and the
need for ends, 176–78; in the debates of the British Moralists, 43–
45, 47–52; in Ross, 52–54; *see
also*: incentives; internalism; motive of duty
motive of duty, 13, 43–44, 55–67,
107–08; Hume's argument that it
cannot be the primary moral motive, 47–48; though it is the usual
motive in the case of the artificial
virtues, 69 *n.13*, 70 *n.21*;
Hutcheson's argument that it is
confused, 49–50; Ross's argument that we cannot be required
to act from it, 52–53; these arguments seem to force rationalists
to be moral realists, 51–52; and
to make it impossible to arrive at
the principle of duty by analyzing
the motive of duty, 47–48, 53;
how Kant's argument in *Groundwork* I overcomes this objection,
60–67; comparison to Aristotle's
acting for the sake of the noble,
51, 71–72 *n.28*, 244; Smith's account, 71 *n.25*, 186 *n.21*; relation
to motives of honor and sympathy, 73 *n.49*, 73–74 *n.51*; Ross
and Prichard's externalist version,
316; *see also*: incentives; internalism; motivation, moral

Nagel, Thomas, 275–310; practical-
ity of reason, 36 *n.1*, 333 *n.11*; in-

purpose of the world, 128–31,
241–43; regress to the Formula of
Universal Law as the law of freedom, 162–67

Universal Law, Formula of, 14, 77–
105, 106–07, 135–37; to be used in
decision-making, 39–40 n.25, 103
n.7, 106, 124; argument for, in
Groundwork I, 55–67; and in
Groundwork II, 46; sense in which
maxims have forms, 75–76 n.58;
three interpretations of the contradiction, 78, 101; tests sufficiency
of reasons, 79, 102; Mill's criticism, 80; is the law of autonomy or
spontaneity, 102, 162–67; allows
lying to the murderer at the door,
136–37, 155 n.2, 155
n.3; other cases in which it is less
rigorous than the Formula of Humanity, 152–53; but is uncompromising, 154; how related to the
Formula of Humanity, 18, 125–28,
143–44; 151–54, 177; *see also*: contradiction in conception test; contradiction in the will test; logical
contradiction interpretation; practical contradiction interpretation;
teleological contradiction interpretation

Universal Principle of Justice, 18–
19, 39–40 n.25, 103 n.7

universalizability, 13, 61–65, 241,
395 n.40; *see also* Universal Law,
Formula of

utilitarianism: problems with rule-
utilitarian readings of Kant's test,
80, 96; a single-level theory, 149;
problems with, as such, 149–50;
equation of two distinctions in
goodness, 253 (*see also* 251–52);
assumes the business of morality

is to bring something about, 275,
299–301; account of agent-
relative reasons, 283; account of
deontological values, 291–93;
problems with that account, 293–
94; on Mill's account, externalist,
315–16, 329; account of the presumption against benevolent lies,
336–38; employs slippery slope arguments, 339–45; appeals to desire for precise concepts and answers, 342–43, 344–45, 353, 355;
that appeal queried, 357–58; emphasizes experience over agency,
363–64, 384–85, 386–88;
whether reductionism about personal identity supports utilitarian
moral views, 380–86, 386–89,
392 n.22; perplexity about
deontological values, 388 n.1, 397
n.48; *see also*: consequentialism;
Mill, John Stuart; Sidgwick,
Henry

value, contributive, 252, 261, 270
value, inherent, 252, 261
value, unconditional vs. conditional: explanation of the distinction, 16–17, 117–19, 256–62,
345–48; unconditional value of
human beings or humanity, 3,.17,
109–10, 124–28, 179; unconditional value of the good will, 16–
17, 55, 239, 256–57, 345–46; how
humanity and good will are related, 123–24; unconditional
value of virtue, 27; conditional
value of happiness, 16, 28, 118,
121–22, 129, 239, 257, 345; conditional value of objects of inclination, 121, 265–68, 345; conditional value of amusements, and

436 INDEX

value, unconditional vs. conditional
(*cont.*)
  of virtuous activity, in Aristotle's
  theory, 232–36, 238–39, 248 n.8;
  unconditional and intrinsic goodness, how related, 117, 227–28,
  257–73, 407; and the argument for
  the Formula of Humanity, 119–24;
  final purpose of the world must be
  unconditionally good, 128–31; Aristotle on the unconditional value
  of contemplation, 230–39, 241; Aristotle's account compared to
  Kant's, 243–46; *see also*: intrinsic
  value; objective goodness
vegetarianism, 342
violence, 82–85, 97–101, 105 n.27
virtue, duties of: are inner duties
  arising from the Supreme Principle of the Doctrine of Virtue, 19–
  20, 178; are duties to have ends,
  20, 110, 178; which ends are duties, 20, 178–79; may not be
  coercively enforced, 20, 84, 382,
  395–96 n.41; are of broad or wide
  obligation, 20, 83–84, 145; but
  some are perfect duties, 20, 83;
  provide reasons to oppose evil,
  146; *see also*: categories of duty;
  justice, duties of
virtue: relation to freedom, 21–22,
  176–83; goes beyond not using
  others as means, 186 n.25; value
  of virtuous activities (the political life), according to Aristotle,
  228–29, 230–31, 233–36, 238; Aristotle's view compared to Kant's,

243–46; virtues as responses to
certain kinds of reasons, 324–25
(*see also* 179–81), including theoretical reasons, 334 n.13; *see also*:
character; virtue, duties of

Wagner, Steven, 388n, 395–96 n.41
war, 31–35; laws of, 33, 42 n.39,
  and non-ideal theory, 154
Warren, Daniel, 307–08 n.31
Wick, Warner, 248 n.10
wide duties, *see* broad or wide duties
will (the): as a cause, 10, 94, 102,
  140–41, 163, 200–05, 219 n.29;
  see also freedom of the will
Williams, Bernard, attitude to the
  concept of obligation, 50, 69 n.11,
  70 n.23, 70–71 n.24; consequences of single-level theories,
  149–50; responsibility and blame,
  216 n.18, 220–21 n.37; unconditional allegiance to agent-neutral
  values contrary to integrity of
  agents, 282; Jim and the Indians,
  292–93, 295–96, 308 n.35, 310
  n.47, 397 n. 48; thinks internalism has Humean implications,
  314, 317, 325–27; this conclusion
  disputed, 327–29, 334 n.16; on
  personal identity, 392 n.24, 392
  n.26, 394–95 n.36
Wolf, Susan, 392 n.23, 393–94 n.33,
  394 n.34, 395 n.37
Wolff, Christian (and Wolffianism),
  4, 5–8, 11, 35, 45, 64
Wood, Allen, 41 n.30, 81

Index of Citations

In this index I have correlated pages in *Kants gesammelte Schriften* with pages in this book on which I have cited or discussed passages from those pages in Kant. The standard method of citing Kant, unlike that of citing, say, Plato or Aristotle, refers to the page rather than specific lines, so, unfortunately, this index cannot be made quite as exact as a traditional *index locorum*. A two or three in parentheses following a page number in this book indicates that there are two or three references to Kant's page on that page.

Printed in the United States
39476LVS00003B/73-90